THE EUROPEAN COMMUNITY, THE EUROPEAN UNION AND THE INTERNATIONAL LAW OF TREATIES

To my beloved late parents.
May I have made them proud.

THE EUROPEAN COMMUNITY, THE EUROPEAN UNION AND THE INTERNATIONAL LAW OF TREATIES

A Comparative Legal Analysis of the Community and Union's External Treaty-Making Practice

Delano R. Verwey

Assistant Professor of European Law
Erasmus University Rotterdam

T·M·C·ASSER PRESS
The Hague

Published by T.M.C.ASSER PRESS
P.O.Box 16163, 2500 BD The Hague, The Netherlands

www.asserpress.nl

T.M.C.ASSER PRESS' English language books are distributed exclusively by:

Cambridge University Press, The Edinburgh Building, Shaftesbury Road,
Cambridge CB2 2RU, UK,
or
for customers in the USA, Canada and Mexico:
Cambridge University Press, 40 West 20th Street, New York, NY 10011-4211, USA

www.cambridge.org

ISBN 90-6704-182-3

PREFACE

This book contains a study comparing the treaty making practices and rules of the European Communities (EC) and the European Union (EU) with those of the International Law of Treaties. Here notably the Vienna Conventions of 1969 and 1986, concluded in the framework of the United Nations, are of importance.

The study illustrates the growing importance of the EC and the EU as international players in an ever globalizing world.

The book is unique to the extent that up to this moment only limited literature is available on this subject.

The European Constitution which has been politically agreed upon on 18 June 2004 by the Representatives of the Member States of the EU, aims at abolishing the pillar structure of the EU, integrating the European Communities into the EU and, finally but not least, formally granting legal personality to the single remaining international organisation, the European Union. In doing so the Constitution, once entered into force, certainly will give more impetus to the state-like characteristics and the identity of the European Union and, thus, to its capacity to act internationally as a fully recognized subject of international law.

The author, Dr Delano R. Verwey, is a specialist both of EU law and of public international law, and therefore pre-eminently well placed to write the book which is in front of you.

Let us hope that the book will give rise to further reading, research and writing regarding the relationship between the European Union legal order and International Law taken in its broadest sense.

Rotterdam, July 2004

Jaap W. DE ZWAAN
Professor of the Law of the European Union
Erasmus Law School
Erasmus University Rotterdam
The Netherlands

TABLE OF CONTENTS

ABBREVIATIONS

AA	Ars Aequi
ACP States	African, Caribbean and Pacific Group of States
AG	Advocate General
AJIL	American Journal of International Law
AVR	Archiv des Völkerrechts
BiH	Bosnia and Herzegovina
Bull.	Bulletin of the European Union
Calif.W.Int'l.L.J.	California Western International Law Journal
CDE	Cahiers de Droit Europeén
CFI	Court of First Instance
CFSP	Common Foreign and Security Policy
C.M.L. Rev.	Common Market Law Review
COP	Conference of Parties
COREPER	Committee of Permanent Representatives
EAEC	European Atomic Energy Community
EC	European Community
ECB	European Central Bank
ECHR	European Convention for the Protection of Human Rights and Fundamental Freedoms
ECJ	European Court of Justice
ECR	European Court Reports
ECSC	European Coal and Steel Community
EDF	European Development Fund
EEA	European Economic Area
EEC	European Economic Community
E.F.A. Rev.	European Foreign Affairs Review
EFTA	European Free Trade Agreement
E.L.Rev.	European Law Review
EU	European Union
EUF	European-led Forces
EUMM	European Union Monitoring Mission
EUPM	European Union Police Mission
FYROM	Former Yugoslav Republic of Macedonia
FRY	Federal Republic of Yugoslavia
GATS	General Agreement on Trade in Services
GDR	German Democratic Republic
GYIL	German Yearbook of International Law
Hague Yb.	Hague Yearbook of International Law
IAEA	International Atomic Energy Agency
ICAO	International Civil Aviation Organization
I.C.J.	International Court of Justice

I.L.C.	International Law Commission
I.L.M.	International Legal Materials
ILO	International Labour Organization
IMO	International Maritime Organization
JCMS	Journal of Common Market Studies
JHA	Justice and Home Affairs
LIEI	Legal Issues of Economic Integration
MJ	Maastricht Journal of European and comparative law
NATO	North Atlantic Treaty Organization
Neth.Yb.Int'l.L	Netherlands Yearbook of International Law
NILR	Netherlands International Law Review
NTER	Nederlands Tijdschrift voor Europees Recht
OECD	Organization for Economic Cooperation and Development
OJ	Official Journal
ÖZoR	Österreichische Zeitschrift für öffentlisches Recht
P.C.I.J.	Permanent Court of International Justice
RTD eur.	Revue trimestrielle de Droit europeén
SEW	Sociaal Economische Wetgeving
TEU	Treaty on European Union
TRIPS	Trade-Related Aspects of Intellectual Property Rights
UNEP	United Nations Environment Programme
UNFCCC	United Nations Framework Convention on Climate Change
v	versus
WTO	World Trade Organization
YEL	Yearbook of European Law
Yale.J.Int'l.L.	Yale Journal of International Law
ZaöRV	Zeitschrift für ausländisches öffentliches Recht und Völkerrecht

GENERAL INTRODUCTION

INTERNATIONAL TREATY LAW

In the international legal system, as opposed to the national legal system, there is no central legislative body that has the authority to enact (binding) rules that apply within the system. Nor is there an international court of justice with comprehensive and compulsory jurisdiction to interpret and enforce the law. Despite their varied nature[1], international treaties are the closest thing to a legislative instrument at international level. Similarly, the adoption and conclusion of international treaties resemble as closely as possible an international legislative process. Treaties are a very important source of international law, for they are the evidence of the express consent of states and international organisations to regulate their interests according to international law. International treaties are thus of paramount importance to the evolution of international law.[2]

Article 38(1) of the Statute of the International Court of Justice[3] refers to international conventions, whether general or particular, establishing rules expressly recognised by the contesting states as a source of international law in accordance with which it will settle disputes.[4] This provision is widely regarded as the most authoritative statement on the sources of international law.[5] There is no express hierarchy between the four sources of international law mentioned in Article 38(1) of the Statute of the International Court of Justice. In general international treaties, which frequently contain codified customary international law, rank as the primary sources of international law.[6]

---

[1] Treaties can be classified depending on the number of participants in bilateral and multilateral treaties. The division can also be made on the basis of geographical criteria (regional or global). Denomination can also be based on the subject matter, for example, trade agreements, peace agreements, treaties delimiting an international border, or an environmental agreement.

[2] M.N. Shaw, *International Law* (2003), at 811. See also the first recital of the preambles of the 1969 and the 1986 Vienna Conventions referring to "the fundamental role of treaties in the history of international relations".

[3] Statute of the International Court of Justice in 39 *AJIL* (1945), Supplement: Official Documents, at 215-229.

[4] Other sources included in Article 38(1) of the Statute of the International Court of Justice are customary international law, general principles of law, judicial decisions and the teachings of highly qualified scholars.

[5] M.N. Shaw, *supra* note 2, at 66 and I. Brownlie, *Principles of Public International Law* (2003), at 4-5.

[6] M.N. Shaw, *supra* note 2, at 66.

The 1969 Vienna Convention on the Law of Treaties governs international treaty law.[7] This Convention deals only with treaties concluded between states. A second source of international treaty law is the 1986 Vienna Convention on the Law of Treaties between States and International Organisations or between International Organisations.[8] This Convention extends the provisions of the 1969 Vienna Convention, *mutatis mutandis*, to international organisations.[9] A third source of international treaty law is customary international law. It is recognised that the two Conventions have codified the customary rules to a great extent, especially the more substantive rules.[10] Secondary sources of international treaty law are the 1978 Vienna Convention on the Succession of States in Respect of Treaties[11], the case-law of the International Court of Justice, its predecessor, the Permanent Court of International Justice and rulings by international arbitration panels.

THE LEGAL PERSONALITY OF INTERNATIONAL ORGANISATIONS

In the domain of international relations, and more specifically in international law, states are the primary actors. Increasingly though, other entities such as international organisations, non-governmental organisations, enterprises and natural persons are the subjects of these laws[12], or derive rights from treaties[13] or are also affected by these laws.[14] Traditionally, the negotiating and signing of international treaties, and in effect, the capacity to engage in international relations have been the prerogative of states. States are the main subjects of international law and *ipso facto* have legal personality.[15] Without legal personality an entity

[7] Reprinted in 8 *I.L.M.* (1969), at 679, hereafter referred to as the 1969 Vienna Convention. The Convention was signed in 1969 and entered into force on 27 February 1980.

[8] Reprinted in 25 *I.L.M.* (1986), at 543 and hereafter referred to as the 1986 Vienna Convention. The Convention was adopted on 21 March 1986 and has not yet come into force.

[9] *Yearbook of the International Law Commission*, 1981, Volume II, part two, at 117-120.

[10] A. Aust, *Modern Treaty Law and Practice* (2000), at 9-11. See also the *Gabcíkovo-Nagymaros* Case, Hungary *v* Slovakia, I.C.J. Reports (1997), at 7 and the *Qatar* v *Bahrain* Case, I.C.J. Reports (1994), at 112.

[11] Reprinted in 17 *I.L.M.* (1978), at 1488. The Convention was adopted on 22 August 1978 and entered into force on 6 November 1996.

[12] The Kyoto Protocol, like the United Nations Framework Convention on Climate Change, UNFCCC, permits that 'regional economic integration organisations' can become a party to the Protocol or the Convention (Article 24 and Article 20 respectively). The Kyoto Protocol reprinted in OJ 2002, L 130/4 and the UNFCCC reprinted in OJ 1993, L 33/13.

[13] An example is the European Convention for the Protection of Human Rights and Fundamental Freedoms reprinted in 45 AJIL (1951), Supplement: Official Documents, at 24-39.

[14] For example, the Agreement on extradition between the European Union and the United States of America, OJ 2003, L 181/27.

[15] Legal personality is the capacity of an entity to engage in activities at international level. In the case of international organisations it is their ability to operate at the international level separate from their member states. N.D. White, *The Law of International Organisations* (1996), at 27.

cannot be a subject of international law and, therefore, it cannot, among other things, conclude international agreements.[16]

With the steady increase of the number of international organisations, especially after the Second World War, the diversification of their activities into a wide range of specialised fields, and their recognition as subjects of international law, the prerogative to conclude international agreements has also been extended to these organisations.[17] The aforementioned 1986 Vienna Convention evidences this.[18] But whereas, as stated before, states possess legal personality *ipso facto*, (academic) opinions have been diverse with regard to the legal personality of international organisations.[19] The problem is further exacerbated by the fact that the majority of the founding treaties of international organisations do not make express reference to the legal personality of the organisations.[20] However, in the *Reparations for Injuries* Case, the International Court of Justice ruled that the United Nations "was intended to exercise and enjoy, and is in fact exercising and enjoying, functions and rights which can only be explained on the basis of the

---

[16] Brownlie points out that the possession of a legal personality by an international organisation in itself does not automatically mean the existence of a treaty-making power. The latter depends on the constituent instrument of the international organisation. I. Brownlie, *supra* note 5, at 651. And in the *LaGrand* Case, *Germany* v *the United States of America*, I.C.J. Reports (2001), the International Court of Justice concludes that Article 36(1) of the Vienna Convention on Consular Relations creates individual rights for detained persons (paragraph 77). The individual is thus perceived as a subject of international law, *in casu* the Convention.

[17] H.G. Schermers and N. Blokker, *International Institutional Law* (2003), at 1114-1115 and I. Pernice, Völkerrechtliche Verträge internationaler Organisationen – Tendenzen und mögliche Grundlagen einer Assimilierung von internationaler Organisationen und Staaten in Lichte der Wiener Konvention über das Vertragsrecht internationaler Organisationen in 48 *ZaöRV* (1988), at 229.

[18] See also the current debate in the International Law Commission on responsibility of international organisations. Examples include the International Law Commission, *Report on the work of its fifty-fifth session*, 2003, Supplement No. 10 (A/58/10) and Special Rapporteur, Mr. Giorgio Gaja, *First report on responsibility of international organisations*, 2003, A/CN.4/532.

[19] Legal theory distinguishes three schools of thought on the legal personality of international organisations. These are the will theory, that is, that international organisations only possess international legal personality if such is the express will of the member states. The second school is the objective personality approach. This theory accepts the existence of a legal personality if the organisation has at least one organ with a will distinct from the member states. The legal personality is not granted by the member states, but is derived directly from international law. The third theory is the implied legal personality. If the organisation is permitted to act at the external level it will only be able to do so if it is accepted that it has international legal personality. H.G. Schermers et al., *supra* note 17, at 978-979. A fourth theory, the presumptive personality, is added to this list by Jan Klabbers. This theory presupposes the existence of a legal personality because of the will to create an international organisation and endowing it with certain competences. J. Klabbers, 'Presumptive Personality: The European Union in International Law' in M. Koskenniemi (ed.), *International Law Aspects of the European Union* (1998), at 231. See in this regard also J.W. de Zwaan, The Legal Personality of the European Communities and the European Union in 30 *Neth.Yb.Int'l. L* (1999), at 75. See also *infra* Chapter 2.

[20] H.G. Schermers et al., *supra* note 17, at 987-988 and N.D. White, *supra* note 15, at 27-28.

possession of a large measure of international personality and the capacity to operate upon an international plane".[21]

The Court furthermore held that the drafters of the United Nations Charter had intended for the United Nations to have such a capacity which was evidenced by the fact that

> "The Charter has not been content to make the Organisation created by it merely "for harmonising the actions of nations in the attainment of these common ends". It has equipped that centre with organs, and has given it special tasks. It has defined the position of the Members in relation to the Organisation by requiring them to give it assistance in any action undertaken by it. Being a subject of international law an international organisation is an entity capable of possessing international rights and having the capacity to maintain its rights by bringing international claims. Although States remain the primary actors in the international arena, this is no longer their exclusive domain".[22]

In this case, the Court's reasoning points in the direction of an acceptance of the implied legal personality doctrine. But the Court only accepts the existence of legal personality when certain conditions are fulfilled. However, in the *Interpretation of the Agreement of 25 March 1951 between the WHO and Egypt* Case[23] the Court appeared to recognize a more general rule that all international organisations have legal personality. The Court stated "International organisations are subjects of international law and, as such, are bound by any obligation incumbent upon them under general rules of international law, under their constitutions or under international agreements to which they are parties".[24]

In the end, however, it all comes down to the intentions of the parties behind the creation of the international organisation, and more precisely the objectives of and the tasks entrusted to it by the member states and the manner in which those objectives and tasks have to be achieved and carried out. If the activities of the organisation carry with them a necessary interaction with other subjects of international law, the organisation will only be capable of achieving its objectives and executing its tasks effectively if it has some measure of legal personality.

The legal personality of the European Community and the European Union

The European Community is an international organisation created under international law, which operates as an entity separate from its Member States. It pos-

---

[21] *Reparations for Injuries Suffered in the Service of the United Nations* Case, I.C.J. Reports (1949), at 174.

[22] *Ibid.*

[23] I.C.J. Reports (1980), at 73.

[24] *Ibid*, at 89-90.

sesses its own organs, called institutions, capable of taking legally binding decisions with which Member States have to comply.[25] These facts were confirmed by the European Court of Justice which, in the landmark *Costa/ENEL* Case, held that the Community has its own institutions, its own personality, its own legal capacity and the capacity of representation on the international plane because the Member States had created this Community for an unlimited period and had transferred part of their sovereignty, albeit in limited fields, to the Community.[26]

The treaty-making power of the Community is derived from Article 281 EC, which bestows international legal personality upon the European Community.[27] As such the Community is capable of establishing contractual links with third countries over the whole field of objectives defined in Part One of the Treaty.[28] The European Court of Justice also held that

> "Such authority arises not only from an express conferment by the Treaty – as is the case with Articles 113 (now 133) and 114 (deleted by the Maastricht Treaty) for tariff and trade agreements and with Article 238 (now 310) for association agreements – but may equally flow from other provisions of the Treaty and from measures adopted, within the framework of those provisions, by the Community Institutions".[29]

The Community is thus not only empowered to conclude international agreements where such has been specifically provided for in the EC Treaty (express powers), but it can also do so on the basis of powers derived from other Treaty provisions and internal measures adopted on the basis of Treaty provisions (implied powers).[30]

The Treaty on European Union, also called the Maastricht Treaty, brought into being a new entity called the European Union[31] , but the Treaty contains no provi-

---

[25] In the literature this latter element is referred to as the supremacy of Community law. P. Craig and G. De Búrca, *EU Law. Texts, Cases and Materials* (2002), at 276-285.

[26] Case 6/64, *Costa/ENEL*, [1964] ECR 585. See also Case 26/62, *Van Gend en Loos*, [1963] ECR 1.

[27] Article 6 of the now defunct European Coal and Steel Community Treaty provided that "The Community shall have legal personality. In international relations, the Community shall enjoy the legal capacity it requires to perform its functions and attain its objectives". Similarly, Article 101 of the Euratom Treaty provides that "The Community may, within the limits of its powers and jurisdiction, enter into obligations by concluding agreements or contracts with a third State or an international organisation".

[28] Case 22/70, *AETR*, [1971] ECR 273. See also the Articles 302-304 EC that require the Commission and the Community to maintain all appropriate relations with the United Nations and its specialised agencies, the Council of Europe, the Organisation for Economic Cooperation and Development and all other international organisations.

[29] Case 22/70, *AETR,* [1971] ECR 273, paragraph 16.

[30] See *infra* Chapter 1.

[31] The European Union consist of the European Communities, supplemented with a Common Foreign and Security Policy and Police and Judicial Cooperation in Criminal Matters (Article 1 TEU).

sion that endows the European Union with international legal personality.[32] The Treaty of Amsterdam did, however, add a new Article 24 TEU to the EU Treaty. Article 24 TEU permits the conclusion of international agreements by the Council on a proposal from the Presidency, with regard to all matters covered by the Common Foreign and Security Policy.[33] The addition of this article to the EU Treaty has spurred a vivid debate within academic circles as to whether the Union possesses international legal personality.[34] The underlying reasoning being that if the competence to conclude international agreements has been granted to the Council as an institution of the European Union, rather than to the Council acting as an intermediary of the Member States, the European Union must have some measure of implied international legal personality. However, with the European Union concluding several international agreements on the basis of Article 24 TEU, the issue has become moot.[35]

Therefore, it can be argued that to a certain extent and in a limited number of fields, the Member States have begun to accept the legal personality of the Union. This conclusion is not only supported by the fact that the Council, on behalf of the Union, thus making the Union a contracting party, has concluded the agreements. The conclusion is also supported by the fact that none of the Member States has invoked the right to conclude the agreements in accordance with its own constitutional procedure.[36] This in itself proves conclusively that the Union has international legal personality. Other developments also point in this direction. The established practice of third countries to accredit their representatives to the European Union is an example to that effect.

---

[32] In the early, post-Maastricht literature, doubts were raised as to whether the European Union qualified as an international organisation. See in this regard D. Curtin, A Europe of bits and pieces in 30 *C.M.L. Rev.* (1993), at 17.

[33] See also Article 38 TEU with regard to matters in the area of Police and Judicial Cooperation in Criminal Matters. However, the precise link between these two provisions is unclear. See *infra* Chapter 2.

[34] Examples include R. Wessel, The International Legal Status of the European Union in 2 *E.F.A. Rev.* (1997), at 109, S. Breitenmoser, Die Europäische Union zwischen Völkerrecht und Staatsrecht in 55 *ZaöRV* (1995), at 951, N. Neuwahl, 'Legal Personality of the European Union – International and Institutional Aspects' in V. Kronenberger (ed.), *The EU and the International Legal Order: Discord or Harmony?* (2001), at 3-22, J.W. de Zwaan *supra* note 19 and J. Klabbers *supra* note 19. See also *infra* Chapter 2.

[35] Agreement between the European Union and the Federal Republic of Yugoslavia on the activities of the European Union Monitoring Mission (EUMM) in the Federal Republic of Yugoslavia, OJ 2001, L 125/2; Agreement between the European Union and the Former Yugoslav Republic of Macedonia on the activities of the European Union Monitoring Mission (EUMM) in the Former Yugoslav Republic of Macedonia, OJ 2001, L 241/2 and the Agreement between the European Union and the North Atlantic Treaty Organisation on the security of information, OJ 2003, L 80/36.

[36] Article 24(5) TEU provides that "No agreement shall be binding on a Member State whose representative in the Council states that it has to comply with the requirements of its own constitutional procedure; the other members of the Council may agree that the agreement shall nevertheless apply provisionally".

On 18 June 2004, the Member States of the European Union adopted a new European Constitution. The failure of the EU Summit, held in Brussels on 16 and 17 December 2003, to come to an agreement had raised some (serious) doubts with regard to the timetable for the adoption and entry into force of this new Constitution. These fears have now been laid to rest. The European Constitution represents a major step forward for the European Union. The Constitution integrates the current EC into the EU, thereby making the Union a more homogenous entity. Under the Constitution there is only one international organisation, namely, the European Union. Article I-6 of the European Constitution grants the European Union as a whole legal personality.

The purpose and scope of the research

In the past decades, the Community, and to a lesser extent the European Union concluded and became a party to a great number of international agreements.[37] Because of its geographical and market size, its unique internal structure (a mix of supranational and intergovernmental elements) and the dominance that (some of) the Member States have in the international arena, the Community and the Union have acquired a place of great prominence in international relations. This prominent role also means that the external activities of the European Community and the European Union will have and indeed do have an impact on the development of international law and, in particular, the law of treaties. The Union's participation in the creation of the World Trade Organisation, the human rights clauses in association agreements and its participation in the Kyoto Protocol are but a few examples to illustrate this point.[38]

The purpose of this study is therefore to conduct an in-depth comparative legal analysis of the relationship between the Community and the Union's international treaty-making practice and the international law of treaties. This will be done in order to outline the manner in which the Community and Union's international

[37] Examples include the Agreement establishing the General Fisheries Commission for the Mediterranean, OJ 2000, L 197/37; the International Cocoa Agreement, 2001, OJ 2002, L 342/2; the Partnership Agreement between the members of the African, Caribbean and Pacific Group of States of the one part, and the European Community and its Member States, of the other part (Cotonou Agreement), OJ 2000, L 317/3; the Protocol of amendment to the International Convention on the Simplification and Harmonisation of Customs Procedures (Kyoto Convention), OJ 2003, L 71 E/33 and the Agreement between the European Union and the North Atlantic Organisation on the Security of Information, OJ 2003, L 80/36.

[38] See also M. Bulterman, *Human Rights in the Treaty Relations of the European Community. Real Virtues or Virtual Reality?* (2001). According to Marise Cremona "in the institutionalization and evolving constitutionalization of the world trading system through the establishment of the WTO, the EC has played a key role and could even be said to have acted as a role model in some respects", M. Cremona, 'External Relations and External Competence: The Emergence of an Integrated Policy' in P. Craig and G. De Búrca (eds.), *The Evolution of EU Law* (1999), at 167.

treaty-making practice and their participation in international agreements affects or may affect the development of international treaty law. The aim is furthermore to determine whether the existing rules of international treaty law, whether as customary international law or as embodied in the two Vienna Conventions, adequately correspond to the unique character of the European Community and the European Union. If analysis reveals that this is not the case, suggestions will be made as to how the rules should be amended in order to best deal with this reality.

It could be rightfully argued that analysing or proposing ways in which the international law of treaties can be modified in order to meet the needs of the European Community and the European Union sets an unacceptable precedence. Indeed, one of the major shortcomings of the 1986 Vienna Convention is the fact that it applies the rules of the 1969 Vienna Convention, which deals with a rather homogenous group, namely states, to a very diverse group, namely international organisations. This has been one of the main reasons why the European Community was hesitant to participate in the negotiations and why it has so far refused to ratify the 1986 Convention.[39]

The 1986 Vienna Convention applies in principle to all international organisations, in particular those organisations that possess treaty-making powers. Article 2(1)(i) defines an international organisation as an intergovernmental organisation. As a result the 1986 Vienna Convention will apply to a wider and more diverse group of international organisations than was probably foreseen.[40] There is, therefore, a genuine need to modify the existing regime. This conclusion is supported by the fact that all multilateral agreements, permitting the conclusion or the accession to these agreements by international organisations, limit this permission to 'regional economic integration organisations'. The definition of the concept of 'regional economic integration organisation' is clearly based upon the structure of the European Union and it represents a clear departure from the general definition used in the 1986 Vienna Convention.[41]

Still, no other international organisation has the same state-like characteristics as the European Union.[42] And none has developed such an extensive practice of

---

[39] Information obtained through personal interviews with the Legal Services of the Commission and the Council in the period November – December 2003. See also P. Manin, The European Communities and the Vienna Convention on the Law of Treaties between States and International Organisations or between International Organisations in 24 *C.M.L. Rev.* (1987), at 468.

[40] See the proposal from the Special Rapporteur, Mr. Giorgio Gaja, to use a more restrictive definition than the one currently used in the 1986 Vienna Convention and some other international instruments. *Supra* note 18, at 12-13.

[41] See *infra* Section 4.3.1 and C. Schreuer, Die Bedeutung internationaler Organisationen im heutigen Völkerrecht in 22 *AVR* (1984), at 363.

[42] R. Bernhardt, 'Europäisches Gemeinschaftsrecht und das Recht internationaler Organisationen: Gemeinsamkeiten und Unterschiede' in G. Hafner, G. Loibl, A. Rest, L. Sucharipa-Behrmann and K. Zemanek, *Liber Amicorum Seidl-Hohenveldern – in honour of his 80th birthday* (1998), at 25.

concluding international agreements with third countries and other international organisations. Therefore, if the study proves that the existing rules do not adequately correspond to the EU structure, it is justified to propose modifications that have to be made in order to develop rules of international treaty law that better suit the needs of the Community and the Union.

The study is divided into two parts. In Part One the focus will be on the external competence of the European Community and the European Union. To understand their interactions at the international level it is imperative to get a clear insight into the basis of the external treaty-making powers of the two organisations. The external competence of the Community will be analysed in Chapter 1, whereas the external competence of the European Union will be described in Chapter 2.

Part Two of the study will focus on the interaction with the rules of international treaty law. The purpose is not to compare the Community and the Union's practice, as it has developed over the years, to every article of the two Vienna Conventions on the law of treaties. Rather the choice has been made to focus on the main substantive elements of international treaty law, namely, the negotiation and conclusion of international agreements, the entry into force of agreements, the application of international agreements, termination and suspension of agreements, the effects of international agreements on the Member States, treaty interpretation and dispute settlement. These elements are directly related to the actual exercise of an external treaty-making competence. They form the core of the Community and the Union's external treaty practice. Excluded are such issues as state responsibility, diplomatic and consular relations and the conclusion of international agreements and depositaries of international agreements.[43] These subject matters fall outside the scope of the present study because they do not relate directly to the actual exercise of the external treaty-making powers. The amendment of international agreements will not be analyzed in detail. From a Community and Union perspective the procedures are similar to the procedures for the conclusion of international agreements. The exception provided for in Article 300(4) EC is analyzed where appropriate.[44]

---

[43] A number of international agreements, especially bilateral agreements, appoint the General Secretariat of the Council of Ministers of the European Union as the depositary of these agreements. Examples include Article 128 of the EC-Latvia Europe Agreement, OJ 1998, L 26/3 and Article 369 of the Fourth ACP-EEC Convention, OJ 1991, L 229/1. It would have been interesting to see how this function is carried out at EU level in relation to the provisions of the Vienna Conventions. It would be equally interesting to know how the Secretariat's work compares to the way in which the Secretary General of the United Nations performs the task of depositary. Unfortunately no information on the daily practice of the Secretariat was available and the subject matter had to be excluded from the study.

[44] By way of derogation from the general procedure for the conclusion of amendments to international agreements (Article 300(2) EC), the Council may authorize the Commission to approve modifications on behalf of the Community. This is only permitted when the amendments are adopted by a simplified procedure or by a body set up by the agreement. The Council may attach conditions for such authorization.

For the purpose of this study the subject matters of international treaty law to be analysed have been divided into two groups. On the one hand there are the provisions related to the coming into being and entering into force of international agreements. These are treated as the more general substantive elements of international treaty law. On the other hand there are the provisions related to the actual implementation and application of international treaties, namely treaty interpretation and dispute settlement. The first group of elements will be analysed in the Chapters 3 and 4. Treaty interpretation and dispute settlement will be analysed in Chapter 5.

In its external relations the Community can act alone or together with the Member States.[45] In the latter case these agreements are referred to as 'mixed agreements'.[46] This practice is the direct result of the internal division of competences between the Community and the Member States and the case-law of the European Court of Justice.[47] The legal effects at the international and internal level of the Community acting alone or together with the Member States are significant.[48] If only for the fact that the 1969 Vienna Convention on the Law of Treaties could be applied if the Member States participate in the agreement. Chapter 3 will focus on the treaty practice of the Community and the Union acting alone, whereas Chapter 4 will focus on the relationship between mixed agreements and the substantive provisions of international treaty law. Chapter 5 deals with treaty interpretation and dispute settlement with regard to both mixed agreements and agreements concluded by the Community or the Union alone.

METHODOLOGY

A few remarks regarding the methodology. There are two key elements involved in a study of this nature. On the one hand there is the international law aspect. On the other hand there is the element related to the law of international organisations. The first aspect focuses on the manner in which the Community and the Union adhere to, implement or influence the rules of international treaty

[45] So far there are no examples of mixed agreements involving the European Union and the Member States.

[46] I. MacLeod, I.D. Hendry and S. Hyett, *The External Relations of the European Communities* (1996), at 142-164, D. McGoldrick, *International Relations Law of the European Union* (1997), at 78-88 and H.G. Schermers and D. O'Keeffe (eds.), *Mixed Agreements* (1983).

[47] See for example Opinion 1/78, *Natural Rubber*, [1979] ECR 2871; Case 12/86, *Demirel*, [1987] ECR 3719 and Opinion 1/94, *WTO*, [1994] ECR I-625.

[48] At international level the joint participation affects the voting rights of the Community in bodies set up based on an international agreement. There is also the matter of liability for non-performance of (parts of) the agreement. At the internal level joint participation may affect the jurisdiction of the European Court of Justice. It also raises questions as to which part of the agreement may have a direct effect, that is, that citizens can derive rights from the agreement, which they can invoke before national courts.

law. It focuses on the active participation of the Community and the Union in the international arena and the consequences of this participation for the development of international law. This part represents the comparative aspects of the research. Of the two aforementioned elements it is the most important aspect of the research. However, in order to understand the interaction between the participation of the Community and the Union in international relations and their influence on the development of international law, it is also necessary to analyse the way the organisations function internally when they negotiate, conclude and implement international agreements. This second element relates to the manner in which the institutions and the Member States interact at Union and Community level in the negotiation, conclusion and implementation of international agreements. It deals with the law of international organisations. It is impossible to gain a full insight into the first element without analysing the second thoroughly. Therefore, the second element will also be the focus of this research.

Under Article 293 EC the Member States are permitted to enter into negotiations with a view to secure certain benefits for their nationals, such as the abolition of double taxation within the Community (second indent). This article has been the legal basis for the conclusion of various international agreements between Member States. These agreements do not form part of Community law although they cannot negatively affect the functioning of the internal market.[49] Therefore, the agreements are not part of the external treaty practice of the EC. These agreements are excluded from the scope of this research. Similarly are excluded agreements between the Community and Member States, for Community law governs these agreements. International treaty law does not apply in this case.

Finally, this study analyses the treaty-making practice of the Community and the Union in relation to the international law of treaties. It is a matter of the inside looking out. That is to say, the study is primarily an analysis of the approach of the European Community and the European Union to these international rules and not *vice versa*. The information is collected up to 25 June 2004.

---

[49] For example Case C-336/96, *Gilly*, [1998] ECR I-2793. See also B. de Witte, 'Internationale verdragen tussen de lidstaten van de Europese Unie' in Mededeling van de Nederlandse Vereniging voor Internationaal Recht, *De plaats van de Europese Unie in het veranderend bestel van de volkenrechtelijke organisatie*, Preadviezen (2001), at 79-131

Part One

Chapter 1
THE EC'S EXTERNAL TREATY-MAKING COMPETENCE

1.1 Introduction

The purpose of this Chapter is to give a detailed overview of the European Community's competence to conclude international agreements with non-member countries and other international organisations.[1] It should be kept in mind that the conclusion of international agreements is but one element of the external activities of the European Community. The Community has the capacity to enter into a variety of international commitments. These commitments include, among others, the establishment of international organisations, the accession to existing international organisations and international agreements, the power to cooperate in the decision-making processes of international bodies, to enter into international commitments that result from these decisions and to maintain diplomatic missions in third countries or with other international organisations.[2]

The first part of the overview involves an in-depth look at the sources of the Community's external competence. This will be done through an analysis of the different types of treaty-making powers, that is, the express powers (Section 1.2.1) and the implied powers (Section 1.2.2). Subsequently, the nature of these powers, whether they are exclusive (that is, the Community alone becoming a

---

[1] On the external relations of the European Community see, among others, I. MacLeod, I.D. Hendry and S. Hyett, *The External Relations of the European Communities* (1996); D. McGoldrick, *International Relations Law of the European Union* (1997); P.J.G. Kapteyn and P. VerLoren van Themaat, *Introduction to the Law of the European Communities* (1998); P.J.G. Kapteyn en P. VerLoren van Themaat, *Het recht van de Europese Unie en van de Europese Gemeenschappen* (2003); R. Barents and L.J. Brinkhorst, *Grondlijnen van Europees Recht* (2003); K. Lenaerts and E. De Smijter, The European Community's Treaty-making Competence in 16 *YEL* (1996), at 1; T. Tridimas, 'The WTO and OECD Opinions' in A. Dashwood and C. Hillion (eds.), *The General Law of EC External Relations* (2000), at 48; J.P. Pescatore, 'Treaty-making by the European Communities' in F. Jacobs and S. Roberts (eds.), *The Effect of Treaties in Domestic Law* (1987), at 171; A. Bleckmann and C.W.A. Timmermans (eds.), *Division of powers between the European Communities and their Member States in the field of external relations* (1980) and H.G. Schermers and D. O'Keeffe (eds.), *Mixed Agreements* (1983). See also Case 22/70, *AETR*, [1971] ECR 263; Opinion 1/75, *OECD Local Cost Standard*, [1975] ECR 1355; Opinion 1/76, *Rhine navigation*, [1977] ECR 741; Joined Cases 3, 4 and 6/76, *Kramer and others*, [1976] ECR 1279; Case 61/77, *Commission* v *Ireland*, [1978] ECR 417; Opinion 1/78, *Natural Rubber*, [1979] ECR 2871; Ruling 1/78, *Draft IAEA Convention*, [1978] ECR 2151; Opinion 1/91, *EEA I*, [1991] ECR I-6079; Opinion 2/91, *ILO*, [1993] ECR I-1061; Opinion 1/92, *EEA II*, [1992] ECR I-2821Opinion 1/94, *WTO*, [1994] ECR I-5267; Opinion 2/94, *ECHR*, [1996] ECR I-1759; Opinion 1/00, *ESA*, [2002] ECR I-3498 and Opinion 2/00, *Cartagena Protocol on Biosafety*, [2001] ECR I-9717.

[2] I. MacLeod, *supra* note 1, at 28-29.

party to an international agreement – Section 1.3.1) or mixed (the Community and the Member States together becoming a party to the agreement – Section 1.3.2) will be looked at. At this point of the study the subject of exclusive versus mixed external competence will only be analyzed in the context of the nature of the Community's external powers. At a later stage, in the course of an analysis of the characteristics of the Community's treaty law and practice, the compatibility of these types of agreements with the principles of international treaty law as codified in the two Vienna Conventions and as accepted under customary international law, will be studied.[3] In the latter part of this Chapter some related topics that play or may play a (n) (important) role in the Community's external relations will be discussed. These related topics include the use of Article 308 EC (Section 1.4.1); the role of Article 10 EC (Section 1.4.2); and the principle of subsidiarity, Article 5 EC (Section 1.4.3).

The question whether the Community has the competence to act in a specific area and if it does so, the extent of that competence, is of fundamental importance in the discussion concerning the division of powers between the European Community and the Member States. This issue manifests itself at both the internal, Community, level as well as at the external level. The European Community is an international organisation and as such it possesses only those powers that have been attributed to it. This is evidenced by Article 5 EC that provides that "the Community shall act within the limits of the powers conferred upon it by this Treaty and of the objectives assigned to it therein". The Community therefore lacks inherent sovereign powers or a general law-making competence similar to a sovereign state. It has been created under international law by the Member States and its powers are decided by the will of the same.[4]

Contrary to other international organisations, the empowerment of the Community is accompanied by a transfer of sovereign powers from the Member States to the European Community. This transfer is one-way and irreversible.[5] Although Article 312 EC provides that the EC Treaty is concluded for an unlimited time, this in itself does not explain the one-way nature of the transfer of competence. The European Court of Justice nevertheless held that the powers of the European Community find their origin in either a limitation of sovereignty or a transfer of powers from the Member States to the Community.[6] But whereas the

---

[3] See *infra* Chapters 3, 4 and 5.

[4] I. MacLeod *et al*, *supra* note 1, at 39-40.

[5] D. Obradovic, Repatriation of Powers in the European Community in 34 *C.M.L. Rev.* (1997), at 59.

[6] Case 6/64, *Costa/ENEL*, [1964] ECR 585. And in Case 7/71, *Commission* v *France*, [1971] ECR 1003, the Court held that "powers thus conferred could not (...) be withdrawn from the Community, nor could the objectives with which such powers are concerned be restored to the field of authority of the Member States alone" (at 1018). See also the Protocol on the interpretation to the Third Stage of Economic and Monetary Union annexed to the Treaty establishing the European Communities and the Conclusions of the Presidency of the Madrid European Council, Bull. 12-1995, point 1.3.4 on the start of the third stage of the Economic and Monetary Union by 1 January 1999.

Treaty very strictly defines the delimitation of the competences between the institutions of the Community, the same cannot be said of the division of competence between the European Community and the Member States.[7]

The transfer of competence from the Member States to the Community and the resulting limitations that the transfer imposes on the Member States' powers to act, in no way affects their standing under international law. The Member States, as sovereign states, retain their status as subjects of international law and are as such capable of engaging in all external activities, including the conclusion of international agreements.[8] These external activities do not require prior authorisation from the European Community.[9] It is precisely this autonomy that carries with it a serious risk of conflict between Community and Member State action regarding the conclusion of international agreements. Whereas conflicts between national laws and Community law can 'easily' be solved with reference to the principles of 'supremacy of Community law' and 'direct effect', the same cannot be done with regard to the conclusion of international agreements. International agreements are governed by international law and any possible conflict between the Community and the Member States concerning the competence to conclude an agreement cannot be solved on the basis of Community law once the agreement has been ratified and has entered into force. It is therefore imperative that the limits of the Community powers vis-à-vis the Member States are, to a certain extent, known beforehand, or at least before the agreement is ratified.[10] It has been the task of the European Court of Justice to establish, through its case-law, the limits of the Community's external competence and its precise scope.[11]

---

[7] Article 7 EC provides that "Each institution shall act within the limits of the powers conferred upon it by this Treaty". This provision is based on a clear delimitation of the powers of the Institution vis-à-vis one another. This division of competence between the Institutions was confirmed by the Court, among others, in Case 327/91, *France* v *Commission*, [1994] ECR I-3641, where it held that "Even though the Commission has the power, internally, to take individual decisions applying the rules of competition, (...), that internal power is not such as to alter the allocation of powers between the Community institutions with regard to the conclusion of international agreements, which is determined by Article 228 (now 300) of the Treaty" (paragraph 41).

[8] Dashwood describes this apparent paradox and the uniqueness of the formal and informal arrangements involved, as 'a constitutional order of states'. A. Dashwood, The Limits of European Community Powers in 21 *E.L.Rev.* (1996), at 113-114.

[9] M. Waelbroeck, 'The Emergent Doctrine of Community Pre-emption – Consent and Re-delegation' in T. Sandalow and E. Stein (eds.), *Courts and Free Markets: Perspectives from the United States and Europe.* Volume II (1982), at 548-549.

[10] This is not to say that there can be no transfer after the agreement has been concluded or that the division must be precise. It is, however, necessary to know at the time of conclusion who possesses the competence to conclude the agreement and assume the international responsibility.

[11] T. Tridimas and P. Eeckhout, The External Competence of the Community and the Case-Law of the Court of Justice: Principle versus Pragmatism in 14 *YEL* (1994), at 143 and D. O'Keeffe, 'Exclusive, Concurrent and Shared Competence' in A. Dashwood and C. Hillion (eds.), *The General Law of EC External Relations* (2000), at 179.

1.2 The concept of express versus implied external competence

1.2.1 The express external competence of the European Community

As stated before, international organisations derive their powers to act from the agreements upon which they are based. They are allowed to act only to the extent that certain powers have been transferred or attributed to them in the founding treaties by the member states. Even in the absence of an explicit treaty establishing an international organisation, as was the case with the Council for Mutual Assistance, the International Wool Study Group or the Asian-African Legal Consultative Committee, will the powers of the organisation to act be limited by the purpose for which it was created.[12] Therefore, international organisations, as subjects of international law, lack a general competence to enter into international commitments similar to the general competence of states.[13]

The International Court of Justice in the *Reparations for Injuries* Case emphatically stated this position.[14] It held that

> "Accordingly, the Court has come to the conclusion that the Organisation [The United Nations] is an international person. That is not the same thing as saying that it is a State, which it certainly is not, or that its legal personality and rights and duties are the same as those of a State. Still less is it the same thing as saying that it is 'a super-State', whatever that expression may mean".[15]

An international organisation is therefore not competent to create or extend its own competence.[16] Its competence to act is determined by the tasks it was created to fulfil and the objectives it has to achieve. It only has those powers which have

[12] H.G. Schermers and N.M. Blokker, *International Institutional Law* (2003), at 153-155. See also Article 101 Euratom, which provides that "the Community may, *within the limits of its powers and jurisdiction*, enter into obligations through the conclusion of agreements or contracts with a third country, an international organisation or a national of a third State" (emphasis added).

[13] In Opinion 2/94, *ECHR*, [1996] ECR I-1759, the ECJ ruled that the Community could not rely on Article 308 EC to become a party to the European Convention on Human Rights of 1950, because this would amount to a modification of the Treaty. Such an amendment was only possible through the procedure provided for in the Treaty (paragraph 30). And in Case 327/91, *France* v *Commission*, [1994] ECR I-3641, the Court annulled the Commission's Decision concluding an agreement between the Community and the United States ruling that the Commission could not increase its own powers beyond those provided for by the Treaty (paragraph 41).

[14] I.C.J. Reports (1949), at 73.

[15] *Ibid*, at 74.

[16] In Opinion 1/94, *WTO*, [1994] ECR I-5267, the ECJ refuted the argument put forward by the Commission that Article 308 EC could be used as a legal basis for the Community's exclusive competence to become a party to the WTO agreement. The Court found that Article 308 EC could not be used to create an exclusive external competence where that competence did not exist internally (paragraph 89). The international organisation is, however, in the absence of any express provisions to that extent, competent to determine the precise scope of its competence, as the European Court of Justice has done repeatedly.

been attributed to it (compétence d'attribution). The attribution of these powers can be made by an express reference in the founding treaties (express powers) or can be derived from the provisions of those founding treaties (implied powers).[17] The principle of attribution of competence applies to both the internal and external activities of international organisations. This was confirmed by the European Court of Justice, which held that

> "It follows from Article 3b (now 5) of the Treaty, which states that the Community is to act within the limits of the powers conferred upon it by the Treaty and of the objectives assigned to it therein, that it has only those powers which have been conferred upon it.
> That principle of conferred powers must be respected in both the internal action and the international action of the Community".[18]

Regarding the external competence of international organisations it must furthermore be observed that these organisations are only capable to act in the external field if they are provided with international legal personality. This is normally done through an express conferment in the founding treaties.[19] However, in the case of the United Nations Charter, such reference did not exist. Still, the International Court of Justice drew the conclusion that the United Nations did possess the legal capacity to bring an international claim. It stated that the functions of the United Nations are of such nature that they could not be effectively discharged if they involved the concurrent action, on the international plane, of fifty-eight or more Foreign Offices. The Court then concluded that the Members have endowed the United Nations with the capacity to bring an international claim when necessary in the course of the discharge of its functions. If an international organisation is to execute the tasks for which it was created, it should be considered to have the power to act on the international plane, and thus have international legal personality, if those tasks so require.[20]

Article 281 EC provides that the Community shall have legal personality. Article 282 EC provides that "In each of the Member States, the Community shall enjoy the most extensive legal capacity accorded to legal persons under their laws; it may, in particular, acquire or dispose of movable and immovable property and may be a party to legal proceedings. To this end the Community shall be represented by the Commission". Read together these provisions lead to the conclusion that the legal personality provided for by Article 281 EC is an internal and external legal personality, permitting the Community to act within the legal orders of the Member States and at the international level.

This was confirmed by the European Court of Justice in the *Costa/ENEL* Case where it ruled, that "the Member States had created a Community of unlimited

[17] H.G. Schermers *et al*, *supra* note 12, at 153-155.

[18] Opinion 2/94, *ECHR*, [1996] ECR I-1763, paragraphs 23 and 24.

[19] See also *supra* General Introduction.

[20] I.C.J. Reports (1949), at 178-179.

duration, having (...) its own legal capacity and *capacity of representation on the international plane*" (emphasis added).[21] And in the *AETR* Case the Court further stressed the external character of Article 281 EC. It ruled that

> "This provision [Article 281 EC], placed at the head of Part Six of the Treaty, devoted to 'General and Final Provisions', means that in its external relations the Community enjoys the capacity to establish contractual links with third countries over the whole field of objectives defined in Part One of the Treaty, which Part Six supplements".[22]

Article 2 of the EC Treaty enumerates the tasks the Community has to perform. These tasks are to be carried out on the basis of the non-exhaustive list of activities mentioned in the Articles 3 and 4 EC. These articles cannot in themselves function as the legal basis for specific Community action, nor do they indicate whether the Community possesses an express treaty-making competence. One would have to look at the individual provisions in Part Three of the Treaty, entitled Community Policies, to find the provisions that grant the Community an express treaty-making competence.[23]

The original EEC Treaty contained only a few provisions, which granted the Community an express external power.[24] The Articles 302-304 EC dealt with administrative cooperation with various international organisations, such as the United Nations and the Council of Europe. Furthermore, the Articles 133 and 310 EC conferred an express power to conclude international agreements. Article 133 EC did so for the conclusion of agreements relating to the Common Commercial Policy, whereas Article 310 EC provided for the conclusion of the so-called association agreements. After several Treaty amendments, the latest being the Treaty of Nice, the current EC Treaty provides the Community with the express power to conclude international agreements in the following areas[25]

- Agreements concerning monetary or foreign exchange regime matters with one or more states or international organisations (Article 111 EC).
- Agreements relating to the common commercial policy (Article 133 EC). These include trade and tariff agreements, agreements in the field of trade in services and the commercial aspects of intellectual property.[26]

---

[21] Case 6/64, *Costa* v *ENEL* [1964] ECR 585, at 593.

[22] Case 22/70, *AETR*, [1971] ECR 263, paragraph 14.

[23] See also A. Dashwood, *supra* note 8, at 116.

[24] See, for example, I. MacLeod *et al*, *supra* note 1, at 45-46; D. McGoldrick, *supra* note 1, at 43-47; P. Pescatore, *supra* note 1, at 172-175; P. Pescatore, External Relations in the Case-Law of the Court of Justice of the European Communities in 16 *C.M.L. Rev.* (1979), at 618-619 and H. Lecheler, Die Pflege der auswärtigen Beziehungen in der Europäischen Union in 32 *AVR* (1994), at 8-11.

[25] See also I. MacLeod *et al*, *supra* note 1, at 44-46; K. Lenaerts *et al*, *supra* note 1, at 6-7; T. Tridimas and P. Eeckhout, *supra* note 11, at 149 and D. O'Keeffe, *supra* note 11, at 180-181.

[26] K. Lenaerts *et al*, *supra* note 1, point out that Article 133 EC can be used for all international agreements "regulating trade with third countries or seeking to influence trade activity and volume"

- Agreements for the implementation of the multiannual framework programme to be adopted under Article 166 EC. The Community may make provision for cooperation with third countries or international organisations. The detailed arrangements for such cooperation may be the subject of an international agreement between the Community and the third party concerned (Article 170 EC).
- Agreements with third states and the competent international organisations in the sphere of environmental matters (Article 174(4) EC). The Community is to cooperate with the third parties concerned in environmental matters. The arrangements for Community cooperation may be the subject of an international agreement. The agreements are to be concluded on the basis of Article 175 EC.[27]
- Agreements within the context of development cooperation (Article 181 EC).
- Agreements concerning economic, financial and technical cooperation with third countries (Article 181a EC).
- Agreements with one or more states or international organisations establishing reciprocal rights and obligations, common action and special procedures (Article 310 EC).

Article 133(6) EC, third subparagraph, makes reference to the negotiation and conclusion of international agreements in the field of transport and stipulates that the negotiation and conclusion of international agreements shall be governed by Title V (Transport) and Article 300 EC. However, none of the provisions of Title V makes any reference to the express powers of the Community to conclude agreements in the field of transport. Similarly, other areas such as Title II, Agriculture and Title VI (Competition, Taxation and Approximation of Laws) make no reference to an express power of the Community to conclude international agreements. Also the Articles 150(3), 151(3) and 152(3) EC allow the Community and the Member States to foster cooperation with third countries and competent international organisations in the fields of education, vocational training and youth, culture, and public health. These articles contain no express reference to the conclusion of international agreements, but such capacity is not ruled out.[28] Finally, Article 301 EC permits the Community to interrupt or to reduce in part or completely economic relations with third countries on the basis of a common position or joint action adopted on the basis of Title V of the Treaty on European Union.

(at 9-10). See also M. Cremona, Rhetoric and Reticence: EU External Commercial Policy in a Multilateral Context in 38 *C.M.L. Rev.* (2001), at 359 and C. Weber, Wirtschaftsabkommen in System der Europäischen Gemeinschaft – Die Rechtsprechung des Europäischen Gerichtshof in 35 *AVR* (1997), at 295.

[27] See Opinion 2/00, *Cartagena Protocol on Biosafety*, [2001] ECR I-9713.

[28] I. MacLeod *et al*, *supra* note 1, at 46 and D. McGoldrick, *supra* note 1, at 47.

1.2.2 The implied powers of the Community

Despite the extensive case-law of the European Court of Justice to that effect[29], the treaty-making powers of the Community have been a matter that raises a number of unanswered questions.[30] To a large extent this is due to the progressive development of Community law. However, this progressive development has not been so much the direct result of the wording of the Treaty but rather the way in which the Court has interpreted and applied the Treaty. As Costonis puts it

> "In many instances the framers failed to provide clear guidelines for shaping important features of the elaborate machinery required in the conduct of a Community treaty-making program. Nor did they always delineate with precision the substantive ambit of the Community's powers. Even when they did address themselves with relative clarity to these questions, their agreement on language may have served only to mask an underlying disagreement on substance. And the very novelty of the experiment has deprived the Community of authoritative precedent for resolving these and other uncertainties that subsequent practice has brought to light".[31]

However, Dashwood states that

> "(...) the logic of implied powers is that they relate to matters which, it is assumed, would have been specifically mentioned in the text, if draftsmen were infinitely wise and prescient. (...), the logic is different. The failure to mention external powers in the Treaty provisions on agriculture or transport, say, is not because the matter slipped the draftsmen's mind: it is because to confer powers in these policy areas that stopped short at the Community's frontiers would simply not have made any sense. In other words, a text that is silent as to its external application should not be interpreted as one that *expressly* confers internal powers only: the natural way of interpreting an express grant of powers is that they are to apply as needed, internally or externally, in furtherance of the objectives specified in the relevant Treaty Articles".[32]

Article 101 Euratom provides the Atomic Energy Community with the power to engage in external relations that are coextensive with its internal competences.[33] Therefore, if an international agreement is intended to further one of the objec-

---

[29] See case-law *supra* note 1.

[30] Questions remain as to the precise division of powers between the Community and the Member States; the precise scope of the Community's exclusive external competence and whether the Member States regain the competence to act when a Community measure granting the Community an exclusive external competence has been repealed, to name just a few. See also P. Pescatore, *supra* note 1, at 173 and R. Holdgaard, The European Community's Implied External Competence after the Open Skies Cases in 8 *E.F.A. Rev.* (2003), at 370-373.

[31] J.J. Costonis, The Treaty-Making Power of the European Economic Community: The Perspective of a Decade in 5 *C.M.L. Rev.* (1967-1968), at 422.

[32] A. Dashwood, *supra* note 8, at 125.

[33] A similar provision could be found in the former Article 6 ECSC.

tives or goals of this Community it will, under these provisions, have the power to act externally. In the European Community there is no similar provision. Prior to the case-law of the ECJ it was generally held that the Community only possessed express powers.[34] In fact, the absence of a similar provision in the EC Treaty, negotiated and signed simultaneously with the Euratom Treaty, was seen as a strong argument in favour of denying the existence of an implied external competence.[35] However, in the absence of a specific provision granting the Community the power to act, the Community has a parallel competence to act externally if this action is necessary to further one of the objectives of the Community. This principle was confirmed in the case-law of the European Court of Justice (the so-called 'AETR doctrine').

In the *AETR* Case the Court ruled that the authority to enter into international agreements did not only arise from an express conferment by the Treaty but could equally flow from other provisions of the Treaty and from measures adopted within the framework of those Treaty provisions, by the Community Institutions.[36] In the *Kramer* Case the Court ruled that the authority of the Community to enter into international commitments did not only arise from an express conferment by the Treaty but could equally flow implicitly from other provisions in the Treaty, in the Act of Accession and from measures adopted within the framework of those provisions by the Community institutions.[37] And in *Opinion 1/76* the Court held that

> "The power to conclude such an agreement is not expressly laid down in the Treaty. However, the Court has already had occasion to state (...), that authority to enter into international commitments may not only arise from an express attribution by the Treaty, but may equally flow implicitly from its provisions. The Court has concluded inter alia that whenever Community law has been created for the institutions of the Community powers within its internal system for the purpose of attaining a specific objective, the Community has authority to enter into the international commitments necessary for the attainment of that objective even in the absence of an express provision in that connection".[38]

Emiliou points to four important principles resulting from the *AETR* Case. These are the 'principle of general powers', that is, the capacity to enter into agreements with third countries over the whole field of objectives defined in Part One of the Treaty; the 'principle of implied powers', that is, that the authority to enter into agreements may also flow implicitly from other provisions of the Treaty; the 'principle of exclusivity', that is, that the Community alone can become a contracting party and the 'principle of parallelism', that is, the external activities

[34] See literature *supra* note 1.
[35] D. McGoldrick, *supra* note 1, at 48.
[36] Case 22/70, *AETR*, [1971] ECR 263, paragraph 16.
[37] Joined Cases 3, 4 and 6/76, *Kramer and others*, [1976] ECR 1279, paragraphs 19-20.
[38] Opinion 1/76, *Rhine Navigation*, [1977] ECR 741, paragraph 3.

should mirror the internal measures.[39] The *AETR* Case makes a distinction between the attribution of the external competence and the exercise of the competence.[40]

The Court thus recognised that the Community possesses an external power that runs parallel with its internal power, something the draftsmen had left out of the Treaty.[41] However, the recognition that the Community possesses an implied external competence does not mean that the concept can be applied extensively. The competence must be coexistent with the principle of attribution referred to in Article 5 EC.[42] Thus, the principle of parallelism cannot be used to widen the substantive scope of the Community's external competence.[43] Furthermore, the doctrine of implied powers is closely connected to the Community's express powers. If the Treaty imposes restrictions on the internal use of the express powers, this will affect the Community's implied external competence.[44]

If the case-law of the European Court of Justice established that the Community has the implied powers to operate in the international arena, it did not do so regarding the exact scope of these powers and the nature of the competence, which arise from applying the principles developed by the Court.[45] These issues have remained unclear and controversial. The successive Treaty amendments have codified the case-law on the implied powers doctrine. As a result, the areas in which the Community has an express external competence have increased. The treaty-making powers of the Community will, therefore, increasingly be determined on the basis of these provisions, rather than with reference to the implied powers doctrine.[46]

Whenever the Community has an internal competence to act it has a corresponding external competence if such is necessary to achieve a specific objective of the Community. The mere existence of an internal competence can give rise to

[39] N. Emiliou, Towards a clearer demarcation line? The division of external relations power between the Community and Member States in 31 *JCMS* (1993), at 79-80. See also A. Barav, 'The Division of External Relations Power between the European Economic Community and the Member States in the Case-Law of the Court of Justice' in A. Bleckmann and C.W.A. Timmermans (eds.), *Division of powers between the European Communities and their Member States in the field of external relations* (1981), at 33.

[40] Case 22/70, *AETR*, [1971] ECR 263, paragraphs 17 and 18. See also J. Auret-Finck, L'Avis 2/91 relatif à la Convention No 170 de l'OIT in 3-4 *CDE* (1995), at 453.

[41] D. McGoldrick, *supra* note 1, at 51.

[42] A. Dashwood, *supra* note 8, at 124.

[43] T. Tridimas *et al*, *supra* note 11, at 153.

[44] D. McGoldrick, *supra* note 1, at 49-50. A point in case is Article 152 EC. This article provides that the Community action must complement national policies in the field of public health. Therefore, the Community is barred from concluding any international agreement that does not meet this requirement of complementarity. Similarly, Article 151 EC prohibits the adoption of harmonising measures at Community level. The Community cannot, therefore, conclude an international agreement that would have such an effect on the laws of the Member States.

[45] I. MacLeod *et al*, *supra* note 1, at 47-49.

[46] However, Declaration No. 10 attached to the Final Act of the Treaty on the European Union, TEU, states that the AETR doctrine remains unaffected by the provisions of the TEU.

a competence to conclude international agreements. The Community need not have exercised this internal competence.[47] The doctrine of implied powers thus recognises the independence of the Community to act in its own right and not merely as a medium for the Member States.[48] The doctrine is closely tied to the internal division of powers between the Community and the Member States. However, it does not affect the division of powers among the institutions. The principle of parallelism does not apply to the powers of the institution when acting externally. The express provisions of the Treaty govern these powers.[49]

In its early case-law, the Court left many questions unanswered concerning the nature of the competence, i.e. whether it was an exclusive Community competence or not.[50] Nor did the case-law say whether the competence also involved a treaty-making competence. The Court only determined that the implied competence existed, and that it could, under certain conditions, be exclusive. The Court, in this early case-law, did not outline all instances where an exclusive competence could occur. Furthermore, the acknowledgement of the existence of an implied external competence does not provide the answer to the type of agreement that can be concluded or the kind of provisions that can be included in the agreement.[51] In its recent case-law the European Court of Justice has clarified some of the controversy surrounding its implied powers doctrine.[52]

In *Opinion 2/91*, for example, the Court held that the

> "authority to enter into international commitments may not only arise from an express attribution by the Treaty, but may also flow from its provisions. In particular, whenever Community law created for the institutions of the Community powers within its internal system for the purpose of attaining a specific objective, the Community had authority to enter into the international commitments necessary for the attainment of that objective even in the absence of an express provision in that connection. At paragraph 20 in its judgment in Joined Cases 3, 4 and 6/76 Kramer and others [1976] ECR 1279, the Court had already pointed out that such authority could flow from other

[47] See I. MacLeod *et al*, *supra* note 1, at 50-51; T. Tridimas *et al*, *supra* note 11, at 151-152; G.L. Close, Self-restraint by the EEC in the exercise of its External Powers in 1 *YEL* (1981), at 46-47; P. Pescatore, *supra* note 1, at 173 and H. Lecheler, *supra* note 24, at 11-12.

[48] M. Cremona, 'External Relations and External Competence: The Emergence of an Integrated Policy' in P. Craig and G. De Búrca (eds.), *The Evolution of EU Law* (1999), at 150.

[49] T. Tridimas *et al*, *supra* note 11, at 152. See also Case 327/91, *France* v *Commission*, [1994] ECR I-3641.

[50] A distinction must be drawn between the existence and the nature of the implied powers of the Community. Existence refers to the capacity or the authority to conclude agreements. The nature refers to whether it is the Community acting alone (exclusive competence) or together with the Member States (mixed agreements). See also A. Maunu, The implied external competence of the European Community after the ECJ Opinion 1/94 – Towards coherence or diversity? in *LIEI* 1995/2, at 115 and R. Holdgaard, *supra* note 30, at 368-370.

[51] P. Eeckhout, 'Expliciete en impliciete externe bevoegdheden na Maastricht – Status quaestiones?' in Asser Instituut Colloquium Europees Recht, *Externe bevoegdheden van de Europese Unie* (1993), at 3.

[52] D. McGoldrick, *supra* note 1, at 61 and A. Barav, *supra* note 39, at 36.

measures adopted by the Community institutions within the framework of the Treaty provisions or acts of accession".[53]

This position was restated in *Opinion 2/92* in which the Court held that the Community's external competence could, in the absence of express provisions in the Treaty, be deduced from its internal powers to act.[54] And in *Opinion 1/94* the Court ruled that the competence of the Community to act internationally "arises not only from an express conferment by the Treaty (...) but may equally flow from other provisions of the Treaty and from measures adopted, within the framework of those provisions, by the Community institutions".[55]

It is clear from *Opinions 2/92* and *1/94* that the Court adopts a more restrictive interpretation of the implied external powers of the Community than in its earlier case-law.[56] The Court utilises a rigorous approach in its interpretation of the condition of necessity before the doctrine of implied powers can be applied. It states that the mere existence of an internal competence does not necessitate a corresponding external competence. Only where the external activity is necessary for the attainment of a specific objective of the Community, does the doctrine apply. Furthermore, the resulting competence can only be exclusive if it is necessary that internal and external action occur simultaneously in order to achieve a Community objective.[57]

On the basis of the Court's case-law there are in fact three ways in which the Community can obtain an implied power.[58] The first involves the situation where measures have been adopted by the institutions on the basis of an internal power.[59] The second situation involves the existence of an external power based upon an internal power, but where no internal measures have been adopted and it is necessary that the external and internal powers are exercised at the same time. The last instance of implied power arises when the power is based on an internal power that has not yet been exercised but where an external power is necessary for the achievement of a specific objective.

---

[53] Opinion 2/91, *ILO*, [1993] ECR I-1061, paragraph 7.

[54] Opinion 2/92, *OECD II*, [1995] ECR I-521, paragraph 29.

[55] Opinion 1/94, *WTO*, [1994] ECR I-5267, paragraph 48.

[56] See also T. Flory and F-P. Martin, Remarques à propos des Avis 1/94 et 2/92 de la Cour de Justice des Communautés Européennes au regard de l'évolution de la notion de Politique Commerciale Commune in 3-4 *CDE* (1996), at 379.

[57] See also K. Lenaerts *et al*, *supra* note 1, at 7.

[58] I. MacLeod *et al*, *supra* note 1, at 48-49 and D. McColdrick, *supra* note 1, at 48-50.

[59] It should be observed that provisions in an internal measure do not confer competence on the Community. They merely recognise the existence of a competence. The competence finds its origin in the Treaty. McGoldrick, *supra* note 1, at 55.

1.3 NATURE OF THE EUROPEAN COMMUNITY'S EXTERNAL COMPETENCE

1.3.1 The exclusive external competence of the Community

The principle of attribution means that within the scope of the EC Treaty, the powers that originally belonged to the Member States have been transferred to the Community. In the ambit of the Treaty, the division of competence between the European Community and its Member State is thus primarily based on the principle of concurrent powers.[60] This means that the division is not based on competence with regard to specific areas (Mittel der Kompetenzausscheidung nach Sachgebieten), but rather one where the competence of the Member States to regulate in a certain areas diminishes as the competence of the Community to legislate in that specific area increases (kumulativ-konkurrierende Zuständigkeit).[61] In some areas, however, the provisions of the Treaty on which the competence to act is based, interpreted in accordance with a stated objective of the Community, can grant the Community an exclusive competence.

The exclusive competence of the Community was confirmed in the case-law of the Court of Justice.[62] The analysis of the Court has been characterised by an examination into the existence of a Community competence followed by a look into the possible exclusive nature of that competence. In accordance with the Court's case-law the European Community has an exclusive competence with regard to both contractual and autonomous measures.[63] For example this is the case with the Common Commercial Policy (Article 133 EC).[64] In *Opinion 1/75* the Court ruled that the Common Commercial Policy was conceived

> "for the defence of the common interest of the Community, within which the particular interests of the Member States must endeavour to adapt to each other. Quite clearly, however, this conception is incompatible with the freedom to which the Member States could lay claim by invoking a concurrent power, so as to ensure that their own

[60] D. McGoldrick, *supra* note 1, at 68.

[61] P.J.G. Kapteyn, Het Advies 1/76 van het Europese Hof van Justitie, de externe bevoegdheid van de Gemeenschap en haar deelneming aan een Europees oplegfonds voor de binnenscheepvaart in 4 *SEW* (1978), at 278.

[62] See, for example, Case 41/76, *Donckerwolcke*, [1976] ECR 1921]; Opinion 1/75, *OECD Local Cost Standard*, [1975] ECR 1355; Opinion 1/76, *Rhine Navigation*, [1977] ECR 741; Opinion 1/78, *Natural Rubber*, [1979] ECR 2871 and Opinion 1/94, *WTO*, [1994] ECR I-5267. See also N. Emiliou, The Death of Exclusive Competence? in 21 *E.L.Rev.* (1996), at 294; D. O'Keeffe and N. Emiliou (eds.), *The European Union and World Trade* (1996); A. Barav, *supra* note 39 and M. Cremona, *supra* note 48.

[63] Contractual measures are bilateral and multilateral agreements concluded by the Community with third countries and other international organisations. Autonomous measures are unilateral Community measures, such as anti-dumping measures, that affect the position of third countries or their nationals. P. Craig and G. De Búrca, *EU Law. Text, Cases, and Materials* (2002), at 128.

[64] The Treaties of Amsterdam and Nice have modified and extended the competence of the Community under Article 133. Agreements concluded on the basis of paragraph 6 must be mixed agreements.

interests were separately satisfied in external relations, at the risk of compromising the effective defence of the common interest of the Community. To accept that the contrary were true would amount to recognizing that, in relations with third countries, Member States may adopt positions which differ from those which the Community intends to adopt, and would thereby distort the institutional framework, call into question the mutual trust within the Community and prevent the latter from fulfilling its task in the defence of the common interest".[65]

In its landmark *AETR* Case the Court had already stated that "each time the Community, with a view to implementing a common policy envisaged by the Treaty, adopts provisions laying down common rules, whatever form these may take, the Member States no longer have the right, acting individually or even collectively, to undertake obligations with third countries which affect those rules".[66] And in Case *804/79*, the Court concluded that since the expiration of the transitional period laid down by the Act of Accession, which was 1 January 1979, the Member States were "no longer entitled to exercise any power of their own in the matter of conservation measures in the waters under their jurisdiction".[67] As from that date the adoption of these conservation measures was a matter of Community law.

In *Opinion 2/91* the Court ruled that

"The exclusive or non-exclusive nature of the Community's competence does not flow solely from the provisions of the Treaty but may also depend on the scope of the measures which have been adopted by the Community institutions for the application of those provisions and which are of such a kind as to deprive the Member States of an area of competence which they were able to exercise previously on a transitional basis. As the Court stated at paragraph 22 in its judgment in Case 22/70 (...), where Community rules have been promulgated for the attainment of the objectives of the Treaty, the Member States cannot, outside the framework of the Community institutions, assume obligations which might affect those rules or alter their scope".[68]

It should be pointed out that the mere fact that the subject matter of an international agreement comes within the competence of the Community does not automatically mean that the Community has an exclusive competence.[69] Still, whenever the Community's external competence is exclusive it will falls to the Community to negotiate and conclude the corresponding international agreements. Only in those instances where, as a consequence of a rule of international law, the Community is barred from exercising its competence will it be up to the Member States to act collectively on behalf of the Community.[70] It is generally

---

[65] Opinion 1/75, *OECD Local Cost Standard*, [1975] ECR 1355, at 1363-1364.
[66] Case 22/70, *AETR*, [1971 ECR 263, paragraph 17.
[67] Case 804/79, *Commission* v *United Kingdom*, [1981] ECR 1045, paragraph 18.
[68] Opinion 2/91, *ILO*, [1993] ECR I-1061, paragraph 9.
[69] K. Lenaerts *et al*, *supra* note 1, at 7 and T. Trimas *et al*, *supra* note 11, at 155.
[70] Opinion 2/91, *ILO*, [1993] ECR I-1061. See also K. Lenaerts *et al*, *supra* note 1, at 7.

accepted that there are four ways in which the Community can obtain an exclusive external competence[71] : 1) express provisions in the Treaty or the Acts of Accession; 2) express provisions in internal measures; 3) where it flows from the scope of an internal measure; and 4) when, in specific circumstances, the internal powers can only be exercised effectively if they are exercised at the same time as the external powers.

1.3.1.1 *Express provisions in the Treaty or Acts of Accession*

It is settled case-law that the European Community has an exclusive external competence with regard to the Common Commercial Policy and the Common Fisheries Policy.[72] In the case of the Common Commercial Policy the Court held that the policy was intended to defend the common interest of the Community and that such an aim could not be achieved if the Member States retained a concurrent external power.[73] Although some question marks may be placed behind the Court's decision as to why the common interest can only be defended through an exclusive competence for the Community, the logic behind the Court's reasoning is quite clear. In a number of areas the Community is called upon to adopt common policies without any reference to the precise scope of these policies.[74] The precise extent of these policies, as a matter of Community law, is subject to the interpretation of the European Court of Justice. The Court has argued that these common policies are the source of an exclusive competence because allowing the Member States to adopt a position vis-à-vis third countries different from the one adopted by the Community could 'distort the institutional framework' and 'call into question the mutual trust within the Community'.[75] Any other conclusion would lead to the Member States adopting a position in their external relations that could seriously undermine the proper functioning of these policies.[76]

McGoldrick questions the validity of the Court's arguments. In his view the Court starts from a pre-established division of competence when it is actually called upon to decide on this very issue.[77] The Court, it would seem, starts from the basic idea that the Common Commercial Policy is an area belonging to the

[71] I. MacLeod *et al*, *supra* note 1, at 56-61; D. McGoldrick, *supra* note 1, at 68-72; P.J.G. Kapteyn *et al* (1995), *supra* note 1, at 1259-1261 and P.J.G. Kapteyn *et al* (2003), *supra* note 1, at 1079-1081.

[72] See Opinion 1/94, *WTO*, [1994] ECR I-5267, Joined Cases 3, 4 and 6/76, *Kramer*, [1976] ECR 1279 and Case C-405/92, *Driftnets*, [1993] ECR I-6133.

[73] N. Emiliou, *supra* note 62, at 299-300; D. O'Keeffe, *supra* note 11, at 35-37; I. MacLeod *et al*, *supra* note 1, at 57 and Chapter 12 and D. McGoldrick, *supra* note 1, at 69-70.

[74] See, for example, Article 133(1) EC read in conjunction with Article 3(1)(e) EC.

[75] Opinion 1/75, *OECD Local Cost Standard*, [1975] ECR 1355. See also D. McGoldrick, *supra* note 1, at 70.

[76] See also Case 22/70, *AETR*, [1971] ECR 263 and Joined Cases 3, 4 and 6/76, *Kramer and others*, [1976] ECR 1279.

[77] D. McGoldrick, *supra* note 1, at 70.

exclusive domain of the Community. The Court subsequently looks at the provisions of the (proposed) international agreement to determine whether they fall completely within the ambit of the Common Commercial Policy or not. If they do, the Community alone must conclude the agreement. If not, the agreement either falls under the competences of the Member States and the Community jointly, or of the Member States only.[78] In Cremona's opinion the Court's position is "a characteristic mixture of pragmatism and (again) the link between external and internal trade policy".[79] However, looking at the Court's case-law, its reason for accepting exclusive external Community competence is to protect the unity of the common market and the uniform application of Community law.[80]

MacLeod *et al* conclude that in the area of EC competition law, more specifically the Articles 81 to 86 EC, the Community also enjoys an exclusive external competence.[81] Their conclusion is based on *Opinion 1/92* where the Court ruled that the Community was empowered under the competition rules in the E (E) C Treaty to conclude international agreements in the field of competition law.[82] They argue that because the European Community has exclusive internal regulatory powers within this field it means that the Community also has an exclusive external competence.

In Case *327/91*, which involved the signing of an international agreement between the Commission and the United States in the area of competition law, the Court annulled the Commission's decision authorising the Vice President of the Commission to sign the said agreement.[83] This was not done because the Community could not conclude such an agreement. The Court annulled the Commission's decision because the Commission had acted in contravention of the procedure laid down in Article 300 EC.[84] This Article stipulates that the Council concludes international agreements (paragraph 2). Because the issue was not raised, the Court did not state whether the Community as such could sign this

[78] See Opinion 1/94, *WTO*, [1994] ECR I-5267. In the *Donckerwolcke* Case, Case 41/76, [1976] ECR 1921, the Court, in the absence of a complete Common Commercial Policy, recognizes the rights of the Member States to adopt protective measures, provided that these measures are in accordance with the EC Treaty, more particularly with Article 134 EC (paragraph 31). However, Member States are not permitted to enact protective measures in anticipation of the possible application of Article134 EC (paragraph 43). Only in cases of urgency Member States are allowed to act without prior authorization from the Commission.

[79] M. Cremona, *supra* note 48, at 154.

[80] K. Lenaerts *et al*, *supra* note 1, at 9 and T. Tridimas *et al*, *supra* note 11, at 156-159.

[81] I. MacLeod *et al*, *supra* note 1, at 57. See also D. McGoldrick, *supra* note 1, at 70.

[82] Opinion 1/92, *EEA II*, [1992] ECR I-2821, paragraphs 38-41.

[83] Case 327/91, *France* v *Commission*, [1994] ECR I-3641. According to AG Tesauro the Commission possesses independent decision-making powers in the field of competition, while only the Council has a general legislative power. Opinion of AG Tesauro, Case 327/91, *France* v *Commission*, [1994] ECR I-3643, paragraph 39.

[84] *Ibid*, paragraph 41. In the words of Hartley "the doctrine of parallelism applies only between the Community and the Member States, not between the Council and the Commission". T.C. Hartley, *The Foundations of European community Law. An Introduction to the Constitutional and Administrative Law of the European Community* (2003), at 174.

agreement. Still, none of the parties in the proceedings contested whether the Community could sign such an agreement.

In his Opinion in Case *327/91*, Advocate General Tesauro states that Article 85 EC does not confer an exclusive power on the Commission with regard to the Articles 81, 82 and 86(3) EC.[85] Article 85 EC requires that the Commission co-operate with the Member States and the national courts. The legislative power in the field of competition remains "firmly vested in the Council".[86] Although the Court has held that with regard to the enforcement of competition rules the Commission and the national courts have concurrent powers, this does not automatically mean that the Community and the Member States share the legislative powers in the field of competition law. In the *BNIC* Case the Court held that although the Articles 81 and 82 EC apply to the behaviour of undertakings and not the legislative and administrative measures of the Member States, the Member States are not allowed to adopt any national measure that could eliminate the useful effect of these Articles.[87] This is not the same as saying that the Member States cannot adopt national legislation or conclude international agreements.[88] Practice shows that the Member States maintain their own competition laws, laws that are concurrent with the Community rules and apply where the intra-Community element is lacking. Within the ambit of the national laws, and in accordance with the limitations Community law places on the Member States, they are permitted to act externally. Therefore, the Community does not possess an exclusive external competence in the field of competition law.

1.3.1.2 *Express provisions in internal measures*

A number of secondary laws contain provisions explicitly authorising the EC to enter into international agreements with third countries and other international organisations.[89] In *Opinion 1/94* the Court confirmed this practice.[90] The Court's statement should be read with some care though. In the Court's reasoning the Community's power would become exclusive "whenever the Community has in-

---

[85] Opinion AG Tesauro, Case 327/91, *France* v *Commission*, [1994] ECR I-3643, paragraph 38.

[86] *Ibid*, paragraph 39. See also Article 83 EC.

[87] Case 136/86, *BNIC* v *Aubert*, [1987] ECR 4789, paragraph 23.

[88] Article 83(2)(e) EC provides that the Council can adopt regulations or directives "to determine the relationship between national laws and the provisions contained in this section or adopted pursuant to this article".

[89] Article 24(4) of Council Regulation 4064/89, OJ 1990, L 257/14, provides that "Whenever it appears to the Commission (...) that a non-member country does not grant Community undertakings treatment comparable to that granted by the Community to undertakings from that non-member country, the Commission may submit proposals to the Council for an appropriate mandate for negotiation with a view to obtaining comparable treatment for Community undertakings". Similarly Article 9(2) of Council Regulation 4056/86, OJ 1986, L 378/4, provides that "Where agreements with third countries need to be negotiated, the Commission shall make recommendations to the Council, which shall authorize the Commission to open the necessary negotiations".

[90] Opinion 1/94, *WTO*, [1994] ECR I-5267, paragraphs 94 and 95.

cluded in its internal legislative acts provisions relating to the treatment of nationals of non-member countries or expressly conferred on its institutions powers to negotiate with non-member countries".[91] This would imply that whenever the Community has adopted internal measures granting the Community the power to conclude an international agreement this power would automatically be exclusive. This cannot be the case.

Exclusivity based upon a Treaty provision is the result of a transfer of competence from the Member States to the Community.[92] This transfer finds its origin in the unique constitutional structure of the Community legal order. It is a legal order based upon a system of concurrent powers between the Community and the Member States. Within the ambit of the Treaty, Community legislation must respect the division of competence between the Community and the Member States.[93] To phrase it differently, an internal measure cannot award the Community an exclusive external competence when the provision that has been used as the legal basis for the Community legislation provides that the Member States and the Community share the competence.

Articles 174(4) and 181(3) EC, allow the Community and the Member States, within their respective spheres of competence to conclude international agreements. Community legislation that excludes actions on the part of the Member States would run counter to these express Treaty provisions. It is established case-law that certain practices, even if accepted by the parties involved, cannot derogate from the Treaty provisions.[94] Member States would thus have the right to enter into international agreements, but under the condition that these agreements are compatible with Community law.[95]

1.3.1.3 *Exclusive competence derived from the scope of an internal measure*

The principle that Member States are excluded from entering into international agreements that may affect the scope of a Community measure, was adopted by the Court in the *AETR* Case and has become known as the 'AETR doctrine'. The Court held that "each time the Community with a view to implementing a common policy envisaged in the Treaty, adopts provisions laying down common rules, whatever form these may take, the Member States no longer have the right, acting individually or even collectively, to undertake obligations which affect those rules".[96] The Court's conclusions make good sense. If in the internal sphere

---

[91] *Ibid*, paragraph 95.

[92] In this case the Member States are, in principle, pre-empted from adopting national legislation or concluding international agreements. See T. Tridimas, *supra* note 1, at 58.

[93] See I. MacLeod *et al*, *supra* note 1, at 60; T. Tridimas, *supra* note 1, at 58; D. McGoldrick, *supra* note 1, at 71 and D. O'Keeffe, *supra* note 11, at 188.

[94] Opinion 1/94, *WTO*, [1994] ECR I-5267, paragraph 52 and Case 327/91, *France* v *Commission*, [1994] ECR I-3641, paragraph 36.

[95] Article 10 EC.

[96] Case 22/70, *AETR*, [1971] ECR 263, paragraph 17.

Member States are precluded from adopting national measures that run counter to or affect Community measures[97] the same principle should apply in the external sphere.[98] Accepting a different view would be tantamount to stating that in the external treaty relations the principles of 'supremacy' of Community law over national law and 'Community loyalty', Article 10 EC, do not apply.[99]

In *Opinion 2/91* the Court elaborated its thesis some more. It held that the exclusive competence of the Community included situations in which the Community had not yet legislated exhaustively.[100] The Member States could not enter into the agreement in question, even though there was no direct conflict between the provisions of Part III of the ILO Convention and the existing Community directives. The Court argued, however, that Part III of the ILO Convention dealt with matters that were already covered to a large extent by Community legislation adopted with a view to achieving an even greater degree of harmonisation.[101] Under the 'AETR doctrine' Member States are precluded from adopting any measure, including the conclusion of an international agreement, that would alter or affect the scope of Community measures. This is not to say that they are precluded from adopting any measures in that particular field. If, within the internal sphere the Member States have the power to adopt more stringent measures, nothing bars them from doing so through an international agreement.[102]

Jans states that the provisions of Article 174(4) EC could be interpreted as allowing the Member States to negotiate and conclude international agreements despite the existence of exhaustive Community legislation.[103] It should be pointed out that although the Articles 174(4) and 181 EC prohibit that Community legislation contains an express provision granting the Community an exclusive external competence, these articles do not stand in the way of the Community acquiring an exclusive external competence through complete or exhaustive harmonisation.[104] Various international agreements require the Community to declare the extent of its competence with respect to matters governed by the agree-

---

[97] See Case 39/72, *Commission* v *Italy*, [1973] ECR 101, paragraph 17; Case 50/76, *Amsterdam Bulb* v *Produktschap voor Siergewassen*, [1977] ECR 137, paragraphs 4-7 and Case 94/77, *Zerbone*, [1978] ECR 99, paragraphs 24-25.

[98] P.J.G. Kapteyn *et al* (1995), *supra* note 1, at 324-325 and P.J.G. Kapteyn *et al* (2003), *supra* note 1, at 1079-1080. See also M. Waelbroeck, *supra* note 9, at 549-550; D. Obradovic, *supra* note 5, at 61-65 and C.W.A. Timmermans, *Het recht als multiplier in het Europese integratieproces. Iets over bevoegdheidsverhoudingen tussen Gemeenschap en Lid-Staten* (1978), at 3-13.

[99] D. O'Keeffe, *supra* note 11, at 182; I. MacLeod *et al*, *supra* note 1, at 58 and D. McGoldrick, *supra* note 1, at 71-72.

[100] Opinion 2/91, *ILO*, [1993] ECR I-1061, paragraph 25. See also I. McLeod *et al*, *supra* note 1, at 58-59.

[101] Opinion 2/91, *ILO*, [1993] ECR I-1061, paragraph 25.

[102] J. Jans, *European Environmental Law* (2001), at 85-87 and D. O'Keeffe, *supra* note 11, at 183-186.

[103] J. Jans, *supra* note 102, at 85.

[104] See Opinion 2/91, *ILO*, [1993] I-1061 and Opinion 1/94, *WTO*, [1994] ECR I-5267.

ments.[105] The Community declarations, as a standard, make reference to the continuing transfer of competence from the Member States to the Community, or list the objectives the Community is permitted to pursue.[106] Because it is not always possible to indicate exactly whether a specific area has been completely occupied by the Community, the Member States could invoke Article 174(4) EC as grounds for denying the Community an exclusive competence. In the end it will be up to the Court to determine in each individual case whether the Community has acquired an exclusive competence. If the existing legislation covers the main elements of the international agreement, the Community will have acquired an exclusive competence.[107]

It should also be said that the mere fact that the Community has the competence to adopt a common policy is in itself not enough to grant the Community an exclusive external competence. In *Opinion 1/94* the Court ruled that where internal rules have not yet been adopted, there is room for the Member States to undertake commitments towards third countries.[108] These external activities by the Member States are subject to the provisions of Article 10 EC and must not hinder the Community in fulfilling its own objectives.

1.3.1.4 *Exclusive competence derived from a simultaneous exercise of the internal and external powers*

In the *Kramer* Case the Court ruled that the competence of the Community to conclude international agreements did not only arise from an express conferment by the Treaty, but could equally flow implicitly from its provisions.[109] In *Opinion 1/76* the Court elaborated its conclusion. It held that

> "Although the internal Community measures are only adopted when the international agreement is concluded and made enforceable, as is envisaged in the present case by the proposal for a regulation to be submitted to the Council by the Commission, the power to bind the Community vis-à-vis third countries nevertheless flows by implication from the provisions of the Treaty creating the internal power and in so far as the participation of the Community in the international agreement is, as here, necessary for the attainment of one of the objectives of the Community".[110]

The Court's reasoning has been open to broad interpretation. Under this broad interpretation the Community would acquire an exclusive external competence ev-

[105] See, for example, Article 24(3) of the Kyoto Protocol to the United Nations Framework Convention on Climate Change, OJ 2002, L 130/4 and Article 34(3) of the Convention on Biological Diversity, OJ 1993, L 23/177.

[106] Declaration by the European Community made in accordance with article 24(3) of the Kyoto Protocol, OJ 2002, L 130/20.

[107] T. Tridimas, *supra* note 1, at 58-59.

[108] Opinion 1/94, *WTO*, [1994] ECR I-5267, paragraph 77.

[109] Joined Cases 3, 4 and 6/76, *Kramer and others*, [1976] ECR 1279.

[110] Opinion 1/76, *Rhine Navigation*, [1977] ECR 741, paragraph 4.

ery time it could not (fully) achieve an objective without bringing third countries into the scheme.[111] In *Opinion 1/94* the Court refined its conclusion. In response to the Commission's argument that the coherence of the internal market would be impaired if the Community was not allowed to conclude the General Agreement on Trade in Services, GATS, on the basis of an exclusive external competence the Court held the following

> "That is not the situation in the sphere of services: attainment of freedom of establishment and freedom to provide services for nationals of the Member States *is not inextricably linked* to the treatment to be afforded in the Community to nationals of non-member countries or in non-member countries to nationals of Member States of the Community" (emphasis added).[112]

Reliance on the 'Opinion 1/76 doctrine' requires a two-step approach. First it has to be proved that a specific objective cannot be attained through the adoption of autonomous measures. Second, the objective can only be fully attained by bringing a third country into the scheme. The competence will, however, only be exclusive if the contractual relation with the third country is inextricably linked to the attainment of the specific objective. Failure to prove the latter requirement will render the agreement a mixed agreement.

1.3.2 **Mixed agreements**

The mixed agreement is a unique instrument in international relations. It is unique in the sense that it involves a shared contractual relationship between an international organisation and its members and one or more third countries and/or international organisations. It is also unique in that it is exclusively used by the European Communities and its Member State. In fact, mixed agreements are of paramount importance to the external activities of the Community.[113] They are

---

[111] See also D. O'Keeffe, *supra* note 11, at 188-189.

[112] Opinion 1/94, *WTO*, [1994] ECR I-5267, paragraph 86.

[113] On the subject of mixed agreements see for example H.G. Schermers *et al*, *supra* note 1; I. Macleod *et al*, *supra* note 1; D. McGoldrick, *supra* note 1; J. Heliskoski, *Mixed Agreements as a technique for Organizing the International Relations of the European Community and Its Member States* (2001); R. Arnold, Der Abschluss gemischter Verträge durch die Europäischen Gemeinschaften in 19 *AVR* (1980-1981), at 419; T. Cottier and A. Caplazi, *Das Genehmigungsverfahren beim Abschluss völkerrechtlicher Abkommen in der Europäischen Union* (1998); J. Temple Lang, The Ozone Layer Convention: A new solution to the question of Community participation in "mixed" international agreements in 23 *C.M.L. Rev.* (1986), at 157; C. Timmermans and E. Völker (eds.), *Division of powers between the European Communities and their Member States in the field of external relations* (1981); N. Neuwahl, Joint Participation in International Treaties and the Exercise of Power by the EEC and Its Member States: Mixed Agreements in 28 *C.M.L. Rev.* (1991), at 717; N. Neuwahl, Shared Powers or Combined Incompetence? More on Mixity in 33 *C.M.L. Rev.* (1996), at 667; J. Megret, *Le Droit de la Communauté Économique Européenne. Commentaire du Traite et des Textes Pris pour son application*, Volume 12, Relations extérieures (1980); P. Pescatore, *supra* note 1; T. Tridimas *et al*, *supra* note 11 and K. Lenaerts *et al*, *supra* note 1.

the direct result of the specific internal structure of the Community and of the jurisprudence of the European Court of Justice.[114] Although the Court did not use the term 'mixed agreement' as such, in *Opinion 1/78*[115] it did stipulate that there are instances where, because of a shared competence between the European Community and the Member States, the latter are empowered to conclude international agreements alongside the Community. Up to that point, the Court's decisions had focused primarily on the existence of an external Community competence[116] and the precise scope of this competence.[117] *Opinion 1/78* added a further elaboration of the rules applying to the Community's external competence and the relation between this competence and the external competence of the Member States in the fields covered by the EC Treaty.

In *Opinion 1/94* the Commission pointed out that problems could arise as regards the administration of the GATS and the Agreement on the Trade Related Aspects of Intellectual Property Rights, TRIPs, agreements if the Community and the Member States shared the competence to participate in the conclusion of these agreements. The Court, although recognising the legitimacy of this concern, replied by saying that

> "It must be stressed, first, that any problems which may arise in the implementation of the WTO Agreement and its annexes as regards the coordination necessary to ensure unity of action where the Community and the Member States participate jointly cannot modify the answer to the question of competence, that being a prior issue. As the Council has pointed out, resolution of the issue of the allocation of competence cannot depend on problems which may possibly arise in administration of the agreements".[118]

And in *Opinion 2/00*[119] the Commission argued that permitting the conclusion of the Cartagena Protocol as a mixed agreement on the basis of the Articles 133 and 175 EC, would bring serious difficulties in its implementation. In the Commission's opinion the agreement should be concluded on the basis of the Com-

---

[114] The EC Treaty, with the exception of Article 133(6) EC, makes no express reference to the conclusion of mixed agreements. There are, however, a number of provisions that provide that the Community competence is without prejudice to the Member States' competence to negotiate and conclude international agreements (Articles 111(5), 174(4) and 181 EC). On the other hand, Article 102 Euratom explicitly recognizes the possibility for the conclusion of mixed agreements involving Euratom and the Member States on the one part and third countries and/or international organisations on the other. Similarly, Article 6(2) of the Act of Accession, Official Journal of 23.9.2003, at 33, obliges the new Member States to accede to agreements and conventions concluded by the current Member States and the Community, acting jointly.

[115] Opinion 1/78, *Natural Rubber* [1979] ECR 2871. In Case 12/86, *Demirel*, [1987] ECR 3719, the Court did use the term mixed agreement in reference to the EC/Turkey Association Agreement (paragraphs 8 and 9).

[116] See, for example, Case 22/70, *AETR*, [1971] ECR 263.

[117] Joined Cases 3, 4 and 6/76, *Kramer and others*, [1976] ECR 1279, Opinion 1/75, *OECD Local Cost Standard*, [1975] ECR 1355 and Opinion 1/76, *Rhine Navigation*, [1977] ECR 741.

[118] Opinion 1/94, *WTO*, [1994] ECR I-5267, paragraph 107.

[119] Opinion 2/00, *Cartagena Protocol on Biosafety*, [2001] ECR I-9713.

munity's exclusive competence ex Article 133 EC. The Court summarily dismissed the Commission's argument by saying that

> "Whatever their scale, the practical difficulties associated with the implementation of mixed agreements, which are relied on by the Commission to justify recourse to Article 133 EC – conferring exclusive competence on the Community so far as concerns common commercial policy – cannot be accepted as relevant when selecting the legal basis for a Community measure".[120]

This has led Dashwood to the following assertion

> "It is an inescapable aspect of the constitutional character of the Community that the competence conferred by the EC Treaty in external as well as in internal matters is limited, and usually shared with the Member States. Mixed agreements are a natural and practical mechanism to enable the Union, with its character as a constitutional order of States, to function effectively on the international plane".[121]

The European Community is a legal order based upon a concurrent sharing of competences between the Community and the Member States. In practical terms this means that in certain, limited areas the Member States have transferred part of their sovereign legislative powers to the Community in order to achieve certain common goals as defined in the Articles 2 and 3 EC.[122] Thus the Community is first and foremost an ongoing integration process. This means that the increment of the fields in which the Community has the capacity to act is a continuous process. The Single European Act, the Maastricht Treaty, the Treaty of Amsterdam and the Treaty of Nice have all added to the number of areas in which the Community has a legislative capacity. The Court has held that being of a supranational character, Community law takes precedence over (conflicting) national legislation.[123] This does not only mean that existing conflicting national laws should be set aside, but also that the Member states are barred from adopting new legislation that may contravene or affect existing EC laws.[124] This principle equally applies in the sphere of the external relations in that in certain areas the Community is the only entity capable of entering into a binding international commitment with third countries and other international organisations.[125]

---

[120] *Ibid*, paragraph 41.

[121] A. Dashwood, Opinion 2/00, Cartagena Protocol on Biosafety in 39 *C.M.L. Rev.* (2002), at 367-368.

[122] See also Case 26/62, *Van Gend en Loos*, [1963] ECR1 and the Preamble to the Treaty establishing the European Community.

[123] See Case 26/62, *Van Gend en Loos*, [1963] ECR 1 and Case 6/64, *Costa/ENEL*, [1964] ECR 585. It must be pointed out that the Court has never used the term 'supranational'. The concept finds its origin in the literature.

[124] See, for example, Case 26/62, *Van Gend en Loos*, [1963] ECR 1; Case 152/84, *Marshall*, [1986] ECR 723 and Case C-213/89, *Factortame*, [1990] I-2433.

[125] The Court held that permitting the Member States to conclude international agreements in the domains reserved for the Community would distort the internal functioning of the Community and undermine the mutual trust. Opinion 1/75, *OECD Local Cost Standard*, [1975] ECR at 1364.

However, as its is a continuous process, there are instances in which the transfer of competences is not complete, that is to say that the Member States have retained a concurrent competence to act in certain areas.[126] There is also the possibility that the Community may not have exercised its competence yet. In the internal arena this means that the Member States remain competent to adopt national legislation.[127] In the situation where the Member States have retained some residual powers they will only loose those powers once the competence to act has been transferred to the Community institutions, or when external action by the Member States, either individually or collectively, could distort or affect existing Community legislation.[128] Where the Member States retain the competence to act externally we find the phenomenon of the so-called mixed agreements.

Mixed agreements are generally defined as agreements to which the European Community and the Member States are a party.[129] A shortcoming of this definition is that it does not make any reference to the exact division of competence between the Community and the Member States. Neither is it clear whether the participation of all the Member States is required for the agreement to be qualified as a mixed agreement. MacLeod *et al* distinguish the following situations in which competence is shared between the Community and its Member States[130]

1. Where the sharing of competence flows from the Treaty provision conferring power on the Community (for example Article 174(4) EC).[131]
2. Where the Community has not yet adopted common rules on the basis of an existing internal competence.[132]
3. Where an international agreement covers subject matters that fall within the competence of both the European Community and the Member States.[133]

---

[126] In his Opinion in Case C-316/91, *Parliament* v *Council*, [1994] ECR I-625, Advocate General Jacobs held that "with regard to development aid to the ACP States, there is nothing in the Treaty, or in the provisions adopted by the Community institutions pursuant to the Treaty, which points to one conclusion that the Community's competence is exclusive. In the absence of any indication to the contrary, it can be accepted that the Community and the Member States share competence in that field" (paragraph 40). Therefore, the conclusion must be that mixed competence between the Community and the Member States is the rule and exclusive competence for the Community the exception. See I. MacLeod *et al*, *supra* note 1, at 64.

[127] Joined Cases 3, 4 and 6/76, *Kramer and others*, [1976] ECR 1279, paragraph 39.

[128] Opinion 2/91, *ILO*, [1993] ECR I-1061.

[129] H.G. Schermers, 'A Typology of Mixed Agreements' in D. O'Keeffe and H.G. Schermers (eds.), *Mixed Agreements* (1983), at 23. Other authors such as I. MacLeod *et al*, *supra* note 1, at 143; D. McGoldrick, *supra* note 1, at 78-79; R. Leal-Arcas, The European Community and Mixed Agreements in 6 E.F.A. Rev. (2001), at 483; and A. Rosas, 'The European Union and Mixed Agreements' in A. Dashwood and C. Hillion (eds.), *The General Law of EC External Relations* (2000), at 203-207 adhere to this definition.

[130] I. MacLeod *et al*, *supra* note 1, at 63-66.

[131] See Case C-316/91, *European Parliament* v *Council*, [1994] ECR I-625, paragraphs 26 and 27. See also the Opinion of AG Jacobs, paragraphs 40 and 41.

[132] See in this regard Joined Cases 3, 4 and 6/76, *Krame and others*, [1976] ECR 1279.

[133] See Opinion 1/78, *Natural Rubber*, [1979] ECR 2871 and Ruling 1/78, *Draft IAEA Convention*, [1978] ECR 2151.

4. Where the internal Community measure consists of rules setting minimum standards.[134]
5. In certain areas, for example intellectual property rights, where the competence of the European Community and the competence of the Member State can coexist without either displacing the other.[135]

Schermers, on the other hand, does not only classify mixed agreements on the basis of their substantive nature, but also with regard to the number of Member States participating in the agreement.[136] Thus he qualifies as "incomplete mixed agreements" those agreements in which only some Member States participate.[137] He also distinguishes between so-called true and false mixed agreements. A false mixed agreement would be an agreement that comes within the exclusive competence of the Community and where the participation of the Member States has no legal substance.[138] A true mixed agreement is an agreement that comes within the shared competences of the European Community and the Member States. Timmermans, however, only distinguishes between what he calls 'classic or real mixed agreements' and 'quasi or sometimes false mixed agreements'.[139] Broadly speaking, his classifications follow those of Schermers.

Alan Rosas provides the most comprehensive classification.[140] Based on Schermers' classification, Rosas also distinguishes between parallel competences and shared competences.[141] In the case of parallel competences the Community and the Member States may become a party, each enjoying the full scale of rights and obligations like any other party to an international agreement.[142] Shared competences presuppose a certain division of competence between the Community and the Member States.

Among the agreements based upon shared competences, Rosas distinguishes between agreements based upon co-existent and concurrent competences.[143] In the case of mixed agreements based upon co-existent competences in principle it is possible to separate the international agreement into two separate parts, with the Community and the Member States being responsible for their respective

---

[134] See Opinion 2/91, *ILO*, [1993] ECR I-1061.

[135] See Opinion 1/94, *WTO*, [1994] ECR I-5267.

[136] H.G. Schermers, *supra* note 129, at 26-28.

[137] *Ibid*, at 26.

[138] *Ibid*, at 27.

[139] C.W.A. Timmermans, 'Organising joint participation of E.C. and Member States' in A. Dashwood and C. Hillion (eds.), *The General Law of E.C. External Relations* (2000), at 241.

[140] A. Rosas, *supra* note 129, at 203-207. See also A. Rosas, 'Mixed Union – Mixed Agreements' in M. Koskenniemi (ed.), *International Law Aspects of the European Union* (1998), at 128-133; and R. Leal-Arcas, *supra* note 129, at 488-493.

[141] A. Rosas, *supra* note 129, at 203.

[142] The most commonly used example is the Agreement establishing the European Bank for Reconstruction and Development, OJ 1990, L 372/1.

[143] A. Rosas, *supra* note 129, at 203-204.

parts.[144] Rosas further divides mixed agreements based upon co-existent competences into agreements where there is a 'horizontal' or 'sectoral' distribution of competences, and agreements with a 'vertical' distribution of competences.[145] In the case of horizontal mixed agreements the Member States would be competent to conclude part of the main substantive parts of the agreements, whereas in the case of vertical mixed agreements the Community would be competent as far as the main substantive provisions are concerned and the Member States would be competent with regard to the remaining or even ancillary matters.[146]

Furthermore, Rosas points out that in case of agreements based upon vertical co-existent competences it can be difficult or even impossible to separate the agreement into a part within the Member States' competence and a part within the Community's competence. In this instance the Community and Member States' competences are concurrent. Therefore, the agreement must be negotiated and concluded by the Community and the Member States. Alan Rosas also distinguishes between mixed agreements in which the participation of the Member States is 'facultative' (optional) and instances where the Member States' participation is 'obligatory' (legally necessary). [147] Mixed agreements are facultative where there are no competences explicitly reserved for the Member States, and obligatory in the event of shared competences.[148]

Finally, depending on the contracting parties of the Community and the Member States, mixed agreements can be divided into bilateral agreements and multilateral agreements. A bilateral mixed agreement is an agreement in which the Community and the Member States, as one party, assume a contractual relation with one single contracting party. This party can consist of one third state or international organisation, as was the case with the Europe Agreements[149], or a group of states and/or international organisations, as in for example the Cotonou Agreement.[150] A multilateral mixed agreement is an agreement involving the Community and one or more Member States, as one party, and two or more third states and/or international organisations, where each party assumes a contractual relation vis-à-vis all the other parties.[151]

The joint participation of the Community and the Member States in international agreements raises some difficulties with regard to the negotiation and conclusion of these agreements. This argument has been used frequently by the

[144] *Ibid*, at 204.

[145] *Ibid.*

[146] Rosas uses the 1982 Law of the Sea Convention as an example of a horizontal mixed agreement and the IAEA Convention, which was the basis for *Ruling 1/78* as an example of a vertical mixed agreement. *Ibid.*

[147] A. Rosas, *supra* note 129, at 205-206.

[148] *Ibid.*

[149] For example, the Europe Agreement with the Slovak Republic, OJ 1994, L 359/2.

[150] OJ 2000, L 317/3.

[151] For example, the United Nations Framework Convention on Climate Change, OJ 1993, L 33/13.

Commission in order to try to convince the Court to rule that the Community should conclude the agreement on the basis of an exclusive competence. The Court has consistently refuted this argument and has held that the difficulties involved in the negotiation and administration of mixed agreements cannot be used to deny the existence of a joint competence.[152] Despite the Court's position the Commission remains adamant that the use of mixed agreement should be limited as much as possible.[153] However, as pointed out at the beginning of this Section, the Court's ruling in *Opinion 2/00* appears to have settled the matter once and for all in favour of the Member States.

In *Opinion 1/94* the Court ruled that

> "Where it is apparent that the subject-matter of an agreement or convention falls in part within the competence of the Community and in part within that of the Member States, it is essential to ensure close cooperation between the Member States and the Community institutions, both in the process of negotiation and conclusion and in the fulfilment of the commitments entered into. That obligation to cooperate flows from the requirement of unity in the international representation of the Community".[154]

Timmermans points out that the duty of close cooperation is in fact more specific than the general principle of Community loyalty under Article 10 EC.[155] According to him the reason for this is that the duty to cooperate is linked directly to the requirement to preserve the unity in the international presentation of the Community.[156] The only way in which the full range of rights under the agreement can be exercised, while at the same time all obligations are carried out, is through a unified and coherent approach of the Member States acting closely together with the Community.

1.4 Related topics

In the previous Sections a comprehensive overview of the different ways in which the Community obtains and exercises its external treaty-making competence was presented. It was outlined that sometimes the exercise of this competence occurs in conjunction with the Member States. The previous Sections have dealt with the main forms of Community external treaty activities. There are some related issues that have not been dealt with yet, but which are also of some (considerable) importance with regard to the subject of the external treaty-making

---

[152] See for example Opinion 1/94, *WTO*, [1994] ECR I-5267, paragraph 104.

[153] Information obtained during personal interviews with the Legal Service of the Commission in the period November-December 2003.

[154] Opinion 1/94, *WTO*, [1994] ECR I-5267, paragraph 108.

[155] C.W.A. Timmermans, *supra* note 139, at 241.

[156] *Ibid.*

competence of the European Community and the manner in which this competence is exercised. These issues include the use of Article 308 EC, the role of Article 10 EC and the relevance of the principle of subsidiarity (Article 5 EC) in the external arena.

1.4.1 The use of Article 308 EC

Article 308 EC provides that

> "If action by the Community should prove necessary to attain, in the course of the operation of the common market, one of the objectives of the Community and this Treaty has not provided the necessary powers, the Council shall take the appropriate measures".[157]

In *Opinion 1/94* the Court ruled that this Article (308 EC) "enables the Community to cope with any insufficiency in the powers conferred on it, expressly or by implication, for the achievement of its objectives".[158]

Article 308 EC contains two elements for its application. First its use must be necessary for the attainment of one of the objectives of the Community. The question that springs to mind is whether the objectives referred to include only those enumerated in the Articles 2 and 3 EC. Kapteyn *et al* argue that the use of Article 308 EC should not be restricted to just the general objectives enumerated in the two aforementioned articles. It should also include the objectives mentioned in the various articles of the Treaty.[159] Or as Leefmans puts it, the objectives of the Community encompass more than just the mere sum of all specific objectives as formulated in the Articles 2 and 3 EC.[160] Olmi even contends that some of these objectives can be deduced from the Preamble of the EC Treaty.[161] However, the Preamble itself cannot be the source of the objectives of the Treaty for it has no legal effect. It can aid in determining the objective of the EC Treaty as a whole or in determining the scope of the objectives contained in the Treaty.[162] But the Preamble itself cannot serve as the legal source of the objectives embodied in the EC Treaty.

---

[157] A similar provision can be found in Article 203 Euratom and the former Article 95 ECSC.

[158] Opinion 1/94, *WTO*, [1994] ECR I-5267, paragraph 89.

[159] P.J.G. Kapteyn *et al* (1995), *supra* note 1, at 236 and P.J.G. Kapteyn *et al* (2003), *supra* note 1, at 184-185 See also T.C. Hartley, *supra* note 84, at 104. Although Article 308 EC cannot be used for the adoption of autonomous measures or the conclusion of international agreements in the area of development co-operation, it can be used, for example, as an additional legal basis for the conclusion of international agreements that do not only pursue the general objectives of development cooperation mentioned in Article 177 EC. See in this regard, K. Lenaerts *et al*, *supra* note 1, at 14-15.

[160] P.J. Leefmans, *Externe milieubevoegdheden. Communautairrechtelijke grenzen aan externe milieubevoegdheden van de EG-lidstaten* (1998), at 37.

[161] G. Olmi, *La place de l'article 235 CEE dans le système d' attribution de compétence à la Communauté* (Volume 2, 1979), at 85.

[162] In Case 26/62, *Van Gend en Loos*, [1963] ECR 3, the Court made use of the Preamble of the EC Treaty as an additional source to confirm that the objective of the EC Treaty is more than a mere agreement which creates mutual obligations between the contracting states.

Article 308 EC stipulates that this article can be used to attain one of the objectives of the Treaty "in the course of the operation of the common market". This phrase should not be interpreted merely in a strict geographical sense. Rather, the application of this article is necessary to guarantee that the internal market as defined by the EC Treaty will continue to function effectively.[163] The Community does not only possess those powers that have been explicitly attributed to it in the EC Treaty, but it also possesses those powers which are necessary for it to fulfil the task for which it was created. Article 308 EC is intended to fill these lacunae.

The second condition for the application of Article 308 EC is that this article can only be used if the Treaty has not provided the necessary powers.[164] However, this provision should not be read in an absolute sense. The use of Article 308 EC is not restricted to only those situations where no express provisions exist at all. Article 308 EC can also be used in those situations where the existing provisions do not provide for a satisfactory and effective solution.[165] Thus, the European Court of Justice, in the *Massey-Ferguson* Case, accepted that the Council could have recourse to Article 308 EC where such action was justified in the interest of legal certainty.[166] Still, Article 308 EC cannot be used in contravention of the Treaty.[167]

The use of Article 308 EC is not restricted, however, to just internal measures. It can also be used as the legal basis for the external treaty relations of the EC. Prior to the Single European Act, the Council frequently used Article 308 EC as legal basis for concluding international environmental agreements.[168] As long as

[163] P.J.G. Kapteyn *et al* (1995), *supra* note 1, at 236; P.J.G. Kapteyn *et al* (2003), *supra* note 1, at 184-185 and T.C. Hartley, *supra* note 84, at 108-109. Dashwood proposes to alter the wording of Article 308 EC to "an objective directly affecting the establishment or functioning of the internal market. A. Dashwood, *supra* note 8, at 123. So far his calls have gone unheeded.

[164] Case 45/86, *Commission* v *Council*, [1987] ECR 1493, paragraph 13; Case C-350/92, *Spain* v *Council*, [1995] ECR I-1985, paragraph 26 and Opinion 2/92, *OECD II*, [1995] ECR I-521, paragraph V-8. See also A. Dashwood, *supra* note 8, at 123.

[165] P.J.G. Kapteyn *et al* (1995), *supra* note 1, at 236; P.J.G. Kapteyn *et al* (2003), *supra* note 1, at 185 and T.C. Hartley, *supra* note 84, at 108-109.

[166] Case 8/73, *Massey-Ferguson*, [1973] ECR 897, paragraph 4.

[167] Article 151(5) EC prohibits any harmonisation of national laws and regulations in the field of Culture. The Community Institutions cannot, therefore, have recourse to Article 308 EC in order to circumvent this express prohibition. Similarly, Article 308 EC cannot be used in conjunction with another Treaty provision that provides for a different decision-making procedure. This would render the other decision-making procedure meaningless. See also Case 300/89, *Titanium Dioxide*, [1991] ECR I-2867 and P. Craig *et al*, *supra* note 63, at 126-127.

[168] For example, Council Decision 81/462 on the conclusion of the Convention on long-range transboundary air pollution, OJ 1981, L 171/11; Council Decision 77/586 concluding the Convention for the protection of the Rhine against chemical pollution, OJ 1977, L 240/35; Council Decision 77/585 concluding the Convention for the protection of the Mediterranean Sea against pollution and the Protocol for the prevention of pollution of the Mediterranean Sea by dumping from ships and aircrafts, OJ 1977, L 240/2 and Council Decision 75/438 concerning Community participation in the Interim Commission established on the basis of Resolution No III of the Convention for the preven-

the requirements for its application are met, there is no objection to the use of Article 308 EC in the external sphere.[169] McGoldrick argues, based on the Court's ruling in *Opinion 1/94*, that Article 308 EC, like the Articles 94 and 95 EC, will only give rise to an external competence where it has been used beforehand as the legal basis for the adoption of internal measures.[170] McLeod *et al*[171] and De Schutter *et al*[172] dispute this conclusion. De Schutter and Lejeune are correct in stating that

> "Toutefois, il n'y a apparemment aucune raison de croire que les conditions de reconnaissance d'une compétence internationale non exclusive de la Communauté puissent être différentes de celles qui viennent d'être rappelées".[173]

Still, wherever its application, internal or external, Article 308 EC cannot be used to enlarge the scope of the Community competence beyond the general framework resulting from the provisions of the Treaties as a whole, and in particular from those defining the Community's objectives and tasks.[174] Allowing Article 308 EC to serve such a purpose would be equal to use it as a tool for the amendment of the Treaty. Thus the Court held that "Article 235 (now 308) cannot be used as a basis for the adoption of provisions, whose effect would, in substance, be to amend the Treaty without following the procedure which it provides for that purpose".[175] It is for the Member States to adopt any measure that goes be-

tion of marine pollution from land-based sources, OJ 1975, L 194/22. See also C.W.A. 'Timmermans, Division of external powers between Community and Member States in the field of harmonisation of national law – A case study' in A. Bleckmann and C.W.A. Timmermans (eds.), *Division of powers between the European Communities and their Member States in the field of external relations* (1980), at 16-18 and P.J. Leefmans, *supra* note 160, at 60-61.

169 One should keep in mind that even if the requirements are met this does not automatically mean that Article 308 EC must be used. It is for the Council to determine whether the adoption of a particular measure is necessary (policy decision). Article 308 EC confers on the Council an option rather than an obligation. Failure to exercise this option cannot affect the validity of the proceedings. See Case 22/70, *AETR*, [1971] ECR 263, paragraph 95 and Opinion 1/94, *WTO*, [1994] ECR I-5267, paragraph 89. At the same time the Council cannot use the intergovernmental approach, the Representatives of the Member States meeting in the Council, if the measure to be adopted can also be based on Article 308 EC. See Case 8/73, *Massey-Ferguson*, [1973] ECR 897, paragraph 4 and P.J.G. Kapteyn *et al* (1995), *supra* note 1, at 238 and P.J.G. Kapteyn *et al* (2003), *supra* note 1, at 186.

170 D. McGoldrick, *supra* note 1, at 66.

171 I. MacLeod *et al*, *supra* note 1, at 55.

172 O. De Schutter and Y. Lejeune, L'Adhésion de la Communauté à la Convention Européenne des Droits de l'Homme à propos de l'Avis 2/94 de la Cour de Justice des Communautés in 3-4 *CDE* (1996), at 570.

173 *Ibid.* In the *Kramer* Case the Court recognised the right of the Community to act externally whenever it possesses an internal competence, even in the absence of implementing measures. This principle equally applies to Article 308 EC. Joined Cases 3, 4 and 6/76, *Kramer and others*, [1976] ECR 1279.

174 Opinion 2/94, *ECHR*, [1996] ECR I-1759, paragraph 30.

175 *Ibid.*

yond the objectives of the Treaty. Adoption of such measures at Community level must be preceded by an amendment of the Treaty in accordance with the procedure of Article 48 TEU.

There are two ways in which Article 308 EC can be used as a legal basis for external activities. The first is where internal measures have been adopted on the basis of Article 308 EC. Depending on the type of internal rules, common rules or rules containing minimum standards, this external competence can either be exclusive or shared with the Member States. The competence can also be exclusive when participation by the Member States is likely to alter or affect the Community rules adopted on the basis of Article 308 EC.[176] However, Article 308 EC in itself cannot vest an exclusive competence in the Community at international level.[177] David O'Keeffe sums it up best

> "(...) Internal legislation under Article 308 should be regarded as an extraordinary measure. At the external level, an uninhibited use of Article 308 to provide for exclusive external competence even where no effective internal measure was taken would be detrimental to the terms of the transfer of sovereignty by the Member States. Despite the strict scrutiny to which Article 308 is subject as regards necessity and the aims of the Community, it nevertheless has a very wide scope and its acceptance as the basis for exclusive Community competence in the absence of internal measures could give rise to an extensive exclusive Community competence of unpredictable range. It therefore seems appropriate that its use as a basis for exclusive Community competence should be tempered by the requirement that there must first be internal measures adopted on the basis of the law-making powers".[178]

The second way in which Article 308 EC can be used is in accordance with the principle set out in *Opinion 1/76*, that is, if the participation of the Community in the international agreement is necessary for the attainment of one of the objectives of the Community and if it is necessary that the internal and external activity occur simultaneously.[179] However, similar to *Opinion 1/94*, the Institutions must prove that the external activity pursued is inextricably linked to the achievement of the internal objective.[180]

It must be stated, however, that the use of Article 308 EC has diminished considerably since the coming into force of the Single European Act, the Treaty on European Union, the Treaty of Amsterdam and the Treaty of Nice. These Treaties have introduced various specific powers in relation to a number of areas, such as monetary capacity, social policy and the environment, to name just a few. These new provisions now serve as legal basis for the Community's internal and exter-

---

[176] Compare the Court's reasoning in Opinion 2/91, *ILO*, [1993] ECR I-1061.

[177] Opinion 1/94, *WTO*, [1994] ECR I-5267, paragraph 89. See also I. MacLeod *et al*, *supra* note 1, at 54 and D. McGoldrick, *supra* note 1, at 66.

[178] D. O'Keeffe, *supra* note 11, at 191.

[179] Opinion 1/76, *Rhine Navigation*, [1977] ECR 741.

[180] Opinion 1/94, *WTO*, [1994] ECR I-5267, paragraph 85.

nal competences. The European Council during its Summit in Edinburgh in 1992 not only excluded the application of Article 308 EC from the fields of education, vocational training and youth, culture and public health, it also stipulated that Article 308 EC must be used in accordance with the principles of subsidiarity and proportionality.[181] The Council thus explicitly recognizes that the principles embodied in Article 5 EC place an additional restriction on the use of Article 308 EC.

1.4.2 **The role of Article 10 EC in the external relations of the Community**

Article 36 *bis* of the Draft Articles of the 1986 Vienna Convention on the Law of Treaties between States and International Organisations or between International Organisations, provided that an international agreement concluded by an international organisation would directly create rights and obligations in relation to the member states of that organisation by the mere fact that the founding treaty of the organisation expressly provided for the agreement to have such effect. This provision, which met with much opposition, was eventually withdrawn.[182] The wording of Article 36 *bis* is similar to the text of Article 300(7) EC that provides that agreements concluded by the Community shall be binding on the institutions of the Community and the Member States. Despite the similarity, the Community was opposed to the inclusion of Article 36 *bis* because under the wording of this article the Members would derive their rights directly from the international agreement itself rather than through the Community.[183] This would entail a right for the Member States to act outside the Community scheme to seek redress for an alleged infringement of the agreement by a third party. And such while the Community alone was the official contracting party.

In Case *327/91* the Court held that "it is the Community alone, having legal personality pursuant to Article 210 (now 281) of the Treaty, which has the capacity to bind itself by concluding agreements with a non-member country or an international organisation".[184] In the *Haegeman* Case the Court stated that

> "This agreement is therefore, in so far as concerns the Community, an act of one of the institutions of the Community within the meaning of subparagraph (B) of the first paragraph of Article 177 (now 234).

---

[181] Bull. EC 12-1992, point I.15.

[182] Article 34 of the Vienna Convention on the Law of Treaties between States and International Organisations or between International Organisations, hereinafter referred to as the 1986 Vienna Convention, provides that international agreements do not create rights or obligations for third states or organisations. Convention adopted on 21 March 1986, not yet entered into force, reprinted in 25 *I.L.M.* (1986), at 543.

[183] P. Manin, The European Communities and the Vienna Convention on the Law of Treaties between States and International Organisations or between International Organisations in 24 *C.M.L. Rev.* (1987), at 468-471.

[184] Case 327/91, *France* v *Commission*, [1994] ECR I-3641, paragraph 24.

The provisions of the agreement, from the coming into force thereof, form an integral part of Community law".[185]

And in the *Kupferberg* Case the Court ruled that

"The Treaty establishing the Community has confirmed upon the institutions the power not only of adopting measures applicable in the Community but also of making agreements with non-member countries and international organisations in accordance with the provisions of the Treaty. According to Article 228(2) (now 300(7)) these agreements are binding on the institutions of the Community and on Member States. Consequently, it is incumbent on the Community institutions, as well as upon the Member States, to ensure compliance with the obligations arising from such agreements".[186]

Under international law the European Community has legal personality and as such has the capacity to engage in contractual relations with third countries and other international organisations "over the whole field of objectives defined in Part One of the Treaty".[187] Nevertheless, the Member States of the Community retain their status as subjects of international law and are as such capable of negotiating and concluding international agreements with third countries and international organisations. However, the exercise of its treaty-making powers by Community entails a loss of the treaty-making power by the Member States in that particular area.[188] Consequently, whenever the Community has concluded an international agreement the Member States are not only barred from concluding other international agreements, either individually or collectively, which would make it difficult or impossible for the Community to carry out its treaty obligations, they are also obliged to take all necessary steps to ensure that the Community will be able to perform in accordance with its international obligations.

The Court phrased this obligation of the Member States as follows

"With regard to the implementation of the provisions of the Treaty the system of internal Community measures may not therefore be separated from that of external relations.

Under Article 5 (now 10), the Member States are required on the one hand to take all appropriate measures to ensure fulfilment of the obligations arising out of the Treaty or resulting from action taken by the institutions and, on the other hand, to abstain from any measure which might jeopardize the attainment of the objectives of the Treaty.

---

[185] Case 181/73, *Haegeman*, [1974] ECR 449, paragraphs 4 and 5.

[186] Case 104/81, *Kupferberg*, [1982] ECR 3641, paragraph 11.

[187] Case 22/70, *AETR*, [1971] ECR 263, paragraph 14.

[188] Article 307 EC, that requires the Member States to eliminate any conflicts or other incompatibilities between Community law and international agreements concluded by the Member States, illustrates this. See also N. Neuwahl, *supra* note 113, at 730 and J. Temple Lang, Community Constitutional Law: Article 5 EEC Treaty in 27 *C.M.L. Rev.* (1990), at 669-670.

> If these two provisions are read in conjunction, it follows that to the extent to which Community rules are promulgated for the attainment of the objectives of the Treaty, the Member States cannot, outside the framework of the Community institutions, assume obligations which might affect those rules or alter their scope".[189]

Article 300(7) EC, which provides that international agreements concluded by the Community shall be binding on the institutions and the Member States, represents a *lex specialis* in relation to the more general obligation incumbent on the Member States on the basis of Article 10 EC. Kapteyn *et al* point out that the extensive case-law of the Court of Justice indicates that the obligations in Article 10 EC are supplementary to the more specific obligations in the EC Treaty.[190]

It is thus evident that, similar to the internal situation of the Community, Article 10 EC, as a general rule of Community loyalty and its more specific applications in such articles as Article 300(7) and 307 EC, plays a fundamental role in the external treaty relations of the Community.[191] Its importance, and, more particularly, its application, are perhaps even greater in the external arena. After all, where Member States fail to comply with their Community obligations, Community law and the case-law of the European Court of Justice provide a wide range of legal remedies to rectify these breaches.[192] At international level such remedies do not exist. Failure by the Member States to comply with their Community obligations can result in the Community being held liable for a breach of its treaty obligations. This breach will have to be settled in accordance with the rules of international treaty law.[193]

Article 10 EC[194] provides that

> "Member States shall take all appropriate measures, whether general or particular, to ensure fulfilment of the obligations arising out of this Treaty resulting from action taken by the institutions of the Community. They shall facilitate the achievement of

---

[189] Case 22/70, *AETR*, [1971] 263, paragraphs 19, 21 and 22.

[190] P.J.G. Kapteyn *et al* (1995), *supra* note 1, at 148-149 and P.J.G. Kapteyn *et al* (2003), *supra* note 1, at 123-124.

[191] On the general subject of Article 10 EC see, for example, J. Temple Lang, *supra* note 188, at 645-681; P.J.G. Kapteyn *et al* (1995), *supra* note 1, at 148-162; P.J.G. Kapteyn *et al* (2003), *supra* note 1, at 123-130; R. Barents *et al*, *supra* note 1, at 61-63 and J. Temple Lang, The Duties of National Authorities under Community Constitutional Law in 23 *E.L. Rev.* (1998), at 109-131.

[192] See Article 226-228 EC, Joined Cases C-6 and 9/90, *Francovich*, [1991] I-5357, Joined Cases C-46 and 48/93, *Brasserie du Pêcheur*, [1996] ECR I-1131 and Case C-224/01, Köbler, [2003] http://www.curia.eu.int.

[193] The Community could be held to have committed a material breach on the basis of the rule codified in Article 60 of the 1986 Vienna Convention. The Community would not be able to argue that the rule embodied in Article 61 of the 1986 Convention, supervening impossibility of performance, applied, since this impossibility of performance was due to a direct fault or omission of one of its Member States.

[194] Similar provisions can be found in Article 192 Euratom and the former Article 86 ECSC. See also Article 11(2) TEU that provides that "The Member States shall support the Union's external and security policy actively and unreservedly in a spirit of loyalty and mutual solidarity".

the Community's task. They shall abstain from any measure which could jeopardize the attainment of the objectives of the Treaty".

This article contains two positive elements, in which the member States are required to take action to help the Community achieve its objectives, and one negative element, in which the Member States must refrain from certain behaviour. The provisions of Article 10 EC represent a general principle of mutual cooperation. Although directed at the Member States this article applies equally to the institutions of the EC.[195] This principle of mutual cooperation can be divided into four distinct elements, namely, 1) an obligation on the Member States and the Community to cooperate with each other; 2) an obligation on the Member States to assist each other; 3) an obligation on the Community institutions to cooperate sincerely with the Member States and 4) an obligation on the Community institutions to cooperate sincerely with each other.[196]

The concept of 'Community loyalty' embodied in Article 10 EC bears a strong resemblance to the principle of *pacta sunt servanda*, a principle that is of fundamental importance to international treaty relations.[197] In the Community, itself being based upon an international treaty, it is obvious that a concept similar to the principle of *pacta sunt servanda* should hold centre stage. However, within the Community context the concept of Community loyalty has a much broader meaning than the principle of *pacta sunt servanda* has in international relations.[198] Barents *et al* point out that the concept of 'Community loyalty' is very similar to the principle of 'Bundestreue' in Germany.[199] This principle of loyalty to the federal interest governs the relationship between the Bund and the Länder in Germany.[200] The concept of Community loyalty embodies both the principle of 'good faith' and the principle of 'due care'.[201] It performs a central role in the relationship between the Community and the Member States as evidenced by the extensive case-law of the Court of Justice.[202]

---

195 See Case C-2/88 Imm, *Zwartveld*, [1990] ECR I-3365 and [1990] ECR I-4405.

196 Kapteyn *et al* (1995), *supra* note 1, at 158-159 and P.J.G. Kapteyn *et al* (2003), *supra* note 1, at 124-129. Kapteyn *et al* indicate that the Court through its case-law has established the fourth element. For example, Case 230/81, *Luxembourg* v *European Parliament*, [1983] ECR 255; Case 204/86, *Greece* v *Council*, [1988] ECR 5233 and Case C-65/93, *European Parliament* v *Council*, [1995] ECR I-643.

197 Article 26 of the 1986 Vienna Convention. Brownlie points out that the principle constitutes a general principle of international law and it requires that agreements must be performed in good faith. I. Brownlie, *Principles of Public International Law* (2003), at 591-592.

198 R. Barents *et al*, *supra* note 1, at 61.

199 *Ibid.*

200 Kapteyn *et al* point out that, due to the case-law of the Court of Justice, the concept of 'Community loyalty' has in fact acquired an importance that exceeds the importance of the concept of '*Bundestreue*'. P.J.G. Kapteyn *et al* (1995), *supra* note 1, at 162.

201 R. Barents *et al*, *supra* note 1, at 63.

202 Examples include Case 14/83, *Von Colson*, [1984] ECR 1891; Case C-106/89, *Marleasing*, [1990] ECR I-4135; Case 61/79, *Denkavit*, [1980] ECR 1205; Case C-213/89, *Factortame*, [1990] ECR I-2433; Case C-340/89, *Vlassopoulou*, [1991] ECR I-2357 and Case C-271/91, *Marshall*, [1993] ECR I-4367.

The primary addressees of Article 10 EC are the Member States. However, the term 'Member State' should not be understood as referring only to the central government. It also includes state, local and regional authorities, state-owned undertakings, undertakings in which the government can exercise a certain amount of influence (Article 86 EC), and the judiciary.[203]

It is settled case-law that in areas where the Community and the Member States hold concurrent powers, both can become a party to an international agreement in accordance with their respective powers.[204] In practice, however, it may prove to be difficult to draw a precise demarcation line between the Community's and the Member States' powers. Sometimes, as the Court ruled in *Opinion 1/94*, the exercise of the respective powers may become meaningless if there is not some type of cooperation between the Community and the Member States.[205] In general, the Court has attempted to discourage any precise allocation of powers between the Community and the Member States.[206] Instead it has emphasised the need for close cooperation between the two parties in the international representation in order to preserve the unity of the external representation of the Community. This duty of close cooperation can be traced back to Article 10 EC.[207]

The concept of close cooperation between the Community and the Member States in the international arena was first introduced by the Court in *Ruling 1/78*.[208] In its judgment the Court held that the draft convention could only be concluded with regard to the Community by means of a close association between the Institutions of the Community and the Member States both in the process of negotiation and conclusion and in the fulfilment of the obligations entered into.[209] In the *Opinions 2/91* and *1/94* the Court reaffirmed its position stating that whenever the subject matter of an international agreement fell within the concurrent competences of the Community and the Member States, they both could become a party to this agreement and they were required to cooperate closely.[210] This close cooperation applies to all aspects of the negotiation, conclusion and imple-

---

[203] R. Barents *et al*, *supra* note 1, at 62; P.J.G. Kapteyn *et al* (1995), *supra* note 1, at 158-162; J. Temple Lang, *supra* note 188, at 647-654 and J.W. de Zwaan, The Netherlands (judiciary and authorities) and Article 10 of the EC-Treaty in 48 *SEW* (2000), at 133.

[204] Ruling 1/78, *Draft IAEA Convention*, [1978] ECR 2151; Opinion 2/91, *ILO*, [1993] ECR I-1061 and Opinion 1/94, *WTO*, [1994] ECR I-5267.

[205] Opinion 1/94, *WTO*, [1994] ECR I-5267, paragraph 109.

[206] In Opinion 2/00, *Cartagena Protocol on Biosafety*, [2001] ECR I-9713, the Court of Justice held that the procedure of Article 300(6) EC could not be used to determine the precise extent of the respective powers of the Community and the Member States, if both had to conclude the agreement (paragraphs 16 and 17).

[207] See also Article 3 TEU, which requires the European Union to "ensure the consistency of its external activities as a whole in the context of its external relations, security, economic and development policies".

[208] Ruling 1/78, *Draft IAEA Convention*, [1978] ECR 2151.

[209] *Ibid*, paragraph 33.

[210] Opinion 2/91, *ILO*, [1993] ECR I-1061, paragraph 36 and Opinion 1/94, *WTO*, [1994] ECR I-5267, paragraph 108.

mentation of the mixed agreement. This obligation "flows from the requirement of unity in the international representation of the Community".[211]

In *Opinion 1/94* the Court indicated that the Community and the Member States were under an obligation of mutual cooperation to guarantee the unity of international representation without indicating how this necessary cooperation should be ensured. MacLeod *et al* conclude that a minimum requirement of this close cooperation is that the Member States and the institutions must inform each other of their positions; attempt to reach a common position on the subject matter of the mixed agreement and act by common accord within the framework of international bodies and conferences.[212] The Article 11(2) TEU confirms this conclusion. This article requires the Member States to support the European Union's external and security policy actively and unreservedly. The Member States must work together to enhance and develop their mutual political solidarity. To that end "they shall refrain from any action which is contrary to the interests of the Union or likely to impair its effectiveness as a cohesive force in international relations" (second subparagraph).

The Court has never indicated what this duty of close cooperation in the international arena entails and its precise extent remains unclear. MacLeod *et al* say that the duty of close cooperation does not mean that the Member States and the institutions must reach a common position; rather that they are only under an obligation to do their best to reach one. Failure to reach such a common position would allow the Member States to express their national views on matters falling within the competence of the Member States.[213] Other authors do not share this latter conclusion. Timmermans points out that the obligation of close cooperation is more specific than the general concept of 'Community loyalty' embodied in Article 10 EC.[214] As a result the Member States, when acting together with the Community "should present a common, coherent approach".[215] O'Keeffe, who holds that in the case of mixed competence Member States are precluded from taking action, which could affect the agreement to be concluded or alter its scope, supports this position.[216] Or as Auvret-Finck puts it

> "Appliquée aux domaines relevants à la fois de la compétence de la Communauté et des Etats membres, l'obligation de coopération constitue un moyen de prévention

[211] *Ibid.*

[212] I. MacLeod *et al*, *supra* note 1, at 149.

[213] *Ibid.* See also S. Hyett, 'The Duty of Co-operation: A Flexible Concept' in A. Dashwood and C. Hillion (eds.), *The General Law of E.C. External Relations* (2000), at 251, who holds that "it does not follow as a matter of law that, in respect of a matter where Member States retain competence, they no longer have the power to act if a common position cannot be agreed amongst all the Member States".

[214] C.W.A. Timmermans, *supra* note 139, at 241.

[215] *Ibid.*

[216] D. O'Keeffe, *supra* note 11, at 197-198.

> contre les risques de désintégration liés à une mise en œuvre inconsidérée du principe de subsidiarité".[217]

Unfortunately, practice shows that the Member States frequently express their views individually when no common position can be agreed upon.[218]

Finally, with regard to the matter of close cooperation, reference should be made to the former Article 116 EC. This article, which was deleted with the Maastricht Treaty, required the Member States to proceed only by common action within the framework of international organisations of an economic character. In the *AETR* Case the Court held that Article 116 EC read in conjunction with Article 300 EC meant "that wherever a matter forms the subject of a common policy the Member States are bound in every case to act jointly in defence of the interests of the Community".[219] Two issues limited the practical application of Article 116 EC with regard to the duty of close cooperation. First Article 116 EC did not require the Member States to adopt a common position, whereas the duty of close cooperation does. The second issue was that not all international agreements were concluded within the framework or under the auspices of international organisations of an economic character. The duty of close cooperation has no such limitations.[220]

Article 15 TEU provides that the Council shall adopt common positions and the Member States shall ensure that their national policies conform to these common positions. This article bears some resemblance with Article 116 EC, although its application is broader than Article 116 EC. Yet, even in this case the application of the article is in principle limited to matters falling under Title V of the EU Treaty. The argument could be made to use it in the case of the EC Treaty too. Still, it will be better to have recourse to the concept of 'Community loyalty' embodied in Article 10 EC to require the Member States to act jointly in order to preserve the unity of the external representation of the Community. Thus, where a Council decision ratifying a mixed international agreement calls upon the Member States to do so simultaneously with the Community, Article 10 EC prohibits one or more Member States to refuse to do so.

1.4.3 The application of the principle of subsidiarity

Since its inclusion in the EC Treaty by the Maastricht Treaty, the principle of 'subsidiarity' has been the source of a great number of academic writ-

---

[217] J. Auvret-Finck, *supra* note 40, at 458.

[218] Information obtained in interviews with the Legal Service of the Commission in the period November-December 2003.

[219] Case 22/70, *AETR*, [1971] ECR 263, paragraph 77.

[220] It could be argued that it would suffice that the subject matter of the international agreement was essentially economic in nature to render Article 116 EC applicable. This would, of course, be up to the discretion of the Member States. See also G.L. Close, *supra* note 47, at 66-67.

ings.[221] Prior to the entry into force of the Maastricht Treaty it was not clear whether the principle could play any role in the external relations of the EC. Although the principle was included in Article 174(4) EC, its application in the external relations of the Community was not self-evident. And even if it were accepted that it did play a part in the external relations of the European Community, its application would be limited to the field of the environment.[222] In the *SPO* Case, the Court of First Instance stated that the principle of subsidiarity did not, before the entry into force of the Treaty on European Union, constitute a general principle of law reference to which the legality of Community acts should be reviewed, nor did it have a retroactive effect.[223]

There are various references to the principle of subsidiarity in the EU and EC Treaty and with varying meanings. Both the Preamble of the EU Treaty and Article 1 TEU refer to the principle in connection with decision-making 'as closely as possible to the citizen'. On the other hand, Article 6(3) TEU provides that the "Union shall respect the national identities of its Member States". These varying meanings of the principle illustrate its complexity and create the impression that the principle of subsidiarity is more than a concept dealing merely with the exercise of competence.[224]

Article 5 EC, which was added by the Treaty on European Union, added the principle of subsidiarity as a general principle into Community law. Its scope is narrower than the provisions in the Preamble and the Articles 1 and 6(3) TEU. On the other hand, Article 2 TEU makes an express reference to the principle as defined in Article 5 EC. It is commonly held, that although the Member States introduced the principle to establish a clear demarcation line between the exercise of Community competence and the exercise of the Member States competence, it has done little in practical terms to address the issue. It remains a cloudy and ambiguous political concept, that offers little legal certainty.[225] This is not to say that the principle does not have legal effect. It is a binding rule and its position at the

[221] G. De Búrca, The Principle of Subsidiarity and the Court of Justice as an Institutional Actor in 36 *JCMS* (1998), at 217; T. Schilling, A New Dimension of Subsidiarity: Subsidiarity as a Rule and a Principle in 14 *YEL* (1994), at 203; J-E. de Cockborne, L. Defalque, C-F. Durand, H. Prahl and G. Vandersanden, *Commentaire Megret. Le Droit de La CEE. Préambules, Principes, Libre Circulation des Marchandises* Volume I (1992); P.J.G. Kapteyn *et al*, *supra* note 1 (1995), at 135-148; C. Callies and M. Ruffert (eds.), *Kommentar des Vertrages über die Europäische Union und des Vertrages zur Gründung der Europäischen Gemeinschaft – EUV/EGV* (2002), at 379-412; V.J.J.M. Bekkers, H.T.P.M. van den Hurk and G. Leenknegt (eds.), *Subsidiariteit en Europese integratie. Een oude wijsheid in een nieuwe context* (1995); A. *Goucha Soares,* Pre-emption, Conflicts of Powers and Subsidiarity in 23 *E.L.Rev.* (1998), at 132; and K. Lenaerts and P. van Ypersele, Le principe de subsidiarité et son contexte: étude de l'article 3B du Traité CE in 1-2 *CDE* (1994), at 3.

[222] See P.J. Leefmans, *supra* note 160, at 38.

[223] Case T-29/92, *SPO*, [1995] ECR II-289, paragraphs 330 and 331.

[224] G. De Búrca, *supra* note 221, at 219.

[225] P.J.G. Kapteyn *et al* (1995), *supra* note 1, at 135-137; P.J.G. Kapteyn *et al* (2003), *supra* note 1, at 117-120 and G. De Búrca, *supra* note 221, at 218-219. But see also T. Schilling *supra* note 221, at 204-211.

beginning of the Treaty underlines its importance. The legal uncertainty lies in that it may prove to be a difficult exercise applying the principle in a straightforward manner.[226] The decision whether to allow the Community to exercise its competence is primarily a political decision. If called upon to assess whether the principle of subsidiarity applies in a specific case, the Court will probably limit itself to an evaluation of a marginal nature.[227]

Article 5 EC stipulates that

> "The Community shall act within the limits of the powers conferred upon it by this Treaty and of the objectives assigned to it therein.
> In areas which do not fall within its exclusive competence, the Community shall take action in accordance with the principle of subsidiarity, only if and in so far as the objectives of the proposed action cannot be sufficiently achieved by the Member States and can therefore, by reason of scale or effects of the proposed action, be better achieved by the Community.
> Any action by the Community shall not go beyond what is necessary to achieve the objectives of this Treaty".

In the application of Article 5 EC three elements can be discerned. First, that the Community shall act within the limits of the powers conferred on it by the Treaty and of the objectives assigned to it therein. The European Community, as an international organisation based upon attributed competences, may only act within the limits of those conferred powers. However, it is rather difficult to establish the precise limits of the Community's competence under the open-textured Treaty.

The second element is that the principle applies in those areas where the Community does not possess an exclusive competence. The exclusive nature of the Community's competences can result from an express conferment or through the adoption of internal measures, such as common policies.[228] It is unclear whether the principle of subsidiarity applies where the Community does possess but has not yet exercised an exclusive competence.[229] However, in Case *C-84/94*, the Court held that the principle did not apply to those areas where the Community is only allowed to adopt minimum norms.[230]

The third element is the principle of proportionality according to which Community action should not exceed the limit, which is necessary for the achieve-

[226] V.J.J.M. Bekkers, H.T.P.M. van den Hurk and G. Leenknegt, 'Subsidiariteit als Europese rechtsnorm' in V.J.J.M. Bekkers et al (eds.), *Subsidiariteit en Europese Integratie. Een oude wijsheid in een nieuwe context* (1995), at 175.

[227] P.J.G. Kapteyn *et al* (1995), *supra* note 1, at 144; P.J.G. Kapteyn *et al* (2003), *supra* note 1, at 119-120 and G. De Búrca, *supra* note 221, at 220-222. See also case C-84/94, *United Kingdom* v *Council*, [1996] ECR I-5755 and Case C-233/94, *Germany* v *Parliament and Council*, [1997] ECR I-2405.

[228] Case 22/70, *AETR*, [1971] ECR 263.

[229] R. Barents *et al*, *supra* note 1, at 136.

[230] Case C-84/94, *United Kingdom* v *Council*, [1996] ECR I-5755.

ment of its objectives. This principle, which was developed as a general principle of law by the ECJ[231], applies to all action by the Community irrespective of whether the Community possesses an exclusive competence or not. The principle of proportionality does not relate to the question as to whether the Community should act at all, but rather to which extent it should act. Proportionality relates to the degree of intervention in national legislation or national policy.[232]

At the outset it must be said that the principle of subsidiarity does not affect the existence of the powers which the Community has been given under the Treaty, that is, its competence to act. It only relates to the manner in which those powers are exercised, that is, whether the Community should act or whether action should be left to the Member States. The principle of subsidiarty is therefore not a principle of attribution of competence, but rather one of use of competence. Thus Article 5 EC cannot be used as a (disguised) means to repatriate powers from the Community to the Member States.[233] The European Council in Edinburgh recognized this.[234] Respect for the existing *acquis* was included in the Interinstitutional Agreement on implementing subsidiarity[235] and was subsequently included in the Amsterdam protocol.[236]

In the exercise of the external powers the principle of subsidiarity cannot be applied in exactly the same way as it is applied with regard to the internal powers of the European Community. Indeed, whenever the Community possesses an exclusive external competence the principle of subsidiarity does not apply. The Community, however, remains constrained by the principle of proportionality in that it should use its external competence only to the extent that such is necessary to achieve its objectives.

In those areas where the Community does not have an exclusive competence, that is, when it shares the competence with the Member States, the principle applies only marginally. This has more to do with the legal consequences of action by the Member States and the difficulty to solve possible future conflicts than with the scope of the principle itself. At the internal level; if action by the Member States should prove to be detrimental to the functioning of the internal market, the situation can easily be remedied through the adoption of a Community measure. After all, the Community already possesses the competence, and Community law supersedes national law. The decision to permit the Member States to adopt the necessary measures was taken by reason of scale and effect.

International agreements concluded by the Member States, without the participation of the Community, which have a negative impact on the functioning of the

---

[231] See, for example, Case 120/78, *Cassis de Dijon*, [1979] ECR 649.

[232] P.J.G. Kapteyn *et al* (1995), *supra* note 1, at 144-146 and P.J.G. Kapteyn *et al* (2003), *supra* note 1, at 120-123.

[233] A. Dashwood, *supra* note 8, at 115 and D. Obradovic, *supra* note 5, at 76-78.

[234] Bull. EC 12-1992, point I.15.

[235] Bull. EC 10-1993, point 2.2.2.

[236] Protocol on the application of the principles of subsidiarity and proportionality annexed to the EC Treaty by the Treaty of Amsterdam.

common market, cannot readily be substituted by a new agreement involving also Community participation. Such action will require the willingness of all the contracting parties involved. Although Article 307 EC requires the Member States to eliminate all international agreements that are incompatible with the EC Treaty, the termination of such agreements is based upon the express provisions to that effect in the agreement itself or in the absence of such provisions on the rules of international treaty law. Until such termination can be achieved, the agreement will remain in force.

1.5 Conclusions

This Chapter has provided a detailed overview of the Community's external treaty-making powers. A thorough understanding of the fundamental principles that underlie the Community's treaty-making practice is imperative in an analysis of this practice vis-à-vis the rules of international treaty law. Study of the Community's external activities reveals practices that do not in any way conform to the general external practice of other international organisations. At the same time it cannot be equated with the external practice of the Member States. For unlike the Member States the Community only possesses those powers that are attributed to it and it is only permitted to act within the limits of those powers.[237]

The exercise of the Community's external treaty-making powers is accompanied by two phenomena that are unique to the Community. On the one hand, the Member States retain their status as subjects of international law and are, therefore, capable of engaging in international contractual relations. However, because of the concept of pre-emption, the Member States are barred from concluding agreements in those areas where the internal competence has been transferred to the Community. Where the transfer is incomplete, the Court has held that it is for the Community and the Member States to act together in the negotiation, conclusion and implementation of the international agreement.[238] This is done in order to preserve the unity of the external representation of the Community.

It is clear that the adoption of the new constitution will considerably alter the existing reality of the Community and the Union. For one, the current situation with distinct entities with specific powers and legal personalities will be a thing of the past. That is not to say that the principles set out by the Court of Justice in its extensive case-law on the external powers of the Community, will also be a thing of the past. On the contrary, the existing *acquis* will continue to apply and many of the concepts elaborated by the Court will find their application in the new setting.

---

[237] Article 5 EC.

[238] Opinion 1/94, *WTO*, [1994] ECR I-5267.

The treaty practice of the European Union is not as elaborate as the Community's. This is understandable given the fact that the Community practice has been developed over a more extensive period than the Union's and the legal nature of the Community is different from that of the Union, supranational *versus* intergovernmental. The landmark *AETR* decision has set in motion an extensive external activity by the Community that has no match in the Union and among other international organisations.[239] The uncertainties surrounding the Union's legal personality and the more limited areas of competence have added to a limited treaty practice. Still, it is interesting to see how the Union's external competence has developed over the past few years.

[239] Case 22/70, *AETR*, [1971] ECR 263.

Chapter 2
THE EU'S EXTERNAL TREATY-MAKING COMPETENCE

2.1 Introduction

In the General Introduction brief reference was made to the treaty-making powers of the European Union. As opposed to the EC, EAEC and the former ECSC Treaties, the Treaty on European Union (Maastricht Treaty) contains no express reference to the Union possessing legal personality. On the contrary, attempts by several Presidencies during successive Intergovernmental Conferences to include such a provision have been rejected by some Member States. Despite renewed attempts to that effect, neither the Treaty of Amsterdam nor the Treaty of Nice has brought about any changes in this situation.[1]

Articles 24 and 38 TEU grant the Council the power to conclude international agreements with one or more states or international organisations in the implementation of Titles V and VI of the Treaty on European Union. It appeared that the power had been granted to the Council as an institution of the Union, rather than the Council acting as an intermediary for the collective Member States. This has led to a vivid debate within academic circles as to whether these provisions could be interpreted in the sense that the European Union does have some form of implied legal personality.[2] In fact, international agreements can only be concluded if the European Union is a subject of international law possessing legal personality. If the provisions of Article 24 TEU were to be understood in the sense that the European Union could conclude international agreements, then it must have legal personality. Not all international organisations have legal personality, but they can only conclude international agreements if they do.[3]

---

[1] Despite the various amendments to the Treaty on European Union made by the Treaty of Nice, including Article 24 TEU, none of these amendments involved awarding of legal personality to the Union.

[2] See, for example, R. Wessel, The International Legal Status of the European Union in 2 *E.F.A. Rev.* (1997), at 109; S. Breitenmoser, Die Europäische Union zwischen Völkerrecht und Staatsrecht in 55 *ZaöRV* (1995), at 951; N. Neuwahl, 'Legal Personality of the European Union – International and Institutional Aspects' in V. Kronenberger (ed.), *The EU and the International Legal Order: Discord or Harmony?* (2001), at 3-22; The European Union – A new international actor (Editorial Comments) in 38 *C.M.L. Rev.* (2001), at 825; J.W. de Zwaan, The Legal Personality of the European Communities and the European Union in 30 *Neth.Yb.Int'l.L* (1999), at 75 and S. Marquardt, 'The Conclusion of International Agreements under Article 24 of the Treaty on European Union' in V. Kronenberger (ed.), *The EU and the International Legal Order: Discord or Harmony?* (2001), at 337.

[3] See in this regard the *Reparations for Injuries* Case, ICJ Reports (1949), at 174. Brownlie stipulates that "the existence of legal personality does not of itself support a power to make treaties, and everything depends on the terms of the constituent instrument of the organization". I. Brownlie, *Principles of International Law* (2003), at 651.

The international agreements between the European Union and the Republic of Yugoslavia, FRY,[4] and between the European Union and the Republic of Macedonia, FYROM,[5] on the basis of Article 24 TEU have rendered the debate regarding the legal personality of the European Union moot. A third agreement concluded with the North Atlantic Treaty Organisation, NATO[6], using the same article as the legal basis and again with the Union acting as contracting party has further added strength to this assessment.[7]

Thus it can be asserted that to a certain extent and in a limited number of fields, related to the Common Foreign and Security Policy, the Member States have accepted and acknowledged the legal personality of the Union.[8] All these agreements were concluded by the Presidency on behalf of the Union on the basis of Article 24 TEU, thus supporting the conclusion that the Union has an implied legal personality. However, it is not just the fact that the agreements were concluded on the aforementioned legal basis, but rather that none of the Member

[4] Agreement between the European Union and the Federal Republic of Yugoslavia on the activities of the European Union Monitoring Mission (EUMM) in the Federal Republic of Yugoslavia, OJ 2001, L 125/2.

[5] Agreement between the European Union and the Former Yugoslav Republic of Macedonia on the activities of the European Union Monitoring Mission (EUMM) in the Former Yugoslav Republic of Macedonia, OJ 2001, L 241/2. See also The European Union – A new international actor, *supra* note 2, at 825-828.

[6] Agreement between the European Union and the North Atlantic Treaty Organisation on the security of information, OJ 2003, L 80/36. Note that in this agreement the wording is "The European Union, hereafter the EU, represented by the Presidency of the Council of the European Union, acting on the basis of Article 24 of the Treaty on the European Union", whereas the two other agreements merely make reference to "The European Union on the one hand".

[7] Other agreements concluded using Article 24 TEU as the legal basis are the Agreement between the European Union and the Former Yugoslav Republic of Macedonia on the status of the European Union-led forces in the Former Yugoslav Republic of Macedonia, OJ 2003, L 82/46; the Agreement between the European Union and Bosnia and Herzegovina (BiH) on the activities of the European Union Police Mission (EUPM) in BiH, OJ 2002, L 293/2 and the Agreement between the European Union and the Republic of Albania on the activities of the European Union Monitoring Mission (EUMM) in the Republic of Albania, OJ 2003, L 93/50. Article 10 of this Agreement provides that the Agreement will apply provisionally from the date of its signature. Another example is the Agreement between the European Union and the Former Yugoslav Republic of Macedonia on the status and activities of the European Police Mission in the Former Yugoslav Republic of Macedonia (EUPOL Proxima), OJ 2004, L 16/66. The European Union has also concluded a number of international agreements with several European nations concerning the participation of their armed forces in the European-led Forces (EUF) in Macedonia. See, for example, the Agreement between the European Union and the Slovak Republic on the participation of the armed forces of the Slovak Republic in the European-led Forces (EUF) in the Former Republic of Macedonia, OJ 2004, L 12/54.

[8] The official position of the Legal Service of the General Secretariat of the Council is that the Agreement on extradition between the European Union and the United States of America is based on Article 38 TEU. Therefore, the legal personality of the Union also extends to matters falling under Title VI, Police and Judicial Cooperation in Criminal Matters. Information obtained through personal interviews with the Legal Services of the Commission and the General Secretariat of the Council in the period November – December 2003

States has invoked the right to ratify the agreement in accordance with its own constitutional procedures that gives added weight to the aforementioned conclusion.[9] The Member States adhered to the letter of the procedure embodied in Article 24 TEU. This lends credence to the conclusion that the Union has acted in its own right as a contracting party and thus that it has legal personality.[10]

It could be argued that these are all exceptional cases in which a relatively limited number of third parties have recognised the European Union as a contracting party, but that this in itself does not prove the existence of legal personality.[11] However, the existence of legal personality does not require an established practice or recognition by a certain minimum number of other subjects of international law. In the absence of an express provision in the EU Treaty, the possession of legal personality is confirmed from the moment the first agreement is concluded and has entered into force. The proliferation of agreements to which the European Union is a party merely reflects its growing acceptance by the international community. However, this proliferation in itself has no bearing on its possession of legal personality. It is true that in international relations the European Union does not fit into the mould of the traditional international organisation. However, in the absence of an express Treaty provision on the legal personality of the Union, the question whether the European Union has legal personality and, therefore, the capacity to act externally is one to be answered on the basis of international law keeping in mind the Union's composition, objectives and tasks.[12]

Declaration No. 23 on the Future of the Union[13] called for a deeper and wider debate, intended, among others, to simplify the Treaties to make them clearer and better understood without changing their meaning.[14] As one of the basic challenges facing the European Union, the Laeken European Summit identified the need "to develop the Union into a stabilising factor and a model in the new, mul-

---

[9] See Article 24(5) TEU.

[10] Article X of the Agreement with FYROM and Article X of the Agreement with FRY provide that the Agreements shall enter into force upon signature. There is no provision in the Agreements alluding to a possible separate ratification by the Member States of the Union. Neither is such provision included in the Council Decisions approving the Agreements (Council Decisions 2001/682/CFSP, OJ 2001, L 241/1 and 2001/352/CFSP, OJ 2001, L 125/1). Article 16 of the Agreement with NATO also provides for its entry into force upon signature. It does not make any reference to a possible derogation by one of the Member States of the EU.

[11] N. Neuwahl, *supra* note 2, at 3-22. She points out, with regard to the pursuit of the objectives of the Union, that 'the replacement of the EU for the Member States is, as yet, discretionary', at 12. The same logic could be applied to the agreements concluded.

[12] See *Reparations for Injuries* Case, I.C.J. Reports (1949), at 179.

[13] Declaration attached to the Final Act of the Conference of the Representatives of the Member States convened for the adoption of the Treaty of Nice, OJ 2001, C 80/70.

[14] Other questions involve the establishment and monitoring of a more precise delimitation of powers between the European Union and the Member States, reflecting the principle of subsidiarity; the status of the Charter of Fundamental Rights of the European Union, adopted in Nice; and the role of national parliaments in the European architecture. *Ibid.*

tipolar world".[15] The Laeken European Council asked itself a number of questions including the one on how to enhance the coherence of the European Foreign Policy; whether the external representation of the Union in international relations should be extended further and whether the distinction between the Union and the Communities should be reviewed.[16]

The Convention, which was convened on the basis of the Laeken Declaration[17], resulted in a "Draft Treaty establishing a Constitution for Europe".[18] According to Cremona the Draft Constitution proposed

> "The integration of the EC and European Union Treaties, the integration of the pillar structure, the integration of policy under one rubric – "The Union's External Action" is the heading of Title V of Part III – and the integration of that action itself into the overall perspective of the Union's objectives".[19]

To this end the Union is granted legal personality[20], which replaces the legal personalities of the European Community and Euratom. As a result, the hybrid structure consisting of two separate international organisations supplemented by the Common Foreign and Security Policy and Police and Judicial Cooperation in Criminal Matters (Article 1 TEU) is replaced by one single organisation, the European Union, capable of concluding international agreements.[21] On 18 June 2004, the Member States adopted the new European Constitution.

---

[15] Presidency Conclusions. European Council Meeting in Laeken, 14 and 15 December 2001. SN 300/1/01 Rev 1, at 21.

[16] *Ibid*, at 21-24.

[17] *Ibid*, at 24-26.

[18] CONV 850/03. Contributions on the European Constitution include, among others, J. Kokott and A. Rüth, The European Convention and its Draft Treaty establishing a Constitution for Europe: Appropriate answers to the Laeken Questions? in 40 *C.M.L. Rev.* (2003), at 1315; M. Cremona, The Draft Constitutional Treaty: External Relations and External Action in 40 *C.M.L. Rev.* (2003), at 1347; B. de Witte, The European Constitutional Treaty: Towards an Exit Strategy for Recalcitrant Member States? in 10 *MJ*1 (2003), at 3; J. Wouters, Exit the Convention, Come the IGC. Some Reflections on the Convention as a Method for Constitutional Change in the EU in 10 *MJ*3 (2003), at 225; P. Gauttier, Horizontal Coherence and the External Competences of the European Union in 10 *European Law Journal* (2004), at 23; R. Grawert, Wie soll Europa organisiert werden? – Zur konstitutionellen "Zukunft Europas" nach dem Vertrag von Nizza – in 38 *Europarecht* (2003), at 971; J-V. Louis, Le Projet de Constitution: Continuité ou Rupture? in 3-4 *CDE* (2003), at 215; J. Schwarze, Ein pragmatischer Verfassungsentwurf – Analyse und Bewertung des Entwurf eines Vertrags über eine Verfassung für Europa – in 38 *Europarecht* (2003), at 535; A.T.J.M. Jacobs, De Europese Grondwet in de wacht gezet in 79 *NJb* (2004), at 366; R. Barents, Hoe Constitutioneel is de Grondwet van Europa? in 52 SEW 2004 at 2; R. Barents, Naar een Europese constitutie? (Parts I-VI) in *NTER* 2002, at 300, *NTER* (2003), at 39, at 100, at 137, 167 and at 218; and B.M.P. Smulders, Kritische kanttekeningen bij de gevolgen van het 'ontwerp-verdrag tot vaststelling van een grondwet voor Europa' voor het institutionele evenwicht in *NTER* 2003, at 246.

[19] M. Cremona, *supra* note 18, at 1347-1348.

[20] Article I-6 of the Constitution.

[21] R. Barents, Part II, *supra* note 18, at 41. The general provisions for the conclusion of international agreements can be found in Article III-227.

The purpose of this Chapter is to provide an overview of the Union's external treaty-making powers as they have developed since the coming into force of the Treaty of Maastricht. A study of the legal personality of the Union as it currently stands (Section 2.3) will be preceded by a brief look at the structure of the Union (Section 2.2). Finally, in Section 2.5 an analysis of the provisions of the European Constitution, as they relate to the external treaty-making powers of the Union, will be conducted.

2.2 The European Union as an international organisation

The European Union came into being with the Maastricht Treaty and one of its objectives is

> "To assert its identity on the international scene, in particular through the implementation of a common foreign and security policy including the progressive framing of a common defence policy, which might lead to a common defence, in accordance with the provisions of Article 17".[22]

Art 1 of the same Treaty furthermore makes reference to the EU Treaty marking "a new stage in the process of creating an ever closer union among the peoples of Europe, in which decisions are taken as openly as possible and as closely as possible to the citizen".

The European Union is founded on the European Communities, the so-called First Pillar, consisting of the European Community and Euratom.[23] Two new forms of cooperation, namely, the Common Foreign and Security Policy and Police and Judicial Cooperation in Criminal Matters (the Second and Third Pillar of the EU), supplement his First Pillar.[24] Whereas the First Pillar has retained its supranational structure, the cooperation in the Second and Third Pillar occurs primarily on the basis of an intergovernmental structure. The unique structure of the European Union immediately became the subject of various analyses regarding its precise status under international law. Already in 1993, Curtin, in a very critical manner, referred to the Union as being a union of 'bits and pieces'.[25] In a later contribution Curtin and Dekker qualified the European Union as a layered organisation.[26]

---

[22] Article 2 TEU, second indent.

[23] The European Coal and Steel Community has ceased to exist and many of its provisions have now been incorporated into the EC Treaty.

[24] Article 1 TEU.

[25] D. Curtin, The Constitutional Structure of the Union: A Europe of bits and pieces in 30 *C.M.L. Rev.* (1993), at 17.

[26] D. Curtin and I. Dekker, 'The EU as a 'Layered' International Organization: Institutional Unity in Disguise' in Craig and De Búrca (eds.), *The Evolution of EU Law* (1999), at 83. Other comments include R. Wessel, *supra* note 2, S. Breitenmoser, *supra* note 2, R. Wessel, 'De Europese

All these analyses and contributions stress the complexity of the new structure created by the Treaty on European Union. This polemic situation has been further exacerbated by the fact that on certain occasions the Member States have refused to grant the Union international legal personality. Although this refusal was more related to the nature of the subject matters of cooperation, especially in the area of the Common Foreign and Security Policy, it can be said that this decision only added more controversy to an already confusing situation.

The Treaty of Amsterdam brought about some changes in the existing structure in that it has moved visa and asylum issues as well as the subject of private international law (conflict of laws) from the Third Pillar to a new Title IV in the EC Treaty.[27] Thus leaving matters related to police and judicial cooperation in the Third Pillar.[28] The Treaty of Nice further refined some of the provisions.[29]

Whereas it is self-evident that the existing Communities are international organisations and have international legal personality[30], questions remained about the precise status of the European Union. The questions centred on whether the European Union was an international entity, separate from the Member States, capable of having international legal personality and possessing international rights and obligations.

That the European Union is not a state is beyond any doubt. It does not possess the qualifications of statehood and has never been presented or viewed as such. Although the EU Treaty speaks of an ever-closer union of the peoples of the Union it is not possible to qualify the Union as a state or being in the process of becoming one.[31] Nor is it a super state, a term used by the ICJ in the *Reparations for Injuries* Case.[32]

Unie in de internationale rechtsorde' in Mededelingen van de Nederlandse Vereniging voor Internationaal Recht, *De plaats van de Europese Unie in het veranderlijke bestel van de volkenrechtelijke organisatie*, Preadviezen (2001), at 1; J-C. Gautron, 'L'Union Européenne et le concept d'organisation internationale' in R. Vitoria (ed.), *L'Union Européenne et les organisations internationales* (1997), at 15 and A. von Bogdandy, The Legal Case for Unity: The European Union as a single organisation with a single legal system in 36 *C.M.L. Rev.* (1999), at 887.

[27] Visas, Asylum, Immigration and Other Policies Related to Free Movement of Persons (Articles 61-69 EC).

[28] Provisions on Police and Judicial Cooperation in Criminal Matters (Articles 29-42 TEU).

[29] For example, Article 24 TEU.

[30] Articles 281 EC and 184 Euratom.

[31] In fact, Article A of the version of the Treaty on Political Union proposed by the Dutch Presidency stipulated that the Treaty marked "a new stage in the process leading gradually to a Union with a federal goal". In the end the word 'federal' was dropped. See, H. Schermers and N. Blokker, *International Institutional Law* (2003), at 25-26. See also S. Breitenmoser, *supra* note 2, at 954. The fourth recital of the Preamble to the Constitution provides that "Convinced that, while remaining proud of their own national identities and history, the peoples of Europe are determined to transcend their ancient divisions and, united ever more closely, to forge a common destiny". Here, too, there is no mention of some form of statehood.

[32] I.C.J. Reports (1949), at 179. Prior to the conclusion of the aforementioned international agreements, it was to this same case that one resorted to in trying to determine whether the European Union possessed international legal personality.

Although questions remain as to what kind of international organisation the European Union is, its status as an international organisation is beyond dispute. In fact, to some it may even seem rather unnecessary to engage in an analysis of the status of the European.[33] Or as Gautron puts it "la tentation de mesurer l'Union européenne à l'aune du concept d'organisation internationale ne serait-elle qu'un exercise de style?"[34] The fact of the matter is that the European Union represents a new and unique entity in the family of international organisations. Its internal structure, the division of competences between the institutions, between the Union and the Member States and its external activities are not matched by any other international organisation.

The Preamble to the EU Treaty stipulates that the Member States have "resolved to mark a new stage in the process of European integration undertaken with the establishment of the European Communities" and have therefore decided to establish a European Union. Article 1 TEU defined the Union as follows

> "The Union shall be founded on the European Communities, supplemented by the policies and forms of cooperation established by this Treaty. Its task shall be to organise, in a manner demonstrating consistency and solidarity, relations between the Member States and their peoples".

Article 1 TEU further establishes that the Union shall have as its task "to organise, in a manner demonstrating consistency and solidarity, relations between the Member States and between their peoples". Article 2 TEU provides the Union with its own tasks whereas the Articles 3 and 5 TEU provide it with its own institutions.

The EU Treaty furthermore provides that a single institutional framework will serve the European Union.[35] These Institutions operate in accordance with the powers provided for under the EC Treaty (Article 5 TEU). Within the European Union the European Council performs a central role. The European Council brings together the Heads of State or Government of the Member States and the President of the Commission, assisted by the Ministers of Foreign Affairs and a Member of the Commission.[36] Its composition is different from the traditional European Council, which only brought together the Heads of State or Government. The main task of the European Council is to provide the Union with the necessary impetus for its development and to define the general political guidelines thereof.[37]

---

[33] R. Wessel, *supra* note 2, at 113.

[34] J-G. Gautron, *supra* note 26, at 34.

[35] At the time of the adoption of the Maastricht Treaty, Curtin asserted that not much should be thought of this provision. She stated, "The putative claim of Article C that the Union shall be served "by a single institutional framework" can, in the light of the substantive provisions of the Treaty, be described, not too unkindly, as mere lip-service to an ideal. It was single only in the sense that the intergovernmental pillars do not have institutions of their own". Curtin, *supra* note 25, at 28. The Treaty of Amsterdam has remedied this alleged ambiguity.

[36] Article 4 TEU, second paragraph.

[37] Article 4 TEU, fourth paragraph.

The Treaty of Amsterdam and, more recently, the Treaty of Nice have made the institutional framework clearer and have broadened the powers of the individual institutions.[38]

As stated before, Article 4 TEU empowers the European Council to provide the Union with the necessary impetus for its development and to define the general political guidelines. This is an autonomous power of the European Council. It is, however, the ordinary Council that must take the decisions necessary to define and implement the Common Foreign and Security Policy and it shall ensure 'the unity, consistency and effectiveness of action by the Union.[39] Furthermore, Article 15 TEU provides that the Council shall adopt common positions to which the Member States are to conform their national policies.[40]

Article 7 TEU should also be mentioned, which grants the Council of Ministers the power to sanction any Member State that has committed a serious, and persistent breach of the principles mentioned in Article 6(1) TEU. In Von Bogdandy's words

> "The Union is thereby made the guarantor of liberal and democratic values when all internal State mechanisms fail, even though individual rights of action are not granted. Herein is thus found a first provision with a material content, which encompasses the whole Union *and* the Member States. The Union becomes not only an organisation, but an organisation with the task and competence to ensure collective order".[41]

2.3 The legal personality of the Union

2.3.1 **Legal theories**

In the *Reparations for Injuries* Case, the International Court of Justice held that

---

[38] De Zwaan, *De toekomst van de Europese Unie. Een aantal constitutionele kanttekeningen* in AA 50 (2001), at 5. On the legal practice of the European Union see, for example, D. Curtin *et al*, *supra* note 26, at 98-103 and M. Koskenniemi, 'International Law Aspects of the Common Foreign and Security Policy' in M. Koskenniemi (ed.), *International Law Aspects of the European Union* (1998), at 27-44.

[39] Article 13(3) TEU.

[40] Examples include Council Common Position 2002/960/CFSP concerning restrictive measures against Somalia, OJ 2002, L 334/1; Council Common Position 2003/140/CFSP concerning exceptions to the restrictive measures imposed by Common Position 2002/402/CFSP, OJ 2003, L 53/62; Council Common Position 2003/280/CFSP in support of the effective implementation of the mandate of the ICTY, OJ 2003, L 101/22 and Council Common Position 2003/297/CFSP on Burma/Myanmar, OJ 2003, L 106/36. See also V. Kronenberger, 'Common Foreign and Security Policy: International Law Aspects of the Association of Third States with the Common Positions of the Council of the European Union' in V. Kronenberger (ed.), *The EU and the International Legal Order: Discord or Harmony?* (2001), at 351.

[41] A. Von Bogdandy, *supra* note 26, at 895. He even asserts that the Articles 23(2) and 35(1) TEU grant the EU certain supranational characteristics.

> "The subjects of law in any legal system are not necessarily identical in their nature or in the extent of their rights, and their nature depends upon the needs of the community. Throughout its history, the development of international law has been influenced by the requirements of international life, and the progressive increase in the collective activities of States has already given rise to instances of action upon the international plane by certain entities, which are not States. This development culminated in the establishment in June 1945 of an international organisation whose purposes and principles are specified in the Charter of the United Nations. *But to achieve these ends the attribution of international personality is indispensable* (emphasis added)".[42]

With the absence of a general constitutional authority capable of awarding legal personality to international organisations, it is up to the member states to do so through the constituent treaty of the organisation. In the absence of provisions to that effect, a functional approach can be used.[43] However, few founding treaties contain a provision granting international organisations legal personality.[44] Schermers *et al* point out that this omission has resulted in the proposition of various theories regarding the status of international organisations under international law.[45] They distinguish three schools of thought. The first school adheres to the will theory, that is, the organisation only possesses legal personality if such is the express will of the member states. This will is expressed though an express provision in the founding treaty granting the organisation legal personality. An example would be Article 281 EC, which grants the European Community legal personality.

The second school relates to the objective personality theory. The reasoning behind this theory is that if the organisation has at least one organ that has a will distinct from that of the member states, it possesses international legal personality. The legal personality is not dependent on the express will of the member states. Rather, it is bestowed on the organisation by international law.

The third, and according to Schermers *et al* most accepted, school is based on the notion that international organisations are legal persons because the status is

---

[42] I.C.J. Reports (1949), at 178.

[43] H. Schermers *et al*, *supra* note 31, at 987-988; I. Brownlie, *supra* note 3, at 648 and N. Blokker and T. Heukels, 'The European Union: Historical Origins and Institutional Challenges', in T. Heukels, N. Blokker and M. Brus (eds.), *The European Union after Amsterdam: A Legal Analysis* (1998), 9-50. "As a general principle under international law and the law of international organisations, there are basically two ways by which national and international legal personality can be obtained by an international organisation. First, through the inclusion of one or more express provisions in the constituent treaty. This must be accompanied by recognition of this legal personality by third states and/or other international organisations. The second option is by implication. The existence of an implied legal personality can be derived from the institutional structure, objectives and instruments for achieving these objectives that characterize the international organisation concerned, again combined with implied or explicit recognition by third states and/or other international organisations" (at 27-28).

[44] It is commonly held that express reference to the legal personality of the organisation in the constituent treaty is the exemption rather than the rule.

[45] H. Schermers *et al*, *supra* note 31, at 988-989.

given to them implicitly. If the organisation is qualified to perform certain external acts, such as the conclusion of international agreements, then it can only do so because it has legal personality. This is an implied personality.[46] Justification for this line of reasoning is found in the *Reparations for Injuries* Case.[47] The International Court of Justice held that the United Nations possesses legal personality because the member states "by entrusting certain functions to it, with the attendant duties and responsibilities, have clothed it with the competence required to enable those functions to be effectively discharged".[48]

Klabbers introduces a new theory, called the presumptive personality.[49] He argues that the International Court of Justice presumed that the fifty states that created the United Nations, and which at that time represented "a vast majority of the members of the international community", had utilised their power to create an international legal person. Klabbers argues as follows

> "In other words: the Court acted on a presumption. It did not actually investigate the truthfulness of its presumption; it satisfied itself by observing that the presumption had not been rebutted".[50]

Klabbers presumptive theory has some elements of a will theory, but not akin to the will theory as outlined by Schermers *et al.* The will theory is based on the notion that there must be an express will to grant legal personality. The presumptive theory stipulates that the will to create an organisation and endowing it with certain capacities presupposes the existence of a legal personality. It is presumed that the personality exists. Why would the member states otherwise create this legal entity and grant it certain powers, powers that can only be effectively exercised on the basis of the possession of legal personality? The will of the member states is thus presumed. Klabbers introduces the presumptive theory because he believes that the International Court of Justice neither accepted nor rejected the will theory and the objective approach.[51]

In the end it does indeed come down to the will of the member states. However, the will of the member states has less to do with an explicit conferral of legal personality on the organisation or not. It has more to do with the underlying reasons for the creation of the organisation. States have moved from the more *ad hoc* approach in the form of international conferences that were so typical in the nineteenth and early twentieth century. They have chosen for a more permanent

---

[46] *Ibid.*

[47] I.C.J. Reports (1949), at 179.

[48] *Ibid.*

[49] J. Klabbers, 'Presumptive Personality: The European Union in International Law' in M. Koskenniemi (ed.), *International Law Aspects of the European Union* (1998), at 231. See also J.W. de Zwaan, *supra* note 2, who refutes this theory where it applies to the Union, stating, "the Union cannot be 'presumed' to be a separate subject of law responsible for the development of cooperation" (at 93).

[50] J. Klabbers, *supra* note 49, at 246.

[51] *Ibid*, at 243-246.

form of international cooperation in the form of international organisations. The intentions behind the creation of the organisation, and more precisely its tasks, will determine whether the organisation also has a corresponding international personality. If the activities carry with them a necessary interaction with other subjects of international law, the organisation will only be capable of executing these tasks if it has some measure of international personality. This is precisely the extent of the *Reparations for Injuries* Case.

Brownlie distinguishes three sets of criteria that must be met for an international organisation to possess legal personality, namely[52]

1. A permanent association of states, with lawful objects, equipped with organs.
2. A distinction, in terms of legal powers and purposes, between the organisation and its members.
3. The existence of legal powers exercisable on the international plane and not solely within the national systems of one or more states.

Brownlie admits, however, that these criteria are not always easy to apply.[53]

2.3.2 The case of the European Union

In the introduction to this chapter, reference was made to the fact that much has been written about the legal personality of the EU, or rather the lack of one. The Member States of the European Union have taken various steps to ensure that the Union's powers, either through a process of pre-emption or creeping integration, did not acquire a broader scope than what was originally intended. The Member States did not want a repeat performance of the developments within the European Community.[54] The explicit refusal to grant the Union legal personality can be seen as an example of this practice. One can, therefore, rightfully argue that because it has been the express will of the Member States not to grant the Union legal personality, it simply does not possess one.

The reality is, however, more nuanced. That the Member States may decide not to allow the Union to exercise its external powers does not alter the fact that the European Union could, theoretically, possess legal personality. It should also be observed, that the refusal is not accompanied by an express reference in the Treaty to that effect or an additional protocol attached to the Treaty explicitly confirming this decision. This leads to the conclusion that this refusal should not be interpreted in absolute terms. The refusal to grant the Union legal personality should be seen for what it represents, a mere political compromise. It was a political compromise that was necessary in the interest of the ongoing integration process. The move to the third and final stage of the Economic and Monetary

[52] I. Brownlie, *supra* note 3, at 649.
[53] *Ibid.*
[54] See *supra* Chapter 1.

Union and the preparation for the inevitable enlargement can be seen as part of this compromise.

One should also keep in mind that the Member States opposed to providing the Union with its own legal personality had different reasons to do so. There was no consensus on awarding legal personality and equally no consensus among the dissenters.[55] In this regard it is also worth mentioning Declaration No. 4[56], which has been used as a supplementary argument to support the position of those who hold that the Union has no legal personality.[57] A closer look at the wording of this Declaration shows that it actually supports both sides of the argument.

If a transfer of competence from the Member States to the Union does not include concluding an international agreement on the basis of Article 24 TEU, then it is correct to say that the Member States and not the Union have in fact concluded the agreement. The Member States are the only ones empowered to act in the area covered by the international agreement. On the other hand, the practice of the European Community and indeed certain Treaty provisions, show that the Community can conclude an international agreement without the Member States losing their competence to act.[58] An analogous application, that is consistent with Declaration No 4, can be used in the case of the European Union. The Member States retain the right to conclude an agreement dealing with the same subject matter as the one concluded by the Union. The conclusion of the agreement by the Union does not pre-empt the Member States from doing so. However, neither the Member States nor the European Union may act in such a way that it would become difficult or impossible for the other to conclude an agreement.[59] Equally, international treaty law prohibits that the Member States conclude an agreement that would run contrary to the agreement concluded by the Union, or *vice versa*, or would make it difficult or impossible for either the Union, or the Member States, to perform its obligations under the international agreement.[60]

Finally, Article 24 TEU, which outlines the procedural steps for the conclusion of international agreements, grants any Member State the right to notify the other Member States that an international agreement concluded on the basis of this article shall not be binding on that Member State until it has complied with

---

[55] See also R. Wessel, *supra* note 26, at 23-25 and N. Blokker *et al*, *supra* note 43, at 29.

[56] Declaration (No 4) on Articles 24 (ex Article J.14) and 38 (ex Article K.10) of the Treaty on European Union in European Union in *Selected instruments taken from the Treaties*, Book I, Volume I, (1999), at 682, provides that "The provisions of Articles 24 and 38 of the Treaty on European Union and any agreements resulting from them shall not imply any transfer of competence from the Member States to the European Union".

[57] For example, J.W. de Zwaan, *supra* note 2, at 100-101.

[58] See Articles 111(5), 174(4) and 181 EC.

[59] In this instance the principle of 'Union loyalty' embodied in Article 11(2) TEU applies.

[60] Articles 26, 46 and 61 of the 1969 Vienna Convention on the Law of Treaties, signed in Vienna 23 May 1969, entered into force 27 January 1980 in 8 *I.L.M.* (1969), at 679. Similar provisions can be found in the 1986 Vienna Convention. The Vienna Convention on the Law of Treaties between States and International Organizations or between International Organizations, signed 21 March 1986, has not yet entered into force in 25 *I.L.M.* (1986), at 543. See also *infra* Chapter 3.

its own constitutional procedure for the ratification of international agreements. However, Article 24 TEU does not require ratification of the agreement by all Member States, in accordance with their respective constitutional traditions, before the agreement can take effect.[61] An agreement concluded by the Council can enter into force in accordance with the provisions of the agreement itself, or, in the absence of such express provisions, in accordance with the rules of international treaty law. If a Member State invokes the right to ratify the agreement in accordance with its own constitutional provisions, the remaining Member States can agree that the agreement will apply provisionally.[62] Agreements concluded on the basis of Article 24 TEU are nevertheless binding on the institutions of the Union.[63]

Still, as stated before, the conclusion of a number of international agreements on the basis of Article 24 TEU has rendered the debate moot. The Member States have accepted that the Union has legal personality. Similarly, the practice of third countries and other international organisations make it clear that as far as they are concerned the Union has legal personality.

2.4 The legal implications of the Articles 24 and 38 TEU

Art. 24 TEU provides that

> "1. When it is necessary to conclude an agreement with one or more States or international organisations in implementation of this title, the Council may authorise the Presidency, assisted by the Commission as appropriate, to open negotiations to that effect. Such agreements shall be concluded by the Council on a recommendation from the Presidency.
>
> 2. The Council shall act unanimously when the agreement covers an issue for which unanimity is required for the adoption of internal decisions.
>
> 3. When the agreement is envisaged in order to implement a joint action or common position, the Council shall act by a qualified majority in accordance with Article 23(2).
>
> 4. The provisions of the Article shall also apply to matters falling under Title VI. When the agreement covers an issue for which a qualified majority is required for the adoption of internal decisions or measures, the Council shall act by a qualified majority in accordance with Article 34(3).

[61] Quite the contrary, the provisions permit that the remaining Member States may agree to apply provisionally the agreement to them. Also noteworthy is the fact that this right of the Member States only comes into effect after the agreement has been concluded internally but before the Union expresses its consent to be bound.

[62] Article 24(5) TEU.

[63] Article 24(6) TEU.

5. No agreement shall be binding on a Member State whose representative in the Council states that it has to comply with the requirements of its own constitutional procedure; the other members of the Council may agree that the agreement shall nevertheless apply provisionally.

6. Agreements concluded under the conditions set out by this Article shall be binding on the institutions of the Union".

This article was added to the EU Treaty with the Treaty of Amsterdam and modified by the Treaty of Nice. As its precise meaning is unclear, it has been clouded with controversy from the start. It contains procedural rather than substantive provisions concerning the negotiation and conclusion of international agreements. Article 24 TEU resembles Article 300 EC in certain aspects, but it is not identical and does not have the same legal effect.[64] The Treaty of Nice has brought about some necessary changes in Article 24 TEU, putting it more on par with Article 300 EC. Article 24 TEU was the compromise text of the two alternatives proposed during the Intergovernmental Conference, IGC, that led to the adoption of the Treaty of Amsterdam.[65] Although the article provides for the possibility to conclude international agreements, it remained unclear whether the agreements concluded were binding on the Union as such, that is, whether the Union is the contracting party.

There are three key issues involved in the application of Article 24 TEU. The first centres on the question as to who concludes the international agreement: the Council as an institution of the Union or the Member States collectively. The second issue focuses on who is bound by the agreement concluded on the basis of this article: the Union, the Union and the Member States, or only the Member States. The third issue concerns the exact relation between the Articles 24 and 38 TEU.

On the basis of Article 24 TEU international agreements are to be negotiated by the Presidency, assisted by the Commission as appropriate, and concluded by the Council. The term international agreement has the same meaning as the term used in 300 EC.[66] The Presidency is not an institution of the Union, but according to Article 18(1) TEU, the Presidency represents the Union in matters resorting under the Common Foreign and Security Policy.[67] The contention was that the negotiations conducted by the Presidency on the basis of Article 24 TEU

[64] Article 300(6) EC permits the Council, the Commission, the European Parliament or a Member State to obtain the opinion of the European Court of Justice as to whether an agreement envisaged is compatible with the EC Treaty. Article 24 TEU does not contain a similar provision. In fact, the Court does not have jurisdiction with regard to matters falling under Title V (Article 46 TEU).

[65] S. Marquardt, *supra* note 2, at 337-338.

[66] See *infra* Chapter 3 and Opinion 1/75, *OECD Local Cost Standard*, [1975] ECR 1355, at 1356.

[67] Curtin and Dekker argue, "Since the entry into force of the TEU, the Presidency has in fact become a separate organ of the Union, notwithstanding the fact that every six months this organ is fronted by another 'subject'. D. Curtin *et al*, *supra* note 26, at 109.

were on behalf of the Union as a separate entity and not on behalf of the Member States collectively.[68] Article 24 TEU refers to the conclusion of international agreements in implementation of this Title, meaning Title V, Provisions on a Common Foreign and Security Policy. This is one argument in favour of the thesis that the Presidency represents the Union.

De Zwaan, citing the 'Mostar experience' as an example, argued that the fact that the Presidency, rather than the Commission, had been appointed to conduct the negotiations on behalf of the Council was illustrative of the intergovernmental character of the negotiations.[69] This was quite true with regard to the Memorandum of Understanding.[70] The negotiations were carried out by the Presidency on behalf of the Member States. The first recital of the Preamble to the Memorandum refers to "The Member States of the European Union acting within the framework of the Union in full association with the European Commission". However, the Memorandum of Understanding was negotiated and concluded before the adoption and entry into force of the Treaty of Amsterdam. At that point in time not only the existence of the Union's international legal personality, but also its status as an international organisation was in dispute.[71]

Within the Community it is the Commission that has the sole authority to conduct negotiations on behalf of the Community, where such negotiations take place on the basis of the Articles 133 and 300 EC. The Commission has to obtain prior authorization from the Council, that shall also issue the necessary negotiating directives. Article 111 EC, on the contrary, does not bestow an exclusive negotiating power on the Commission. Paragraph 3 provides that by way of derogation from Article 300 EC, the Council, acting by qualified majority, shall decide the arrangements for the negotiation and for the conclusion of such agreements. In this specific instance the Council can authorise the Presidency, the Commission or the European Central Bank to negotiate and conclude such agreements.[72] In the case of the Common Foreign and Security Policy and Police and Judicial Cooperation in Criminal Matters the Presidency, assisted by the Commission as appropriate, conducts the negotiations upon authorization from the Council.

---

[68] As pointed out before in all the international agreements concluded so far, the Union is mentioned as the only contracting party on the side of the Union and the Member States.

[69] J.W. De Zwaan, *supra* note 2, at 103. See S. Marquardt, *supra* note 2, at 339-340, for an opposing view. Marquardt also argues that if the agreement deals with matters covered by the EC Treaty and Title V the Council could authorise the Commission to conduct all the negotiations. The Presidency will, probably, still be in charge of the negotiations involving matters falling under Title V of the EU Treaty.

[70] Memorandum of Understanding on the European Union Administration of Mostar, signed in Geneva on 5 July 1994, Tractatenblad 1994, No 183.

[71] See D. Curtin, *supra* note 25.

[72] "Agreements concluded in accordance with this paragraph shall be binding on the institutions of the Community, on the ECB and on the Member States" (Article 111(3) EC, second subparagraph). See also *infra* Chapter 3.

The Council concludes the agreements.[73] The Council, together with the European Parliament, the Commission, the Court of Auditors and the Court of Justice are the institutions of the EU (Article 3 TEU). Contrary to Article 300 EC, which refers to agreements between the Community and one or more states or international organisations, Article 24 TEU does not make express reference to the Union. One could argue that the Council is acting on behalf of the Member States and not of the European Union. However, the omission in itself is not enough proof for such a conclusion. The Council is acting in its capacity as an institution of the Union. Nothing in Article 24 TEU or the other provisions in Title V allows for a different conclusion. On the contrary, Article 3 TEU, read in conjunction with Article 7(1) EC, supports such conclusion.

There have also been several instances where the Member States have used the Council as an intergovernmental framework to approve Community action in a specific field without imposing any legal obligation on the Community.[74] The European Court of Justice has even sanctioned this type of behaviour.[75] However, recent developments show that where the Council concludes agreements on the basis of Article 24 TEU it is acting in its capacity as an Institution of the EU. There is no allusion in either of the agreements, or in the Council Decisions ratifying the agreements, that the Member States have used the intergovernmental framework to conclude the agreements.

At this point reference should be made to the agreement between the Council of the European Union and Iceland and Norway.[76] The first recital of the 1999 Agreement referred to the Agreement of Luxembourg of 19 December 1996 between the thirteen Member States of the European Union as Schengen contracting parties and Iceland and Norway, referred to as being the start of ongoing talks between the parties on the application, implementation and further development of the Schengen *acquis*. The 1999 Agreement was a direct result of these negotia-

---

[73] The term 'conclude' has the same meaning as in Article 300 EC. It has two components, an internal component meaning that the text of proposed agreement has been approved of and the internal procedure has been finalised. The external (international law) component is that the Council or its representative expresses the Union's consent to be bound by depositing the instrument of ratification with the depositary of the agreement or, as is usually the case with bilateral agreements, by exchanging the instruments of ratification.

[74] See, for example, Decision 2002/234/ECSC of the Representatives of the Governments of the Member States meeting within the Council on the financial consequences of the expiry of the ECSC Treaty and on the research fund for coal and steel, OJ 2002, L 79/42.

[75] In Joined Cases C-181 and C-248/91, *Bangladesh*, ECR [1993] I-3685, the European Court of Justice held that the Member States are not only permitted to use the Institutions as an intermediary for their external actions, but that these actions are not subject to judicial review on the basis of Article 230 EC.

[76] Agreement concluded by the Council of the European Union and the Republic of Iceland and the Kingdom of Norway concerning the latter's association with the implementation, application and development of the Schengen *acquis*, OJ 1999, L 176/36, hereafter referred to as the 1999 Agreement.

tions and an implementation of Article 6(1) of the 'Schengen Protocol'.[77] The Council concluded this agreement after the entry into force of the Treaty of Amsterdam. De Zwaan pointed out that in international relations this was an unprecedented approach.[78]

This was indeed the case. The 1999 Agreement was an international agreement according to the definition of Article 2 of the 1969 Vienna Convention. There was, however, one contracting party, the Council, that did not have international legal personality. Therefore, it was unclear, in which capacity the Council had acted, whether in its own right, on behalf of the Union or as a medium for the Member States, and on which legal basis. The official position of the Legal Service of the General Secretariat of the Council has been that this agreement was concluded on behalf of the European Union and with article 38 TEU as legal basis.[79] There was, however, nothing in the agreement itself to substantiate such a conclusion. To eliminate the existing ambiguity, the decision has been made to renegotiate the agreement and substitute the Union for the Council as contracting party.[80]

Article 24(4) TEU provides that the provisions of Article 24 TEU also apply to agreements on matters falling under Title VI, Police and Judicial Cooperation. Article 38 TEU, on the other hand, provides that agreements concluded under Article 24 TEU may also cover matters under Title VI. The precise relation between these two provisions has been unclear and controversial. De Zwaan, for example, argued that Articles 24 and 38 TEU had to be read in conjunction, and that it had apparently not been the intention of the Member States to allow the conclusion of international agreements on the basis of only Article 38 TEU.[81] The official position of the Legal Services of the Commission and the General Secretariat of the Council is that Article 38 TEU applies the procedure embodied in Article 24 TEU, and that it can be used as the single legal basis for the negotiation and conclusion of international agreements.[82]

Recent events prove that the assertion by the Legal Services of the Commission and the General Secretariat of the Council is correct. The first case involves the extradition agreement between the European Union and the United States of

[77] Protocol integrating the Schengen *acquis* into the framework of the European Union, OJ 1997, C 340/93. A second agreement was concluded implementing Article 6(2) of the 'Schengen Protocol'. Agreement concluded by the Council of the European Union and the Republic of Iceland and the Kingdom of Norway on the establishment of rights and obligations between Ireland and the United Kingdom of Great Britain and Northern Ireland, on the one hand, and the Republic of Iceland and the Kingdom of Norway, on the other, in areas of the Schengen *acquis* which apply to these States, OJ 2000, L 15/2.

[78] J.W. de Zwaan, *supra* note 2 at 102.

[79] Information obtained in personal interviews with the Legal Services of the Commission and the General Secretariat of the Council in the period November – December 2003.

[80] *Ibid.*

[81] J.W. de Zwaan, *supra* note 2, at 103-104.

[82] Information obtained in personal interviews with the Legal Services of the Commission and the General Secretariat of the Council in the period November-December 2003.

America.[83] The Agreement contains no express reference to the legal basis utilised by the European Union, but Article 2(1) of the Agreement stipulates that the European Union and the United States of America are the contracting parties.[84] Article 3(1) of the Agreement provides that the

> "European Union, pursuant to the Treaty on European Union, (...), shall ensure that the provisions of this Agreement are applied in relation to bilateral extradition treaties between the Member States and the United States of America, in force at the time of the entry into force of this Agreement".

The subject matters referred to all relate to police and judicial cooperation in criminal matters and are thus within the scope of Title VI of the EU Treaty.[85] It is, therefore, evident that this Agreement was concluded on the basis of Article 38 TEU.[86]

A more recent international agreement provides even more conclusive evidence of the use of Article 38 TEU as the single legal basis for concluding international agreements.[87] This Agreement is intended to apply those provisions of the Mutual Assistance Convention and the Mutual Assistance Protocol, that do not apply by virtue of the 1999 Agreement between the Council of the European Union, Iceland and Norway, to the relations between Iceland and Norway and between Iceland and Norway and the Member States of the European Union.[88] The matters referred to in the Agreement are those that come exclusively within the domain of Title VI of the EU Treaty. The Agreement was concluded on the basis of Articles 24 and 38 TEU.[89] However, the reference to Article 24 TEU is merely

[83] Agreement on extradition between the European Union and the United States of America, OJ 2003, L 181/27. See also V. Mitsilegas, The New EU-USA Cooperation on Extradition, Mutual Legal Assistance and the Exchange of Police Data in 8 *E.F.A. Rev.* (2003), at 515.

[84] Article 18 of the Agreement permits the conclusion of future bilateral agreements between individual Member States and the United States of America. The explanatory note on Article 18, attached to the Agreement, requires the Member State involved and the United States to try, through consultations, to eliminate any operational difficulties that may arise between the Agreement and their bilateral agreement. "Where it is not possible to address such operational difficulty through consultation alone, it would be consistent with the Agreement for future bilateral agreements between the Member State or Member States and the United States of America to provide an operationally feasible alternative mechanism that would satisfy the objectives of the specific provision with respect to which difficulty has arisen." From the foregoing it is clear that this Agreement takes precedence over any future agreement between the United States of America and a Member State.

[85] Article 2(3) defines the term 'Minister of Justice'. No other officials are referred to.

[86] A similar conclusion can be drawn for the Agreement on mutual legal assistance between the European Union and the United States of America, OJ 2003, L 181/34.

[87] Agreement between the European Union and the Republic of Iceland and the Kingdom of Norway on the application of certain provisions of the Convention of 29 May 2000 on Mutual Assistance in Criminal Matters between the Member States of the European Union and the 2001 Protocol thereto, OJ 2004, L 26/3.

[88] Article 1. See also the eight and ninth recital of the Preamble to the Agreement.

[89] Council Decision of 17 December 2003 on the signing of the Agreement between the European Union and the Republic of Iceland and the Kingdom of Norway on the application of certain

intended to indicate that the procedure embodied in Article 24 TEU was used.

Fortunately, the adoption of the Constitution in the course of the present Intergovernmental Conference will put an end to this mixed and confusing situation. The European Union is granted international legal personality and the conclusion of international agreements will occur on the basis of one single legal basis. This will not only facilitate the internal operations of the Union but will also provide greater clarity for third states and other international organisations.

2.5 The new European Constitution

2.5.1 The legal personality of the European Union

As stated before, Article I-6 of the European Constitution provides that the Union shall have legal personality. Within the Convention, Working Group III on legal personality was given the task to examine a number of matters related to a possible conferral of legal personality on the Union.[90] These were[91]

- The consequences of explicit recognition of the Union's legal personality.
- The consequences of a merger of the Union's legal personality with that of the Community.
- The impact on the simplification of the Treaties.

Within the Working Group there was a broad consensus to recommend that legal personality be conferred on the Union. The Working Group's position was that

> "The present situation was found to be ambiguous in a number of ways and likely to undermine affirmation of the Union's identity at international level and legal certainty, both of which are essential in international relations with third States and international organisations".[92]

The Working Group identified two possible solutions to the current complex situation. The first solution was to grant the Union legal personality alongside those of the European Community and Euratom. The second option was to provide for one single legal personality for the Union thereby replacing the legal personalities of the existing Communities.[93] Within the Working Group the second option was preferred.[94] The argument put forward was that providing the Union with a sepa-

provisions of the Convention of 29 May 2000 on Mutual Assistance in Criminal Matters between the Member States of the European Union and the 2001 Protocol thereto, OJ 2004, L 26/1.

[90] Final Report of Working Group III on Legal Personality, CONV 305/02.

[91] *Ibid*, at 1.

[92] *Ibid*, at 3. Only one member of the Working Group was opposed to granting the Union legal personality.

[93] *Ibid.*

[94] Again, with one member opposing.

rate legal personality alongside the personalities of the Community and Euratom, would not go far enough in 'providing the clarification and simplification necessary in the Union's external relations'.[95] The complications that might present themselves in the conclusion of cross-pillar mixed agreements were considered unacceptable, since such agreements would involve participation of the Community and the Union acting under Titles V and VI.

The Working Group agreed that conferral of legal personality on the European Union would bolster its profile at the international level. The Working Group concluded that

> "Explicit conferral of a single legal personality on the Union does not per se entail any amendment, either to the current allocation of competences between the Union and the Member States or to the allocation of competences between the current Union and the Community. Nor does it involve any amendments to the respective procedures and powers of the institutions regarding in particular the opening, negotiation and conclusion of international agreements".[96]

The arguments put forward by the Working Group involve recognition of the existence, at the present time, of an implied legal personality for the Union as a result of the provisions of Articles 24 and 38 TEU.[97] As pointed out, the Union has concluded a number of international agreements on the basis of Articles 24 and 38 TEU. This practice was seen as evidence of the existence of an implied legal personality.[98] However, the fact that the existence of an implied legal personality is not generally accepted necessitated the introduction of an express provision conferring legal personality on the Union.

2.5.2 The conclusion of international agreements

Article I-1 of the European Constitution provides that

> "Reflecting the will of the citizens and States of Europe to build a common future, this Constitution establishes the European Union, on which the Member States confer competences to attain objectives they have in common. The Union shall coordinate the policies by which the Member States aim to achieve these objectives, and shall exercise in the Community way the competences they confer on it".

Article I-2 of the European Constitution stipulates that

> "The Union is founded on the values of respect for human dignity, liberty, democracy, equality, the rule of law and respect for human rights. These values are common to the

[95] *Ibid*, at 3-4.

[96] *Ibid*, at 6.

[97] J. Kokott *et al*, *supra* note 18, at 1323.

[98] See V. Mitlilegas, *supra* note 83, at 533, note 87.

Member States in a society of pluralism, tolerance, justice, solidarity and non-discrimination".

According to Article I-3(4) of the European Constitution these values upon which the Union is founded will form the basis of the external objectives of the European Union. Thus, according to Cremona, this represents the first time in which 'the Union will have a set of overall principles, values and objectives guiding its external policy'.[99] The European Constitution unites the different objectives that define the different policy areas, into one set of objectives formulated in Article III-193.

The unification process brought about by the merging of the Community and Union objectives will be accompanied by an institutional unification. First, the Constitution provides for the creation of the Minister for Foreign Affairs.[100] The Minister for Foreign Affairs will be responsible for the Common Foreign and Security Policy as a member of the European Council and Chair of the Foreign Affairs Council. He will also be entrusted with the task of coordinating the Union's external activities as a Vice-President of the Commission.[101]

The second institutional innovation is the dominant role of the European Council in the external relations of the European Union. The European Constitution provides that it is for the European Council to identify the strategic interests and objectives of the European Union.[102] Contrary to the current EU Treaty, the policy statements of the European Council will not be limited to Common Foreign and Security Policy matters. They will extend to other areas of the Union's external relations. The policy statements will be adopted in the form of a European Decision on the basis of a recommendation from the Council of Ministers.[103] Depending on the subject matter (Common Foreign and Security Policy or other external policies) the proposals for these recommendations may come from the Minister for Foreign Affairs, the Commission or both acting jointly.[104]

Article I-1 of the European Constitution requires that the Union exercises its competences in a Community way. No explanation is provided as to what constitutes "the Community way". This is all the more interesting given the fact that the Community will cease to exist. Within the Community structure three fundamental concepts play an important role. These are the concepts of 'direct effect', 'supremacy of Community law' and 'pre-emption'. Application of the latter concept to the new structure would mean that in all areas of shared competence between

---

[99] M. Cremona, *supra* note 18, at 1348-1349.

[100] Article I-27(1) of the European Constitution. The office of the Minister for Foreign Affairs represents a unification of the functions of the Commissioner for External Relations and those of the High Representative of Common Foreign and Security Policy.

[101] Article I-27(3) of the European Constitution.

[102] Article III-194 of the European Constitution.

[103] A European decision is a non-legislative act that is binding in its entirety (Article I-32(1), fifth sub-paragraph of the European Constitution).

[104] *Ibid.*

the Union and the Member States an action by the European Union will pre-empt any action by the Member States which is likely to affect or distort existing Union law.[105] However, Article I-13, which lists the shared competences, does not include the Common Foreign and Security Policy. Thus, the concept of pre-emption will not apply in this particular area. It is unclear whether the principles of 'supremacy' and 'direct effect' will apply.

With regard to the actual conclusion of international agreements the drafters of the Constitution have attempted to combine the unification of the existing Treaty provisions with a codification of the jurisprudence of the European Court of Justice. This applies both to the power to conclude agreements in general as to the exclusive competence to conclude agreements. Thus Article III-225 of the European Constitution provides that

> "The Union may conclude agreements with one or more third countries or international organisations where the Constitution so provides or where the conclusion of an agreement is necessary in order to achieve, within the framework of the Union's policies, one of the objectives fixed by the Constitution, where there is provision for it in a binding Union legislative act or where it affects one of the Union's internal acts".

And Article I-12(2) of the European Constitution stipulates that

> "The Union shall have exclusive competence for the conclusion of an international agreement when its conclusion is provided for in a legislative act of the Union, is necessary to enable it to exercise its internal competence, or affects an internal Union act".

It must be said that the drafters have not fully managed to codify the complex case-law of the European Court of Justice on the external relations of the European Community. This is not surprising given that the case-law is not complete and remains a work in progress. Still, even in those areas where the Court has pronounced itself, the drafters have failed to include all the relevant doctrines. Thus, the Court has held that the Community has an exclusive external competence where the internal and external competence must be exercised simultaneously in order to achieve a Community objective.[106] In fact, Article I-12(2) makes no reference to external action related to the achievement of Union's objectives.

It will be interesting to see how the Court will apply these provisions. In any event, the provisions represent a certain setback from the current situation. The Court cannot be expected to adhere to the precise wording of the text of the Ar-

---

[105] On the subjects of pre-emption and repatriation of powers see D. Obradovic, Repatriation of Powers in the European Community in 34 *C.M.L. Rev.* (1997), at 59 and M. Waelbroeck, 'The Emergent Doctrine of Community Pre-emption – Consent and Re-delegation' in T. Sandalow and E. Stein (eds.), *Courts and Free Markets: Perspectives from the United States and Europe*, Volume II (1982), at 548.

[106] Opinion 1/94, *WTO*, [1994] ECR I-5267, paragraphs 85 and 86.

ticles I-12(2) and III-225 of the European Constitution. This would represent a reversal of its own case-law on the external relations of the Community. In that sense it is rather unfortunate, but understandable given the sensitivity of the matters involved, that the drafters have not seen it fit to extend the Court's jurisdiction to Common Foreign and Security Policy matters.

Article III-227 of the European Constitution sets out the procedural aspects for concluding international agreements. In line with the proposal from the Working Group the article represents a merger of the Articles 300 EC and 24 and 38 TEU.[107] One major advantage of this approach is that it will eliminate the ambiguity resulting from the provision of Article 24(5) TEU. The Working Group argued that if the Union is granted legal personality and it concludes an agreement, there would be no justification for national ratification procedures.[108] Thus Article III-225(2) of the European Constitution, in line with Article 300(7) EC, provides that agreements concluded by the European Union are binding on the institutions and the Member States.

Article III-227(3) of the European Constitution provides that either the Commission or the Minister for Foreign Affairs will negotiate agreements on behalf of the Union.[109] The Council of Ministers, on the basis of a European Decision, shall authorise these negotiations.[110] The EC and EU Treaty do not mention the legal instrument the Council can use to authorise the negotiation of agreements. Article II-227(3) of the European Constitution requires that this must be a European Decision. Another innovation is that the Council must nominate the negotiator or leader of the Union's negotiating team. It is not clear what the added value of this provision is. Perhaps it is intended to avoid disputes that may arise at the time of the conclusion of agreements. The Commission negotiated the WTO agreement on behalf of the Community and the Member States. The Commission saw this as sufficient evidence to assume that the agreement came within the domain of the exclusive competence of the Community.[111] Although Articles I-12

---

[107] CONV 305/02, at 7-10.

[108] *Ibid*, at 9. According to the Working Group, the deletion of the provision embodied should not be read as meaning that national parliaments are barred from scrutinising the government's position on the decision-making concerning the conclusion of the agreement. The only aim of the deletion is to eliminate the legal uncertainty that may arise if a Member State were to refuse to ratify the agreement. It would not be clear, and damaging to the Union's external policy, if the agreement would apply to the Member State as a matter of Union law.

[109] Only agreements involving matters that relate exclusively or principally to the Common Foreign and Security Policy may be negotiated by the Minister for Foreign Affairs. At present such agreements are negotiated by the Presidency, assisted by the Commission where appropriate (Article 24(2) TEU).

[110] Article III-228(3) of the European Constitution provides that agreements on matters relating to the monetary or exchange rate system shall be negotiated on the basis of the arrangements provided for by the Council of Ministers. The Council must ensure that the Union expresses a single position. The last sentence of the paragraph stipulates that the Commission must be fully associated with the negotiations. Literally this means that the Commission can never carry out the negotiations alone.

[111] Opinion 1/94, *WTO*, [1994] ECR I-5267.

and I-13 of the European Constitution draw a distinction between those matters that fall under the exclusive competence of the Union and those that are part of the shared competence, nothing prevents matters that are listed as belonging to the shared competences to become part of the Union's exclusive competence. Also, by appointing the negotiator or leader of the Union's negotiating team, third parties will know whom to turn to during the actual negotiations. This will guarantee, or at least enhance, the unity of the external representation. However, the provision does not exclude the Member States' participation in the delegation during the negotiations of mixed agreements.

A major improvement in the procedure is the increased role of the European Parliament. At present, the role of the European Parliament is primarily one of advisor to the Council. In matters related to Titles V and VI of the EU Treaty the Parliament has no official role. Even in areas where the co-decision procedure applies for the adoption of internal measures, the Parliament is only to be consulted.[112] Under the provisions of Article III-227(7) of the European Constitution the Parliament's consent, or assent, will also apply to agreements covering fields to which the legislative procedure applies. However, the role of the Parliament in the area of Common Foreign and Security Policy remains as it currently is. That is, it has no role to play.[113] Article III-227(11) of the European Constitution, furthermore, provides that the European Parliament is to be fully informed at all stages of the procedure. This represents a codification of the existing practice of the Commission and the Council.[114]

2.6 Conclusions

This Chapter set out to analyse the external treaty-making powers of the European Union. Whereas the existence of such powers, where the European Community is concerned, is clear, the same could not be said of the Union. The conclusion of a number of international agreements has gone a long way in answering the relevant questions.

On the basis of an interpretation of the relevant provisions of the EU Treaty and in the light of the subsequent practice of the Union and the Member States, it can be concluded that the European Union has an implied legal personality and the provisions of Article 24 TEU provide the necessary legal basis for the conclusion of international agreements. Agreements can also be concluded on the basis of Article 24 TEU in conjunction with Article 38 TEU or only Article 38 TEU.

---

112 Article 300(3) EC.

113 The same applies regarding the Common Commercial Policy agreements (Article III-217 of the European Constitution) and agreements on matters relating to the monetary or exchange rate system (Article III-228(3) of the European Constitution.

114 See Commission Notice of 31 January 2001, Guide pratique de l'accord-cadre sur les relations entre le Parlement européen et la Commission européenne, SP(2000)3785/5.

This means that technically speaking, agreements can also be concluded on the basis of Article 300 EC in conjunction with Article 24 TEU. This would qualify as a new type of mixed agreements in which the Community and the Union or the Community, the Union and the Member States act as joint contracting parties.[115]

The European Constitution adopted within the current Intergovernmental Conference is intended, among others, to solve this confusing duality between the Community and the Union in the external activities. Under the new treaty, the existing Treaties are merged and the Union is granted legal personality. The Community ceases to exist and the Member States loose the right to insist on an own national ratification process when the agreement deals with matters falling under the Common Foreign and Security Policy. Furthermore, the Union has to carry out its tasks in a 'Community way'. This will not only guarantee transparency and legal certainty, both internally and externally, but it will also preserve and extend the extensive treaty-making practice and *acquis* of the European Community.

[115] The European Union – A new international actor, *supra* note 2, at 827-828. See also S. Marquardt, *supra* note 2, at 39.

Part Two

Chapter 3
THE EC AND THE EU AND THE INTERNATIONAL LAW OF TREATIES

3.1 INTRODUCTION

International treaty law[1] is governed by the 1969 Vienna Convention[2], the 1986 Vienna Convention[3] and customary international law to the extent that these provisions have not been codified in the aforementioned Conventions. The 1969 and 1986 Conventions are essentially uniform. Still, the existence of two analogous conventions dealing with two distinct categories of subjects of international law, namely, states and international organisations raises questions as to their underlying relationship and whether there is some kind of hierarchy between the two.[4] The answer to this question is all the more important in the case of the European Community and the European Union, given their unique character, which sets them apart from all other international organisations.[5]

---

[1] For an extensive analysis of international treaty law see I.M. Sinclair, *The Vienna Convention on the Law of Treaties* (1973); P. Reuter, *Introduction to the Law of Treaties* (1995); S. Rosenne, *Developments in the Law of Treaties 1945-1986* (1989); M.N. Shaw, *International Law* (2003); I. Brownlie, *Principles of Public International Law* (2003) and A. Aust, *Modern Treaty Law and Practice* (2000).

[2] Vienna Convention on the Law of Treaties, signed at Vienna 23 May 1969, entered into force 27 January 1980 in 8 *I.L.M.* (1969), at 679, hereafter referred to as the 1969 Vienna Convention.

[3] Vienna Convention on the Law of Treaties between States and International Organisations or between International Organisations, signed 21 March 1986, not yet entered into force in 25 *I.L.M.* (1987), at 543, hereafter referred to as the 1986 Vienna Convention.

[4] This issue was raised in the International Law Commission at the time of the drafting of the 1986 Convention. The Special Rapporteur, Mr. P. Reuter, indicated that within the International Law Commission there was a general consensus on the differences between states and international organisations. There were two important questions that needed to be answered. The first question was whether agreements concluded implied a fundamental equality between states and international organisations as subjects of international law. The second issue concerned the independence of the draft Convention from the 1969 Vienna Convention. Was it necessary to adhere as closely as possible to the text of the 1969 Convention, or should the International Law Commission prepare the draft Convention independent from the 1969 Convention? In the end the Commission chose a draft that possessed some distinctive characteristics owing to the extremely close relationship between the draft Convention and the 1969 Vienna Convention. *Yearbook of the International Law Commission*, 1981, Volume I, at 2-5 and Volume II, Part Two, at 117. See also Special Rapporteur, Mr. G. Gaja, *First report on responsibility of international organisations*, 2003, A/CN.4/532.

[5] Within the International Law Commission the members debated whether the definition of an international organisation as an intergovernmental organisation would suffice. It was proposed to define an international organisation as an intergovernmental organisation having the capacity to conclude treaties. The proposal was rejected. The argument being that international organisations either had the power to conclude treaties or they did not. *Yearbook of the International Law Commission*, 1981, Volume I, at 6.

Given the fact that states are still the primary actors, whereas international organisations derive their powers from the will of the member states, it can be argued that the 1986 Convention is of a lesser degree than the 1969 Convention. However, the large number of provisions that these two Conventions have in common shows that the distinction between the two is merely a matter of political will rather than hierarchy.[6]

The 1969 Convention is open to states alone.[7] The European Community, the European Union, and for that matter all other international organisation, cannot become a party to this Convention. The 1986 Convention, which deals with agreements concluded between states and international organisations, and between international organisations, has not yet entered into force. To the extent that the 1986 Convention codifies customary international law, these provisions as sources of customary international law bind the European Community and the European Union.[8] It is generally accepted, partially in light of some of the judgements of the International Court of Justice[9], that almost all the substantive provisions of the Vienna Convention constitute customary international law.[10]

In its early case-law the European Court of Justice has indirectly used the 1969 Vienna Convention as its source of law. In *Opinion 1/91*, for example, the Court explicitly invoked Article 31 of this Convention.[11] In more recent cases both the European Court of Justice and the Court of First Instance have made reference to the 1986 Vienna Convention.[12] The direct consequence of not having a complete set of rules applicable to the Community and the Union, means that there may be instances where doubts will remain as to the precise rules of international treaty law that apply to the Community's and the Union's treaty practice.[13] In the final Chapter recommendations will be made on how to remedy these legal lacunae.

The purpose of this chapter is, therefore, to conduct the first part of a thorough analysis of the Community's treaty-making practice in the light of the international law of treaties. The aim is to establish whether the Community's and the

---

[6] Except for a number of specific provisions, due to the structure of international organisations, the regime of treaties where the parties include several international organisations, conforms to the regime of inter-state agreements. P. Reuter, *supra* note 1, at 20.

[7] Article 81.

[8] Examples include Case 104/81, *Kupferberg*, [1982] ECR 3641; Case C-327/91, *France* v *Commission*, [1994] ECR I-3641; Case C-162/96, *Racke*, [1998] I-3655 and Opinion 2/00, *Cartagena Protocol on Biosafety*, [2001] ECR I-9713.

[9] Most notably the 1997 *Gabcíkovo-Nagymaros* Case, *Hungary* v *Slovakia* of 25 September 1997, I.C.J. Reports (1997), at 7 and the *Qatar* v *Bahrain* Case, I.C.J. Reports (1994), at 112.

[10] A. Aust, *supra* note 1, at 9-11.

[11] Opinion 1/91, *EEA I*, [1991] ECR I-617.

[12] This happened in the *Opel Austria* Case, Case T-115/94, [1997] ECR II-39. However, in Case C-162/96, *Racke*, [1998] ECR I-3655, both the European Court of Justice and AG Jacobs referred to the 1969 Vienna Convention as their primary source.

[13] The official position of the Legal Service of the Commission is that it adheres to the provisions of the 1969 Vienna Convention. Information obtained through personal interviews with the Legal Services of the Commission and the Council in the period November-December 2003.

Union's treaty-making practices are comparable with treaty-making practice of States or other international organisations, or whether they form a system *sui generis*.

The European Community and the European Union have a very complex system of rules and practices. In the case of the European Community, it is not only a unique supranational structure with a monistic relation with the national legal orders of the Member States, but it also has a highly developed system of checks and balances between the various institutions. The European Court of Justice, as the judicial organ endowed with extensive powers, plays a pivotal role in this system. Understanding the way in which this important, near-state like international organisation interacts with other subjects of international law, and more specifically adheres or contributes to the development of international treaty law is very important and, therefore, requires detailed analysis.

This chapter is not intended, however, to compare every aspect of the law of treaties to the Community's practice as it has developed over the years, and has been confirmed by the European Court of Justice. Rather, the aim is, as was indicated in the General Introduction, to select a number of key aspects, such as the negotiation and conclusion of international agreements, entry into force, application of international agreements, invalidity, termination and suspension of international agreements and to compare the Community and Union practice to the applicable provisions of the international law of treaties. Although there may be some incidental reference to mixed agreements, this Chapter primarily will focus on agreements to which the Community alone is a party. Agreements concluded by the European Union will also be mentioned. Mixed agreements will be analysed in Chapter 4 and the subjects of treaty interpretation and dispute settlement will de dealt with in the Chapter 5.[14]

3.2 The negotiation and conclusion of international agreements

3.2.1 **The concept of agreement**

International agreements play a very important role in international relations. Not only is this the case in the relation between states, but also, increasingly, between states and international organisations, and between international organisations. Although Article 38(1) of the Statute of the International Court of Justice does not establish a clear hierarchy amongst the various sources of law, it is generally accepted that international agreements constitute the primary source of international law.[15] The various attempts made to codify the law of treaties are further evidence of the importance of treaties in international relations. Or as Shaw puts

[14] See *supra* General Introduction.

[15] M.N. Shaw, *supra* note 1, at 66-67.

it "The concept of treaty and how it operates becomes of paramount importance to the evolution of international law".[16] In fact, numerous international disputes involve the validity and interpretation of international agreements. International agreements embody and reflect the practical content of state relations and the agreed objectives of states. It can thus be argued that international agreements are the closest thing to legislation at international level.[17]

The development of an acceptable definition of the concept international agreement is of paramount importance. It is, therefore, rather remarkable that given the importance of internationals agreements to the organisation of international relations that international treaty law uses the very narrow definition of the two Vienna Conventions. What is even more noteworthy is the fact that given the wide variety of international agreements in force the international community has limited itself to the adoption of just these two aforementioned Conventions.

Although the name 'treaty' is commonly used in the context of international agreements, a great number of names are used to express the same concept. In fact, the International Law Commission, in its preparations for the 1969 Vienna Convention, identified 16 different names.[18] Examples include such concepts as convention, protocol, covenant, and act. In accordance with the two Vienna Conventions it is generally accepted that the designation of an international agreement is irrelevant from a legal perspective. The determining factor is whether the instrument is intended to establish binding commitments between the contracting parties. In return, this is dependent on the will of the parties involved. Thus, in a number of cases the International Court of Justice has qualified the instrument in effect between the parties as an international agreement, although *prima facie* they did not appear to be so.[19]

John King Gamble asserts, however, that although it may be generally accepted that the name of the instrument has no bearing on its legal significance, state practice may prove a definite pattern in the use of the name of the same.[20] He states that of the various names used, treaty, convention, agreement, protocol and exchange of notes are the most commonly used. He concludes that of these aforementioned names 'treaty' is the most formal instrument; 'convention' is a formal, proper document more frequently used for multilateral than for bilateral treaties, and predominantly used when international organisations are directly involved in the treaty-making process; 'agreement' is used for informal intergovernmental contracts; 'protocols' are often subsidiary documents to a convention

[16] M.N. Shaw, *supra* note 1, at 811.

[17] G.M. Danilenko, *Law-making in the International Community* (1993), at 44-54. Reuter asserts, "if international law does rest in the will of States, the law of treaties is the most constructive and rational expression of that will". P. Reuter, *supra* note 1, at 28.

[18] H.G. Schermers and N. Blokker, *International Institutional Law* (2003), at 1111-1112.

[19] A good example is of course the *Qatar* v *Bahrain* Case, I.C.J. Reports (1994), at 112.

[20] J. King Gamble, Multilateral Treaties: The significance of the name of the instrument in 10 *Calif.W.Int'l L.J.* (1980), at 1-24. See also H. Hongju Koh, The President versus the Senate in Treaty Interpretation: What's all the fuss about? in 15 *Yale J.Int'l L.* (1990), at 331-344.

and 'exchange of notes' tends to deal with fairly trivial matters and almost always on the bilateral level.[21]

The 1969 and 1986 Vienna Convention only apply to written agreements.[22] Both Conventions do recognise, however, the validity of other types of treaties, specifically oral agreements (Article 3 of the 1969 Vienna Convention and of the 1986 Vienna Convention). Both Conventions also accept the possibility of international agreements being concluded between subjects other then states and international organisations.[23] This can be seen as a recognition of a basic concept of contract law, namely, that parties, irrespective of whether they are subjects of international law, are free to give any designation to the contract in force between them as well as to the laws governing this contract.

Within the Community the word 'agreement' is used whenever reference is made to a concept that traditionally carries the name of treaty under international law.[24] The reason for this use is that the word 'treaty' is used when reference is made to the Treaty establishing the European Communities, the Treaty establishing the European Atomic Energy Community and the Treaty on European Union. Even so, in international relations it is common practice to designate treaties concluded by international organisations as agreements. In fact, the documents usually bear the name agreement.[25] Though the underlying reason for the use of the term 'agreement' may be different, the result remains the same, in that the concept involves a written document concluded between two or more subjects of international law, which is binding under international law. In the course of this research this (Community) practice and use of the term 'agreement', whenever reference is made to an international treaty to which the Community or the Union is a party, will be adhered to.

Article 2 of the 1969 Vienna Convention on the Law of Treaties defines a treaty (an international agreement) as "an international agreement concluded between States in written form and governed by international law, whether embodied in a single instrument or in two or more related instruments and whatever its particular designation" The 1986 Vienna Convention on the Law of Treaties copies this definition with the addition that a treaty constitutes an agreement signed between States; between (a) State(s) and (an) international organisation(s); or between international organisations. The first sentence of the article in question provides that this definition is used solely for the purpose of the Vienna Conventions.[26]

As indicated before, the two Conventions represent a substantial codification of existing state practice in the field of international treaty law. Still, there is

---

[21] J. King Gamble, *supra* note 20, at 4-8.

[22] Article 1(a) of both Conventions.

[23] Article 3 of both Vienna Conventions.

[24] I. MacLeod, I.D. Hendry, and S. Hyett, *The External Relations of the European Communities* (1996), at 73. See also the Articles 111, 133, 174, 181, 181a, 300 and 310 EC and 24 and 38 TEU.

[25] Schermers *et al*, *supra* note 18, at 1111-1112.

[26] "For the purposes of the present Convention: (...)".

nothing that would suggest that this definition represents customary international law. The fact that Article 2 begins with the sentence "For the purpose of the present Convention" can be seen as a clear indication that the definition used does not represent customary international law but that it is merely a working definition. However in the *Qatar* v *Bahrain Delimitation* Case[27], the International Court of Justice's reasoning could lead to a different conclusion. Using the 1969 Convention as its source of reference, and without verifying whether the Convention was ratified by both parties and, therefore, applicable in the present case, the Court went on to conclude that the exchange of notes between the parties was an international agreement. Klabbers correctly argues that such reasoning could mean that the International Court of Justice has concluded that the definition, embodied in Article 2 of the 1969 Vienna Convention, constitutes customary international law.[28] What has led the Court to this conclusion remains unclear, however.

As stated, both Conventions make reference to an agreement concluded in written form. This reference does not, however, exclude oral agreement. As indicated above, Article 3 of the 1969 Vienna Convention and Article 3(iii) of the 1986 Vienna Convention make special reference to oral agreements, stipulating that they, too, can have legal effect and are therefore binding. Furthermore, the two Vienna Conventions make reference to agreements signed between States, States and International Organisations and between International Organisations. The term 'agreement' would not, therefore, seem to apply to agreements that involve a different actor as one of the treaty parties. Article 3 of both Vienna Conventions recognises the legal force of international agreements concluded between states or international organisations and other subjects of international law, or between such other subjects of international law. Examples of these subjects of international law include the Holy See, the International Committee of the Red Cross and some liberation movements, such as the Palestinian Liberation Organisation. However, the article provides that the provisions of the Conventions do not apply to these international agreements. Also excluded from the definition provided for in the Vienna Conventions are natural persons, multinational corporations and non-governmental organisations.[29]

In the *Nuclear Test* Cases[30], the International Court of Justice concluded that in certain cases and under very specific conditions unilateral statements could qualify as international agreements. The Court held that

---

[27] I.C.J. Reports (1994), at 112.

[28] J. Klabbers, *Qatar* v *Bahrain*: the concept of "treaty" in international law in 33 *AVR* (1995), at 361. If this is true, then the same can be said of the definition of the term 'agreement' in Article 2 of the 1986 Vienna Convention.

[29] In the *Anglo-Iranian Oil Company* Case, I.C.J. Reports (1952), at 20, the International Court of Justice held that an oil concession granted by Iran to an oil company did not qualify as an agreement, because the state whose nationality the company had was not a party to the concession.

[30] *Nuclear Test* Cases, I.C.J. Reports (1974), at 253.

> "It is well recognized that declarations made by way of unilateral acts, concerning legal or factual situations, may have the effect of creating legal obligations. Declarations of this kind may be, and often are, very specific. When it is the intention of the State making the declaration that it should become bound according to its terms, that intention confers on the declaration the character of a legal undertaking, the States being thenceforth legally required to follow a course of conduct consistent with the declaration. *An undertaking of this kind, if given publicly, and with an intent to be bound, even though not made within the context of international negotiations, is binding.* In these circumstances, nothing in the nature of a *quid pro quo* nor any subsequent acceptance of the declaration, nor even any reply or reaction from other States, is required for the declaration to take effect, since such a requirement would be inconsistent with the strictly unilateral nature of the juridical act by which the pronouncement by the State was made" (paragraph 43, emphasis added).

The Court did not elaborate on what these specific conditions are and it remains to be seen whether the Court's ruling can be qualified as a general rule of international treaty law.[31] The International Court of Justice itself recognises in paragraph 44 of its judgement that not all unilateral acts imply consent to be bound. In the *Legal Status of Eastern Greenland* Case[32], for example, the Permanent Court of International Justice denied legal effect to the statements made by the Norwegian Foreign Minister, M. Ihlen. In response to the Danish argument that Denmark had relied on M. Ihlen's declaration as recognition of an existing Danish sovereignty in Greenland, the Court held that

> "The Court is unable to accept this point of view. A careful examination of the words used and of the circumstances in which they were used, as well as of the subsequent developments, shows that M. Ihlen cannot have meant to be giving then and there a definitive recognition of Danish sovereignty over Greenland, and shows also that he cannot have been understood by the Danish Government at the time as having done so".[33]

The conclusion to be drawn from these cases is that international treaty law recognizes the possibility that unilateral statements can have legal effect equivalent to an international agreement, provided that the state making this declaration had such an intention. This consent to be bound must be clear from the person(s) making the statements on behalf of the state and the circumstances under which these statements are made.

In international relations states make frequent use of informal non-treaty instruments, such as a Memorandum of Understanding.[34] These documents are

---

[31] See in this regard D.J. Harris, *Cases and Materials on International Law* (1991), at 736-741.

[32] *Legal Status of Eastern Greenland Case*, P.C.I.J. Reports (1933), Series A/B, No. 53.

[33] *Ibid*, at 1933.

[34] Not all Memoranda of Understanding are informal agreements. The Memorandum of Understanding on the European Union Administration of Mostar, signed in Geneva on 5 July 1994, Tractatenblad 1994, No 183, is an example of a binding international agreement.

usually non-binding, confidential and easy to amend. The purpose of these instruments is very clear, namely, the creation of a non-binding instrument, usually expressing a political position without the assumption of any legal obligations. In the *Qatar* v *Bahrain* Case, the International Court of Justice stipulated that attention has to be paid to all actual terms, the circumstances in which the document had been drawn up and the facts of the case. The Court came to the conclusion that in this particular instance the Minutes dated 25 December 1990 qualified as an international agreement.[35]

While it is recognized that there may be a state practice whereby unilateral statements made by persons on behalf of the state could qualify as an international agreement, the same cannot be said of international organisations. Although in international organisations it is very common for, for example, the Secretary General, as Head of the organisation's Secretariat, to make public statements on behalf of the organisation, it cannot be readily assumed that these statements can and do constitute the acceptance of an international obligation. Given the traditional structure of international organisations and the prominent role played by the member states, it is very unlikely that the Secretary General, through unilateral statements, can accept international obligations binding on the organisation and its members. This is not to say that the Secretary General or any other organ of the organisations could not assume, within the limits of their powers, international obligations that are binding upon him/it alone. These arrangements are administrative arrangements and have a different legal significance than international agreements. Still, the commitments assumed under these administrative arrangements must be fulfilled and the other organs of the organisations and the member states are obliged to assist the Secretary General or the organ in question in fulfilling these obligations.

The European Community and the European Union, as two distinct and unique international organisations, have rules applying to them that set them apart from other international intergovernmental organisations. Within the European Community the European Parliament plays an active, yet not general role, in the external relations of the organisation. Although the general rule is that the European Parliament is to be consulted whenever the EC is to conclude an international agreement[36], there are instances where this consultation is not mandatory.[37] Although certain inter-institutional arrangements have been set up to allow the Parliament a certain level of involvement in the external relations of the Community in the Articles 111 and 133 EC, these arrangement do not have any legal

[35] M.N. Shaw, *supra* note 1, at 813-814.

[36] Article 300(3) EC makes reference to various instances where the assent of the European Parliament has to be obtained. An example would be an international agreement concluded on the basis of Article 310 EC (association agreements).

[37] See Articles 111 and 133 EC. See also Commission Notice of 31 January 2001, Guide pratique de l'accord-cadre sur le relations entre le Parlement européen et la Commission européenne, SP (2000)3785/5. The arrangements between the Commission and the European parliament embodied in this agreement have legal force.

force.[38] Where there is no parliamentary involvement, it could be argued that unilateral statements made by the Presidency of the Union on the basis of a common position adopted by the Council, could qualify as binding international commitments, provided they were made by someone who can commit the European Union at the international level, and the wording of the common position and the subsequent statement is such that it can readily be assumed that the Union intended itself to be bound by these statements.[39]

Each year the European Union issues a number of common positions.[40] These common positions are adopted within the sphere of the Common Foreign and Security Policy, CFSP. These common positions adopted by the Council are expressed by the Presidency of the European Union. A remarkable feature of this practice is the adherence of third countries, especially candidate Member States, to these common positions.[41] Although this practice alone does not provide sufficient evidence for the unilateral acceptance of international obligations on the part of the Union, it does provide some valuable information and warrants further study.

In his Introduction to the Law of Treaties, Reuter proposes a broader definition than the one used by the Vienna Conventions.[42] He defines a treaty as "an expression of concurring wills attributable to two or more subjects of international law and intended to have legal effects under the rules of international law".[43] His reasoning behind this broader definition is, as he puts it, "to convey the general sense of the problem".[44] In Reuter's view the rules applicable to written agreements between states are so numerous that the Vienna Convention had to use a more restrictive definition. In his words "the broader the definition, the

[38] The Luns Procedure and the Luns-Westerterp Procedure (Luns II). See also C. Tomuschat, 'Abkommen der Gemeinschaft' in H. von der Groeben (ed.), *Kommentar zum EG-/EU-Vertrag* (1997), at 488-494; J. Megret, *Le Droit de la Communauté Economique Européenne. Commentaire du Traité et des Textes Pris pour son Application*, Volume 12, Relations extérieures (1980), at 42-46 and the Commission Notice, *supra* note 37.

[39] According to Megret, with regard to Article 300 EC, "le terme <<accords>> ne peut être limité aux accords écrits ou verbaux. Les négociations internationals ne doivent pas nécessairement aboutir à un accord écrit ou oral mais peuvent également avoir pour résultat des actions unilatérales (bien que souvent concertées) des parties qui ont mené ces négociations, comme par exemple dans le cas des préférences généralisées". J. Megret, *supra* note 38, at 22.

[40] Examples include Council Common Position 2002/960/CFSP concerning restrictive measures against Somalia, OJ 2002, L 334/1; Council Common Position 2003/280/CFSP in support of the effective implementation of the mandate of the ICTY, OJ 2003, L 101/22; and Council Common Position 2003/297/CFSP on Burma/Myanmar, OJ 2003, L 106/36.

[41] V. Kronenberger, 'Common Foreign and Security Policy: International Law Aspects of the Association of Third States with the Common Positions of the Council of the European Union' in V. Kronenberger (ed.), *The EU and the International Legal Order: Discord or Harmony?* (2001), at 351.

[42] P. Reuter, *supra* note 1, at 28-33.

[43] *Ibid*, at 28-29.

[44] *Ibid*, at 28.

fewer the rules applying to all the cases it covers".[45] But with the International Court of Justice, apparently, recognizing the 1969 Vienna Convention definition as being a rule of customary international law, and, it seems logic, the same applying to the 1986 Vienna Convention, this debate becomes moot.

The only outstanding issue to be analysed is whether the European Community adheres to the Vienna Conventions' definition. As stated before, the Community and the Union are bound by the rules of international treaty law to the extent that international treaty law constitutes customary international law. The European Court of Justice's eventual use of a definition that has a different legal meaning from the current international definition, in the light of the International Court of Justice's decision in the *Qatar* v *Bahrain* Case, does not necessarily mean that it may have to revise its existing case-law. After all, there have been various instances where the European Court of Justice has stated that concepts mentioned in the EC Treaty should be interpreted within the Community context.[46] The Court could, therefore, provide its own Community definition of the term agreement. Given the fact that rules of public international law are binding on the Community and that a great number of international agreements are concluded by the Community, and the Member States (mixed agreements) and the European Union, it is highly unlikely that the European Court of Justice's definition will deviate much, if any, from the definition used in the Vienna Conventions.

In *Opinion 1/75* the Court defined an international agreement as "any undertaking entered into by entities, subject to international law which has binding force, whatever its formal designation".[47] The conclusion has to be that the Court's definition of the term 'agreement', although broader in scope than the Vienna Conventions' definition, encompasses the definition provided in the 1969 and the 1986 Vienna Conventions.[48] The Court's definition is slightly broader, because it includes oral agreements. It does, however, exclude unilateral statements with binding force along the line of the *Nuclear Test* Cases. But as we have already seen, neither the EC Treaty nor the EU Treaty explicitly excludes this possibility. Case 327/91, *France* v *Commission*, further substantiates the conclusion that the Court uses a broader definition than the Vienna Conventions.[49]

The Vienna Conventions stipulate that other types of international arrangements do not fall under the definition provided. Although they may be binding, the determining factor is whether the arrangement is governed by international law. The European Court of Justice's definition clearly includes these additional

[45] *Ibid.*

[46] See, for example, Case C-54/96, *Dorsch Consult*, [1997] ECR I-4983, concerning the interpretation of the term 'tribunal' within the meaning of Article 234 EC.

[47] Opinion 1/75, *OECD Local Cost Standard*, [1975] ECR 1355, at 1356.

[48] See also MacLeod *et al*, *supra* note 24, at 75-77.

[49] [1994] ECR I-3666. First the Court used the Vienna Convention definition. After it had confirmed that the agreement fell within the definition it subsequently referred to its own definition. If the two definitions are identical in meaning, why make this distinction?

forms of international agreements. The definition in the 1969 and the 1986 Vienna Conventions only applies to states and international organisations. The European Court of Justice, using the phrase entities rather than subjects of international law, should not, however, be seen as recognition of a general power of the Community to conclude international agreements with a wide variety of parties, with the only condition that the agreement is subject to international law and has binding force. The Court's definition is restricted to international agreements concluded with other subjects of international law. Community law or the law of one of the Member States usually governs agreements concluded with other parties.

Besides the conclusion of ordinary international agreements, the Community regularly, through the Commission, engages in various other international arrangements, such as administrative agreements. In fact, Article 302 of the EC Treaty explicitly entrusts the Commission with the task of maintaining all appropriate administrative relations with the United Nations and its specialized agencies as well as all other international organisations.[50] However, these administrative agreements are also concluded with third countries, for example, with regard to the diplomatic missions of the European Union in those countries. The Commission is not subject to any formal control by the Council but despite the broad formulation of the Commission's powers under Article 302 EC, it can be argued that the Commission's powers only relate to general administrative cooperation and that it does not include the power to conclude international agreements.[51] This conclusion is, furthermore, emphasized by the very precise constitutional arrangements provided for in Article 300 EC, and more particularly the pre-eminent role of the Council in the conclusion of international agreements.[52] However, to the extent that these administrative arrangements are governed by international law, as would be the case of diplomatic missions, they do fall under the general definition of an international agreement as provided for by international treaty law and the European Court of Justice's own case-law.

According to Article 300(2) EC, international agreements to which the Community is a party are to be concluded by the Council. The Court of Justice held in Case *327/91* that this is a constitutional arrangement from which deviation is only possible under the conditions set out in the Treaty itself. In certain circumstances the Council is empowered to authorise the Commission in signing an international agreement.[53] An example would be the Council Decision 93/726/EC

[50] See also Article 303 EC concerning the maintenance of all appropriate forms of cooperation with the Council of Europe and Article 304 EC regarding close cooperation with the Organisation for Economic Cooperation and Development.

[51] I. MacLeod *et al*, *supra* note 24, at 166-168.

[52] The Court of Justice, in Case 327/91, *France* v *Commission*, [1994] ECR I-3666, confirmed this conclusion.

[53] Paragraph 4 stipulates that: "When concluding an agreement, the Council may, by way of derogation from paragraph 2, authorize the Commission to approve modifications on behalf of the

of 23 November 1993.[54] Article 3 of this Decision stipulates that "For the purposes of Article 13 of the Agreement, the Commission is hereby authorized to conclude the necessary acts amending the Agreement, in accordance with the procedure laid down in Article 83 of Regulation (EEC) No 822/87".[55]

The Commission is of the opinion that when the Council delegates the power to conclude additional technical agreements, the Council renounces its power to conclude these agreements.[56] The Commission can opt to negotiate the agreement alone, or it can request the assistance of a committee appointed by the Council. With regard to the committee appointed by the Council, the Commission has two options. It can make use of a standard Article 300 EC committee or it can cooperate with a comitology committee. In general the Commission prefers to utilise the specific expertise of the comitology committee rather than the more general expertise of Article 300 EC committees. Although the Commission uses a comitology committee, the comitology procedure itself does not apply.[57] Should the Council disagree with the contents of the agreement negotiated by the Commission, there is not much the Council can do with regard to that particular agreement. Its only option is to seek the annulment of the Commission Decision concluding the agreement on the basis of Article 230 EC. To this day, this has never happened.[58]

It is clear, however, that the Commission lacks an autonomous power to sign and conclude international agreements.[59] The administrative agreements are part of the external activities of the Commission.[60] As stated before, it could be argued that they do not fall under the definition of the term international agreement as used by the European Court of Justice, and which, as indicated before is in line with the definition under international treaty law, because the Commission is not acting on behalf of the Community and it is not a subject of international law. According to this line of reasoning these documents lack legal force as far as the

---

Community where the agreement provides for then to be adopted by a simplified procedure or by a body set up by the agreement; it may attach specific conditions to such authorization".

[54] Council Decision 93/726/EC of 23 November 1993 concerning the conclusion of an Agreement between the European Community and Romania on the reciprocal protection and control of wines, OJ 1993 L 337/177.

[55] A similar arrangement can be found in Article 3 of Council Decision 93/725, OJ 1993 L 337/172.

[56] Information obtained through personal interviews with the Legal Services of the Commission and the Council in the period November-December 2003.

[57] *Ibid.*

[58] *Ibid.*

[59] However, the Commission has the authority to initial international agreements.

[60] These agreements are usually concluded on the basis of an exchange of letters. They deal, among others, with the privileges and immunities of the Union's diplomatic missions, the granting of special travel documents and the establishment of task forces to conduct joint research (for example in the field of biotechnology). See A-P. Allo, 'Les accords administratifs entre l'Union Européenne et les organisations internationales' in D. Dormoy (ed.), *L'Union européenne et les organisations internationales* (1997), at 56.

Community is concerned and there is no obligation to perform. The agreements do not qualify as international agreements and do not, therefore, bind the Community and Member States as provided for in Article 300(7); they only bind the Commission.[61] Only in the event that the Council, having fulfilled the procedural requirements of Article 300 EC, sanctions these arrangements through a subsequent act, will they become an international agreement binding upon the Community and the Member States.

Contrary to Articles 303 and 304 EC, which authorize the Community to maintain the necessary relations with the Council of Europe and the Organisation for Economic Co-operation and Development, OECD, Article 302 EC provides the Commission with the power to maintain the appropriate relations with the United Nations, its specialised organs and all other international organisations. However, the difference in terminology has no legal significance.[62] The Commission, as the Community's executive power, is entrusted with a general task of ensuring the proper functioning and development of the common market (Article 211 EC). All its activities are in the interest of the Community. International commitments assumed by the Commission, within the limits of its powers, are, therefore, always on behalf of the Community as a whole.[63] Therefore, the conclusion must be that these administrative agreements could qualify as international agreements.

In Case *327/91* the Court ruled that the agreement concluded between the Commission and the Antitrust Division of the United States Department of Justice and the Federal Trade Commission fell squarely within the definition of Article 2(1)(a)(i) of the 1986 Vienna Convention.[64] The Court went on to say, in reference to *Opinion 1/75*, that the expression agreement as referred to in Article 300 EC should be read in a general sense and subsequently repeated its definition of the term agreement.[65] The Court went on to say, that although the Commission had violated the internal procedures of the Community, there was now a binding international agreement, committing not only the Community but also the Member States at the international level.[66]

In its case-law the Court has maintained the aforementioned definition of the term agreement. However, the type of instrument used, whether it is in the form of a bilateral or multilateral agreement, or an exchange of letters, or a gentleman's agreement, is irrelevant. In the words of the European Court of Justice, the formal designation of an agreement envisaged under international law

[61] Although the 1999 Agreement was concluded between the Council of the European Union and Iceland and Norway, it was believed that the Council acted on behalf of the Union and not in its own right. See *supra* Chapter 2.

[62] Conf. P. Léger (ed.), *Commentaire article par article des traités UE et CE* (2000), at 1920-1926; J. Megret, *supra* note 38, at 64-66; H. von der Groeben (ed.), *supra* note 38, at 5692-5705.

[63] See also MacLeod *et al*, *supra* note 24, at 166-167.

[64] Case 327/91, *France* v *Commission*, [1994] ECR I-3666, paragraph 25.

[65] Case 327/91, *France* v *Commission*, [1994] ECR I-3666, paragraph 27.

[66] Case 327/91, *France* v *Commission*, [1994] ECR I-3666, paragraph 25.

was not decisive.[67] It does not matter in which form the agreement was concluded, written or oral, or which type of document it is, a bilateral or multilateral agreement, a letter of exchange or whatever other type of document used. What matters, is that it has to be an agreement between the Community or the Union and one ore more subjects of international law, governed by international law and being legally binding on the parties concerned. As outlined before, this definition excludes unilateral statements that have binding force equivalent to an international agreement.

In the *Van Gend en Loos* Case the Court ruled that the Member States had created a new, yet separate legal order, separate from international law proper.[68] Separate though it may be, the Community and the European Union are still bound by international law. It is therefore not remarkable that the Court has used a definition of the term 'agreement' that is similar to the definition provided for by international law.

3.2.2 The classification of international agreements

International treaty law is rather silent where it comes to the classification of international agreements. This is not very surprising given the large number of international agreements concluded. Both Vienna Conventions only stipulate that the agreement has to be in written form and governed by international law, without engaging in any type of systematic classification of international agreements. Therefore, with this in mind it may seem rather superfluous to attempt to classify the different types of international agreements concluded by the European Community and the European Union. This problem is further exacerbated by the fact that there is a multitude of international agreements and any single factor can be used as the determining element to classify international agreements. However, given the fact that this study is not only about the Community's and the Union's treaty law but also about their practices, it is relevant to see whether some type of classification at the international level is discernible. If such a classification is visible, a similar attempt must be made at the Community and Union level, followed by a comparison between the international and the Community/Union classifications.

International agreements can be subdivided in two ways. The first deals with the form and substance (the nature) of the agreements. Although form and substance are not the same concept, they do go hand in hand. The chosen form always mirrors the substance of the international agreement.[69] The second way of

---

[67] Opinion 1/75, *OECD Local Cost Standard*, [1975] ECR 1355, at 1356. Also confirm MacLeod *et al*, *supra* note 24, at 75.

[68] Case 26/62, *Van Gend en Loos*, [1963] ECR 1.

[69] C. Osakwe, 'The Concept and Forms of Treaties Concluded by International Organisations' in K. Zemanek (ed.), *Agreements of International Organisations and the Vienna Convention on the Law of Treaties*, Supplementum I to ÖZoR (1971), at 180-181.

subdividing international agreements has to do with the number of contracting parties involved. International agreements are commonly divided into bilateral and multilateral agreements.[70]

A bilateral agreement is an agreement establishing rights and obligations between two parties. Each contracting party may consist of more than one member.[71] The determining factor is, however, that the agreed rights and obligations do not apply between the members of one contracting party, but only between the two contracting parties themselves.

A multilateral agreement is an agreement establishing reciprocal rights and obligations between three or more parties. In general, the rights and obligations that apply between the parties A and B also apply between A and C, A and D, B and C, B and D, and C and D.[72] Each contracting party is individually responsible for the performance of all the duties enshrined in the international agreement. Multilateral agreements can deal in a general or particular manner with matters of concern to the contracting parties. This, however, has no bearing on its qualification as a multilateral agreement.

Osakwe distinguishes the following groups of international agreements concluded by international organisations: formal agreements, exchanges of notes, disjunctive exchange of notes (consisting of a direct offer, accepted subsequently and separately by the other party) and parallel resolutions.[73] These forms of international agreements result in headquarters agreements, operational agreements, peacekeeping agreements, relationships agreements, private contracts and miscellaneous agreements.

The European Community, and to a much lesser extent the European Union, is party to a wide variety of international agreements. The overwhelming majority of these international agreements are bilateral agreements. This is even the case in those instances where the Community and the Member States act jointly as contracting parties, so-called mixed agreements, or where the agreements are concluded with more than one third country, such as the Cotonou Agreement.[74] The rights and obligations are established between the European Community alone or jointly with the Member States on the one hand, and the third country or coun-

[70] Reuter identifies four models of international agreements taking into account three main variables, namely, the number of parties, the length of the procedure and the number of instruments involved. P. Reuter, *supra* note 1, at 53.

[71] Osakwe refers to these agreements as being bipartite. C. Osakwe, *supra* note 69, at 188-189.

[72] Deviation from this general rule would be when one or more of the parties have made a reservation with regard to certain parts of the agreement and one or more of the parties involved have accepted this reservation. On the subject of reservations see *infra* Sections 3.4 and 4.5.

[73] C. Osakwe, *supra* note 69, at 180-188. See also H.G. Schermers *et al*, *supra* note 18, at 1114.

[74] The same reasoning applies when the two Communities act as joint contracting parties. See, for example, the Europe Agreement establishing an association between the European Economic Communities and their Member States, of the one part, and Romania, of the other part, OJ 1994, L 357/2. On the Community side the contracting parties were the European Community, Euratom and the Coal and Steel Community. See also Council Decision 94/907/ECSC, EC, Euratom on the conclusion of the EC-Romania Europe Agreement, OJ 1994, L 357/1.

tries on the other. The agreement does not establish reciprocal rights and obligations between the European Community and its Member States or amongst the third countries. Community law governs the rights and obligations between the Community and the Member States.[75]

With regard to their form, Lenaerts and De Smijter distinguish three types of international agreements concluded by the European Community.[76] The first type concerns improvement of the economic relations between the parties. The second type is a further elaboration of the first type with the addition of cooperation in specific areas of policy. Finally, the third type contains a specific section dealing with political dialogue. A fourth category can be added to these three groups, namely, agreements concluded in the areas of the Common Foreign and Security Policy and Police and Judicial Cooperation in Criminal Matters. Formal agreements and exchanges of notes are the most common forms through which the Community concludes international agreements. The main provisions are usually adopted in the form of a formal agreement. Additional protocols and other supplementary provisions are generally concluded through an exchange of notes. Throughout this research no examples of oral agreements concluded by the European Community or the European Union have been found.[77]

3.2.3 **Negotiating an international agreement**

Article 300(1) EC provides that

> "Where this Treaty provides for the conclusion of agreements between the Community and one or more States or international organisations, the Commission shall make recommendations to the Council, which shall authorize the Commission to open the necessary negotiations. The Commission shall conduct these negotiations in consultation with the special committees appointed by the Council to assist it in its task and within the framework of such directives as the Council may issue to it.
> In exercising the powers conferred upon it by this paragraph, the Council shall act by a qualified majority, except in the cases where the first subparagraph of paragraph 2 provides that the Council shall act unanimously".

Article 300 EC sets out the standard procedure to be followed whenever the Community decides to conclude an international agreement with a third state or another international organisation. A point worth making though is that prior to the entry into force of the Treaty on European Union, the old Article 228 (now Article 300) EC was never used as the legal basis for the Community's external activity. Traditionally the Treaty article providing the Community with an ex-

[75] Mixed agreements will be analysed *infra* Chapter 4.

[76] K. Lenaerts and E. De Smijter, The European Community's Treaty-making Competence in 16 *YEL* (1996), at 1.

[77] The Legal Services of the Commission and the Council have confirmed this in the course of interviews conducted in the period November-December 2003.

press power to act was referred to.[78] The significance of this policy was at the internal level, being that the decision-making procedure for the adoption of Community legislation was also the decision-making procedure for the conclusion of an international agreement.

In case the Community action was based on secondary EC legislation, the legal basis of this secondary legislation was thought to be the legal basis for the Community's external action. Still, there have been times when the legal basis for the conclusion of an international agreement was not exactly identical to the legal basis used for the adoption of the internal measure.[79]

International treaty law governs neither the negotiating process nor the negotiating powers of subjects of international law. This is a remarkable fact given the central role negotiations play in the bringing about of international agreements. It is for the parties involved to determine the manner in which they want to conduct their negotiations.[80] There is a distinction, though, between, the power to negotiate (that is the power to represent the entity at the international level) and the actual representation. The former is a matter of the constitutional provisions of the entity, a state or international organisation.[81] The latter is governed by international law on the basis of Article 7 of the 1969 and 1986 Vienna Conventions. States and international organisations do not act on their own but are represented by persons. It is, therefore, necessary that the parties involved are able to ascertain whether the person in question has the authority to commit the entity he/she represents. This is an essential safeguard in international relations.

[78] The standard practice used to be that the Commission would send a proposal to the Council requesting a formal decision from the Council. The proposal contained a preamble with recitals and a reference to the proper legal basis. This practice has been discontinued the last fifteen years. At present, the Commission will send a recommendation to the Council. The recommendation does not require a formal Council decision. The Council can limit itself to merely authorizing the Commission to negotiate. Upon completion of the negotiations the Commission will send a communication to the Council. The communication consists of two parts. The first part outlines the reasons for the negotiations. The second part contains the draft Council Decision. Information obtained in personal interviews with the Legal Services of the Commission and the Council in the period November-December 2003. See also Commission Proposal of 13 March 2002 for a Council Decision concerning the conclusion, on behalf of the Community, of the Cartagena Protocol on Biosafety, COM(2002), 127 final. The agreement was concluded on the basis of Council Decision 2002/628/EC of 25 June 2002, OJ 2002, L 201/48. In this particular case the Commission disputed the legal basis chosen by the Council and requested an opinion from the Court on the basis of Article 300(6) EC, Opinion 2/00, *Cartagena Protocol on Biosafety*, [2001] ECR I-9717. The Court concluded that the legal basis chosen by the Council, Article 175(1) EC, was the proper legal basis for the conclusion of the agreement.

[79] The Council Decision by which the Bonn Convention was concluded was based exclusively on the old Article 235 (now 308) EEC, whereas the legal basis of Directive 76/464 was the Articles 100 (now 94) and 235 (now 308) EEC. It must be stated, however, that the Council did not make any reference to the internal powers of the Community to combat water pollution. In the Bonn Convention itself reference is made to the internal measures adopted by the EEC.

[80] M.N. Shaw, *supra* note 1, at 815-816 and I. Brownlie, *supra* note 1, at 591-582.

[81] Even in this case there is no cohesive practice among states and among international organisations.

In the literature distinction is made between people with full powers, for example, Heads of State or Government and Ministers of Foreign Affairs, and people with special full powers.[82] In the latter case the power to negotiate is granted to the people representing the entity by the person who actually holds the power. The person negotiating is thus acting on a mandate from the authorising agency.

In a number of international agreements to which the Community is a party special reference is made to the powers of the parties representing the Community and the third party. The Association agreement with the Slovak Republic[83], for example, stipulates in its Preamble that the Member States, and the Community, and the Slovak Republic "Have decided to conclude this Agreement and to this end have designated as their plenipotentiaries (...) Who, having exchanged their full powers, found in good and due form (...)".[84]

This is a recurring theme in a number of the international agreements[85] to which the Community is a party, but it is not commonplace in all international agreements concluded by it.[86] Nor can it be said that this formulation has been used because it only involved an agreement to which the Community and the Member States are a party. The Cooperation Agreement with the Association of South-East Asian Nations is an agreement concluded by the EC alone as contracting party, but with the aforementioned formulation.[87] Furthermore, not even in the case where the Community and the Member States act as a joint contracting party is this type of reference standard practice. The Europe Agreement with the Republic of Latvia is an international agreement that contains no such refer-

---

[82] *Ibid.* Conf. I.M. Sinclair, *supra* note 1, at 27-32; D.J. Harris, *supra* note 31, at 745; and P. Reuter, *supra* note 1, at 60.

[83] Europe Agreement establishing an association between the European Communities and their Member States, of the one part, and the Slovak Republic, of the other part, OJ 1994 L 359/2.

[84] *Ibid*, at 3-4.

[85] See, for example, the Framework Agreement for commercial and economic cooperation between the European Communities and Canada, OJ, 1976 L 260/2; the Additional Protocol to the Europe Agreement establishing an association between the European Communities and their Member States, of the one part, and the Republic of Poland, of the other part, OJ, 1995 L 317/35; the Cooperation Agreement between the European Community and the Republic of India on partnership and development, OJ 1994, L 223/24 and the Interregional framework cooperation Agreement between the European Community and its Member States, of the one part, and the Southern Cone Common Market and its member countries, of the other part, OJ 1996, L 69/4.

[86] Examples include the Agreement on Partnership and Cooperation between the European Communities and their Member States, of the one part, and the Russian Federation, of the other part, OJ 1997, L 327/3; the Agreement between the European Community and Hong Kong, China on cooperation and mutual administrative assistance in customs matters, OJ 1999, L 151/21 and the Agreement on the European Economic Area between the European Communities, their Member States and the Republic of Austria, the Republic of Finland, the Republic of Iceland, the Principality of Liechtenstein, the Kingdom of Norway, the Kingdom of Sweden and the Swiss Confederation, OJ 1994, L 1/3.

[87] Cooperation Agreement between the European Communities and Indonesia, Malaysia, the Philippines, Singapore and Thailand – member countries of the Association of South-East Asian Nations, OJ 1980, L 144/2.

ence.[88] The international agreements concluded with the European Union acting as one of the contracting parties similarly contain no reference to the exchange of full powers.[89] Therefore, the conclusion must be that there is no specific pattern and no coherence with regard to this part of the Community's practice. It could be argued that this lack of coherence may be due to internal procedures and/or division of powers within the Commission.[90] The Commission negotiates these agreements and helps prepare the final text. But the fact that even the Europe Agreements, which contain a fairly identical text, lack any coherence in this regard undermines this conclusion somewhat.[91]

In the case of international organisations, the power to conclude, and thus, negotiate international agreements is determined by the founding treaty.[92] Because of the great diversity among international organisations regarding their structure and capacity it is simply not possible to lay down a general rule similar to the rule applicable to states.[93] In the end, the power to negotiate will be held by the supreme organ competent to conclude international agreements.[94] This organ may conduct these negotiations itself or delegate the power to another organ or another member state. The constituent treaties once again determine the extent to which this delegation can occur. In the absence of express provisions the delegation of powers will be based on the internal practice of the organisation.

---

[88] Europe Agreement establishing an Association between the European Communities and their Member States, of the one part, and the Republic of Latvia of the other part, OJ 1998, L 26/3. Remarkably enough the Protocol adjusting trade aspects of the Europe Agreement between the European Communities and their Member States, of the one part, and the Republic of Latvia, of the other part, to take account of the accession of the Republic of Austria, the Republic of Finland and the Kingdom of Sweden to the European Union and the outcome of the Uruguay Round negotiations on agriculture, including improvements to the existing preferential arrangements, OJ 1999, L 317/3, does not contain any reference to the exchange of full powers or their having been found in good and due form.

[89] Agreement between the European Union and the Former Yugoslav Republic of Macedonia on the activities of the European Union Monitoring Mission (EUMM) in the Former Yugoslav Republic of Macedonia, OJ 2001, L 241/2 and the Agreement between the European Union and the Federal Republic of Yugoslavia on the activities of the European Union Monitoring Mission (EUMM) in the Federal Republic of Yugoslavia, OJ 2001, L 125/2.

[90] In principle, the External Relations Directorate-General is responsible for the negotiation of international agreements. Throughout the years it has become customary for other Directorates-General to develop their own expertise in negotiating agreements. The decision to negotiate is taken by the Commission as a whole. This is mandatory, but the delegation conducting the actual negotiation may be led by the Directorate-General in charge of the specific subject matter, supported by the External Relations Directorate-General. Information obtained through personal interviews with the Legal Services of the Commission and the Council in the period November-December 2003.

[91] Article III-227(4) of the Draft Constitution provides that the Council of Ministers shall nominate the negotiator or the leader of the Union's negotiating team. However, this does not mean that this person will be referred to in final text.

[92] Article 6 of the 1986 Vienna Convention.

[93] See also P. Reuter, *supra* note 1, at 60.

[94] Schermers *et al*, *supra* note 18, at 1128-1129.

In the case of the European Community the power to negotiate is given to the Commission. The use of this power, however, is subject to approval by the Council. This means that although the Commission, in the course of its activities, is free to maintain all necessary relations with third countries and other international organisations, it has to seek prior approval from the Council if these talks are to be the basis of negotiations that can result in the conclusion of an international agreement.[95] In the authorizing decision the Council will set out the precise guidelines to be followed by the Commission and it will appoint the special committee to assist the Commission during the negotiations.[96] In general, this authorization also includes the right to initial the final text.[97] Still, the Commission has what was earlier referred to as full powers, because the Council is not delegating its negotiating powers to the Commission. The Commission has an autonomous power to negotiate, but it can only do so after it has received the approval of the Council and in accordance with such guidelines as the latter deems necessary.[98]

---

[95] It must be said that the Council is not under any obligation to approve the Commission's proposal. Similar to ordinary legislative proposals, the Council can propose amendments or reject the proposal. See also MacLeod *et al*, *supra* note 24, at 87.

[96] Article 300(2) EC. The preparations for a request to negotiate a specific international agreement can take place in one of two ways. The first is in the course of the daily activities of the Commission. The Commission regularly looks into the need to conclude agreements related to the areas of the Community competences. It can also happen that an additional protocol needs to be added to an existing agreement. In the second situation the Commission is overtaken by events or the Member States are already involved in the actual negotiations. Using the 'AETR doctrine' the Commission will seek permission to initiate or to participate in the negotiations. In the latter case the Member States may be somewhat reluctant to grant the Commission permission to join the negotiations or it may simply be too late for the Commission to participate because of the advanced stage of the negotiations. Information obtained through personal interviews with the Legal Services of the Commission and the Council in the period November-December 2003.

[97] T. Cottier and A. Caplazi, *Das Genehmigungsverfahren beim Abschluss völkerrechtlicher Abkommen in der Europäische Union* (1998), at 13-14. Initialling is the process through which the parties indicate agreement upon the final text to be submitted for ratification by the competent authorities (Art. 10 of the 1969 and 1986 Vienna Conventions). Initialling has no specific legal effect. See also I.M. Sinclair, *supra* note 1, at 35. The Framework Agreement for Peace in Bosnia and Herzegovina is a unique example where initialling had legal effect. The Agreement on Initialling the Framework Agreement provided that the parties that had initialled the Agreement were not only committed to signing the texts of the Agreement but had also expressed their consent to be bound. Shaw, *supra* note 1, at 638. In certain instances involving the Community an exchange of letters between the heads of the delegations is used instead of initialling to indicate approval of the final text. J. Megret, *supra* note 38, at 34.

[98] The negotiating directives issued by the Council are confidential. A summary of the general parts may be published, but the precise guidelines are not revealed to the public. The purpose of this secrecy is to avoid informing the other party or parties on the precise extent of the Commission's negotiating mandate. It does happen occasionally that the other party somehow gains possession of the directives. The instructions usually provide the Commission with sufficient room for manoeuvring during the negotiations. On certain occasions the Council will include a hard bottom line in the directive. This bottom line establishes the maximum concessions the Commission can make. On the other hand, the directives will never include incorrect information. Information obtained through personal interviews with the Legal Services of the Commission and the Council in the period November-December 2003.

As a general rule, the constitutional arrangements of the European Community thus stipulate that the Commission is the only entity that can negotiate on behalf of the Community.[99] The entity that has the actual power to authorize the negotiations and approve the end result (that is to conclude the resulting international agreement) cannot itself conduct these negotiations.[100] Megret summarises this as follows

> "La répartition de tâches entre les institutions dans le domaine externe reflète le jeu interinstitutionnel connu dans le domaine interne de la CEE (la Commission propose, le Conseil décide), et traduit la particularité du système communautaire qui se distingue de celui d'un Etat souverain dont l'exécutif, ou son représentant, détient le pouvoir tant de négocier que de ratifier".[101]

The only exceptions are where the Treaty makes special arrangements for the negotiation of international agreements in derogation of the procedure of Article 300 EC[102] or where the rules of the conference negotiating an international agreement exclude the Community, and therefore the Commission, from participating. In the latter case the Member States, most likely through the Presidency of the Union, will conduct the negotiations on behalf of the Community, but in close cooperation with the Commission.[103]

Throughout the negotiations, the Commission is assisted by such committees as appointed by the Council on the basis of Article 300(2) EC. In the past there used to be great uncertainty concerning the extent of the powers of these committees. Prior to the Maastricht Treaty, the majority of the international agreements were trade agreements. These agreements were concluded on the basis of Article 133 EC. Article 133 committees traditionally have a stronger influence in the ne-

[99] From the perspective of the Council there is no encroaching on the competence of the Commission to negotiate agreements. The Commission is the chief negotiator of the Community and this is respected. Information obtained through personal interviews with the Legal Services of the Commission and the Council in the period November-December 2003.

[100] The opposite is not possible, however. In other words, the Council cannot oblige the Commission to initiate the necessary negotiations. Article 208 EC stipulates, "The Council may request the Commission to undertake any study the Council considers desirable for the attainment of the common objectives, and to submit to it any appropriate proposal". This article should not be read, though, as meaning that the Council can compel the Commission to come up with a proposal to obtain the Council's permission to initiate the necessary negotiations with a third party.

[101] J. Megret, *supra* note 38, at 24.

[102] This would be the case with Article 111(3) EC which states: "By way of derogation from Article 300, where agreements concerning monetary or foreign exchange regime matters need to be negotiated by the Community with one or more States or international organisations, the Council, acting by a qualified majority on a recommendation from the Commission and after consulting the ECB, shall decide the arrangements for the negotiation and for the conclusion of such agreements. These arrangements shall ensure that the Community expresses a single position. The Commission shall be fully associated with the negotiations". In this instance the Council could authorize a party other than the Commission to conduct the negotiations on behalf of the Community.

[103] Opinion 2/91, *ILO*, [1993] ECR I-1061 and Article 10 EC.

gotiating process. On several occasions the Council has tried to extend the practice of the Article 133 committee to the committees appointed on the basis of Article 300(2) EC. The provisions are clear, however. The committees must assist the Commission. The Commission remains adamant that the committees should only have an advisory role to play. The Council and the Member States, while respecting the position of the Commission as chief negotiator would like the committees to be more directly involved in the actual negotiations.[104]

It should be noted that the European Parliament plays no formal role in the actual negotiations. The Parliament's role is formally limited to the actual conclusion of the agreement. Article 300(3) EC provides that the Council is either to consult the European Parliament or to obtain its assent, depending on the subject matter of the proposed agreement. In the case of agreements concluded on the basis of Article 133 EC, the EC Treaty even explicitly excludes Parliamentary involvement. This is not to say, however, that the European Parliament is not involved in anyway in the negotiating process.[105]

Until the mid-1990s there were two inter-institutional arrangements in force, specifically intended to allow the European Parliament an indirect role during the negotiation of international agreements. The Parliament was thus kept informed and had an indirect channel to influence the negotiation and conclusion of international agreements.[106] These non-binding arrangements were the "Luns Procedure" and the "Luns-Westerterp Procedure".[107] The use of these procedures depended on whether the international agreement being negotiated was an association agreement or any other agreement concluded on the basis of Article 300 EC (Luns I) or an agreement concluded on the basis of Article 133 EC (Luns II).[108]

The Luns I procedure was introduced by the Council on 25 February 1964 and consisted of a three-step involvement of the European Parliament. Prior to the start of the negotiations there was the possibility for a plenary debate in the European Parliament. Throughout the negotiation of the international agreement there was a constant exchange of information between the Commission and the relevant Parliamentary committees. At the end of the negotiations, but prior to the signing of the agreement, the Council, or its representative, informed the aforementioned committees in an informal and confidential manner on the substance of the agreement.[109]

---

[104] Information obtained through personal interviews with the Legal Services of the Commission and the Council in the period November-December 2003.

[105] Members of the European Parliament are permitted to participate as observers in the Community delegations. They are sometimes permitted to sit in during the plenary sessions, but the Parliamentarians cannot participate in the closed negotiating sessions. *Ibid.*

[106] I. MacLeod *et al*, *supra* note 24, at 98.

[107] Also known as 'Luns II'.

[108] J. Megret, *supra* note 38, at 42-44.

[109] *Ibid.*

In order to assure a certain level of Parliamentary involvement in the negotiation and conclusion of commercial agreements (Article 133 EC), on 15 October 1975 the Council introduced the Luns II Procedure. This Procedure also involved a three-step approach. Before the start of the negotiations the Council informed the relevant Parliamentary committees. If necessary, the European Parliament could, on the basis of the information provided, hold a plenary debate. At the end of the negotiations, but prior to signing the agreement, the President of the Council or his representative informed the aforementioned committees in an informal and confidential manner on the substance of the international agreement. After the signature of the agreement but before its ratification the Council informed the European Parliament on the scope of the agreement.[110]

The rules of cooperation between the European Parliament, the Commission and the Council have been updated. The procedure known as 'PROBA 20' is no longer in use.[111] This is to a large extent due to the fact that the Member States have accepted that the Commission alone should negotiate commodity agreements. The Luns I and Luns II procedures have been modernised. The Framework Agreement of 5 July 2000 governs the cooperation between the Commission and the European Parliament.[112] Annex II deals with international agreements and provides for the following procedures

> "Dans le cadre des accords internationaux, y compris les accords commerciaux (la phase de préparation de ces accords, le projet de directives de négociation et les directives de négociation adoptées), la Commission informe le Parlement européen, clairement et sans délai, pour pouvoir tenir dûment compte, des vues du Parlement européen.
>
> La Commission, au travers de la commission parlementaire compétente, et, le cas échéant, en séance plénière, tient le Parlement européen pleinement et régulièrement informé du déroulement et de la conclusion des négociations internationales. Les informations évoquées au point précédent sont transmises au Parlement européen dans des délais suffisants pour lui permettre d'exprimer, le cas échéant, ses points de vue. Le Parlement européen s'engage, pour sa part, a établir les procédures et les mesures visant a préserver la confidentialité, conformément aux dispositions de l'annexe III.
>
> La Commission prend les mesures nécessaires pour veiller à ce que le Parlement européen soit immédiatement et pleinement informé:

[110] *Ibid.*

[111] Generally speaking, commodity agreements have become outdated. The notion that markets, and more particularly, the prices of commodities, can be regulated in some form no longer appeals to the developed countries. It was a mechanism designed to assist the developing countries, but with the demise of the Tin Council the developed countries have lost interest. There are still a few commodity agreements, such as the Cocoa Agreement 2001, in force. There are also agreements establishing study groups for specific commodities such as copper and tin. At present there is a 'PROBA 20 *bis*' in place for the negotiation of the agreements establishing the study groups, but few Member States use this procedure. The negotiations are left to the Commission. Information obtained through personal interviews with the Legal Services of the Commission and the Council in the period November-December 2003.

[112] See Commission Notice of 31 January 2001, *supra* note 37.

(i) des décisions concernant l'application provisoire ou la suspension d'accords, et
(ii) de la définition d'une position commune dans un organe institué par un accord en vertu de l'article 310 du traité CE".[113]

The overall conclusion is that the Community's formal procedure is in line with the 1986 Vienna Convention, in particular Article 2(1)(c). Although the Council's decision authorizing the Commission to negotiate on behalf of the Community is not published, the practice of the Community whereby it is the Commission that represents the Community is well known and accepted by states and international organisations alike. The European Community's procedure is furthermore in conformity with Article 7(3) of the 1986 Vienna Convention, which stipulates that

> "A person is considered as representing an international organisation for the purpose of adopting or authenticating the text of a treaty (...) if (a) that person produces full powers; or (b) it appears from the circumstances that it was the intention of the States and international organisations concerned to consider that person as representing the organisation for such purposes, in accordance with the rules of the organisation, without having to produce full powers".

In those cases where the competence to conclude an international agreement is shared between the Community and the Member States, the power to negotiate is also shared. In various cases the European Court of Justice has held that whenever the Community and the Member States must, by reason of this division of powers, act together, they must do so in close cooperation in order to preserve the unity of the external representation of the Community.[114] They do not need, however, to indicate, during the negotiations, the limits of their respective powers to the other contracting parties. The division of powers is an internal matter to be settled in accordance with the internal rules of the Community. As in the case of agreements falling within the exclusive competence of the Community, the Commission must, in the case of mixed agreements, obtain the Council's authorization concerning its participation in the negotiations. Traditionally, the authorization will include provisions concerning the coordination between the Community and the Member States. Although in theory both parties are free to pursue their own negotiation, this is never the case.[115]

With regard to the European Union the Member States have decided on a different approach. On the basis of Article 24 TEU it is the Presidency, assisted by

---

[113] *Ibid*, Annex II, at 28-30, paragraphs 2-4.

[114] Opinion 2/91, *ILO*, [1993] ECR I-106 and Opinion 1/94, *WTO*, [1994] ECR I-5267. See also *supra* Chapter 1.

[115] In the case of the Uruguay Round Multilateral Trade Negotiations the Commission acted on behalf of the Community and the Member States. J. Heliskoski, *Mixed Agreements as a Technique for Organizing the International Relations of the European Community and its Member States* (2001), at 80. See also MacLeod *et al*, *supra* note 24, at 151-153.

the Commission as appropriate, who negotiates on behalf of the Union.[116] The same applies to Article 38 TEU.[117] In theory, this distinction between negotiations on behalf of the Community or the Union should not and does not create much confusion. This changes when the negotiations involve matters that come clearly within the scope of the EC and the EU Treaties. This could, for example, be the case where the (trade) negotiations involve so-called dual use goods. Security reasons may require that the negotiations are conducted on the basis of the EC and EU Treaties.[118] The same security concerns may result in Member States wanting to have a direct participation in the negotiations. The resulting mix could lead to the necessary confusion on the part of the opposing contracting party or parties. It is essential that at these times the Council sets out clear guidelines with regard to the negotiating powers of the various parties representing the Community's/Union's interest.[119]

3.2.4 The signing and concluding of international agreements

An international agreement can only give rise to rights or obligations after the state or international organisation has expressed its consent to be bound. Article 34 of the 1986 Vienna Convention stipulates, "A Treaty does not create either obligations or rights for a third State or a third organisation without the consent of that State or that organisation". Conclusion, approval or ratification are all different names for the process whereby the state indicates to the other contracting parties its consent to be bound by the adopted international agreement (Article 2(2)(b) of the 1986 Vienna Convention). In the case of international organisations the phrase "act of formal confirmation" is used (Article 2(2)(b) *bis*). Manin believes that this insertion sets a new precedent and may become the stan-

---

[116] From the wording of Article 24 TEU it is clear that the Presidency is negotiating on behalf of the Union and not the Member States. S. Marquardt, 'The Conclusion of International Agreements under Article 24 of the Treaty on European Union' in V. Kronenberger (ed.), *The EU and the International Legal Order: Discord or Harmony?* (2000), at 342. The role of the Minister for Foreign Affairs being discussed in the context of the Draft Constitution is unclear. Lately, it has become customary, within the Community, to use the Common Foreign and Security Policy umbrella to increase the role of the Presidency in the actual negotiations. The Commission is afraid that this can lead to an erosion of its position as chief negotiator. The Council and the Member States dispute this. The Commission's position is, that if the new Minister for Foreign Affairs acts in his capacity as a member of the Commission, there will be no problem, if he leads the negotiations. However, if he is closely associated with the Council, this could be construed as a further undermining of the position of the Commission. Information obtained through personal interviews with the Legal Services of the Commission and the Council in the period November-December 2003.

[117] On the external powers of the European Union see *supra* Chapter 2.

[118] In this case the Council will adopt a common position based on Article 23(1) TEU. This will be the legal basis of the negotiations. The actual agreement will be concluded based on the EC Treaty.

[119] Much of this will change now that the European Constitution has been adopted. For an analysis of the relevant provisions see *supra* Chapter 2, Section 2.5.

dard practice in international forums.[120] This will, for example, be the case in the adoption of a multilateral instrument where ratification is open to states and international organisations. The various multilateral agreements analysed do not confirm this prediction.

From a legal standpoint there is no difference between the terms 'conclusion', 'ratification' and 'approval'. Usually ratification involves two distinct procedural acts. The first is related to the constitutional (internal) laws of a contracting party. It involves the internal procedure that must be fulfilled before the state or international organisation can assume the international obligations enshrined in the international agreement. In many instances this involves approval by the national parliament. The second element deals with the external (international) level. It is the process through which the contracting party indicates its consent to be bound to the other contracting parties. The consent to be bound can be expressed "by signature, exchange of instruments constituting a treaty, ratification, acceptance, approval or accession or by any other means if so agreed".[121]

'Signature' is a process that has different legal meanings depending on the circumstances in which it is performed. Its precise meaning is to be deduced from the arrangements made in the international agreement. For example, the parties can agree beforehand that signature of the international agreement also constitutes ratification.[122] Article 11(2) of the 1986 Vienna Convention stipulates that "The consent of an international organisation to be bound by a treaty may be expressed by signature (...)". Although this process is becoming more common in international relations[123], the more commonly used procedure is still signature followed by ratification at a later stage. For states this usually means that the international agreement has to be put before the national parliament for approval, thereby giving the people a direct say in the external activities of the state. In the case of international organisations this process is determined by the rules of the organisation.[124] Usually this will involve putting the agreement before the organ in which all members of the organisation are assembled.[125]

---

[120] P. Manin, The European Communities and the Vienna Convention on the Law of Treaties between States and International Organisations or between International Organisations in 24 *C.M.L. Rev.* (1987), at 468.

[121] Article 12 of both Vienna Conventions.

[122] Article 18 of the 1969 and 1986 Vienna Conventions stipulates that the contracting parties should refrain from acting against the object and purpose of a signed agreement. When the parties to the agreement have not agreed that signature also constitutes ratification, parties that have signed the agreement must refrain from all activities that can affect the object and purpose of the agreement.

[123] Article 12 of the 1986 Vienna Convention.

[124] For example Article 300(2) EC.

[125] A distinct exception is the now defunct European Coal and Steel Community. In this case, the organ that concluded the international agreement was the Commission if these agreements were concluded on the basis of the ECSC Treaty without mentioning a specific legal basis. However, agreements concluded on the basis of Article 95 ECSC required the assent of the Council and the opinion of the Consultative Commission. I. MacLeod *et al*, *supra* note 24, at 106-107.

The EC and EU Treaty both use the term conclusion. Under Community law the term has a dual meaning. The first meaning is related to the internal Community procedure involving the various institutions that, within the limits of their powers, decide together to approve the international agreement. It also concerns the authorization of the Community representative to take the steps mentioned in the agreement to notify the other contracting part(y)(ies) of the Community's consent to be bound.[126]

> "Der Begriff "Abschluss" in den Vertragen ist nach unbestrittener Auffassung von Lehre und Praxis gemeinschaftsrechtlich auszulegen und nicht mit dem völkerrechtlichen Ratifikationsakt gleichzusetzen. (...) Die entsprechenden Gemeinschaftsnormen beziehen sich somit allein auf das notwendige innergemeinschaftliche Genehmigungsverfahren zur Eingehung dieser völkerrechtlichen Bindung, sei es in Bezug auf die Rolle und Mitwirkung der Organe oder auf deren interne Beschlussfassung".[127]

The internal procedure is completed through the adoption of a Council Decision.[128] This is a decision *sui generis*. This decision (Beschluß) is different from the decision (Entscheidung) referred to in Article 249 EC. Still, the decision *sui generis*, like the decision mentioned in Article 249 EC is subject to judicial review. In the *Les Verts* Case[129], the European Court of Justice held that all Community measures that produce legal effect are amenable to judicial review. The decision authorizing the Commission to initiate negotiations does not in itself produce legal effects. It is the result of the negotiations, the international agreement, which produces legal effect. Article 300(7) EC confirms a binding general principle of law (*pacta sunt servanda*) and also assures the contracting parties that the commitments are assumed by the Community, supported by the Member States. The institutions, and, more particularly, the Member States should be able to challenge the legality of the decision approving the international agreement.[130] The decision *sui generis* produces legal effect and is, therefore, subject to judicial review on the basis of the Articles 230 and 234 EC.

---

[126] I. Macleod *et al*, *supra* note 24, at 91-92; J. Megret, *supra* note 38, at 35-38; and T. Cottier *et al*, *supra* note 97, at 13-15.

[127] T. Cottier *et al*, *supra* note 97, at 13.

[128] In certain cases a regulation is used. In fact, until 1969, with the introduction of the decision *sui generis*, it was commonplace to use a regulation as the legislative act to conclude international agreements. The current Communities practice is very incoherent and does not allow generalised conclusion. If the international agreement contains provisions that deal with ECSC matters, the Council and the Commission adopt the decision.

[129] Joined Cases 294-297/83, [1986] ECR 1339.

[130] Article 10 EC imposes an unconditional obligation on the Member States to assist the Community in achieving its goals. If the Member States are of the opinion that the Community has exceeded the limits of its powers or that the commitments assumed impose an onerous burden upon them, they should be able to seek judicial redress.

The EC Treaty empowers the Community to conclude international agreements. Remarkably enough, the text of the decisions adopted to conclude international agreements, rarely uses the term 'conclusion'. The titles of the Council Decision usually contain the term conclusion. Examples include Decision 98/98/EC, ECSC, Euratom on the conclusion of the Europe Agreement with the Republic of Latvia[131]; Council Decision 87/149/EEC concerning the Conclusion of the Agreement with the United States on the Mediterranean preferences, citrus and pasta[132] and Council Decision 80/271/EEC concerning the conclusion of the Multilateral Agreements resulting from 1973 to 1979 trade negotiations.[133] The preambles to the majority of the Council Decisions (and Council and Commission Decisions) stipulate that the negotiated agreement "should be approved". Examples include Council and Commission Decision 91/400/ECSC, EEC on the conclusion of the Fourth ACP-EEC Convention[134]; Council Regulation 2616/85 concerning the conclusion of a Trade and Economic Cooperation Agreement with the People's Republic of China[135] and Council Decision 96/219/EC concerning the conclusion of the Agreement for Scientific and Technological Cooperation between the European Community and Canada.[136] In the operative parts of these decisions and regulations the agreement is subsequently approved.

There are a number of exceptions to this Community practice. The fourth recital of the preamble to Council Regulation 1440/80 stipulates that "whereas the conclusion of the cooperation agreement (...) appears necessary for the attainment of the aims of the Community in the sphere of external economic relations: (...)".[137] Other examples include Council Decision 82/461/EEC on the conclusion of the Convention on the conservation of migratory species of wild animals[138] and Council Regulation 3179/78 concerning the conclusion by the European Community of the Convention on Future Multilateral Cooperation in the North-west Atlantic Fisheries.[139]

---

[131] OJ 1998, L 26/1.

[132] OJ 1987, L 62/22.

[133] OJ 1980, L 71/1.

[134] "Whereas the Fourth ACP-EEC Convention, signed in Lomé on 15 December 1989, should be approved". OJ 1991, L 229/1, fourth recital.

[135] "Whereas the Trade and Economic Cooperation Agreement between the European Economic Community and the People's Republic of China should be approved". OJ 1985, L 250/1, fourth recital.

[136] "Whereas the Agreement for Scientific and Technological Cooperation between the European Community and Canada should be approved". OJ 1996, L 74/25.

[137] Council Regulation 1440/80 concerning the conclusion of the Cooperation Agreement between the European Economic Community and Indonesia, Malaysia, the Philippines, Singapore, and Thailand – member countries of the Association of South-East Asian Nations, OJ 1980, L 144/1. In Article 1 of the Regulation the agreement is yet again approved.

[138] OJ 1982, L 210/10.

[139] OJ 1978, L 378/1.

The preamble to Council Regulation 2300/76[140] shows yet a different practice. The fourth recital makes reference to the conclusion of the agreement. Article 1 of the Regulation stipulates, "The Framework Agreement (...) is hereby concluded on behalf of the European Economic Community". A similar wording is used in Council Decision 75/437 concluding the convention for the prevention of marine pollution from land-based sources.[141] Yet again other Council decisions make no reference in their preamble to such terms as conclusion, approve, or ratify.[142] Council and Commission Decision 96/300/Euratom, EC[143] stipulates in its seventh recital that, "Whereas the Commission has negotiated, on behalf of the European Community and the European Atomic Energy Community, an Additional Protocol to the Europe Agreement with the Slovak Republic". In Article 1 the agreement is approved. A similar wording is used in Council and Commission Decision 95/561/Euratom[144] and Council and Commission Decision 95/560/EC, Euratom.[145]

All these examples and others that could be mentioned have two elements in common. The first concerns the legal effect of the various wordings. It can be safely said that the different wording has no bearing whatsoever on the legal effect of these decisions and regulations. They all constitute the final act of the Council, or the Council and the Commission, signalling that the internal procedures have been concluded and that the Community can proceed to express its consent to be bound in accordance with the provisions of the international agreement. The second element concerns the diversity of practices within the Community, particularly the Commission. Although all proposals emanate from the Commission as a body the preparatory work is done by the various Directorates-General. The result is a very varied use of language[146], language that in the end generates the same end result. A more standardised use of language is recommendable. It avoids unnecessary confusion and makes the intentions of the institution clear.[147]

[140] Council Regulation 2300/76 concluding the Framework Agreement for commercial and economic cooperation between the European Communities and Canada, OJ 1976, L 260/1.

[141] OJ 1975, L 194/5.

[142] For example Council Decision 94/800/EC concerning the conclusion on behalf of the European Community, as regards matters within its competence, of the agreements reached in the Uruguay Round multilateral negotiations (1986-1994), OJ 1994, L 336/1.

[143] Council and Commission Decision concluding the Additional Protocol to the Europe Agreement establishing an association between the European Communities and their Member States, of the one part, and the Slovak Republic, of the other part, OJ 1996, L 115/42.

[144] Council and Commission Decision concluding the Additional Protocol to the Europe Agreement establishing an association between the European Communities and their Member States, of the one part, and Romania, of the other part, OJ 1995, L 317/39.

[145] Council and Commission Decision concluding the Additional Protocol to the Europe Agreement establishing an association between the European Communities and their Member States, of the one part, and the Republic of Poland, of the other part, OJ 1995, L 317/34.

[146] This study revealed more than 15 different types of wording in the preamble to the decision or regulation approving the international agreement.

[147] See also *supra* note 90 and the corresponding text.

3.2.4.1 *Signature*

Article 12(1) of the 1986 Vienna Convention stipulates that

> "1. The consent of a State or of an international organisation to be bound by a treaty is expressed by the signature of the representative of that State or that international organisation when:
>
> (a) the treaty provides that signature shall have that effect;
> (b) it is otherwise established that the negotiating States and negotiating international organisations or, as the case may be, the negotiating organisations were agreed that signature should have that effect; or
> (c) the intention of the State or organisation to give that effect to the signature appears from the full powers of its representative or was expressed during the negotiation.
>
> 2. For the purposes of paragraph 1:
>
> (a) the initialling of a text constitutes a signature of the treaty when it is established that the negotiating States and negotiating organisations or, as the case may be, the negotiating organisations so agreed;
> (b) the signature ad referendum of a treaty by the representative of a State or an international organization, if confirmed by his State or organization, constitutes a full signature of the treaty".

As already stated, consent to be bound by signature followed by ratification remains by far the most common practice in international relations, although consent to be bound by signature alone has its merits and its use is becoming more widespread. Ratification by signature speeds up the approval process and avoids unnecessary delays[148]. Still, in the case of international organisations, it may not be desirable to make frequent use of this procedure. The international agreement will have binding force on the organisation and perhaps even additional obligations for its members. Although the entity negotiating on behalf of the organisation will act in accordance with strict guidelines set up by the responsible organ, or the rules provided for in the founding treaty, states might prefer to have a discussion regarding the content and scope of the proposed agreement. There may also be the need to put the agreement before a parliamentary body, whether national or within the organisation, for approval. Where, however, the constitutional procedures do not explicitly require parliamentary approval, signature should suffice.

In the case of the European Community it would appear, *prima facie*, that the Community couldn't conclude an international agreement by signature alone if the agreement is concluded on the basis of Article 300 EC. This article sets out precise rules for the Council when ratifying an international agreement. Among

---

[148] I. Brownlie, *supra* note 1, at 582-583 and M.N. Shaw, *supra* note 1, at 817-818.

others, the Council has the obligation to either consult the European Parliament or to obtain its assent. Nowhere in this article the possibility is explicitly created to allow the Council to ratify an international agreement without Parliamentary involvement, thereby creating the possibility for ratification by signature alone. The reality is different, however.

The EC Treaty requires that, as a general rule, the Council is to consult the European Parliament prior to the conclusion of an agreement. Article 300 EC does not stipulate at which points the Parliament is to be consulted. It is obvious that it has to be after the negotiations have been concluded and the final text approved, and initialled by the Commission, but before the Council adopts its final decision. If the international agreement provides that signature constitutes consent to be bound, the Council will use the so-called simplified procedure.[149] Parliament's approval will be sought on the basis of the adopted and initialled text. Once Parliament's advice has been obtained, the Council will adopt the necessary decision. The Council's decision will authorize the Presidency or the Commission to sign the agreement.

Consent to be bound by signature depends on the will of the contracting parties. This means that if the Community is to agree that signature shall have that effect, the Commission should make this clear to the Council in its request. The Council's decision authorizing the Commission to initiate the negotiations, will make reference to this possibility. Of course this decision can also be taken at a later date.

International agreements to which the Community is a party are not concluded on the basis of the procedural requirements of Article 300 EC alone. Articles 111 and 133 EC can also function as the legal basis. Contrary to Article 300(3) EC, Article 133 EC does not require Parliamentary involvement. Agreements concluded within the sphere of the Community's Common Commercial Policy and monetary or exchange-rate matters can thus easily provide that signature amounts to consent to be bound. As shown, the Commission is usually not authorized by the Council to sign the negotiated international agreement. The Commission is only permitted to initial the agreement. In general, the Council Decisions provide for signature by the Presidency or someone to be appointed by the Council at a later date.[150] In the case of agreements negotiated on the basis of Article 133 EC or Article 111 EC, the Council decision authorizing the negotiation of the agreement, the granting of full powers, could also authorize the Commission to sign the agreement and thereby expressing the Community's consent to be bound.

[149] I. MacLeod *et al*, *supra* note 24, at 93 and J. Megret, *supra* note 38, at 38-39.

[150] The Council act normally provides who will express the consent to be bound on behalf of the Community. Article 4 of Council Decision 1999/790/EC on the conclusion of a Protocol with Latvia authorizes the Council to give the notification provided for in Article 7 of the Protocol, OJ 1999, L 317/1 and Article 2 of Council Decision 81/850/EEC on the provisional application of the 1980 International Cocoa Agreement stipulates that the President of the Council will designate the person empowered to deposit the notification, OJ 1981, L 313/1

This would be in line with Article 12(1)(c) of the 1986 Vienna Convention.[151]

Analysis of various international agreements concluded by the European Community provides the following picture. The Council signs most agreements after which they are ratified in accordance with Article 300 EC. Article 125 of the Europe Agreement with Romania[152], for example, stipulates, "This Agreement will be approved by the Parties in accordance with their own procedures. This Agreement shall enter into force on the first day of the second month following the date on which the Parties notify each other that the procedures referred to in the first paragraph have been completed". The Council on the basis of Council and Commission Decision 94/907/ECSC, EC, Euratom, concluded the agreement.[153] Article 4 of the Additional Protocol between the European Communities and the Slovak Republic[154] also provides for the entry "into force on the first day following the date upon which the parties notify each other of the completion of the procedures necessary for that purpose". Ratification has taken place on the basis of a Council and Commission Decision of 22 April 1996.[155]

There are, however, also agreements that provide that they will enter into force upon signature. Examples include the Agreement between the European Communities and the Government of Canada regarding the application of their competition laws[156]; the Agreement between the Government of the United States of America and the European Communities regarding the application of their competition laws[157]; the Memorandum of Understanding between the United States of America and the European Economic Community on government procurement[158] and the Agreement between the European Economic Community and the People's Republic of China on trade in textile products.[159]

Agreements concluded by the European Union on the basis of the Articles 24 and 38 TEU do not require any level of Parliamentary involvement. This in itself is a highly unsatisfactory situation. Unfortunately, the new European Constitution does not remedy this omission. The agreements concluded on the basis of Articles 24 and 38 TEU could, therefore, easily be concluded on the basis of signature alone. This is indeed the case. The agreement between the European Union and the Federal Republic of Yugoslavia and the agreement between the European

---

[151] Where the Council has authorized the Commission on the basis of Article 300(4) EC to approve modifications on behalf of the Community, it can be agreed by the parties that signature of the new agreement also constitutes consent to be bound.

[152] Europe Agreement between the European Communities and their Member States, of the one part, and Romania, of the other part of 01.02.1994, OJ 1994, L 357/1.

[153] OJ 1994, L 357/1.

[154] Additional Protocol to the Europe Agreement establishing an association between the European Communities and their Member States, of the one part, and the Slovak Republic, of the other part of 11 December 1995, OJ 1996, L 115/43.

[155] OJ 1996, L 115/42.

[156] OJ 1999, L 175/50, Article XII(1).

[157] OJ 1995, L 95/47, Article XI(1).

[158] OJ 1993, L 125/2, Article 7(1). This is a binding agreement.

[159] OJ 1990, L 352/2, Article 20(1).

Union and the Former Yugoslav Republic of Macedonia both provide that the agreement "shall enter into force upon signature".[160]

Looking at the Community practice the following conclusion can be drawn. Consent to be bound by signature alone will only be used in the case of bilateral agreements. Multilateral agreements are usually signed and ratified at a later date. Signature is a formal event. Especially in the case of multilateral agreements negotiated within or under the auspices of an international organisation, it is common practice to have a closing session at which the authorized representatives will sign the international agreement. In general, bilateral agreements that establish an association between the Community and one or more states will also provide for signature followed by ratification.[161] Only bilateral agreements between the Community or the Union with one single contracting party or common commercial policy agreements may enter into force upon signature.

3.2.4.2 *Ratification*

Article 14 of the 1986 Vienna Convention provides that

> "(...)
>
> 2. The consent of an international organisation to be bound by a treaty is expressed by an act of formal confirmation when:
>
> (a) the treaty provides for such consent to be expressed by means of an act of formal confirmation;
> (b) it is otherwise established that the negotiating States and the negotiating organisations or, as the case may be, the negotiating organisations were agreed that an act of formal confirmation should be required;
> (c) the representative of the organisation has signed the treaty subject to an act of formal confirmation; or
> (d) the intention of the organisation to sign the treaty subject to an act of formal confirmation appears from the full powers of its representative or was expressed during the negotiation".

The process of consent by ratification is a well-established one. Historically, it was intended to avoid that the representative exceeded his powers or instructions with regard to the making of a particular agreement.[162] With the decline of absolute sovereigns and the increase of parliamentary democracies the consent by ratification has acquired a new meaning. Although it still gives the contracting parties the chance to weigh and consider their options under the proposed agree-

[160] Article X in both cases.
[161] These agreements require the European Parliament's assent.
[162] M.N. Shaw, *supra* note 1, at 819-820

ment, its most important role is to give the national parliament, and therefore the citizens, a direct say in the public affairs of the state.[163]

In the case of international organisations the process, which is referred to as the act of formal confirmation, is governed by the organisation's own internal provisions as stipulated in its founding treaties or through its own established practice. Usually ratification is done through the organ in which all members are represented, such as the General Congress, Assembly, or whatever other name may be used to indicate the collective membership.[164] This does not, however, mean that other organs are not capable of concluding international agreements.[165] In matters involving international peace and security it is the Security Council of the United Nations and not the General Assembly that holds the power to conclude international agreements and, therefore, bind the United Nations.[166]

In the case of the European Community the Council primarily ratifies international agreements. Article 300(2) EC explicitly confers this power on the Council. Article 300(2) EC only stipulates that the international agreement is to be concluded by the Council. It does not indicate, however, what kind of act needs to be adopted. Such, while the article contains detailed provisions with regard to the voting procedure. As outlined above, the Council usually adopts a decision *sui generis*, and in some cases a regulation, by which it ratifies the international agreement.

If the contracting parties agree that the agreement will come into force upon signature followed by ratification, the Community could use the so-called solemn procedure.[167] The solemn procedure is used whenever the Parliament's assent has to be obtained prior to the approval of the agreement by the Council, for example in the case of association agreements concluded on the basis of Article 310 EC. But also in cases where the Parliament only has to be consulted the solemn procedure may be used. In the end, the use of the procedure depends on the ratification procedure provided for in the international agreement. As already indicated,

---

[163] *Ibid.*

[164] H.G. Schermers *et al*, *supra* note 18, at 1114-1121.

[165] See also H. Neuhold, 'Organs competent to conclude International Agreements for International Organisations and the Internal Procedure Leading to the Decision to be bound by a Treaty and Negotiation and Conclusion of Treaties by International Organisations' in K. Zemanek (ed.), *Agreements of International Organisations and the Vienna Convention on the Law of Treaties*, ÖZoR, Supplementum 1 (1971), at 196-199.

[166] Other examples include UNICEF, the International Maritime Organisation, IMO, and the International Atomic Energy Agency, IAEA, among others. *Ibid.*

[167] In the solemn procedure the Council adopts an act authorizing the President or a representative of the Commission to sign the agreement. The signature does not represent consent to be bound, although Article 18 of both Vienna Conventions stipulates that the contracting party is barred from acting against the "object and purpose" of the agreement. The signed agreement is put before Parliament for its opinion or assent. Once these requirements have been fulfilled the Council will adopt an act approving the agreement and authorize the Presidency or the Commission to take the necessary steps to express the Community's consent to be bound to the other contracting parties or the depositary of the agreement. See also I. MacLeod *et al*, *supra* note 24, at 93 and J. Megret, *supra* note 38, at 39-44.

nearly all agreements concluded by Community provide for signature followed by ratification.[168]

3.2.4.3 *Exchange of instruments*

Article 13 of the 1986 Vienna Convention stipulates that

> "1. The consent of a State or of an international organisation to be bound by a treaty constituted by instruments exchanged between them is expressed by that exchange when:
>
> (a) the instruments provide that their exchange shall have that effect; or
> (b) it is otherwise established that those States and those organisations or, as the case may be, those organisations were agreed that the exchange of instruments should have that effect".

The International Law Commission in its Commentary on the 1969 Vienna Convention pointed out that the expansion of interactions between states has resulted in the use of less formal types of international agreements.[169] These less formal types of international agreements include the exchange of instruments, such as notes and letters. The terminology itself has no legal significance. The exchange of instruments is commonly used for its ease and convenience. Its use depends on the willingness of the parties concerned. The parties must declare that the exchange shall have that effect or it should be established otherwise that the contracting parties have agreed that the exchange of instruments shall have that effect.[170]

Although it started out as a rather informal way of concluding international agreements, the exchange of instruments has now gained in importance and is being used at all levels and for all subject matters.[171] Aust points out that about one-third of all international agreement registered with the United Nations each year are in the form of an exchange of instruments.[172] Exchanges of instruments are frequently used to amend existing international agreements, but their use is not restricted to this secondary function. They can also be self-standing and dealing with matters of great importance.[173] Exchanges of instruments almost always take place in a bilateral fashion, although in the *Qatar* v *Bahrain* Case, the agreement was formed by a double exchange of letters between Qatar, Bahrain and Saudi Arabia.

---

[168] See also Commission Notice of 31 January 2001, *supra* note 37.
[169] *Yearbook of the International Law Commission*, 1966, Volume II, at 197-198.
[170] A. Aust, *supra* note 1, at 80 and M.N. Shaw, *supra* note 1, at 818-819.
[171] A. Aust, *supra* note 1, at 80-81.
[172] *Ibid.*
[173] *Ibid.*

The Community frequently uses the exchange of letters as a means of concluding international agreements. The exchange of letters is never used to conclude primary international agreements, such as association agreements, but rather to deal with a specific issue such as a trade dispute[174]; to promote trade in a specific area[175]; to amend an existing agreement[176]; to adopt an additional protocol[177] or to execute (part of) an international agreement[178], to name just a few examples.

Just as the parties are free to use the exchange of instruments as the way to express their consent to be bound, they are free to choose the form in which this is to take place. Traditionally the exchange of letters follows a specific pattern. This standard pattern includes one contracting party sending a letter to the other contracting party. In this letter the terms of the agreement are stipulated as well as an invitation to the other contracting party to confirm the agreement. In the responding letter the second contracting party will reproduce the complete text of the first letter followed by the confirmation of its acceptance.[179] In certain cases the agreement is attached as an annex to the letters.[180] Unlike in the *Qatar* v *Bahrain* Case, there are no examples in the case of the Community or the European Union involving double exchanges of letters.

3.2.4.4 *Accession*

Consent to be bound by accession is the procedure by which a state or an international organisation becomes a party to an international agreement signed by others, but which the state or organisation has not signed. The accession can take place before the agreement has entered into force or after.[181] The rules governing

---

[174] Agreement in the form of an Exchange of Letters between the European Economic Community and the United States of America, OJ 1987, L 62/23.

[175] Agreement in the form of an Exchange of Letters between the European Community and Romania on the reciprocal establishment of tariff quotas for certain wines, OJ 1993, L 337/173.

[176] Agreement in the form of an Exchange of Letters between the European Community and the Slovak Republic concerning fish, OJ 1994, L 294/27.

[177] Agreement in the form of an Exchange of Letters between the European Community and the Republic of Poland regarding a Protocol on a European Conformity Assessment Agreement, OJ 1998, L 237/9.

[178] Arrangement in the form of an Exchange of Letters between the European Economic Community and the Government of Canada on the establishment of a scientific observation programme in the Regulatory Area of the NAFO Convention. OJ 1984, L 292/8. The term 'Arrangement' in the title does not affect the legal status of this international agreement. The Council concluded the Arrangement in conformity with the normal Community procedures for the conclusion of international agreements. See Council Regulation 3114/84, OJ 1984, L 292/7.

[179] For example, the Agreement in the form of an Exchange of Letters between the European Community and Slovakia, *supra* note 176.

[180] As in the case of the Protocol on a European Conformity Assessment Agreement, *supra* note 177.

[181] A. Aust, *supra* note 1, at 88, M.N. Shaw, *supra* note 1, at 820-821 and I. Brownlie, *supra* note 1, at 583.

consent to be bound by accession are provided for in Article 15 of the 1986 Vienna Convention. This article stipulates that

> "The consent of a State or of an international organisation to be bound by a treaty is expressed by accession when:
>
> (a) the treaty provides that such consent may be expressed by that State or that organisation by means of accession;
> (b) it is otherwise established that the negotiating States and negotiating organisations or, as the case may be, the negotiating organisations were agreed that such consent may be expressed by that State or that organisation by means of accession; or
> (c) all parties have subsequently agree that such consent may be expressed by that State or that organisation by means of accession".

Accession is a simple but delayed procedure that excludes the preliminary stages like signature. Whether a state or an international organisation has participated in the adoption of an international agreement is irrelevant where accession is concerned. Accession usually takes place in the context of multilateral agreements, but the parties to a bilateral agreement can agree to open it to accession by a third party, thereby transforming the agreement into a multilateral agreement. Aust gives the examples of the Franco-German Convention on the Construction and Operation of a Very High Flux Reactor 1967 and the France-United Kingdom European Air Group Agreement 1998 as bilateral agreements that allowed accession of third states.[182] There are instances where the only way to become a party to a multilateral agreement is by means of accession. That would be the case of a convention approved by the General Assembly of the United Nations.[183]

Accession is a process that contains two elements, one of which is especially important in the case of international organisations. Article 15 of the 1986 Vienna Convention regulates the first element, which is the international law aspect. The international agreement must provide for the possibility to accede or the parties to the agreement must have agreed to that effect. The second element has to do with the internal powers of the international organisation. An international organisation can only accede to an existing international agreement if the subject matter of the agreement falls within the explicit powers of the organisation or forms part of the objectives for which the organisations was created. Unlike states, international organisations do not have general powers; the constituent treaties determine their powers. They are not allowed to act outside the limits of those powers. Accession subject to ratification is without legal effect and it is rarely used in modern treaty practice. It is seen as a declaration of intention.[184]

---

[182] A. Aust, *supra* note 1, at 89-90.
[183] I. Brownlie, *supra* note 1, at 583.
[184] P. Reuter, *supra* note 1, at 65 and A. Aust, *supra* note 1, at 90.

As outlined above, the Community is empowered to conclude international agreements in a wide variety of subject matters. The corresponding procedures can be found in the Articles 111, 133 and 300 EC. All provisions refer to the conclusion of international agreements. This term should be interpreted to include accession to existing international agreements. In *Opinion 2/94*[185], the Court was asked to rule whether the European Community could accede to the European Convention on Human Rights and Fundamental Freedoms. The Court's negative opinion was not related to the subject of accession *per se*, but rather to the fact that the Community lacked the necessary powers to do so. Article 22 of the Convention for the prevention of marine pollution from land-based sources provides that the states invited to the diplomatic conference and the European Economic Community could sign the Convention.[186] The Convention is subject to ratification (Article 23). Article 24 provides for accession by the states referred to in Article 22 and the European Economic Community after 30 June 1975. However, the Community signed the Convention and on 3 March 1975 adopted Council Decision 75/437/EEC concluding the Convention, and did not, therefore, accede to the agreement.[187]

3.3 Provisional application of international agreements

It was pointed out earlier that signature subject to ratification remains by far the most common way of expressing consent to be bound. This method has its limitations in that it can take a long time before the ratification process is completed. Especially in the case of multilateral agreements this may complicate matters. Not only the large number of contracting parties may prove to be a problem, very often a minimum number of ratifications is required for the agreement to enter into force. The provisional application of the international agreement, or part of the agreement, may be a useful tool to overcome the delay brought about by the need for constitutional approval. Of course, if none of the parties to the agreement needs to submit the agreement for constitutional approval, there is also no need to apply the agreement provisionally. Parties could agree that signature will suffice as consent to be bound.[188]

Contracting parties may have various reasons to render necessary the provisional application of agreements. Among these reasons the urgency of the matter

[185] [1996] ECR I-1763.

[186] OJ 1975, L 194/6.

[187] OJ 1975, L 194/5. See also Council Decision 2003/EC concerning the accession of the European Community to the Kyoto Convention, OJ 2003, L 86/21 and Council Decision 98/416/EC on the accession to the General Fisheries Commission for the Mediterranean, OJ 1998, L 190/34.

[188] A. Aust, *supra* note 1, at 139-141 and R. Lefeber, 'The Provisional Application of Treaties' in J. Klabbers and R. Lefeber (eds.), *Essays on the Law of Treaties. A collection of Essays in honour of Bert Vierdag* (1998), at 81-83.

dealt with in the agreement ranks among the most important reasons. A peace treaty intended to end hostilities could become rather obsolete if its application would have to wait for constitutional approval. At the time of nuclear incident at the Chernobyl nuclear power plant, for example, the 1986 IAEA Convention on Early Notification of a Nuclear Incident[189] and the 1986 IAEA Convention Assistance in the Case of a Nuclear Incident[190] were responses to an immediate international crisis. In both cases it was agreed that the agreement would apply provisionally.[191]

Although provisional application would be impractical in the case where it is agreed that signature expresses consent to be bound, it all comes down to the will of the contracting parties. Parties are free to decide on the provisional application whenever they deem it necessary. Article 25 of the 1986 Vienna Convention recognizes this freedom of contract. It stipulates that "A treaty or part of a treaty is applied provisionally pending its entry into force if: (a) the treaty itself so provides; or (b) the negotiating States and negotiating organisations or, as the case may be, the negotiating organisations have in some other manner so agreed".

A state or international organisation is only obliged to apply the agreement provisionally if there is a provision to that extent in the agreement and the state or organisation has signed the agreement. If the decision to apply the agreement provisionally is in the form of an additional agreement or protocol, this agreement will only apply to the contracting parties that have approved the decision or have indicated that they consider themselves bound by the agreement or protocol.[192]

Article 25 of the 1986 Vienna Convention provides that the provisional application is permitted pending entry into force. This provision should not be read as an absolute condition. There may be parties who have signed but not yet ratified the agreement, although the necessary number of ratifications has been achieved, or the date agreed for the entry into force has passed. The contracting parties may agree to allow the provisional application of the agreement between them and the party concerned. However, international agreements cannot be applied provisionally in relation to states or organisations that have not yet signed the agreement.

The provisional application is seen by some as a way of circumventing the obligation of constitutional approval. After all, provisional application is either on the basis of a provision of the agreement, permitting such application, or an additional agreement or protocol between the contracting parties. Until recently, it was common practice to adopt this additional instrument allowing the provisional application of the main agreement. The increased use of this instrument has resulted in the inclusion of provisions in the agreement to that effect. To avoid abuses of the provisional application and to safeguard the rights of the parties in-

---

[189] 25 *I.L.M.* (1986), at 1370.
[190] 25 *I.L.M.* (1986), at 1377.
[191] R. Lefeber, *supra* note 188, at 82-83.
[192] A. Aust, *supra* note 1, at 139 and R. Lefeber, *supra* note 188, at 90-91.

volved, Article 25(2) of the 1986 Vienna Convention allows for the unilateral termination of the provisional application.[193] The parties are thus free to stipulate the conditions regarding the provisional application, as well as the termination of the provisional application.

The provisional application of agreements is also dependent upon the constitutional provisions of the contracting parties. In general, states will encounter less constitutional restraints on the provisional application of international agreements. It can be expected that the number of states whose constitution prohibits the provisional application of certain types of international agreement will be small and the number of subjects limited. The same cannot be said of international organisations. In the absence of a specific reference in the founding treaty it will be very difficult to assert if, when and what kind of international agreement can be applied provisionally. The internal practice of the organisation can be useful but it will certainly not provide a definitive answer. Even if one were to have recourse to the internal practice of the organisation, the great diversity between international organisations makes it a rather useless effort to try to come up with some kind of generalized rule.

Article 300(2) EC, as amended by the Treaty of Amsterdam, explicitly empowers the Council, upon the conclusion of the international agreement, to provide for its provisional application. The same possibility applies with regard to agreements concluded on the basis of Article 133 EC, since this article itself refers to the general provisions of Article 300 EC. Apparently the same cannot be said of Article 111(3) EC. The article does not provide for the possibility of provisional application of international agreement, nor is there any express reference or link to Article 300(2) EC. It is likely, however, that the provisions of Article 111(3) EC only deviate from the general procedure with regard to the negotiations of international agreements and not with regard to the remainder of the provisions. Article 111(3) EC introduces the European Central Bank as one of the advisory organs of the Council and the Commission must be associated with the negotiations. It must, therefore, be assumed, also in the light of the need to preserve the cohesion of the Community's foreign policy, that even in the case of Article 111(3) EC provisional application is permitted. This conclusion is further supported by the provisions of Article 24 TEU, which also allows for the provisional application of international agreements, even in the case where a Member State's representative in the Council has indicated that it needs to comply with its constitutional provisions.

Although it was not until the Treaty of Amsterdam that provision has been made for the provisional application of international agreements, Community

[193] "Unless the treaty otherwise provides or the negotiating States and negotiating organisations, or as the case may be, the negotiating organisations have otherwise agreed, the provisional application of a treaty or part of a treaty with respect to a State or an international organisation shall be terminated if that State or that organisation notifies the States or organisations with regard to which the treaty is being applied provisionally of its intention not to become a party to the treaty".

practice shows that this had been done in the past. An example would be the International Cocoa Agreement 1980.[194] Article 65 of this Agreement allows for its provisional application by a signatory government which intends to ratify, accept or approve the Agreement, but which has not yet been able to deposit the necessary instrument. The depositary has to be notified about the provisional application and the notifying party may indicate when the provisional application will commence and whether the contracting party will be an exporting or an importing member. On 30 June 1981 the European Council adopted Decision 81/850/EEC approving the provisional application of the aforementioned Agreement.[195]

An example in the post-Amsterdam era is Decision No 1/2000 of the ACP-EC Council of Ministers regarding transitional measures valid from 2 August 2000 until the entry into force of the ACP-EC Partnership Agreement.[196] Article 1 of this Decision provides for the provisional application of parts of the Agreement. This ACP-EC Council of Ministers Decision was accompanied by Decision 2000/771/EC of the Representatives of the Governments of the Member States, meeting within the Council, on the provisional application of the Internal Agreement between the Representatives of the Member States, meeting within the Council, on measures to be taken and procedures to be followed for the implementation of the ACP-EC Partnership Agreement.[197] In this instance the adoption of transitional measures was necessary because the predecessor of the ACP-EC Partnership Agreement, Lomé IV, had already expired and ratification and entry into force of the new agreement would take a certain time. To avoid having a period in which there would be no legal instrument governing the relationship between the Community and the ACP countries it was agreed within the ACP-EC Council of Ministers to apply parts of the Partnership Agreement provisionally in the form of a transitional measure.

The decision on provisional application of an international agreement is one usually agreed upon by the parties or a majority of the parties to the agreement. International treaty law does not prohibit, however, that a party, in the absence of such a provision unilaterally decides to apply the agreements provisionally. This unilateral decision does not create any obligations on the part of the other contracting parties. Article 300 EC does not impose any restriction on the Council's powers to apply international agreements provisionally. As a result the Council has the authority to adopt a unilateral decision to apply an international agreement even if the agreement does not contain any provision to that effect or the parties to the agreement have not agreed to do so.

Article 300 EC does not stipulate how the decision permitting the provisional application of an international agreement is to come about. Although the provisionally applied agreement brings with it legal rights and obligations, these legal

[194] OJ 1981, L 313/3.
[195] OJ 1981, L 313/1.
[196] OJ 2000, L 195/46.
[197] OJ 2000, L317/375.

effects are remarkably different from a concluded international agreement. There is, therefore, no need for the Council to mention the appropriate legal basis or consult the European Parliament. Community practice shows that the Council sometimes cites the required legal basis for the conclusion of the agreement. In the past, the opinion or assent of the European Parliament was almost never sought before the adoption of the decision on the provisional application.[198] The decision was adopted on the basis of the majority required for the conclusion of the agreement. The advantage of the inclusion of the provision in Article 300 EC is that the Community does not need to have recourse to additional agreements or protocols to provide for the provisional application of international agreements.[199]

3.4 Reservations

Article 5(1) of the International Convention on the simplification and harmonisation of customs procedures permits, that the parties to the Convention can enter reservations.[200] The Community became a party to the convention by adopting Council Decision 75/199/EEC.[201] The Community entered reservations on some "Standards and Recommended Practices". Because Article 5(2) of the Convention requires that the parties that have made reservations review at least every three years the Standards and Recommended Practices in respect of which they have entered reservations, the Council adopted Decision 94/167/EC of 10 March 1994 amending the reservations entered by the Community.[202]

In this specific instance the agreement permitted that parties enter reservations. Reservations are a useful tool in international relations in that they make it possible for states and international organisations to become a party to an agreement they would otherwise have rejected completely, because they have objections to one or a few provisions of the agreement. It illustrates the principle of state sovereignty, because the state can refuse to give its consent to provisions it cannot accept.

Still, the subject of reservations[203] remains one of the most contentious subjects in international treaty law. Although the provisions of the Vienna Conven-

[198] See I. MacLeod *et al*, *supra* note 24, at 91, who provide the example of the European Energy Charter. In this case, exceptionally, the opinion of the European Parliament was sought. The most common examples of provisionally applied agreements are fisheries and commodities agreements. See also the Commission Notice of 31 January 2001, *supra* note 37.

[199] P. Léger, *supra* note 62, at 1900.

[200] OJ 1975, L 100/2.

[201] OJ 1975, L 100/1.

[202] Council Decision concerning the amendments to the reservations entered by the Community in respect of some provisions of certain Annexes to the international Convention on the simplification and harmonisation of costumes procedures, OJ 1994, L 76/28.

[203] Reservations should not be confused with derogation. Derogation is a provision in the agreement permitting a party to temporarily suspend the application of parts of the agreement in order to protect a higher interest, such as public policy, public order, or public morality.

tions broadly reflect current state practice, the codification is not complete and still has a rather long and uncertain way to go.[204] Traditionally the subject of reservations centred on two opposing views. The first was born out of state practice. International agreements were traditionally negotiated and adopted on the basis of unanimity. This unanimity requirement ensured that the contracting parties had to draw up a text acceptable to all or, where possible, unanimously decide on which provisions would be set aside for the parties that could not accept all the commitments included in the agreement.[205]

The advent of adopting multilateral text on the basis of a two-third-majority rule has brought a shift in international treaty-making practice. This resulted in the second point of view. States or international organisations could be overruled by a majority decision and be forced to accept the final outcome despite their opposition. The only remaining option would be a complete rejection of the agreement. This solution is not very satisfactory, especially if the agreement in question regulates subject matters that are of great importance to the party concerned. Treaties provide for their own rules on reservation. However, this may not be in conformity with the wishes of the party concerned. In the absence of specific provisions on reservation the problem may be further exacerbated. In the *Convention on the Prevention and Punishment of the Crime of Genocide* Case[206] the International Court of Justice recognized, although emphazising the principle of the integrity of a convention, a general right of states to make reservations on agreements provided that the proposed reservations do not jeopardise the object and purpose of the agreement.[207]

The regime outlined by the Vienna Conventions reflects these two viewpoints. The applicable rules can be found in the Articles 2 and 19-23 of the 1969 and 1986 Vienna Conventions. Although the International Law Commission had some reservations on equating the rules applicable to international organisations to those applicable to states, it was decided in the end to assimilate international organisations to states. Practice shows that international organisations rarely make use of reservations. In fact, these rules primarily concern the treaty practice of the European Community.[208]

The European Commission's stance on reservations is usually a neutral one. If there is a need for a Community reservation or a Community response to a proposed reservation, the Commission will prepare a proposal for a Council Decision.[209] The primary source of information for the Council is COJUR. COJUR is

---

[204] A. Aust, *supra* note 1, at 100-101 and P. Reuter, *supra* note 1, at 77-81.

[205] P. Reuter, *supra* note 1, at 77-80, M.N. Shaw, *supra* note 1, at 641-645 and I. Brownlie, *supra* note 1, at 584-585 and A. Aust, *supra* note 1, at 100-101.

[206] I.C.J. Reports (1951), at 15.

[207] P. Reuter, *supra* note 1, at 79-80.

[208] *Ibid*, at 62.

[209] Information obtained through personal interviews with the Legal Services of the Commission and the Council in the period November-December 2003.

a working group within the Council consisting of representatives from the Member States. These representatives are usually legal experts. The experts meet twice a year and discuss various matters related to the development of international law, including the law of treaties. Proposals for a Community reservation or a Community response to a proposed reservation are usually debated and prepared within COJUR.[210]

On 12 October 2001, the Commission presented a proposal to the Council for a Council Decision, on behalf of the European Atomic Energy Community, objecting to a reservation entered by the Islamic Republic of Pakistan to the Convention on Physical Protection of Nuclear Material.[211] The Commission was of the opinion that although the aforementioned Convention does not prohibit the formulation of specific or general reservations, the Community should object to Pakistan's reservation as being incompatible with the object and purpose of the Convention.[212] This example is illustrative of the practice of reservations. Although the reservation is entered as a unilateral statement, its validity depends on the acceptance of at least one other contracting party.

Even though international law does not restrict the application of the rules on reservations just to multilateral agreements, their use in bilateral agreements in general has no practical meaning and function. In this instance a reservation would merely signal a wish on the part of the reserving state to reopen negotiations. Of course this would be the case if the bilateral agreement involved just two parties. In the event that one or both of the contracting parties is made up of more than one party[213], the issue could be different. In this particular instance parties could agree to permit reservations. The usefulness of such a practice is not clear, however.

Reservations become meaningful in multilateral agreements in close connection with the rules governing the adoption of the agreement.[214] Reservations are permitted during signature, acceptance, approval, ratification or accession.[215] Deviation from this rule is only permissible if the agreement permits or if the parties have agreed to this option. Their use will be dependent on the mode of expressing consent to be bound used by the contracting party.[216] The term unilateral does not

---

[210] *Ibid.* COJUR does not issue any official statements or documents. Its expertise is particularly essential when the Community has to conclude agreements involving Islamic countries, because of their use of the Shari'a. The Shari'a consists of the Qur'an, or revealed word of God, given to the Prophet Mohammed in 610 C.E., and Sunnah, or life-experiences of the Prophet Mohammed. See also S.L. Bunn-Livingstone, *Juricultural Pluralism vis-à-vis Treaty law* (2002), at 88-97.

[211] COM(2001) 583 final.

[212] *Ibid.* at 2. In the explanatory notes the Commission makes express reference to the Vienna Convention on the Law of Treaties, in particular Article 20 (5), although it does not mention which one of the two Conventions it is referring to. See, however, note 13.

[213] This was referred to in Section 3.2.2 as a bipartite agreement.

[214] P. Reuter, *supra* note 1, at 79-80; A. Aust, *supra* note 1, at 106-107; and Council of Europe (ed.), *Treaty making – Expression of consent by States to be bound by a Treaty* (2001), at 13.

[215] Article 2(1)(d) of the 1986 Vienna Convention.

[216] Council of Europe, *supra* note 214, at 13.

exclude the possibility that more than one contracting party may agree to submit the same reservation. The purpose of the reservation must be to exclude or to modify the legal effect of certain provisions of the agreement in their application to the state or international organisation entering the reservation.

As shown above, the European Community is allowed to make reservations to international agreements subject to the rules of international treaty law and the terms of the agreement. This includes the right to restrict the territorial application of an international agreement. Reservations are an integral part of the agreement and, therefore, entail the assumption of binding commitments. This means that the Community and the institutions, must abide by the same decision-making processes that apply to the case of the conclusion of the agreement itself. Usually the reservation is included in the same decision that approves the international agreement.

Reservations must be distinguished from statements and declarations made at the time of the signing, ratification or accession to an international agreement. These declarations are usually made for domestic political purposes and have no legal significance. That is not to say that all declarations have the same meaning. Special attention must be paid to the precise wording. There are instances in which the declaration concerns a specific interpretation given to one or more provisions in the international agreement. At times these interpretive declarations can amount to actual reservations.

In certain instances international agreements specifically demand that international organisations, more specifically regional economic integration organisations such as the European Community, declare the extent of their competence in respect of the matters governed by the agreement. Article 25(3) of the Rotterdam Convention[217] contains such a demand for a declaration. In Decision 2003/106/EC[218] concerning the approval of the Convention the Council authorized the Presidency to designate the person(s) to deposit the instrument of approval[219] and to deposit the declaration of competence in accordance with Article 27 of the Rotterdam Convention.[220]

In Annex B, attached to the Decision, the Community outlines the extent of its powers by citing in full Article 175(1) EC. This is the legal basis for the Council Decision. The final sentence of the Declaration reads, "The exercise of Community competence is, by its nature, subject to continuous development". Although not thus intended, the Declaration could be read by others as a reservation in that the Community announces that it reserves the right to alter its competence in relation to the stated limits outlined in the Declaration. Parties to the Rotterdam Convention could object to this Declaration because it leaves them in uncertainty

[217] Rotterdam Convention on the Prior Informed Consent Procedure for Certain Hazardous Chemicals and Pesticides in International Trade, OJ 2003, L 63/29.

[218] OJ 2003, L 63/27.

[219] Article 2(1).

[220] Article 2(2).

concerning the precise extent of the Community's competence under the Convention. However, this Declaration does not amount to a reservation but is rather a recognition of the very fluid division of powers between the Community and its Member States. It recognizes that the competence of the Community can increase as a result of the adoption of internal measures. This transfer of competence does not alter the fact that the European Community and the Member States assume the totality of international obligations embodied in the international agreement.

3.5 Entry into force of international agreements

In Section 3.2.1 it was pointed out that in international relations international agreements are the closest thing to a legislative process. Despite the similarities that (may) exist between the national legislative process and international treaty law, international agreements do not have the same legal effects as national laws. Whereas national laws are not dependent on the consent of the subjects for their entry into force, international agreements need to be ratified, approved, accepted or acceded to in order to become binding on the parties concerned. Furthermore, contrary to national laws, international agreements that have entered into force do not have a general application. They are only binding on the parties that have ratified the agreement.

Therefore, it is imperative that the states or international organisations that have expressed their consent to be bound by an agreement know when that consent takes effect and in relation to which other contracting parties. International agreements are similar to contracts. The entry into force is thus dependent on the will of the parties. International treaty law, in particular Article 24(1) of the two Vienna Conventions, recognizes this contractual freedom. This article mentions the manner in which and the date on which treaties can come into force. It is only in the absence of such provisions that the Vienna Conventions provide the answer regarding the entry into force of the agreement. They stipulate that in this particular instance the agreement will enter into force as soon as the consent to be bound of all the contracting states and international organisations has been established (Article 24(2)).

Community law does not mention when international agreements to which the Community is a party come into force. It only stipulates the procedure that must be completed at the internal level for the Community to express its consent to be bound (Articles 111, 133 and 300 EC). These articles do not say at which point the agreement becomes binding on the European Community and the Member States. The external consent to be bound requires an internal Council decision concluding the agreement after, the European Parliament where applicable, or in the case of Article 111 EC after the European Central Bank, has been consulted or the Parliament's assent obtained. The Treaty specifies that consent to be bound cannot be expressed when the international agreement is incompatible with the

EC Treaty (Article 300(5) EC). The Member States can assess that for themselves or obtain a binding advisory opinion from the European Court of Justice (Article 300(6) EC). If the agreement is incompatible with the EC Treaty it can only be concluded after the Treaty is first amended in accordance with the provisions of Article 48 TEU. Still, the provisions of the international agreement determine the actual entry into force.

There are a variety of ways in which international agreements to which the Community is a party come into force. This depends on whether the agreement in question is a bilateral or multilateral agreement and whether the Community and the Member States together, or the Community alone, are a party to the agreement. There are instances where the European Community, because of the internal transfer of powers from the Member States to the Community, becomes bound by the substantive parts of the agreement without actually being a party to the agreement itself. This is the case when the agreement is only open to states or if the other contracting parties do not want the Community to accede to the agreement.[221] In this particular case, the European Community is not a party and, therefore, international treaty law does not apply.

Article 102 of the UN Charter stipulates that international agreements must be deposited with the Secretary General of the United Nations (paragraph 1). Paragraph 2 of the same article provides that only when the agreement has been deposited with the Secretary General can the agreement be invoked before any of the organs of the Organisation. However, the failure to deposit the agreement with the Secretary General does not affect the validity of the agreement.

The Secretary General, and depositaries in general, plays an important role with regard to the entry into force of international agreements. Multilateral agreements usually require a minimum amount of ratifications to enter into force. Sometimes a specific date is set to put pressure on the parties to speed up the ratification process. It is the depositary that has to notify the parties when the requirements have been met and the agreement has entered into force.

Within the European Union the General Secretariat of the Council performs the role of depositary. This is part of the activities of the Secretariat. However, the Council does not issue specific instructions and particular tasks are not expected. The General Secretariat performs the standard duties ascribed to depositaries of international agreements under international law. Whenever a party enters a reservation to an agreement for which the Secretariat acts as the depositary, it will communicate the information to all the other parties.[222] On the Com-

[221] This was the case with the GATT Agreement. See also Joined Cases 21-24/72, *International Fruit Company*, [1972] ECR 1219.

[222] Article 9(1) of the Agreement between the European Union and Iceland and Norway on the application of certain provisions of the 2000 Convention on Mutual Assistance in Criminal Matters and the 2001 Protocol, OJ 2004, L 26/3, has appointed the General Secretariat as the depositary of the Agreement. Article 9(2) provides that the "depositary shall make public information on any notification made concerning this Agreement".

munity side it is left to COJUR to advise the Council of Ministers on the position the Community should adopt. The Commission is not associated in any way with the work of the General Secretariat as the depositary of international agreements. The General Secretariat also maintains all appropriate contacts with other depositaries, especially the Secretary General of the United Nations.[223]

3.6 Application of international agreements

3.6.1 Non-retroactivity

As a general rule of international law, international agreements cannot have a retroactive effect unless the parties so agree. This applies to facts, acts or situations prior to the acceptance of the agreement.[224] EC law does not restrict the powers of the Community with regard to a possible retroactive effect of agreements to which it is a party. The only restriction is that the agreement must be compatible with the EC Treaty itself.[225]

3.6.2 Territorial application of agreements

Article 29 of the 1986 Vienna Convention provides that "unless a different intention appears from the treaty or is otherwise established, a treaty between one or more States and one or more international organisations is binding upon each State party in respect of its entire territory". Not all international agreements have a territorial scope or application. But where the territorial application is relevant there can be a complication with regard to international organisations. By definition international organisations do not have a territory of their own, but Community practice occasionally shows a deviation from this general rule.[226] Usually the rules of the organisation apply to the entire territory of the member states. But

---

[223] Information obtained through personal interviews with the Legal Services of the Commission and the Council in the period November-December 2003. Unfortunately, no information on the day-to-day operations of the Secretariat, as the depositary of international agreements, was available. See also *supra* General Introduction.

[224] Article 28 of the 1986 Vienna Convention.

[225] See Article 300(5) and (6) EC.

[226] Article 1(1) of Council Regulation 3155/90 extending and amending Regulation 2340/90 preventing trade by the Community as regards Iraq and Kuwait, OJ 1990, L 304/1, provides, "Without prejudice to the provisions introduced by Regulation (EEC) No 2340/90, the provision of non-financial services with the object or effect of promoting the economy of Iraq or Kuwait carried out in or from Community territory, including its air space, (...)". Similar references to the 'Community territory' can be found in the Articles 1, 2 and 3 of Council Decision 90/414/ECSC of the Representatives of the Governments of the Member States of the European Coal and Steel Community, meeting within the Council, OJ 1990, L 213/3. See also P.J. Kuijper, 'Trade Sanctions, Security and Human Rights and Commercial Policy' in M. Maresceau, *The European Community's Commercial Policy after 1992; The Legal Dimension* (1993), at 387.

even this may be a source of contention as members may have overseas territories or their jurisdiction over certain territories may be subject to an international dispute with another state.

Article 299 EC regulates the territorial application of the EC Treaty. Therefore, international agreements concluded by the Community can also be applicable to the territories mentioned in this article and additional protocols. Wherever the Community competence is exercised, international agreements to which the Community is a party will be applicable. Deviation from this general rule is only possible in the event that the agreement so provides or where such can be deduced from the intention of the contracting parties.[227] Still, it must be borne in mind that the concept of territory when applied to the Community is not the same as when applied to states. But the state-like character of the Community gives the concept a meaning that is different from that of a typical international organisation.[228]

There are a number of international agreements that contain varying provisions concerning their territorial application. Paragraph 3 of the Community's Declaration to the Agreement on the implementation of provisions relating to the conservation and management of highly migratory fish stocks[229] provides that the Agreement shall apply "to the territories in which the Treaty establishing the European Community is applied and under the conditions laid down in that Treaty, in particular Article 227 (now 299) thereof". A similar provision can be found in Article 92 of the Annex to Decision No 1/2000 of the ACP-EC Council of Ministers on transitional measures valid until the entry into force of the ACP-EC Partnership Agreement.[230] Article XIII of the Agreement establishing the General Fisheries Commission for the Mediterranean[231] requires the parties to state explicitly to which territories the Agreement will apply. In the absence of such a declaration the Agreement will apply to all the territories of the international relations for which the party is responsible. However, the territorial application may be modified by a subsequent declaration.[232] Because the International Convention on liability and compensation for damage in connection with the carriage of hazardous and noxious substances by sea (HNS Convention)[233] is only open to sovereign states, the Council of the European Union adopted Council Decision 2002/971/EC authorizing the Member States to ratify or to accede to the aforementioned Convention.[234] In this particular instance the Member States are acting as

[227] MacLeod *et al*, *supra* note 24, at 67-72 and 132-133.

[228] See also P. Manin, *supra* note 120, at 478-479.

[229] OJ 1998, L 189/39. The Agreement was concluded by Council Decision 98/414/EC of 8 June 1998, OJ 1998, L 189/4.

[230] OJ 2000, L 317/1.

[231] OJ 2000, L 197/37. The Agreement was concluded by Council Decision 2000/487/EC, OJ 2000, L 197/35.

[232] Article XIII in conjunction with Art. XIV.

[233] OJ 2002, L 337/57.

[234] OJ 2002, L 337/55.

custodians or guardians of the Community interest.[235] Article 1(3) of the Decision stipulates, "The term 'Member State' shall mean all Member States with the exception of Denmark". The Community Notification to the Secretary General of the Customs Cooperation Council[236] adopted in accordance with Article 11 of the Revised Kyoto Convention[237] provides that the customs territory of the Community is to be taken as single territory thereby listing the exact territories of each Member State.[238]

To the extent that there are problems concerning the territorial application of agreements, these problems most often occur in the sphere of the accession of new Member States. The practice is that the Commission notifies the other contracting parties that the agreements will apply to the area in which the EC Treaty applies. The Community thus takes a unilateral decision to extend the territorial application of international agreements to which it is a party to the new Member States.[239]

This Community practice can meet with opposition on the part of the other contracting parties. A good example is the extension of the territorial scope of the EC-Russia Cooperation Agreement to the new Member States. The Russian Federation was opposed to its application to the Republics of Estonia and Latvia. Both these countries have laws that negatively affect the position of the Russian minority living in their territories. The Commission had notified the Russian authorities that the extension was automatic, because the Agreement contains a provision to that effect. The Russian government did not accept this interpretation of the Agreement. The issue was settled through negotiations, because the Community preferred a negotiated settlement rather than the use of arbitration. Of course, both the Community and the Russian Federation had the right to denounce the Agreement if a settlement had not been reached.[240]

3.6.3 **Successive treaties**

The proliferation of international agreements brings with it the risk of overlapping provisions in subsequent agreements. The drafters of an international agreement should keep possible relations with other agreements in mind. In the case of bilateral agreements it is in principle easier to assess such a relationship. Where

[235] I. MacLeod *et al*, *supra* note 24, at 236-237. See also Joined Cases 3, 4 and 6/76, *Kramer and others*, [1976] ECR 1279.

[236] OJ 2003, L 71 E/56.

[237] International Convention on the simplification and harmonisation of customs procedures (as amended), OJ 2003, L 71 E/35.

[238] For example the territory of the Kingdom of Spain, except Ceuta and Melilla; the territory of the Kingdom of Denmark, except the Faroer Islands and Greenland and the territory of the French Republic, except the overseas territories and Saint-Pierre-et-Miquelon and Mayotte.

[239] Information obtained through personal interviews with the Legal Services of the Commission and the Council in the period November-December 2003.

[240] *Ibid.*

multilateral agreements are being negotiated this may prove much more difficult. In the end it all comes down to the interpretation of the relevant provisions by the parties to the agreements. A general guide on how the parties are to proceed is provided for in Article 30 of the 1986 Vienna Convention.[241]

The specific characteristics of the European Community, and more particularly, its unique powers as an international organisation creates a variety of situations were subsequent international agreements are concerned. In the context of this research the following situations are relevant, namely, a) the Community concludes an agreement with the same parties the Member States had concluded an agreement with prior to the Community assuming the power to act in that particular field; b) the Community concludes the agreement with some of the original contracting parties; c) the European Community concludes an international agreement with the same parties it had originally concluded an agreement with together with the Member States in a field where it now has exclusive competence; d) the Community alone concludes an agreement with not all of the original contracting parties of the original mixed agreement; e) the European Community concludes a subsequent agreement with the same parties it had previously concluded an agreement with and f) the Community concludes an agreement with parties that include some of the previous contracting parties.

In the case of sub a) it is evident that the contracting parties are aware of and have accepted the fact that the Community has assumed the internal competence to act in a particular field. If the provisions of the later agreement are compatible with the earlier agreement there is no conflict of agreements and both apply. If the later agreement provides that it is subject to the earlier agreement, but there are provisions that are incompatible with the previous agreement, then the earlier agreement will prevail.[242] If the earlier treaty is not suspended or terminated then its provisions will apply to the extent that they are compatible with the latter agreement.[243] The same conclusions apply in the cases of sub c) and sub e).

In the case of sub b), d) and f), Article 30(4) of the 1986 Vienna Convention applies. In the case of sub b) the earlier agreement will apply between the non-participating parties in the new agreement and the Member States. Under Article 307(1) EC the Community is to ensure that the rights of the contracting parties are respected and the Member States are allowed to fulfil their obligations under the original agreement.[244] The new agreement will apply between the Community and the remaining contracting parties to the extent that the original agreement has

---

[241] See also I. Brownlie, *supra* note 1, at 624-625; M.N. Shaw, *supra* note 1, at 871-875 and A. Aust, *supra* note 1, at 181-183.

[242] Article 30(2) of the 1986 Vienna Convention.

[243] Article 30(3) of the 1986 Vienna Convention.

[244] See in this regard Case C-124/95, *Centro-Com*, [1996] ECR I-81. The Court held that "the purpose of the first paragraph of Article 234 (now 307) of the Treaty is to make clear, *in accordance with the principles of international law*, that application of the Treaty does not affect the commitment of the Member State concerned to respect the rights of non-member States under an earlier agreement and to comply with its corresponding obligations" (emphasis added).

not been suspended or terminated as between them, and that the provisions of the earlier agreement are compatible with the latter agreement. In the cases of sub d) and sub f) the same rules as sub b) will apply with the exception that the previous agreement will apply between the Community and the non-participating parties rather than the Member States and the non-participating parties.

Although neither the European Community nor the European Union is a member of the United Nations, they are barred from assuming obligations under an international agreement that are incompatible with the obligations assumed by the Member States under the UN Charter. Article 30(6) of the 1986 Convention provides that "the preceding paragraphs are without prejudice to the fact that, in the event of a conflict between the obligations under the Charter of the United Nations and obligations under a treaty, the obligations under the Charter shall prevail". The obligation to refrain from concluding international agreements in violation of the UN Charter is provided for by Article 307 EC. In certain cases Article 297 EC may also be applicable.[245]

There have been instances in the past where the Community encountered problems with regard to agreements previously concluded by the Member States. The Community acceding to the agreements usually solved the problem. A current problem is presented by the new Member States. Shortly after their independence, or after their internal political changes, these countries negotiated bilateral investment agreements with the United States of America. The agreements were concluded for a very extensive period, usually ten years. The overwhelming majority of these agreements are incompatible with the EC Treaty. The agreements would guarantee the United States, after the accession of the new Member States, a preferential access to the internal market. This is not permitted on the basis of current Community legislation and existing agreements between the Community and the United States of America. This conflicting situation was communicated to both the candidate Member States and the United States. The Commission's position was clear, either the United States agreed to negotiate a new agreement with the Community, to substitute the existing agreements, or the new Member States would have to denounce the existing bilateral agreements. The final arrangement, in the form of a Memorandum of Understanding, provides that the American Administration will negotiate a new agreement with the Commission and in return the Commission will not insist on a denunciation of the existing bilateral agreements. The Memorandum of Understanding still needs to be approved by the US Senate. Approval is expected in the summer of 2004.[246]

---

[245] Member States shall consult each other with a view to taking together the steps needed to prevent the functioning of the common market being affected by measures which a Member State may be called upon to take in the event of serious internal disturbances affecting the maintenance of law and order, in the event of war, serious international tension constituting a threat of war, or in order to carry out obligations it has accepted for the purpose of maintaining peace and international security.

[246] Information obtained through personal interviews with the Legal Services of the Commission and the Council in the period November-December 2003.

3.7 Invalidity, termination and suspension of international agreements

Article 300(2) EC, second subparagraph, provides that "by way of derogation from the rule laid down in paragraph 3, the same procedures shall apply for a decision to suspend the application of an agreement (...)". The term 'the same procedure' refers to the procedure mentioned in the first subparagraph of Article 300(2) EC. The Treaty does not stipulate under which circumstances an international agreement may be terminated or suspended. The Vienna Convention or customary law therefore governs the relevant rules. Article 300(5) EC also stipulates that agreements which call for amendments of the EC Treaty can only be concluded after the amendments have been adopted in accordance with Article 48 TEU. The conclusion would be that agreements concluded in violation of this express Treaty provision are invalid.[247] From the perspective of Community law this may be the case, but given that this involves an international agreement concluded between two or more subjects of international law, the assessment regarding validity needs to be made on the basis of international law. It is only when rules of international treaty law provide that such agreements shall be invalid that the Community may terminate the application of the agreement.

3.7.1 **Invalidity of international agreements**

International agreements that have entered into force are binding on the parties that have consented to be bound by it. The contracting parties are under an obligation to perform all the necessary duties that are required (*pacta sunt servanda*) and they must do so in good faith.[248] They are also entitled to all the rights recognised under the agreement. Still, in certain circumstances parties to an agreement may wish to impeach their consent to be bound by the agreement. In this case the Vienna Convention provides that this impeachment can only occur on the basis of the rules provided in the Convention itself.[249] Parties are, therefore, not free to make up their own rules concerning the (unilateral) denunciation of an international agreement they have consented to.

It is therefore not surprising that the EC Treaty does not contain any provisions concerning the invalidity and termination of international agreement.[250] There is not even any need for a specific reference to the rules of the Vienna Convention. It also means that the provisions of Article 300(5) EC do not have

[247] See for example Opinion 1/91, *EEA I*, [1991] ECR I-6079 and Opinion 2/94, *ECHR*, [1996] ECR I-1759. See also T. Hartley, International Law and the Law of the European Union – A Reassessment in 33 *Neth.Yb.Int.L* (2002), at 18-20.

[248] Article 26 of the 1986 Vienna Convention.

[249] Article 42 of the 1986 Vienna Convention. This article applies to the denunciation, withdrawal or suspension of an agreement.

[250] Article 300(2) EC only refers to the procedure for the suspension of international agreements.

an absolute nature. Rather its meaning must be assessed in the light of the applicable rules of international treaty law.[251] The EC Treaty can only suffice with stipulating the internal procedure the institutions of the Community must follow when they want to terminate or suspend the Community's consent to be bound. Although none of the articles makes reference to the relevant procedure in the event of the termination of an international agreement, it is obvious that the same procedure applies to the conclusion of agreements, at least as far as the Council is concerned.

International law makes a distinction between international agreements that are void and international agreements that are voidable. An agreement is void if the consent of the party has been obtained through coercion. Article 51 of the 1986 Vienna Convention provides that the consent to be bound by an international agreement of the state or international organisation will be without legal effect, that is the agreement will be invalid, if the consent was obtained through the coercion of the representative of the party or through acts or threats directed against the representative. The coercion would have to be directed at the representative of the Commission negotiating on behalf of the Community. The Commission traditionally conducts these negotiations in constant contact with the special committees appointed by the Council to assist the Commission. It is difficult to see how in the process of these negotiations the Commission could be coerced or threatened to express consent to be bound on behalf of the Community. This is different when this coercion occurs in the context of informal contacts between the Commission and a third party.

On the basis of the internal division of powers it is evident that only the Council of the European Union can invoke Article 51 and the other relevant provisions of the Vienna Convention. It is the party that officially concludes the agreement on behalf of the Community.[252] It is not clear, however, whether in this particular instance the Council would have to consult the European Parliament or obtain its assent if for the conclusion of a similar agreement the Council would either have to consult the Parliament or obtain its assent. In urgent cases the Council could suffice with simply notifying the European Parliament. The Council decision must, however, be based on either a qualified majority vote or unanimity depending on the corresponding voting procedure for the conclusion of a similar agreement. It must also state the proper reasons for its decision.

International agreements are also void, if they are in conflict with an existing or emerging peremptory norm of general international law (*jus cogens*).[253] The

[251] An international agreement is, therefore, not invalid merely because the conclusion of the agreement constitutes an amendment of the EC Treaty.

[252] The 1986 Vienna Convention speaks of the competent organ. This refers to the organ entitled to renounce the agreement and not to the organ entrusted with its performance. All the Community institutions are entrusted with the performance of international agreements, but only the Council can conclude them.

[253] Article 53 of the 1986 Vienna Convention. This article defines a peremptory norm of international law as "a norm accepted and recognized by the international community of States as a whole

agreement will be invalid if the peremptory norm is of an earlier date than the agreement. The parties to the agreement will also have to terminate the agreement once it becomes evident that the agreement is in conflict with an emerging binding rule of international law. In this latter case the parties may try to severe the parts of the agreement that are in conformity with the norm. The severance will only be possible if the provisions are separable with regard to their application; the acceptance of those clauses was not an essential basis of the consent to be bound of the other party or parties to the agreement and the continued performance of the remainder of the agreement is not unjust.[254] In case of an existing peremptory norm of international law, the invalidity will be *ab initio*. In the case of an emerging norm the agreement will be terminated from the moment the norm comes into existence. There is no retroactive effect.[255]

In certain cases a party to an agreement must invoke a ground of invalidity. The agreement will remain in force until the party claims that a representative who, under internal law, lacked the necessary competence to do so, concluded the agreement[256], his authority was restricted[257], or because of error[258], fraud[259] or corruption of the representative.[260] Remarkably enough, despite the relatively large number of articles involved, renunciation of consent to be bound is a very rare practice in international relations.[261]

The European Community has one case in which a representative lacking the necessary competence to do so, concluded an agreement. This involved the competition law cooperation agreement between the Community and the competent US authorities. As pointed out earlier, the Commission has the standard practice of concluding administrative agreements with its administrative counterparts in other international organisations and third countries. This practice is accepted by the Member States because they see these agreements as mere administrative arrangements that do not bind the Community.[262] In Case 327/91, *France* v *Commission*, the Commission relied on this practice to assert its powers to conclude international agreements on the basis of Article 300 EC. The Court, in paragraph 26 of the judgment, summarily dismissed this claim by stating, "mere practice cannot override the provisions of the Treaty". Still, in this case the Court only annulled the Commission's decision permitting the conclusion of the agreement.

---

as a norm from which no derogation is permitted and which can be modified only by a subsequent norm of general international law having the same character".

[254] Art. 44 of the 1986 Vienna Convention. See I. Brownlie, *supra* note 1, at 598-599.

[255] Art. 64 of the 1986 Vienna Convention.

[256] Art. 46 of the 1986 Vienna Convention.

[257] Art. 47 of the 1986 Vienna Convention.

[258] Art. 48 of the 1986 Vienna Convention.

[259] Art. 49 of the 1986 Vienna Convention.

[260] Art. 50 of the 1986 Vienna Convention.

[261] A. Aust, *supra* note 1, at 252 and P. Reuter, *supra* note 1, at 134-135.

[262] See also the Opinion of AG Tesauro in Case 327/91, *France* v *Commission*, [1994] ECR I-3643.

The agreement itself remained valid. It was unclear what the precise consequences of the Court's judgement would have been had the United States refused to allow the Council to conclude the international agreement. It is evident that the European Community could not have invalidated the agreement. Although the Commission had violated an internal rule of fundamental importance, Article 300 EC, the breach was not manifest to the American representative.[263] In any event, the Community did not invoke Article 46 of the 1986 Vienna Convention.

3.7.2 **Termination of international agreements**

International treaty law recognizes other grounds for the termination of agreements. These include state succession, operation of the provisions of an agreement or with the consent of all the parties (Article 54), a material breach (Article 60), supervening impossibility to perform (Article 61), and fundamental change of circumstances (Article 62).

3.7.2.1 *State succession*

The 1969 Vienna Convention also makes reference to state succession and war and armed conflict (Article 73). There are no corresponding provisions in the 1986 Convention. In the case of state succession the rules are governed by international practice.

There are two possibilities. One is that the state has concluded an international agreement prior to it becoming a member of an international organisation. The second situation is where a state member of the organisation merges with another non-member state. The problems will be less acute in traditional intergovernmental organisations where there is in principle no transfer of sovereign powers from the members to the organisation. In the case of so-called supranational organisations, such as the European Community, where the organisations, because of the renunciation of sovereign powers by the member states, have state-like features, the story is quite a different one.

The general rule of *pacta sunt servanda* prohibits that a state evades its obligation under an agreement with other subjects of international law by becoming a member of an international organisation. The accession will always be in the form of an international agreement with the states that are parties to the founding treaty of the organisation. The organisation either has to allow the state concerned to perform its duties or assume the duties on behalf of the member state. Of course this latter part depends on the consent of the other contracting parties. Ar-

[263] See also P.J. Kuijper, The Court and the Tribunal of the EC and the Vienna Convention on the Law of Treaties 1969 in *LIEI* 1998/1, at 12-14 and C. Kaddous, L'arrêt France c Commission de 1994 (accord concurrence) et le contrôle de la légalité des accords externes en vertu de l'article 173 CE: la difficile réconciliation de l'orthodoxie communautaire avec l'orthodoxie internationale in 5-6 *CDE* (1996), at 613-633.

ticle 307 of the EC Treaty permits the Member States to honour their commitments assumed before the date of their accession.[264] The EC Treaty will not affect the rights and obligations arising from these agreements. The Community will usually strive to open negotiations with the other parties and conclude its own agreement. Until such becomes possible it will allow the Member State to extend and honour the commitments provisionally.[265]

The collapse of the Berlin Wall and the subsequent reunification of Germany is another case in point. The Unification Treaty[266] between the two German States provided that most of the international agreements concluded by the Federal Republic of Germany would apply to the German Democratic Republic (Articles 11 and 12). Although under the *pacta tertiis nec nocent nec prosunt* maxim this agreement did not bind any party other than the two German states, the other parties were willing to accept the terms of the Unification Treaty. Still, by virtue of this state accession the Federal Republic of Germany could have been bound by agreements that are incompatible with the EC Treaty.[267] In its main document on German reunification, the Commission proposed a number of solutions. The first solution was that the Community should renegotiate the agreement if the agreement falls under the exclusive competence of the EC. The second solution was that in the case of mixed agreements the Community and a united Germany had to seek renegotiation. Two other solutions included the GDR denouncing the agreements that were incompatible with the Community Treaty before unification if the terms of the agreement made this possible and, secondly, the autonomous adaptation of Community law to meet the terms of the agreements. In the end, the solution chosen was to invoke the *clausula rebus sic stantibus* principle and declare the GDR agreements terminated.[268]

---

[264] It should be noted, however, that these agreements do not become part of Community law. Article 307 EC does not impose any obligation on the Community in relation to the other parties, Case 812/79, *Burgoa*, [1980] ECR 2787. See also I. MacLeod *et al*, *supra* note 24, at 229-231.

[265] As seen, in the *International Fruit Company* Case, Joined Cases 21-24/72, [1972] ECR 1219, the European Court of Justice recognized that the Community had succeeded the Member States as a party to the GATT agreement. Because the GATT only permitted states to become a party, the Community could not accede to the GATT, although the Commission became the main negotiator in the successive trade rounds. It was not until the creation of the WTO that the Community became a party to the WTO Agreement and a member of the WTO. In Opinion 2/94, *ECHR*, [1996] ECR I-1759, the Court held that the Community lacked the internal power to act in the field of fundamental rights. Therefore, there was no transfer of competence to the European Community. The Community must allow the Member States to perform their duties under the European Convention for Human Rights and Fundamental Freedoms. However, the Court's sometimes differing interpretation of the Human Rights Convention, in relation to the European Court of Human Rights, has raised some questions as to whether the Community is really living up to its end of the bargain.

[266] 29 *ILM* (1991), at 457.

[267] See also C. Tomuschat, A United Germany within the European Community in 27 *C.M.L. Rev.* (1990), at 415 and P.J. Kuijper, 'The Community and State Succession in Respect of Treaties' in D. Curtin and T. Heukels (eds.), *Institutional Dynamics of European Integration. Essays in Honour of Henry G. Schermers* (1994), at 619.

[268] P.J. Kuijper, *supra* note 267, at 623-633.

3.7.2.2 *Operation of the provisions of agreements*

The overwhelming majority of international agreements contain express provisions specifying the conditions of their termination or denunciation. In the case of bilateral agreements, Article 56(1) of the 1986 Vienna Convention provides that in the absence of specific provisions regarding the termination, denunciation of, or withdrawal from an agreement, this agreement cannot be denounced or withdrawn from unless: a) it is established that the parties intended to admit the possibility of denunciation or withdrawal or b) a right of denunciation or withdrawal may be implied by the nature of the agreement. In any event, the party will have to give the other contracting parties at least twelve months' notice of its intention to denounce or withdraw from the agreement (Article 56(2)).

An assessment of some of the agreements to which the Community is a party shows a very diverse picture. Article 39(1) of the Cartagena Protocol on Biosafety[269] provides that a party may withdraw from the Protocol two years from the date on which the Protocol has entered into force for that party, by giving written notification to the depositary. The withdrawal will become effective one year after the date of its receipt by the depositary or 'on such later date as may be specified in the notification of the withdrawal' (paragraph 2). The Agreement between the European Union and NATO on the security of information permits that any party may denounce the agreement by written notice given to the other party. The denunciation will take effect six months after receipt of the notification.[270]

Other examples include the International Cocoa Agreement, 2001[271], which stipulates that the Agreement will remain in force until the end of the fifth full cocoa year after its entry into force, Article 63(1), but the International Cocoa Council may also decide at any time, by special vote, to terminate the Agreement, Article 63(4). The Fourth ACP-EEC Convention provides that the Community may denounce the Convention in respect of each ACP State and each ACP State may do so in respect of the European Community upon six months' notice.[272] Article 17(5) of the Agreement on international humane standards between the Community, Canada and the Russian Federation permits a withdrawal by giving at least six months' notice in writing.[273] Although the association agreement between the European Community and Poland is concluded for an unlimited period, each party is allowed to denounce the agreement.[274] The agreement ceases to apply six months after the notification.

Analysing these various agreements, the conclusion is that they contain a variety of provisions concerning their termination. A general rule seems to be that in

[269] COM (2002) 127 final.
[270] OJ 2003, L 80/36, Article 17.
[271] OJ 2002, L 342/2.
[272] OJ 1991, L 229/3, Article 367.
[273] OJ 1998, L 42/43.
[274] OJ 1993, L 348/2, Article 118.

the case of bilateral agreements the denunciation becomes effective six months after the other party has been notified in writing of the other's intention. There are some exceptions, though. The Agreement between the European Community and Canada regarding the application of their competition laws provides that the Agreement shall remain in force "until 60 days after the date on which either Party notifies the other Party in writing that it wishes to terminate the Agreement".[275] Termination or denunciation of multilateral agreements is governed by the rules of the international agreement and these are very diverse rules.

3.7.2.3 *Material breach*

Under international treaty law a party may withdraw from or suspend an international agreement if another party commits a breach of its obligations under the agreement. This is in effect a reprisal or counter-measure. The offended party may not, however, simply declare the agreement as terminated. Rather, it must invoke the breach as grounds for the suspension or termination of the agreement.[276] Of course the question is when a breach qualifies as a sufficient enough reason to suspend or terminate the agreement. Article 60 of the 1986 Vienna Convention regulates the subject. Basically two criteria must be met for a state or international organisation to invoke a breach of an international agreement. There must be a violation of the agreement and it has to be a material breach.[277]

Where the breach occurs in a bilateral agreement, the non-offending party may invoke the breach as a ground for the suspension or termination (of the operation) of part of or of the entire agreement (Article 60(1)). In case of a multilateral agreement different problems occur, because a material breach does not necessarily affect the rights of all other parties, whose interests must also be taken into account. Article 60(2) of the 1986 Vienna Convention provides three solutions. The parties may agree unanimously to suspend or terminate the operation of the agreement in part or in whole in relation between themselves and the defaulting party or between all parties. The second option is that the party specially affected by the breach may invoke it as a ground for suspending the agreement in part or in whole between it and the offending party. Finally, any party may invoke the breach as a grounds for suspending the operation of the agreement in whole or in part in respect to itself if the agreement 'is of such a character that a material breach of its provisions by one party radically changes the position of every party with respect to the further performance of its obligations under the treaty'.

In Case *C-268/94*, *Portugal* v *Council*, the European Court of Justice was not asked to determine whether the Community could suspend an agreement because

[275] OJ 1999, L 175/50, Article XII(2).

[276] A. Aust, *supra* note 1, at 236-237; I. Brownlie, *supra* note 1, at 593; M.N. Shaw, *supra* note 1, at 853-855.

[277] A material breach consists in: a) a repudiation of the agreement not sanctioned by the 1986 Vienna Convention or b) the violation of a provision essential to the accomplishment of the object or purpose of the agreement (Article 60(3)).

of a material breach, but rather whether it could include such a provision in the Cooperation Agreement with India.[278] Portugal was of the opinion that the inclusion of a human rights clause was in violation of the chosen legal basis, namely Article 181 EC. In its view, respect for human rights was only foreseen as a general goal of the Community. The inclusion of a provision to that effect at the beginning of the Agreement and as a ground for the automatic suspension or termination of the agreement required a different legal basis, namely, Article 308 EC. The Council, in its arguments, referred to Article 60 of the Vienna Convention and the Court concurred that such a human rights provision could be, in conformity with international treaty law, an important tool for the suspension or termination of the agreement. The European Community had to be allowed to use the remedies that international treaty law permits in its international relations.[279]

3.7.2.4 *A fundamental change of circumstances*

The principle that a contracting party may terminate an agreement or withdraw from it if there is a fundamental change of circumstances finds its origin in domestic law. This doctrine is referred to as the *clausula rebus sic stantibus*. Accepted though it may be at the international level, there is still considerable discord with regard to its precise application to international agreement. This disagreement is born out of a fear for abuses. The absence of any system for compulsory jurisdiction in the international legal order could result in the principle having a disrupting influence upon international relations.[280] The modern approach is, therefore, to severely restrict the scope of the doctrine.

In the *Fisheries Jurisdiction* Case[281] the International Court of Justice held that

> "One of the basic requirements embodied in Article 62 is that the change of circumstances must have been a fundamental one.
> (...)
> Moreover, in order that a change of circumstances may give rise to a ground for invoking the termination of a treaty it is also necessary that it should have resulted in a radical transformation of the extent of the obligations still to be performed. The change must have increased the burden of the obligations to be executed to the extent of rendering the performance something essentially different from that originally undertaken" (paragraphs 37 and 43).

---

[278] *Portugal* v *Council*, [1996] ECR I-6207.

[279] See also M. Bulterman, *Human rights in the Treaty Relations of the European Community. Real Virtues or Virtual Reality* (2001) and E. Riedel and M. Will, 'Human Rights Clauses in External Agreements of the EC' in P. Alston (ed.), *The EU and Human Rights* (1999), at 723 and Article 5 of the Lomé IV Convention.

[280] M.N. Shaw, *supra* note 1, at 855-858.

[281] I.C.J. Reports (1973), at 3 reprinted in M. Dixon and R. McCorquodale, *Cases and Materials on International Law* (1995), at 100-101.

The European Court of Justice had to deal with the *clausula rebus sic stantibus* doctrine in the context of the suspension of trade concessions granted under the Cooperation Agreement with the former Yugoslavia.[282] The Bundesfinanzhof, the highest German Court in customs matters, had referred two preliminary questions to the ECJ. The German Court wanted to know whether Regulation 3300/91 was valid and whether the Council had properly applied the procedural requirements imposed by international treaty law on the application of the *clausula rebus sic stantibus* principle in light of the immediacy of the suspension (Article 65 of the 1986 Vienna Convention).

In the second paragraph of the preamble to Regulation 3300/91 the Council indicated that the pursuit of hostilities and their consequences on economic and trade relations, both between the Republics of Yugoslavia and with the Community, constituted a radical change in the conditions under which the Cooperation Agreement was concluded and it therefore called into question the application of the Agreement. In the subsequent paragraphs the Council indicated the various efforts undertaken to obtain compliance with the cease-fire agreement reached in The Hague on 4 October 1991. The Council also made an express reference to UN Security Council Resolution 713 (1991), which held that the prolonged situation constituted a threat to international peace and security. That the refusal by Yugoslavia to do so was the reason why the trade concessions granted had to be suspended with immediate effect. A similar reasoning was used in Decision 91/586.

In his Opinion[283], Advocate General Jacobs argues that, although not all the rules contained in the 1969 Vienna Convention constitute customary international law, the *clausula rebus sic stantibus* does (paragraphs 25-29). Remarkably, the Advocate General restricts himself to application of the 1969 Vienna Convention to the extent that it embodies customary international law. Only a minor reference is made to the 1986 Convention. Advocate General Jacobs points out that Article 62 of the 1969 Vienna Convention imposes strict conditions on the application of the *clausula rebus sic stantibus* principle. The principle has to be applied in a restrictive and objective manner. In his argument he clearly adheres to the International Court of Justice's decision in the *Fisheries Jurisdiction* Case.

Advocate General Jacobs begins his analysis of the *clausula rebus sic stantibus* doctrine from the perspective of direct effect (paragraphs 73-90). He concludes that recourse to the *clausula rebus sic stantibus* doctrine is only possible if it constitutes a rule of customary international law capable of having direct effect,

[282] Case C-162/96, *Racke*, [1998] ECR I-3655. See Council Decision 91/586/ECSC, EEC of the Council and the Representatives of the Governments of the Member States meeting within the Council suspending the application of the Agreements between the European Community, its Member States and the Socialist Federal Republic of Yugoslavia, OJ 1991, L 315/47 and Regulation 3300/91 suspending the trade concessions provided for by the Cooperation Agreement between the EEC and the Socialist Federal Republic of Yugoslavia, OJ 1991, L 315/1. See also P.J. Kuijper, *supra* note 263, at 18-22 and P.J. Kuijper, *supra* note 226, at 413-417.

[283] Opinion of Advocate General Jacobs in Case C-162/96, *Racke*, [1997] ECR I-3655.

that is, if the breach of the rule of customary law has serious negative consequences for the private individual (paragraphs 89 and 90). Here he also makes an express reference to the *Opel Austria* Case[284] where the Court of First Instance had decided that the customary rule of *pacta sunt servanda* protects individuals against violations of their legitimate expectations (paragraph 87). The Advocate General points out that the procedural requirements on the application of the *clausula rebus sic stantibus* doctrine as codified in Article 65 of the 1969 Vienna Convention do not constitute customary international law. Racke is thus barred from invoking this rule. Jacobs states, furthermore, that even if Article 65 constituted a rule of customary international law, only Yugoslavia could rely on it and not a private party (paragraphs 96 and 97). In his opinion the Community had good reason to assume that the *clausula rebus sic stantibus* doctrine applied and had, therefore not been unreasonable in suspending the agreement (paragraphs 92-94).

In its judgment, the European Court of Justice uses a different approach. The Court begins by pointing out that

> "The European Community must respect international law in the exercise of its powers. It is therefore required to comply with the rules of customary international law when adopting a regulation suspending the trade concessions granted by, or by virtue of, an agreement which it has concluded with a non-member" (paragraph 45).

The Court concludes that the *clausula rebus sic stantibus* doctrine is binding on the Community (paragraph 46). It holds, furthermore, that because the plaintiff is only marginally challenging the validity of a Community regulation under those rules, the subject of direct effect is not at stake (paragraph 47). The Court goes on to say, with reference to the *Gabcíkovo-Nagymaros* Case[285], that deviation of the *pacta sunt servanda* principle, which is a fundamental principle of any legal order, can only be permitted in exceptional cases.

It held that

> "However, because of the complexity of the rules in question and the imprecision of some of the concepts to which they refer, judicial review must necessarily, and in particular in the context of a preliminary reference for an assessment of validity, be limited to the question whether, by adopting the suspending regulation, the Council made manifest errors of assessment concerning the conditions for applying those rules" (paragraph 52).

In assessing whether the Council had made a manifest error in the application of the *clausula rebus sic stantibus* doctrine, the Court uses the two conditions laid down in Article 62(1) of the Vienna Convention. The European Court of Justice concludes that the maintenance of the peace in Yugoslavia was an essential condition for initiating and pursuing cooperation. This condition was an essential ba-

---

[284] Case T-115/94 [1997] ECR II-39.

[285] I.C.J. Reports (1997), at 7.

sis of the consent of the parties to be bound. The first condition was thus met. The Court went on to say that the Council was not unreasonable to assume that the ongoing hostilities and their consequences on economic and trade relations constituted a radical change of the conditions under which the Agreement was concluded.

As a matter of judicial review the Court of Justice thus limited itself to analyse whether the Council, in the present case, had correctly applied the *clausula rebus sic stantibus* doctrine as a matter of policy. The Court did not set out precise guidelines on how the principle is to be applied. Nor did it look at the procedural requirements of Article 65 of the Vienna Conventions and whether the Council properly adhered to them. It restricted itself to saying that as long as the Council does not commit a manifest error, it is permitted to apply the principle. What constitutes a manifest error and the precise conditions for the application of the doctrine remains unclear, however.

3.8 The effect of international agreements concluded by the Community on its Members

The recognition of international organisations as subjects of international law capable of concluding international agreements with states and other international organisations brings with it an important legal problem, namely, the legal effects of those agreements for the member states of the organisation. Although the organisation is acting under its own powers, as attributed to it by the members in the constituent treaty, a restrictive application of the *pacta tertiis* rule does not fully reflect the legal relation between the members and the organisation. Nor does the general rule that the members are bound to the same extent as the organisation. The problem is furthermore exacerbated by the fact that international organisations exist in varying degrees. Not all international organisations have an express legal personality and, therefore, the capacity to act externally, nor do all international organisations involve a transfer of sovereignty comparable to the European Community.

The effect of an international agreement concluded by an international organisation on its members was the most contentious and complex issue the Vienna Convention had to deal with.[286] Article 36 *bis* was proposed to regulate this relationship, exposing as it were the transparency of the organisation while preserving the egalitarian system of the law of treaties.[287] The article proposed by the Special Rapporteur provided that an agreement concluded by an international organisation directly created rights and obligations in relation to its member

[286] P. Manin, *supra* note 120, at 468-469.

[287] C. Brölmann, 'The 1986 Vienna Convention on the Law of Treaties: The history of draft article 36 *bis*' in J. Klabbers and R. Lefeber (eds.), *Essays on the Law of Treaties. A collection of Essays in honour of Bert Vierdag* (1998), at 121-122.

states by the mere fact that the constituent instrument of the organisation expressly provided for a treaty to have such effects.

This proposed article resembles the provisions of Article 300(7) EC and Article III-225(2) of the European Constitution. The Community, as its Member States, has its own legal personality. It is empowered to act externally, separate from the Member States. The conclusion of an international agreement by the European Community should, therefore, not have any direct legal consequences for the Member States. The Member States are not parties to the agreement and have no legal obligations in relation to the other contracting parties. This even applies where the Member States are involved in the actual implementation of the agreement, such as a customs agreement. In the case of mixed agreements, the Member States' obligations are also restricted to the areas falling within their competence.[288] The transfer of powers is not only limited to the internal field but extends to the external activities too.[289]

Then what is the precise scope of Article 300(7) EC? The leading case in this matter is the *Kupferberg* Case.[290] In paragraph 17 of the judgment the Court held that

> "It is true that the effects within the Community of provisions of an agreement concluded by the Community with a non-member country may not be determined without taking into account the international origin of the provisions in question. In conformity with the principles of public international law Community institutions, which have power to negotiate and conclude an agreement with a non-member country are free to agree with that country what effect the provisions of the agreement are to have in the internal legal order of the contracting parties. Only if that question has not been settled by the agreement does it fall for decision by the courts having jurisdiction in the matter, and in particular by the Court of Justice within the framework of its jurisdiction under the Treaty, in the same manner as any question of interpretation relating to the application of the agreement in the Community".

The conclusion must be that failure by the Member States to assist the Community in performing its obligations under an international agreement does not result in liability under international law for the Member States. It is the European Community that is in breach. Under Community law, in particular Article 10 EC, the Member States are under a general obligation to take all necessary measures to assist the Community in fulfilling its tasks. This applies at both Community and international level. Failure to do so can result in the use of Community infringement procedures (Articles 226-227 EC).

The conclusion must be that at present neither Community law nor international law provides a conclusive answer concerning the responsibility of the members of an international organisation that has concluded an international

[288] I. MacLeod *et al*, *supra* note 24, at 125-128.
[289] Case 22/70, *AETR*, [1971] ECR 263.
[290] Case 194/81 [1982] ECR 3641.

agreement. Because of the opposition during the Vienna Conference, the International Law Commission withdrew Article 36 *bis*. In the end the precise extent of the member states' obligation is to be determined in accordance with the third party rules of the Articles 34-36 of the Vienna Conventions.

3.9 The Community's participation in the preparation of international agreements

Article 9(2) of the 1986 Vienna Convention provides that

> "The adoption of the text of a treaty at an international conference takes place in accordance with the procedure agreed upon by the participants in that conference. If, however, no agreement is reached on any such procedure, the adoption of the text shall take place by the vote of two-thirds of the participants present and voting, unless by the same majority they shall decide to apply a different rule".

The original proposal from the International Law Commission contained a specific reference to international organisations. Whenever states and international organisations are participating in an international conference, they both shall have a vote on the adoption of the text. This proposal met a lot of opposition and was eventually amended to its present form.

In itself this is not surprising. International conferences usually take place under the auspices of international organisations, in particular the United Nations. Very often the multilateral agreements are drafted by the General Assembly and open to signature, ratification and accession. Like many international organisations, the United Nations only permits states as its members. International organisations are only permitted to participate as observers.

This reality does not alter the fact that Article 9 of the 1986 Vienna Convention is not practical from the Community's point of view. The European Court of Justice has held that the European Community represents a new legal order in international law for the benefit of which the Member States have limited their sovereignty.[291] There are instances where this transfer is complete, with other words that the Community has acquired, at the internal level, an exclusive power. It is established case-law that where the Community enjoys an exclusive power at the internal level this also applies at the external level. Any other conclusion carries with it the risk that the Member States, in their external activities, could undermine the Community's internal policies.[292] The European Community therefore

[291] Case 26/62, *Van Gend en Loos*, [1963] ECR 1 and Case 6/64, *Costa* v *ENEL*, [1964] ECR 585.

[292] Opinion 1/75, *OECD Local Cost Standard*, [1975] ECR 1355.

needs to able to participate in international conferences.[293] Not allowing it to do so, as in the case of Article 9 of the 1986 Vienna Convention, is therefore a major shortcoming. Article 9 of the Vienna Convention merely preserves the right of states, as the primary actors under international law, to adopt multilateral agreements.

3.10 Conclusions

The conclusion that the European Community and the European Union are neither states nor mere intergovernmental organisations is an accurate assessment when it comes to their compliance with international treaty law. The Community and the Union are not like any other international organisation and so far international law has yet to provide the proper solution to the many questions surrounding their participation in international relations.

In international treaty law the European Community and the European Union are in fact positioned between international organisations and states. In certain instances their treaty practice resembles state practice. For example, in the Community, like in the case of states, it is the executive, the Commission, who holds the power to negotiate international agreements. Although the Commission needs the approval of the Council to negotiate, and in the end it is the Council that has a general power to conclude international agreements, these agreements cannot be negotiated, safe for the exception of Article 111 EC, by any other party than the Commission. In the Community context the Commission and the Council can decide whether negotiations are necessary but only the Commission can put a proposal before the Council requesting permission to initiate and carry out the actual negotiations.

On the other hand, the treaty-making practice of the Union resembles the practice of other international organisations in that the Presidency negotiates agreements on behalf of the Union. Although the Commission is associated with these negotiations as appropriate, it is the Presidency that seeks approval for the start and execution of the negotiations.

Even so, it is difficult to compare the Community treaty-making practice to the practice of international organisations in general. This is because not all organisations have legal personality and not one of them involves such a complete transfer of sovereignty from the member states to the organisation. Any attempt to equate the Community and the Union with other international organisations is by definition self-defeating. But despite their unique features, the Community and the Union are still international organisations. Their powers are

[293] The Community was only allowed to participate as an observer in the drafting of the 1982 Convention on the Law of the Sea, but was permitted to become a party. On the other hand, it has participated as full member in the negotiation of various international trade rounds, including the Uruguay Round of Trade Negotiations that led to the creation of the World Trade Organisation.

not general but rather determined by the constituent treaties. The Community and the European Union have conferred powers. It is, therefore, not surprising that both the Court of First Instance and the Court of Justice make reference to both Vienna Conventions in the analysis of the Community's treaty practice. This is not only because the two Conventions are more or less identical and represent a significant amount of codified customary treaty law, but also because this is the only correct way to capture an entity that finds itself somewhere between the two most important subjects of international law, the state and the traditional international organisation.

Chapter 4
MIXED AGREEMENTS AND THE INTERNATIONAL LAW OF TREATIES

4.1 Introduction

This Chapter represents the second instalment in the analysis of the Community's and Union's treaty practice in light of substantive rules of international treaty law. Whereas the previous Chapter, although making ancillary references to mixed agreements, was primarily about international agreements to which the Community or the Union alone is a party (exclusive competence) this Chapter will focus almost entirely on mixed agreements. The analysis will be completed when, as pointed out earlier, the next Chapter will focus on treaty interpretation and dispute settlement.[1]

In Chapter 1 the subject of mixed agreements was analysed in the context of a general overview of the external powers of the Community.[2] Although much has been written about this unusual practice in international treaty relations[3], little research has been done into its precise relation to international treaty law.[4] That the Community can conclude such agreements is an established fact.[5] This practice

---

[1] See *supra* General Introduction.

[2] Section *supra* 1.3.2.

[3] Examples include H. Schermers and D. O'Keeffe (eds.), *Mixed Agreements* (1983); I. MacLeod, I. Hendry, and S. Hyettt, *The External Relations of the European Community* (1996); D. McGoldrick, *International Relations Law of the European Union* (1997); J. Heliskoski, *Mixed Agreements as a Technique for Organising the International Relations of the European Community and Its Member States* (2001); R. Arnold, Der Abschluss gemischter Verträge durch die Europäischen Gemeinschaften in 19 *AVR* (1980-1981), at 419; T. Cottier and A. Caplazi, *Das Genehmigungsverfahren beim Abschluss völkerrechtlicher Abkommen in der Europäischen Union* (1998); J. Temple Lang, The Ozone Layer Convention: A new solution to the question of Community participation in "mixed" international agreements in 23 *C.M.L. Rev.* (1986), at 157; C. Timmermans and E. Völker (eds.), *Division of powers between the European Communities and their Member States in the field of external relations* (1981); N. Neuwahl, Joint Participation in International Treaties and the Exercise of Power by the EEC and Its Member States: Mixed Agreements in 28 *C.M.L. Rev.* (1991), at 717; N. Neuwahl, Shared Powers or Combined Incompetence? More on Mixity in 33 *C.M.L. Rev.* (1996), at 667 and J. Megret, *Le Droit de la Communauté Économique Européenne. Commentaire du Traité et des Textes Pris pour son application*, Volume 12, Relations extérieures (1980).

[4] See A. Bleckmann, 'The Mixed Agreement of the EEC in Public International Law' in H.G. Schermers and D. O'Keeffe (eds.), *Mixed Agreements* (1983), at 155.

[5] Although the compatibility of mixed agreements with the EC Treaty has been called into question in the past, analogous application of Article 102 Euratom, prior to the Single European Act, to the EC and ECSC Treaties have proven that this is not the case. At the present, Treaty provisions, such as the Articles 174(4) and 181 EC, explicitly provide for the conclusion of such agreements. See also D. McColdrick, *supra* note 3, at 79-82.

has not only been recognized and endorsed at the internal level by the European Court of Justice[6], it has also been recognized and accepted by the international community.[7] In fact, mixed agreements are of paramount importance to the external activities of the Community. As indicated in the aforementioned Section 1.3.2 of Chapter 1, the Community and some, or all, of the Member States, acting as joint contracting parties, have concluded dozens of international agreements. But it remains unclear as to how this practice fits into the general rules of international treaty law. The purpose of this Chapter is, therefore, to conduct this analysis with regard to mixed agreements.

The mixed agreement is a unique instrument in international relations. It is unique in that it involves a shared contractual relationship between an international organisation and its members. It is also unique in that exclusively the European Communities and their Member States use it. It is the direct result of the jurisprudence of the European Court of Justice. Although the Court did not use the term 'mixed agreement' as such, it did stipulate in *Opinion 1/78*[8] that there are instances where, because of a shared competence between the European Community and the Member States, the latter are empowered to conclude international agreements alongside the Community. Up to that point, the Court's decisions had focused primarily on the existence of an external Community competence[9] and the precise scope of this competence.[10] *Opinion 1/78* added to a further elaboration of the rules applying to the Community's external competence and the relation between this competence and the external competence of the Member States in the fields covered by the EC Treaty.

In the preceding Chapter it was pointed out that the Community's treaty relations are governed by the rules of customary international law. Although the Court of First Instance and the Court of Justice have made frequent references to the 1969 and 1986 Vienna Convention, this could only be done to the extent that these international Conventions embody customary international law.[11] The 1969

[6] Examples of the Court's case-law include Ruling 1/78, *Draft IAEA Convention* [1978] ECR 2151, Opinion 1/78, *Natural Rubber* [1979] ECR 2871, Opinion 2/91, *ILO* [1993] ECR I-1061; Opinion 1/94, *WTO* [1994] ECR I-625 and Opinion 2/00, *Cartagena Protocol on Biosafety*, [2001] ECR I-9717.

[7] This is not only the case in the Community's bilateral relationships but also in a wider context. Many multilateral agreements allow for regional economic integration organisations, such as the EU, to become a party, alongside its members, to the agreement. Usually the international agreement contains a provision requesting that the organisation and its member state the precise limits of their respective competences.

[8] Opinion 1/78, *Natural Rubber* [1979] ECR 2871. In Case 12/86, *Demirel*, [1987] ECR 3719, the Court did use the term 'mixed agreement' in reference to the EC-Turkey Association Agreement, paragraphs 8 and 9.

[9] See, for example, Case 22/70, *AETR*, [1971] ECR 263.

[10] Joined Cases 3, 4 and 6/76, *Kramer and others*, [1976] ECR 1279, Opinion 1/75, *OECD Local Cost Standard*, [1975] ECR 1355 and Opinion 1/76, *Rhine Navigation*, [1977] ECR 741

[11] Examples of this case law include Case 104/81, *Kupferberg*, [1982] ECR 3641; Case T-115/94, *Opel Austria*, [1997] ECR II-39; Case 12/86, *Demirel*, [1987] ECR 3719; C-162/96, *Racke*, [1998] ECR I-3655 and Case C-124/95, *CentroCom*, [1996] ECR I-81.

Vienna Convention has already entered into force, but is only open to states. The 1986 Convention on treaties between states and international organisations and between international organisations is open to organisations such as the European Community, but it has not been signed and ratified by the Community and it has not yet entered into force.

This presents a rather curious situation in the case of mixed agreements. In the event that this agreement is concluded with one or more states, the 1969 Vienna Convention governs the relation between these states and the Member States of the European Union, insofar as these contracting parties have ratified this Convention.[12] Customary law governs the treaty relations with the contracting states that have not yet ratified the 1969 Vienna Convention. The relation between the European Community and the other contracting party, irrespective of whether it is a state or an international organisation, is also governed by customary international law, as will the treaty relationship between the EU Member States and another international organisation.

This complicated problem can be further exacerbated if customary law does not govern the issue at stake. As indicated in the previous chapter, this will involve only minor areas, for it is generally accepted that most of the substantive rules embodied in the two Vienna Conventions represent customary law.[13] To the extent that this is not the case, it will be up to the parties to decide upon the applicable rules, keeping in mind the object and purpose of the agreement and the general rules of international law.

4.2 Negotiating mixed international agreements

In *Ruling 1/78*[14] the European Court of Justice held that

> "Where it is apparent that the subject matter of an agreement or convention falls in part within the competence of the Community and in part within that of the Member States, it is essential to ensure close cooperation between the Member States and the Community institutions, both in the process of negotiation and conclusion and in the fulfilment of the commitments entered into. That obligation to cooperate flows from the requirement of unity in the international representation of the Community" (paragraph 3).

In *Opinion 2/91*[15] the Court held that

[12] Article 73 of the 1986 Vienna Convention specifically provides that the treaty relationship between states that are parties to agreements concluded between states and international organisations will be governed by the rules of the 1969 Vienna Convention.

[13] A. Aust, *Modern Treaty Law and Practice* (2000), at 9-11.

[14] Ruling 1/78, *Draft IAEA Convention*, [1978] ECR 2151.

[15] Opinion 2/91, *ILO*, [1993] ECR I-1061.

"Cooperation between the Community and the Member States is all the more necessary in view of the fact that the former cannot, as international law stands at the present, itself conclude an ILO Convention and must do so through the medium of the Member States" (paragraph 37).

And in *Opinion 1/94*[16] the ECJ went even further by stipulating that

"This duty to cooperate is all the more imperative in the case of agreements such as those annexed to the WTO agreement, which are inextricably interlinked, and in view of the cross-retaliation measures established by the Dispute Settlement Understanding. Thus, in the absence of close cooperation, where a Member State, duly authorized within its sphere of competence to take cross-retaliation measures, considered that would be ineffective if taken in fields covered by GATS or TRIPS, it would not, under Community law, be empowered to retaliate in the area of trade in goods, since that is an area which on any view falls within the exclusive competence of the Community under Article 113 (now 133) of the Treaty. Conversely, if the Community were given the right to retaliate in the sector of goods but found itself incapable of exercising that right, it would, in the absence of close cooperation find itself unable, in law, to retaliate in the areas covered by GATS or TRIPS, those being within the competence of the Member States" (paragraph 109).

At the hearing leading up to *Opinion 1/94* the Commission had argued that problems would arise "as regards the administration of the agreements, if the Community and the Member States were recognized as sharing competence to participate in the conclusion of the GATS and TRIPS agreements" (paragraph 106). The Court responded by saying

"That concern, which is quite legitimate, it must be stressed, first that any problems which may arise in the implementation of the WTO Agreement and its annexes as regards the coordination necessary to ensure unity of action where the Community and the Member States participate jointly cannot modify the answer to the question of competence, that being a prior issue. (...) resolution of the issue of the allocation of competence cannot depend on problems which may possibly arise in administration of agreements" (paragraph 107).

Thus the institutions of the European Community and the Member States are under a binding obligation to cooperate closely in the negotiation, conclusion and implementation of international agreements wherever the competence to act in the field of the subject matter of an agreement is shared by the Community and the Member States. This duty is a fundamental principle that has its basis in Article 10 EC. However, it should be pointed out that the European Court of Justice only spoke of a duty of close cooperation and not of a unity of representation. The Member States must thus co-operate with the Community institutions and

---

[16] Opinion 1/94, *WTO*, [1994] I-5267.

vice versa.[17] There is, therefore, no need for a unified representation. This point will be further elaborated later on. In this Section the negotiation of such mixed international agreement will be analysed.

In the previous Chapter it was pointed out that international treaty law is rather silent where the negotiation of an international agreement is concerned.[18] The law limits itself to recognizing the right of the contracting parties to set out their own rules. International treaty law makes no reference to the negotiating process or the negotiating powers of the contracting parties. The law limits itself to the actual representation at international level of the negotiating parties (Article 7 of the 1969 and 1986 Vienna Conventions). States and international organisations are entities that are represented by persons. It is imperative that the other parties be allowed to establish whether the person involved has the authority to commit the state or international organisation he represents. This is all the more necessary in the case of mixed agreements. States or international organisations negotiating with the European Community and its Member States will like to know who has the authority to conduct these negotiations and commit the Community and its Member States.

International law of treaties also stipulates that a party cannot invoke the nullity of an international agreement where the person negotiating on its behalf lacked the proper authority to commit the state or international organisation.[19] The only exception permitted is where it was manifest to the other party that the person negotiating the agreement lacked the proper authority to enter into a binding arrangement on behalf of the party he represented.[20] The designation of the negotiating authority is based upon the internal laws of the state or international organisation[21]. In the setting of a bilateral negotiation the rules of procedure are determined by the parties involved.[22]

In the case of multilateral agreements, the rules are usually determined before the start of the international conference that is convened to negotiate the agree-

[17] See also S. Hyett, 'The Duty of Cooperation: A Flexible Concept' in A. Dashwood and C. Hillion (eds.), *The General Law of E.C. External Relations* (2000), at 250-251.

[18] See *supra* Chapter 3, Section 3.2.3.

[19] Article 46(1) of the 1969 and 1986 Vienna Conventions.

[20] *Ibid.* It must be a violation of 'a rule of its law of fundamental importance'. The party invoking this provision must prove that the violation of its fundamental rules is 'objectively evident' to any state or international organisation acting in accordance 'with normal practice and in good faith' (Article 46(2) of the 1969 and 1986 Vienna Conventions).

[21] The Preamble of the 1986 Vienna Convention recognizes this principle and provides "that nothing in the present Convention should be interpreted as affecting those relations between an international organisation and its members which are regulated by the rules of the organisation".

[22] The standard procedure in the negotiation of the 'Europe Agreements' is that the Presidency of the Council of Ministers of the EU presents the negotiating positions agreed by the Council and also chairs the negotiating sessions at the level of ministers and their deputies. The applicant state appoints its own Chief Negotiator, with a supporting team of experts. The draft negotiating positions are proposed by the Commission, which works in close contact with the applicant country to seek solutions to problems arising during the negotiations. http://www.europa.eu.int/enlargement/negotiations/index.

ment, or they are established by the General Assembly of the United Nations if the negotiations are to take place under its auspices.[23] For example, the Secretary General of the United Nations was requested by the General Assembly of the United Nations, on the basis of Resolution 3029 (XXVII) of 18 December 1972, to convene the first and second session of the Third United Nations Conference on the Law of the Sea.[24] General Assembly Resolution 3067 (XXVIII) of 16 November 1973 authorized the Secretary General to invite the specialized agencies of the United Nations and several international organisation, including the European Economic Community, to cooperate fully with the Secretary General in the preparations for the Conference and to send observers to the Conference.[25] The Community participated as an observer in the negotiations.[26]

The European Economic Community was among the parties invited to participate in the Conference of Plenipotentiaries of the Coastal States of the Mediterranean Region for the Protection of the Mediterranean Sea against Pollution from Land-Based Sources.[27] The Conference was convened by the Executive Director of the United Nations Environment Programme on the basis of a recommendation adopted by the Intergovernmental Review Meeting of Mediterranean Coastal States and First Meeting of the Contracting Parties to the Convention for the Protection of the Mediterranean Sea against Pollution and its related Protocols.[28]

The Convention for the Prevention of Marine Pollution from Land-Based Sources was negotiated and adopted by a diplomatic conference. The European Community participated as a party.[29] Although Article 10 of the Convention called upon the Contracting Parties to have due regard to the work carried out by the appropriate international organisations and agencies, without allowing for these organisations and agencies to become a party to the Convention, the European Community was among the parties authorized to conclude the agreement

[23] Other multilateral settings include, amongst others, the United Nations Conference on Trade and Development, the Food and Agriculture Organisation, and the United Nations Environment Programme.

[24] Third United Nations Conference on the Law of the Sea: Final Act in 21 *I.L.M.* (1982), at 1245.

[25] *Ibid.* See also K. Simmonds, The Community's Declaration upon Signature of the U.N. Convention on the Law of the Sea in 23 *C.M.L. Rev.* (1986), at 521.

[26] During the Eighth (Resumed) Session of the Conference, the parties debated whether to allow the Community to participate in the meetings as an equal contracting party. A political compromise, following fierce opposition by the then Socialist countries resulted in the adoption of Resolution IV, permitting the limited participation of liberation movements, governments that were not fully independent, and Namibia. In return Annex IX, permitting the conclusion of the agreement by regional economic integration organisations, was added to the Draft Convention. K. Simmonds, *supra*, note 25, at 524-528.

[27] Conference of the Plenipotentiaries of the Coastal States of the Mediterranean Region for the Protection of the Mediterranean Sea against Pollution from Land-Based Sources 1980: Final Act in 19 *I.L.M.* (1980), at 863.

[28] *Ibid.*

[29] Conference on the Prevention of Marine Pollution from Land-Based Sources in 13 *I.L.M.* (1974), at 352.

(Article 24). It was again invited to participate as a party in the diplomatic conference of the contracting parties that negotiated and adopted the Protocol amending the Convention to include pollution through the atmosphere.[30]

The Vienna Convention on the Protection of the Ozone Layer was adopted following the Conference of Plenipotentiaries on the Protection of the Ozone Layer.[31] The Conference was convened by the Executive Director of the United Nations Environment Programme, pursuant to Decision 12/14 of the Governing Council of UNEP on 28 May 1984.[32] The European Economic Community was among the various specialized agencies and international organisations invited to participate as an observer in the Conference. A request by the Community to include a clause enabling it, by name, to become a party to the Convention was denied. In the end the more general definition of regional economic integration organisation was used.[33]

Philippe Manin correctly points out that the aforementioned practice seriously hampers the exercise of the Community's competence to conclude international agreements.[34] International Conferences, convened to negotiate an international agreement, are usually only open to states. As a result the European Community is unable to influence directly any decision, not even in areas coming under its exclusive competence, concerning the negotiating formula. Both Vienna Conventions compound the problem. Article 9(2) of the 1969 Vienna Convention provides that in an international conference an agreement shall be adopted by two thirds of the states present and voting, or by a different rule agreed upon by the same two third majority. This provision affirms the supremacy of states in international relations.

In its proposal for the 1986 Vienna Convention, the International Law Commission wanted to eliminate any secondary role that international organisations would play to states in international conferences with regard to the voting procedure. Fierce opposition from states to the proposed text resulted in the current text of Article 9(2) of the 1986 Vienna Convention, which provides that the agreement will be adopted in accordance with the procedure agreed upon by 'the participants'. If there is no agreement the text will be adopted by two thirds of the participants present and voting, unless by the same majority they have agreed to apply a different rule. Article 9(2) of the 1986 Vienna Convention contains no

---

[30] Contracting Parties to the Convention for the Prevention of Marine Pollution from Land-Based Sources: Protocol Amending the Convention in 27 *I.L.M.* (1988), at 625.

[31] Final Act of the Conference of the Plenipotentiaries on the Protection of the Ozone Layer in 26 *I.L.M.* (1987), at 1520.

[32] *Ibid.*

[33] J. Temple Lang, *supra* note 3, at 163-166.

[34] P. Manin, The European Communities and the Vienna Convention on the Law of Treaties between States and International Organisations or between International Organisations in 24 *C.M.L. Rev.* (1987), at 474-476.

explicit reference to international organisations, nor is it clear what 'all participants' means.[35]

From the foregoing it is clear that, insofar as it concerns the issue of who is to negotiate on behalf of the Community and the Member States, there is ample room for the Community and the Member States to develop an internal practice that is (considerably) different from the standard practice in international relations and unique to the European Community. Although an international conference may only be open to states, there is nothing that prevents the Member States to include representatives of the Commission in their delegations and permit them to speak at the various meetings. However, the (possible) involvement of multiple parties on the Community's side can be confusing for the other contracting parties. Even in the case where, for example the Commission represents the Community and the Member States[36], the other parties involved may want to obtain some measure of clarity as to the precise scope of the Commission's negotiating powers before the start of the negotiations.[37]

This is all the more relevant because the Commission is acting on the one hand on the basis of negotiating directives issued by the Council and on the other on the basis of the instructions issued by the Member States. The Member States are sovereign nations who have the right to negotiate separately from the Community. Their negotiating directives may not undermine the Community's interest but need not be identical to the Council's directives. During the negotiations the Commission will, therefore, be acting in two capacities. Parties may not know, and even be confused, regarding the exact capacity in which the Commission, or its representative, is acting at any given time. The same principle applies if the Presidency of the European Union acts as the sole negotiator on behalf of the Community and the Member States.

---

[35] *Ibid.*

[36] During the Uruguay Round of Trade Negotiations the Commission was authorized to negotiate on behalf of the Community and the Member States. It was stipulated by the Member States that this did not involve the recognition of an exclusive Community competence over the whole range of subject matters being negotiated. The Court finally settled the dispute concerning the division of competence in Opinion 1/94, *WTO*, [1994] ECR I-5267.

[37] In the previous Chapter reference was made to the fact that the other parties frequently obtain copies of the negotiating directives prior to the start of the negotiations. Still, the Community and the Member States are not obliged to outline the precise division of their competences. It can even happen that the Community's competence may evolve in the course of the negotiations as in the Case C-25/94, *Commission* v *Council*, [1996] ECR I-1469. What started out as a shared competence transformed into an exclusive competence. However, if there are changes that exceed the initial negotiating directives, the Commission will inform the Council and seek additional authorization. In this particular instance the committees appointed by the Council to assist the Commission cannot provide the additional mandate. The authorization must come from the Council itself. The changes in the negotiating directives require political assessments and are sensitive in nature. Authorization can be obtained on the basis of direct contacts between the Commission and the Council of Permanent Representatives, COREPER, in the case of bilateral negotiations, or on the basis of *ad hoc* consultations with the delegations of the Member States in the case of international conferences. Information obtained through personal interviews with the Legal Services of the Commission and the Council in the period November-December 2003.

Although reference is made to the concept of mixed agreements whenever the Community and the Member States act together as contracting party, Chapter 1 has illustrated that there are different types of mixed agreements.[38] The division of powers between the Community and the Member States does not present itself in a well-defined unitary manner. Where an international agreement deals with matters falling partly within the exclusive domain of the Community and partly within that of the Member States, mixed agreements are used. Although in this case it is not mandatory that the two act together, it is common that they do so. A mixed agreement is also used where the Community and the Member States hold concurrent powers. In this instance it would be necessary to draw the precise demarcation line between the Community's and the Member States' competence. But this is easier said than done. Therefore, in this instance it is necessary that the Community and the Member States act closely together so as to guarantee the unity of the international representation of the Community and the Member States.

A specific type of mixed agreement is used where the Community has an exclusive competence but is barred from participating in an international agreement because the rules of procedure do not permit the participation of international organisations.[39] Or where there are provisions within the agreement related to its execution that require the participation of the Member States.[40] This was the case in *Opinion 1/78*. This kind of mixity was also commonplace in commodity agreements.[41]

In all these cases of mixed agreements the negotiating has to be done by the Member States and the European Communities together. The Community involvement is determined by the rules of the EC Treaty, that is Article 300(1) EC.[42] The Commission, following a qualified majority Council decision authorizing the Commission to conduct these negotiations, carries out the negotiations.[43] As mentioned before, on the basis of such guidelines the Commission carries out these negotiations as the Council may decide. A committee appointed by and representing the Council assists the Commission. It was also pointed out that although the Commission has to seek the approval of the Council, the power

---

[38] For an overview of different types of mixed agreements see H.G. Schermers, 'A Typology of Mixed Agreements' in H.G. Schermers and D. O'Keeffe (eds.), *Mixed Agreements* (1983), at 23-33.

[39] These mixed agreements are commonly referred to as false mixed agreements. This is done because the Community does not actually participate in the agreement, despite the fact that the agreement deals with matters that come within the domain of its exclusive competence. Schermers, *supra* note 38, at 26.

[40] Prior to the Maastricht Treaty recourse could be had to Article 116 EC, although this provision was not specifically designed for the joint conclusion of international agreements. See *supra* Chapter 1.

[41] See *supra* Chapter 3.

[42] The exception to this rule is where the negotiations are carried out on the basis of Article 111 EC. In this case the Council decides who will negotiate on behalf of the Community.

[43] Article 300(1) EC provides, that in accordance with Article 300(2) EC the Council decision must be unanimous.

to negotiate is an autonomous one, that is to say that the Commission cannot be compelled to negotiate the agreement and that no else can be authorized to negotiate the agreement if the Commission does not want to carry out these negotiations.[44]

In the case of the European Union, acting on the basis of Article 24 TEU, or Article 24 TEU in combination with Article 38 TEU, or Article 38 TEU, the negotiations are to be carried out by the Presidency, assisted by the Commission where appropriate. So far, the agreements concluded on the basis of Article 24 TEU, have not been mixed agreements.[45] But it was pointed out that the new practice of concluding international agreements on the basis of the Second Pillar procedure could lead, in future to new types of mixed agreements.[46] In the event of a mixed agreement involving the Community and the Union, the Commission would negotiate on behalf of the Community, and the Presidency on behalf of the Member States.[47] Where the Union and the Member States act together as one contracting party, the negotiations will be carried out by the Presidency on behalf of the Union. In the case of a 'double mixity', that is, the Community, the Union and the Member states acting together, the negotiating delegation could consist of the Commission acting on behalf of the Community, and the Presidency acting on behalf of the Union. The Commission's position is that the Member States tend to favour negotiations under the leadership of the Presidency. The Council disputes this fact, saying the primary role of the Commission with regard to Community matters is respected.[48]

Whereas the EC and EU Treaties determine unambiguously who is to negotiate on behalf of either entity, the Member States are free to choose who will represent them. They can allow the Commission to negotiate the entire agreement on their behalf.[49] This was, for example, done in the case of the Uruguay Round of

[44] On the official positions of the Commission, the Council and the Member States see *supra* Chapter 3.

[45] See *supra* Chapter 2.

[46] See *supra* Chapter 2, Section 2.6. The adoption of the European Constitution results in the creation of one single organisation, the European Union, and under the new regime only mixed agreements involving the Union and the Member States will be possible.

[47] On 12 July 2002 the Council adopted negotiating directives authorizing the Commission to negotiate a Trade and Cooperation agreement with Iran. In its decision the Council stipulated that instruments on political dialogue and cooperation against terrorism should be negotiated in parallel with the aforementioned agreement. It was therefore determined that the Union delegation would consist of the Commission and the Presidency. The negotiations were initiated on 12 December 2002. Given the various subjects to be negotiated, and especially the matters falling within the Common Foreign and Security Policy, it is possible that the agreement will be concluded as a mixed agreement involving the Community, the Union, and (possibly) the Member States. Press release by the Danish Presidency of 12 December 2002 accessed from http://www.europa.eu.int. The negotiations have not yet been formalized.

[48] Information obtained through personal interviews with the Legal Services of the Commission and the Council in the period November-December 2003.

[49] Megret points out that in the case of mixed bilateral agreements two forms of negotiation are used. One is where the Commission is permitted to negotiate on behalf of the Community and the

Trade Negotiations.[50] In this particular instance the Commission is dependent on the instructions of the Member States. It cannot act in contravention of these guidelines and has to accept any and all instructions given to it by the Member States. The autonomous power belongs to the Member States. The Commission is merely acting as an intermediary.[51] In the end the choice will be made for the Community and the Member States to exercise their combined negotiating power to its fullest extent. The modality chosen will determine how their individual and combined objectives can best be achieved.[52]

There are two components to the negotiation of a mixed agreement, an internal and an external one.[53] As already mentioned, the parties negotiating with the Community and its Member States will want to establish the ground rules at the offset.[54] They will want clarity as to the precise limits of the competence of the Community and the Member States respectively, and who correspondingly will be responsible for which part of the negotiations.[55] This drawing of a demarca-

Member States. The second form is where the Presidency is permitted to negotiate. This second option is clearly a violation of the EC Treaty because the power to negotiate on behalf of the Community is, with the exception of Article 111 EC, an autonomous power of the Commission. Under the 'PROBA 20' arrangement (Council Decision of 30 March1981, unpublished) the Commission agreed not to pursue the legal arguments. In return the Council assured the Commission that negotiations would be conducted in a way that will improve the external image of the Community. In the case of mixed multilateral agreements the negotiations are conducted by a delegation consisting of the Commission and representatives of all Member States, the so-called 'délégation unique' or by a group of delegations consisting of the Commission delegation and the delegations of all the Member States. J. Megret, *supra* note 3, at 50-51. With the demise of commodity agreements, 'PROBA 20' has become a thing of the past. The Commission alone has negotiated the few commodity agreements in existence. See also *supra* Chapter 3.

[50] I. MacLeod *et al*, *supra* note 3, at 87.

[51] This means that where the Commission represents the Community it has full powers, but where it represents the Member States it has special full powers. See also P. Reuter, *Introduction to the Law of Treaties* (1995), at 60.

[52] S. Hyett, *supra* note 17, at 252-253.

[53] For a detailed analysis of the internal procedure see J. Groux, 'Mixed Negotiations' in H.G. Schermers *et al* (eds.), *Mixed Agreements* (1983), at 87-96.

[54] This was recognized by the European Court of Justice in Opinion 1/78, *Natural Rubber*, [1979] ECR 1979, when it held that "when a question of powers is to be determined it is clearly in the interests of all the States concerned, including any non-member countries, for such a question to be clarified as soon as any particular negotiations are commenced" (paragraph 35). However, in Ruling 1/78, *Draft IAEA Convention*, [1978] ECR 417, the Court held that "the exact nature of the division of powers is a domestic question in which third parties have no need to intervene" (paragraph 35). This may seem as a contradiction of the Court's statement in *Opinion 1/78*. Standard practice reveals, however, that third countries not only have a need for clarity, but that they demand that this clarity be provided before the start of the negotiations. Although it is not necessary that the Community and the Member States indicate the precise limits of the division of competence, some dividing line must be presented. The standard Community practice is to provide general statements to that effect.

[55] The third countries can also insist on the mixed formula because they are unfamiliar with the internal system of the Community or because they want additional guarantees from the Member States with regard to the rights these third parties acquire under the agreement. J. Groux, *supra* note 53 at 90-91.

tion line between the Community's and the Member States' competence is not a major issue in a bilateral setting. In multilateral negotiations the reality is different. In this instance, the other contracting parties, for various political and legal reasons, will insist on a clear division between the Community and the Member States. The most notorious example is the case of the negotiation of the 1982 United Nations Convention on the Law of the Sea.[56] The standard practice is that the European Community and its Members issue a declaration outlining the precise limits of the powers of both parties.[57]

It must be pointed out that the negotiation of an international agreement on behalf of the Community is almost always preceded by a Council decision.[58] Even in the case where the subject matter of the agreement falls within the exclusive domain of the Member States an assessment must be made *ex ante* to determine to what extent the agreement may affect the Community's interest. Arrangements will have to be made for some form of Community participation in order to safeguard its interest, even if only as an observer. Once it is established that no Community interests are at stake, the Member States will be free to pursue whichever course of action they prefer. They may even decide to use a common approach, authorizing the Presidency on the basis of a decision of the Representatives of the Member States meeting within the Council, to conduct the negotiations on their behalf.[59]

With the exception of certain well-defined cases, it is usually virtually impossible to determine at any given time the precise division of competence between the Community and the Member States. In the areas in which the Community or the Member states have an exclusive competence the division is very straightforward. Also in certain areas, such as public health, Article 152 EC, the Community is barred from adopting binding legislation. The precise limits of its competence, are self-evident. In all other areas the division is difficult to establish and subject to constant change. Despite these complications, which are particular to the unique nature of the Community, the conclusion must be that the established practice of the Community and its Member States is in line with international law, because international law itself leaves it to the parties to set out the

---

[56] For a detailed analysis see K.R. Simmonds, *supra* note 25, at 521-544.

[57] McGoldrick argues that in light of the duty of close cooperation it is up to the Member States to seek a clause that will permit Community participation in the negotiations under the most favourable conditions for both the Community and the Member States. This depends in part on the negotiating strength of the European Community and the Member States. D. McGoldrick, *supra* note 3, at 86-87.

[58] In the case of the multilateral trade negotiations known as the Tokyo Round, there was only tacit consent on the part of the Member States, but no express Council decision. J. Groux, *supra* note 53, at 88.

[59] It was pointed out in previous Chapters that it is an accepted practice that the Member States use the institutions and organs of the Community to further their common goals without such actions becoming a Community action. This intergovernmental framework makes it possible for the Member States to alter their approach at any given time and pursue a different course of action.

ground rules for the negotiation of an international agreement and to appoint the authority to negotiate on their behalf.

In the case of mixed negotiations the decision of the Council is normally accompanied by a decision of the Representatives of the Member States meeting within the Council authorizing the Commission or the Presidency to negotiate the agreement on their behalf.[60] The latter is the more commonly used format. Whereas the Commission has full powers to negotiate on behalf of the Community, it or the Presidency, whichever represents the Member States, will have only special full powers. Because the representative of the Member State holding the Presidency is acting on behalf of the collective group of Member States, it will not be possible to separate his action from his representation of his own Member State. Without any explicit or tacit agreement between the Member States he will not be permitted to act in two different capacities.

A supplementary issue involves the negotiation of the Community's accession to an existing agreement to which one or more Member States are already a party. In this instance, neither the Community nor the Member State(s) is (are) competent to act with regard to the entire range of subject matters dealt with by the agreement. The Community's accession is given because of the transfer of the power to act from the Member States to the Community. Although it may not be necessary for the Member States to participate directly in the negotiation, they will have to undertake coordinated action to assist the Community in achieving its objective.[61] It may also be necessary for the Community and the Member States to issue a prior declaration, explaining the extent of the Community's competence.

4.3 The signing and concluding of mixed agreements

4.3.1 Defining the concept of 'regional economic integration organisation'

It was pointed out in the previous Section that it is established case-law that where the subject matter of an international agreement falls within the shared

[60] Article 133 EC, as amended by the Treaty of Nice, provides a clear example of this possibility. Paragraph 6 provides that the Council may not conclude an international agreement if the agreement "includes provisions that would go beyond the Community's internal powers". In addition to the Community decision authorizing the negotiation of the agreement, there shall be a common accord of the Member States on the negotiation of the aforementioned agreement. The negotiated agreement is to be concluded as a mixed agreement.

[61] On 11 April 2002 the Commission submitted a Recommendation to the Council requesting its permission to initiate negotiations with the International Civil Aviation Organisation, ICAO, and the International Maritime Organisation, IMO, on the conditions and arrangements for accession by the European Community, SEC(2002)381 final. Accession would be to the Chicago Convention and the 1948 Geneva Convention respectively. The Commission called upon the Council to decide on the appropriate action by the Member States *vis-à-vis* the ICAO in support of the Commission's request and to explain to the third countries the internal developments within the European Community that have led to this new situation. A similar proposal was made with regard to the Community accession to the IMO.

competence of the Member States and the Community, Community law, in particular Article 10 EC, imposes an obligation on the European Community and its Member States to associate closely in the negotiation, conclusion and implementation of the agreement. Although the Community institutions and the Member States may agree to use a single negotiating authority, for example the Commission, and even permit this authority to initial the adopted text on their behalf, the actual expression of consent to be bound must be established in conformity with the individual constitutional procedures of each participating party.[62]

Consent to be bound can be expressed in a variety of ways. It can be done through signature, signature subject to ratification, approval or conclusion, exchange of instruments, ratification, accession, or any other means if so agreed.[63] The applicable procedure will be provided for in the international agreement itself. International treaty law is silent on the manner in which an international organisation and its members are to express their consent to be bound in the event that they act together as a contracting party. There are provisions concerning the expression of consent to be bound by the organisation[64] and provisions for the member states[65], but none for the expression of consent to be bound by both at the same time. Yet, the numerous multilateral agreements to which the Community and the Member States are parties, and the corresponding state practice in the light of this established reality provide insight into a developing trend. Some examples will be subsequently analyzed.

Multilateral agreements permitting ratification by an international organisation and its members traditionally include an article defining the concept of international organisation. Reference is generally made to regional economic integration organisations. Although at present, it is very rare that specific reference is made to the European Community[66], the definitions clearly indicate that it is the Community the parties have in mind.[67] The different definitions have a number of ele-

---

[62] The established Community practice is that the Commission initials the final negotiated text. There is no such established practice with regard to mixed agreements. The manner in which the agreement is negotiated will determine who will initial the final text. If the Commission carries out the entire negotiations on behalf of the Community and the Member States, it will also initial the final text. If it is not the sole negotiator, the representatives of the Member States will do so jointly with the Commission.

[63] Article 11 of the 1969 and 1986 Vienna Conventions.

[64] Articles 12-16 of the 1986 Vienna Convention.

[65] Articles 12-16 of the 1969 Vienna Convention.

[66] Article 4 of the International Cocoa Agreement makes express reference to the European Union, without granting the Union special privileges. The Agreement is also open to 'any intergovernmental organisation having responsibilities in respect of the negotiation, conclusion and application of international agreements, in particular commodity agreements'. OJ 2002, L 342/2.

[67] Numerous international agreements prior to the United Nations Convention on the Law of the Sea did make specific reference to the European Economic Community as a party permitted to ratify these agreements. See J. Feenstra, 'A Survey of the Mixed Agreements and their Participation Clauses' in H.G. Schermers and D. O'Keeffe, *Mixed Agreements* (1983), at 216-228.

ments in common, but it cannot be said that the definitions are identical. None of the definitions accurately describes the European Community.[68]

The Protocol of Amendment to the International Convention on the Simplification and Harmonisation of Customs Procedures permits that customs or economic unions may become a Contracting Party (Article 5). Article 1, sub k, defines a customs or economic union as

> "A union constituted by, and composed of States which has competence to adopt its own regulations that are binding on those States in respect of matters governed by this Convention, and has competence to decide, in accordance with its internal procedures, to sign, ratify or accede to this Convention".[69]

The United Nations Convention to combat desertification in those countries experiencing serious drought and/or desertification, particularly in Africa provides in Article 1, sub j, that

> "A regional economic integration organisation means an organisation constituted by sovereign States of a given region which has competence in respect of matters governed by this Convention and has been duly authorized, in accordance with its internal procedures, to sign, ratify, accept, approve or accede to this Convention".[70]

A similar definition can be found in Article 2, sub h, of the Rotterdam Convention on the Prior Consent Procedure for Certain Hazardous Chemicals and Pesticides in International Trade.[71]

The Convention on the Conservation and Management of Fishery Resources in the South-East Atlantic Ocean[72] and the Agreement on the international dolphin conservation programme[73] use a definition that is similar to the definition used by the Food and Agriculture Organisation. On the other hand, the Protocol to the 1979 Convention on Long-range Transboundary Air Pollution on Heavy Metals[74] utilizes the definition of organisations

---

[68] In its proposal to the Council, seeking permission to initiate the necessary negotiations for the accession of the Community to the ICAO and the IMO, the Commission acknowledges this diverse practice. It points out that during negotiations and if necessary, it will propose a definition of regional economic integration organisation along the lines of the definition provided for in Article II of the Statute of the Food and Agriculture Organisation. The aforementioned Article defines a regional economic integration organisation as "one constituted by sovereign States, a majority of which are Member of the Organisation, and to which its Member States have transferred competence over a range of matters within the purview of the Organisation, including the authority to make decisions binding on its Member States in respect of those matters". SEC(2002)381 final, at 20.

[69] OJ 2003, L 86/23.

[70] OJ 1998, L 83/3.

[71] OJ 2003, L 63/29.

[72] OJ 2002, L 234/40.

[73] OJ 1999, L 132/3.

[74] OJ 2001, L 134/41.

> "Constituted by sovereign States members of the Commission (United Nations Economic Commission for Europe), which have competence in respect of the negotiation, conclusion and application of international agreements in matters covered by the Protocol, provided that the States and organisations concerned are Parties to the Convention" (Article 14 (1)).

Finally, Article 27 of the Convention on the Transboundary Effects of Industrial Accidents[75] defines a regional economic integration organisation as one

> "Constituted by sovereign States members of the Economic Commission for Europe to which their member States have transferred competence in respect of matters governed by this Convention, including the competence to enter into treaties in respect of these matters".

All these agreements make reference to regional economic integration organisations. Although, as outlined in the previous paragraphs, all definitions used have some common elements, none specifically explains or defines the concept of 'economic integration'. John Temple Lang is right in arguing that no indication is given as to what economic integration entails.[76] A direct result of this omission is that in order to qualify an organisation would merely have to indicate economic integration as one of its objectives. Compounding the problem is that not all conventions and international agreements require that the organisation has so-called 'supranational powers'.[77]

Temple Lang points out that this unclear situation can result in a state being a party to an agreement, while at the same time it could be a member of two or more international organisations, party to the same agreement.[78] This can have serious consequences for the voting procedure within any institutional framework set up on the basis of the agreement. Such a development will be a direct contradiction of international law. A party to an agreement cannot have more than the sum of all the rights and obligations embodied in the agreement. Temple Lang therefore proposes to use a definition that includes only organisations with some exclusive competence.[79] This proposal would solve the problem, for no state can, simultaneously, be a member of two or more international organisations that have exclusive competence with regard to the same subject matter.

The 1986 Vienna Convention on the Law of Treaties has limited itself in Article 2(1)(i) to define an international organisation as an 'intergovernmental organisation'. The members of such an international organisation are traditionally states, but membership could also include one or more international orga-

[75] OJ 1998, L 326/5.

[76] J. Temple Lang, *supra* note 3, at 164-166.

[77] See, for example, the definition provided for in the United Nations Convention to combat desertification, OJ 1998, L 83/3, Article 1(i).

[78] J. Temple Lang, *supra* note 3, at 164-166.

[79] *Ibid.*

nisations. The multilateral treaty practice demonstrates, however, that in the context of a mixed international agreement a narrower concept is used. The various definitions used have in common that the organisation has to be a regional organisation, that is, it has a limited number of members, is composed of only sovereign states and it must have legislative powers, both internally and externally.

The conclusion is, therefore, that on the one hand state practice clearly takes into account the unique character of the Community, something the Vienna Convention has failed to do. That the existing Convention on the Law of Treaties between States and International Organisations or between International Organisations does not take into account the specific features of the European Community is not surprising given the fact that the 1986 Vienna Convention was more about recognizing the increasingly prominent role being played by international organisations as subjects of international law and extending the general rules and practices that govern international treaty relations between states and these organisations.

The 1986 Vienna Convention permits the development of the 'normal practice' of international organisations.[80] The interaction between the European Community and third countries and, more importantly, the recognition of the role the Community plays in international treaty relations by these third countries, is resulting in the normal practice in which specific international organisations, vaguely defined as regional economic integration organisations, are permitted to participate in multilateral international agreements. What is needed is a more proper codification of the rules of international treaty law in order to deal with this new reality.

4.3.2 The concluding of mixed agreements

The conclusion of international agreements has two components. One is the internal (constitutional) procedure and the second is the external one. In the first, the party has to go through its own internal rules to approve the agreed text. Once the international agreement has been accepted and approved at the internal level, the state or international organisation will proceed to express its consent to be bound, that is, notify the other contracting parties that it considers itself bound by the provisions of the agreement. The second procedure involves this expression of consent to be bound. Parties to an international agreement are free to determine the manner in which their consent to be bound is to be expressed. The law of treaties governs the rules applicable to the various procedures.

Irrespective of the internal division of competence between the Community and the Member States, the conclusion of mixed agreements has to be in conformity with the rules of the European Community, where the Community is con-

[80] P. Reuter, *supra* note 51, at 20.

cerned, and the constitutional rules and traditions of the Member States, where they are concerned. Yet once again, the rule is that the use of domestic procedures cannot undermine the coherence and efficiency of the Community system or make it difficult for the Community to achieve its goals. It was pointed out that the conclusion of international agreements by the Community is governed by the general procedure of Article 300 EC. Exceptions to this general procedure can be found in the Articles 111 and 133 EC. These procedures apply irrespective of whether the Community's participation in the agreement is exclusive or in combination with the Member States.

Analysis of a number of national procedures provides a very diverse picture.[81] First it should be mentioned that none of the Member States has a separate constitutional provision for the conclusion of mixed agreements, despite their unique character. One would have to look at separate statutory laws or other provisions to see whether such provisions have been made. Heliskoski mentions that in the United Kingdom's European Community Act 1972 reference is made to mixed agreements. However, this reference does not concern the procedural aspects for the conclusion of these agreements. They just point out that the agreements do not qualify as 'Community Treaties'.[82]

Article 55 of the French Constitution provides that treaties or other agreements duly ratified or approved rank, upon their publication, higher than statutes, 'loi', in the hierarchy of national laws. Condition for this application of international agreements is, however, that the other contracting parties apply the agreement on a reciprocal basis. The President negotiates and ratifies all international agreements (Article 52 of the French Constitution). He has to be notified of all negotiations that lead to the conclusion of agreements not subject to ratification. Article 54 of the French Constitution furthermore provides that all international agreements listed in this Article must be ratified by Parliament. Some other agreements are merely signed by the President. International agreements that are incompatible with the French Constitution must not be ratified.[83] The President, the Premier, the President of the National Assembly, the President of the Senate or sixty Deputies or sixty Senators may refer an international agreement to the 'Conseil Constitutionnel' for a decision on its compatibility with the Constitution before the ratification (Article 61). If the 'Conseil' decides that the international

---

[81] See in this regard also J. Heliskoski, *supra* note 3, at 89-92.

[82] J. Heliskoski, *supra* note 3, at 91. Article 88-4 of the French Constitution provides that "Le Gouvernement soumet à l'Assemblée Nationale et au Sénat, dis leur transmission au Conseil des Communautés, les propositions d'acts communautaires comportant des disposition de nature legislative". 'Articles 88-1 through 88-4 inserted by Constitutional Law No. 93-952 of 27 July 1994' reprinted in A. Blaustein and F. Flanz (eds.), *Constitutions of the Countries of the World. Special Supplement France* (1994), at 11-12. This provision could be read as including mixed international agreements. But once again no reference is made to any specific procedural requirement in the negotiation and conclusion of mixed agreements.

[83] J. Bell, S. Boyron and S. Whittaker, *Principles of French Law* (1998), at 18-19.

agreement is incompatible with the French Constitution, the agreement can only be ratified after the Constitution has been amended (Article 54).[84]

In Germany the Federal President, 'Bundespräsident', is Head of State. Yet, his function is politically neutral.[85] Though it is socially integrating. Article 55 of the 'Grundgesetz' (GG) obliges the President to protect the constitutional values as is underlined by his oath of office.[86] Article 59 I GG provides that the President represents Germany at international level, concludes international agreements with third states and accredits and receives envoys. Treaties concerning political relations require the approval or the contribution of the authorized legislative bodies.[87] This provision should be read in conjunction with Article 25 GG, which stipulates that general rules of international law form an integral part of German law without the need of any act of transformation. Parliamentary involvement is thus necessary. Although these general rules rank lower than the German Constitution, they are still superior to ordinary national law.[88]

The prerogative to conclude international agreements belongs to Ministers in the United Kingdom.[89] The prerogative powers used to belong to the Crown but nowadays the Ministers exercise them. This is a direct result of the rise of Cabinet Government and stems from the time democracy developed in the United Kingdom.[90] Although the power to conclude international agreements rests with Ministers these agreements can only become a source of national law after they have been incorporated into the legal system through an Act of Parliament. Still, in *R* v *Secretary of the Home Department ex P Ahmed (Mohammed Hussain)* (1998) a British court held that the fact that the government has entered into a treaty obligation might provide a person with 'legitimate expectations'. The government will, therefore, have to comply with its obligations even if the international agreement has not yet been incorporated into national law.[91]

Joni Heliskoski writes that in Finland international agreements are concluded by the President in the Council of State and approved by the Parliament under the Parliament's general competence.[92] Practice shows that Parliamentary involvement is less frequent. Parliamentary approval has been obtained for a number of Europe and other association agreements. The 1982 UN Convention on the Law of the Sea and the Energy Charter Treaty are among the few multilateral agree-

[84] Note the similarity between this provision and Article 300(6) EC.

[85] This does not mean that he cannot have any political affiliation. The current President, Horst Köhler, is a member of the CDU.

[86] N. Foster and S. Sule, *German Legal System and Laws* (2000), at 189-192. For a detailed analysis see *Bonner Kommentar zum Grundgesetz*. Part 6 (2002).

[87] Article 59 II GG.

[88] See also A. Freckmann and T. Wegerich, *The German Legal System* (1999), at 33-34.

[89] There is no formal document listing comprehensively the prerogative powers of Ministers.

[90] A. Le Sueur, J. Herberg and R. English, *Principles of Public Law* (1999), at 33.

[91] *Ibid*, at 49-50. See also J. Heliskoski, *supra* note 3, at 91-92.

[92] J. Heliskoski, *supra* note 3, at 90-91.

ments approved by Parliament since Finland's accession to the European Union.[93]

In Belgium foreign relations and defence traditionally form part of the prerogatives of the Crown. Prior to the revision of the Constitution, in 1993, it was for the King to conclude international agreements. Agreements that create obligations for the State or individual Belgian citizens had to be ratified by both Chambers of Parliament. Other types of international agreement need not be approved by Parliament. Nowadays the Government, under the scrutiny of the Parliament, conducts foreign relations.[94]

The Belgian Constitution provides for its own system of mixed international agreements. These are agreements between the Kingdom of Belgium and one or more states and international organisations. However, because of the constitutional division of competence between the Federal Government and the Communities and Regions, these agreements also have to be approved by Communities and Regions Councils.[95] These agreements are negotiated by a mixed delegation consisting of federal and local representatives. They operate on an equal footing, but the Minister of Foreign Affairs coordinates the negotiations. However, this mixed delegation can only conduct negotiations after the Inter-ministerial Conference, 'Interministeriële Conferentie', has established, within sixty days after it has been notified of the mixed nature of the proposed agreement, the composition of this national delegation.[96]

Similar to the German Constitution, Article 9(1) of the Austrian Constitution provides that general rules of international law apply automatically within the Austrian legal order. International agreements can also be a source of law in the Austrian legal order (Article 50). On a proposal from the Federal Government the Federal President concludes the agreements. The international agreements have to be ratified by the National Council if they have a political character or if they can change or supplement statutory laws. Upon ratification the National Council can also decide that the agreement is non-self-executing. In this instance it must be transformed into national law through a subsequent Act of the Council. The precise position international agreements assume in the hierarchy of national laws is determined by their content. The highest possible ranking is that of a constitutional regulation. The implemented agreement will be on a constitutional level and subject to the requirements of constitutional amendment.[97]

Finally, Article 91(1) of the Dutch Constitution, 'Grondwet', provides that international agreements cannot bind the Kingdom of the Netherlands, nor can international agreements to which the Netherlands is a party be terminated without the approval of the Dutch Parliament, 'Staten-Generaal'. International agree-

[93] *Ibid.*

[94] J. vande Lanotte, *Overzicht van het Publiekrecht* (1997), at 673

[95] *Ibid*, at 674.

[96] *Ibid*, at 675-676.

[97] H. Hausmaninger, *The Austrian Legal System* (1998), at 24.

ments that are incompatible with the Constitution have to be approved by both Chambers of Parliament, 'Eerste' en 'Tweede Kamer', on the basis of a two-third majority (Article 91(3) GW).[98]

Until 1983, the Dutch Constitution itself provided which international agreements did not require parliamentary approval. In 1994, the Statute Law on the ratification and publication of international agreements, 'Rijkswet goedkeuring en bekendmaking verdragen', entered into force. Article 7 of this Statute Law lists the various types of agreements that do not require parliamentary approval. These include, amongst others, agreements adopted to implement an earlier agreement (sub b); agreements that do not bring about important financial obligations for the Kingdom and which will be in force for a period of not more than one year (sub c); and international agreements that modify the annexes of existing agreements (sub f).

Article 3 of the Statute Law also provides that parliamentary approval can be explicit or implicit. If neither of the Chambers of Parliament or at least one-fifth of the Members of either Chamber of Parliament indicates, within a period of 30 days, that the agreement has to be approved explicitly by Parliament it will be deemed to have been approved implicitly (Article 5(1)). To avoid unnecessary delays the Government will, when it submits the agreement for approval, of its own motion request that Parliament explicitly approve those agreements that the Government considers important enough to warrant parliamentary approval. International agreements are concluded on the basis of a law, 'Koninklijk Besluit'.

Contrary to Article 102 Euratom, the EC Treaty does not contain any provision concerning the order in which the Community and the Member States must conclude an international agreement.[99] The European Court of Justice has only ruled that the obligation of close cooperation also extends to the conclusion of international agreements without making any reference to what this means in reality or in which way this close cooperation is to take effect.

MacLeod *et al*, supported by Neuwahl, argue that the obligation of close cooperation should be interpreted as meaning that the Member States have to make a concerted effort to reach a common position. If such a common position cannot be agreed upon, the Member States are free to pursue their own national objec-

---

[98] P. Kooijmans, *Internationaal publiekrecht in vogelvlucht* (2002), at 93-96. Kooijmans also points out that the recent ratification of the Statute of the International Criminal Court, ICC, led to a debate on the application of the provision of Article 91(3) GW. The King and the Members of Parliament are exempted from prosecution (Articles 42(2) and 71 GW). However, Article 27 of the Statute of the ICC provides that a person cannot invoke his official function to escape prosecution by the Court. In the end the Statute was approved without further complication.

[99] The old Article 116 EEC did provide the legal base for a common approach by the Community and the Member States in the negotiation and conclusion of international agreements of particular interest to the internal market. The Maastricht Treaty has deleted this Article. Perhaps the time has come to consider its reinsertion, albeit in a different form, in the EC Treaty. See also J. Megret, *supra* note 3, at 51-53.

tives subject to the limitations that general EC law imposes upon them.[100] Hyett points out that

> "It does not follow as a matter of law that, in respect of a matter where Member States retain competence, they no longer have the power to act if a common position cannot be agreed amongst all the Member States. The duty of cooperation is a flexible concept which allows the Community and the Member States to reach a practical solution tailored to the particular case".[101]

Rosas takes a different point of view, one that reflects Community law more accurately. He makes a distinction between mixed agreements involving parallel competences and mixed agreements involving concurrent competences. He argues that indeed the Member States are allowed to pursue their own agenda in the event of parallel competence and in the absence of a common position. However, if the Community and the Member States have concurrent powers, Article 10 EC prohibits the Member States from negotiating an international agreement if they cannot agree on a common position.[102]

Similar rules apply to the actual conclusion of mixed agreements. In the case of parallel powers in principle there is no need for the Community and the Member States to conclude the agreement at the same time. Where the international agreement involves concurrent competences it is customary that conclusion by the Community occurs simultaneously with conclusion by the Member States.[103] In this instance, the need to await ratification by the Member States could result in (unnecessary) complications.[104] This may be a cause for concern for not only the Member States that have ratified the agreement in time, but also for the other contracting parties. The delayed ratification by some of the Member States can also negatively influence the actual implementation of the agreement.[105]

---

[100] I. MacLeod *et al*, *supra* note 3, at 148-150 and N. Neuwahl (1996), *supra* note 3, at 670.

[101] S. Hyett, *supra* note 17, at 251.

[102] A. Rosas, 'The European Union and Mixed Agreements' in A. Dashwood and C. Hillion (eds.), *The General Law of EC External Relations* (2000), at 207-208.

[103] It is common for Council Decisions approving international agreements to contain reference to the order of ratification. Article 6(2) of Council Decision 2002/358/EC concerning the approval of the Kyoto Protocol provides that "Member States shall endeavour to take the necessary steps with a view to depositing their instruments of ratification or approval simultaneously with those of the European Community and the other Member States (...)", OJ 2002, L 130/1. Article 2(1) of Council Decision 98/414/EC on the ratification of UN Convention relating to the conservation and management of straddling stocks simply provides that the instrument of ratification shall be deposited simultaneously with the instruments of all the Member States, OJ 1998, L 189/14. And Article 3(1) of Council Decision 2003/231/EC on the accession to the Protocol of Amendment of the Kyoto Convention stipulates that the deposit of the instruments of accession of the EC and the Member States shall take place at the same time, OJ 2003, L 86/21.

[104] A. Rosas, *supra* note 102, at 207-208.

[105] The General Secretariat of the Council keeps a record of the instruments of ratification deposited by the individual Member States. The Member States are never told by the Secretariat to speed up the national ratification process. The Presidency keeps all the Member States informed on the

This dilemma can be solved by one of the following options. The Community and the other parties can agree on the provisional application of the agreement pending ratification.[106] It is not uncommon for international agreements to provide for the provisional application of the agreement or parts of the agreement.[107] The advantage of this option is that it allows the Community to agree on the provisional application without compromising the position of the Member States under the agreement.

The second option is that the Community concludes the agreement in respect of the parts falling within its competence. This option would only be useful where it is possible to establish the precise limits of the Community's competence. A possible downside is that the parts of the agreement to which it is not a party may indirectly affect the European Community's position. Yet it will lack the proper competence to respond appropriately.[108]

Simultaneous conclusion of a mixed agreement also has added political and legal significance. In its proposal for the conclusion of the Montreal Convention[109], the Commission stressed that it was necessary for the European Community and the fifteen Member States to accede simultaneously because this would allow the Convention 'to be properly and seamlessly incorporated throughout the Community'.[110] The political and legal value of simultaneous ratification lies in the support for the New Convention and, in particular, in the new liability system it introduces. This is all the more necessary because the liability system under the Warsaw Convention is very outdated.[111]

An additional argument for the simultaneous conclusion or accession is the fact that many multilateral agreements do not count the deposit of the instruments of ratification by regional economic integration organisations in addition to the instruments of ratification of its members.[112] If the Community ratifies the agree-

number of instruments deposited and, perhaps, encourages those Member States that have not yet ratified the agreement do so as soon as possible. Information obtained through personal interviews with the Legal Services of the Commission and the Council in the period November-December 2003.

[106] Although based on a different reasoning, this possibility is expressly foreseen in Article 24 TEU. There is no argument, however, why it should not be applied, *mutatis mutandis*, in the case of the European Community.

[107] See also Article 300(2) EC.

[108] Look at the Court of Justice's reasoning in paragraph 109 of Opinion 1/94, *WTO*, [1994] ECR I-5267.

[109] COM(1999) 435 final.

[110] *Ibid*, at 3.

[111] *Ibid.*

[112] See, for example, Article 36(3) of the United Nations Convention to combat desertification in those countries experiencing serious drought and/or desertification particularly in Africa, OJ 1998, L 83/3; Article 25(4) of the Kyoto Protocol, OJ 2002, L 130/4; and Article 30(2) of the Convention on the Transboundary Effects of Industrial Accidents, OJ 1998, L 326/5. On the other hand, Article 18 of Kyoto Convention merely provides that the Convention will enter into force after five entities have signed or deposited their instruments of ratification, OJ 2003, L 86/23. Similarly Article XXVII(1) of the Agreement on the international dolphin conservation programme provides that the Agreement will enter into force on deposit of the fourth instrument of ratification, OJ 1999, L 132/3.

ment before all the Member States, its instrument will be counted, unless one of the Member States deposits its instrument prior to the entry into force of the agreement. In that case, the instrument deposited by the Community will no longer count. With all fifteen Member States becoming a party, where all twenty-five can do so, the Community and Member States' position will obviously be enhanced. Of course the best solution still remains conclusion by the Community alone on the basis of an exclusive external competence. The reality is, however, that mixed agreements are an indispensable part of the Community's external treaty relations. Therefore, simultaneous ratification is the next best solution.

4.3.2.1 *Signature*

International treaty law permits that parties can agree that their signature constitutes consent to be bound. It has been stated in the preceding chapter, that although consent to be bound by ratification is still the most prominent form of treaty approval, consent to be bound by signature is gaining in importance. The need to avoid unnecessary delays brought about by lengthy national ratification procedures has made consent to be bound by signature an interesting alternative in, for example, simple cooperative technical agreements.

Under Community law, the Council is free to agree to any form of consent to be bound. As long as it assures that the European Parliament is given enough time to exercise the powers attributed to it by Article 300 EC, that is, to express its opinion or give its assent prior to the conclusion of the agreement, the procedural requirements will have been met. In case of agreements concluded on the basis of Articles 111 and 133 EC, formally the Parliament is not directly involved.[113] In these instances the use of consent to be bound by signature is, therefore, more feasible.

But whereas the Community side of the ratification procedure may appear rather straightforward, the same cannot be said of the Member States. Each Member State has its own rules regarding the expression of consent to be bound. The involvement of up to twenty-five different constitutional procedures can thus generate added difficulties to the use of consent to be bound by signature. The added delays could undermine the effectiveness of this technique. As a result one would come to expect that in the case of mixed agreements, consent to be bound by signature will only be used in simple technical agreements or in the case of complementary protocols, dealing with ancillary matters, to international agreements. Remarkably enough, in these instances it is usually the Community alone

[113] See Commission Notice of 31 January 2001, Guide pratique de l'accord-cadre sur les relations entre le Parlement européen et la Commission européenne, SP(2000)3785/5.

that concludes the additional protocols. This is especially the case in bilateral mixed agreements.[114]

An example of an international agreement that requires only signature to express consent to be bound is the International Convention on Liability and Compensation for Damage in Connection with the Carriage of Hazardous and Noxious substances by Sea, 1996 (HNS Convention).[115] This agreement was concluded by the Member States (with the exception of Denmark) in the interest of the Community pursuant to Council Decision 2002/971/EC.[116] Article 45(2) of the HNS Convention provides that states may express their consent to be bound by 'signature without reservation as to ratification, acceptance or approval'. In the end the Member States were authorized to ratify or accede to the Convention.[117]

Another example is the Kyoto Convention.[118] Article 18(1) of this Convention provides that "this Convention shall enter into force three months after five of the entities referred to in paragraphs 1 and 5 of Article 8 have signed the Convention without reservation of ratification or have deposited their instruments of ratification or accession". The Community acceded to this Convention pursuant to Council Decision 2003/231/EC.[119]

4.3.2.2 *Ratification*

The involvement of one or more Member States in the conclusion of international agreements alongside the Community has resulted in the use of consent to be bound by ratification being the principle manner in which mixed agreements are concluded. This is irrespective of whether these agreements are bilateral or multilateral agreements. As seen in the previous Section, even in instances where the

[114] For example, the Agreement in the form of an exchange of letters between the European Community and the Republic of Poland regarding a Protocol on a European Conformity Assessment Agreement, OJ 1998, L 237/9; Agreement in the form of an exchange of letters between the European Community and the Slovak Republic concerning fish, OJ 1994, L 284/27 and the Agreement in the form of an exchange of letters between the European Community and the Republic of Poland amending Annex IVb to the Interim Agreement between the European Coal and Steel Community and the European Economic Community, of the one part, and the Republic of Poland, of the other part, and to the Europe Agreement between the European Communities and their Member States, of the one part, and the Republic of Poland, of the other part, OJ 1994, L 202/20.

[115] OJ 2002, L 337/57.

[116] OJ 2002, L 337/55. The Convention only permits sovereign states as a party to it. Article 5 of Council Decision 2002/971 provides that the "Member States shall, at the earliest opportunity, use their best endeavours to ensure that the HNS Convention is amended to allow the Community to become a contracting party". Community accession to this Convention is necessary because the Community has sole competence in a number of fields covered by the Convention and because the Convention affects the provisions of Regulation 44/2001 (paragraph 3 of the recital to the Council Decision).

[117] Article 1(1) of Council Decision 2002/971.

[118] Kyoto Convention, OJ 2003, L 86/23.

[119] OJ 2003, L 86/21.

international agreement itself provides for the possibility of consent to be bound by signature, the choice is made for a formal act of ratification in accordance with the national constitutional procedures. This is not surprising in the light of the national parliaments' need to assess for themselves to what extent there has been or there is the likelihood of a transfer of competence from the Member States to the Community. They also want to assess the obligations that the Member States will take upon themselves on the basis of the agreement, and whether these commitments are in conformity with national laws.

The process of 'pre-emption', whereby the European Community gradually becomes empowered to act in a particular field, can take place through the adoption of internal legislation in the form of common policies, or through the conclusion of international agreements.[120] Permitting the conclusion of an international agreement on the basis of signature alone would deprive national parliaments of a very important supervisory power vis-à-vis their own government. Although national procedures may sometimes allow the government to conclude international agreements without obtaining the express approval of the national parliament, the Member States themselves may insist, for their own political reasons, on the use of the ratification procedure. This may provide individual Member States with some leverage within the Council to pursue other political objectives, which they would otherwise not be able to do.

4.3.2.3 *Exchange of instruments*

Exchange of instruments is never used to conclude a principal international agreement. It is a form of consent to be bound that is used in a bilateral setting dealing with amendments to the primary agreement. An exchange of letters as an instrument of consent to express approval of a mixed agreement may prove to be unworkable where a (large) number of Member States is involved. Although the European Community and the Member States are acting as one contracting party, the exchange still involves approval of all individually. Even in international relations there are no examples of multiple exchanges of instruments. It was pointed out that the double exchange of letters between Qatar, Bahrain and Saudi Arabia was an exception and was probably not intended. It was the International Court of Justice that held that the exchange qualified as an international agreement.[121]

So far, no examples have been found of the use of exchange of letters as a means to express consent to be bound in case of mixed agreements. The conclu-

---

[120] See D. Obradovic, Repatriation of Powers in the European Community in 34 *C.M.L. Rev.* (1997), at 59; M. Waelbroeck, 'The Emergent Doctrine of Community Pre-emption – Consent and Re-delegation' in T. Sandalow and E. Stein (eds.), *Courts and Free Markets: Perspectives from the United States and Europe*, Volume II (1982), at 548; Joined Cases 3, 4 and 6/76, *Kramer and others*, [1976] ECR 1279; Opinion 1/76, *Rhine Navigation*, [1977] ECR 741 and Opinion 1/78, *Natural Rubber*, [1979] ECR 2871.

[121] *Qatar* v *Bahrain*, I.C.J. Reports (1994), at 112.

sion of the principal mixed agreement is always on the basis of signature subject to ratification or accession. Treaty practice of the Community shows that there are instances in which the Community alone is permitted to conclude additional protocols with the other contracting party and that these protocols are concluded on the basis of an exchange of letters.[122] This is always done in a bilateral setting and always involves the actual implementation of the primary agreement or ancillary matters.

4.3.2.4 *Accession*

From the perspective of the Community, an international agreement can become a mixed agreement when the European Community alone or the European Community and one or more Member States accede to an agreement to which one or more Member States are a party. An agreement can also become a mixed agreement where the Community and one or more Member States become a contracting party to an international agreement to which one or more new Member States are a party and accession to the agreement is necessary because of membership of the Union.[123]

However, in principle accession by one or more Member States to an international agreement, where the subject matter of that agreement falls entirely within the exclusive domain of the Community, is not possible. The European Court of Justice has held that the transfer of sovereignty can only take place from the Member States to the Community and not *vice versa*. To accede to the agreement it would be necessary for the Member States that the agreement is amended and the amendments fall partially or entirely under the exclusive competence of the Member States.

A number of international agreements contain provisions recognizing the right of a regional economic integration organisation to become a party or to accede to the agreement without its members.[124] It is, therefore, possible for the European Community to become a party or to accede to the agreement, while the Member States accede to it at a later date. It must be kept in mind, however, that the agreements are of a mixed nature. Although the Community assumes all the rights and obligations embodied in the agreement, it does so because the international agree-

[122] See previous Section.

[123] An example is the current debate between the Commission and the US Administration concerning the application of the bilateral investment agreements between the United States and all new Member States. At present the Memorandum of Understanding is up for approval before the US Senate.

[124] Examples include the Rotterdam Convention on the Prior Informed Consent Procedure for Certain Hazardous Chemicals and Pesticides in International Trade, OJ 2003, L63/29; the United Nations Convention to combat desertification in those countries experiencing serious drought and/or desertification, particularly in Africa, OJ 1998, L 83/3; the Kyoto Protocol to the United Nations Framework Convention on Climate Change, OJ 2002, L 130/4 and the Convention on the Transboundary Effects of Industrial Accidents, OJ 1998, L 326/5.

ment so stipulates. It does not, however, acquire these rights or assumes the obligations because it has acquired an exclusive competence. Should one or more of the Member States accede to the agreement, it will be up to the organisation and its members to decide on their respective responsibilities for the performance of their combined obligations. The Community and the Member States will not be allowed to exercise their rights concurrently, that is, simultaneously. Furthermore, they will be required to declare the extent of their competence with the deposit of the instrument of accession.

4.4 Provisional application of mixed agreements

The provisional application of international agreements is a very useful tool where the urgency of the matter involved and the lengthy ratification process are irreconcilable. To avoid negative consequences because of this problem, parties may agree, through an express provision in the agreement itself or in the form of an additional protocol or any other form they may choose, to permit the provisional application of the agreement. Both Vienna Conventions recognize this right of the contracting parties (Article 25).

It is common practice that the decision to apply an agreement provisionally is adopted by all parties involved or by a majority of the parties to the agreement.[125] International treaty law does not prohibit, however, that any of the parties may decide unilaterally to apply the agreement provisionally. The party must have signed the agreement, however. Of course, this decision cannot bring any obligations with it for the other contracting party. There is no obligation to reciprocate.

Theoretically, mixed agreements can be a source of confusion where it is decided that the agreement will be applied provisionally. The confusion can be brought about by the refusal of one or more Member States to apply the agreement provisionally. Parties to the agreement may be in doubt as to the precise range of obligations assumed. Provisional application does not entail the same range of obligations as ratification. Yet, the parties that agree to do so must apply the agreement in good faith. The useful effect of provisional application may be undermined where one or more Member States refuse to or refrain from applying the agreement provisionally.

Once again, in the case of parallel competences the argument can be made that it is not necessary that the Community and the Member States act at the same time when provisional application is concerned. In the case of concurrent competences, Article 10 EC once again obliges the Community and the Member States to act together. Permitting the Member States to refrain from applying the agreement provisionally, where there is a Community decision to do so, would

[125] Article 57(1) of the International Cocoa Agreement 2001, OJ 2002, L 342/2, allows signatory governments that intend to ratify, accept, approve or accede to the Agreement to apply the Agreement provisionally upon its entry into force or at a specified date after its entry into force.

not only be a violation of the EC Treaty but would seriously undermine the unity of the external representation of the Community.

In the light of the provisions of Article 24 TEU, it could be argued that even in the case of concurrent competences there is no need for the simultaneous provisional application of an international agreement. Article 24 TEU allows the Member States to agree to apply an agreement concluded on the basis of Article 24 TEU provisionally in the event that the representative of a Member State in the Council has indicated that the Member States need to comply with its own constitutional provisions. However, this parallel cannot be drawn. The provision of Article 24 TEU serves a different function. Its purpose is directly related to the intergovernmental form of cooperation between the Member States of the European Union in the area of the Common Foreign and Security Policy.

The scope of Article 24 TEU is different from Article 300(2) EC. Article 300(2) EC envisions the provisional application of an agreement signed by the Community. The Community and the Member States share the competence concerning the matters covered by the agreement concurrently. This concurrent sharing of competence is not the case regarding matters falling under the Common Foreign and Security Policy and Police and Judicial Cooperation in Criminal Matters. It is precisely the concurrent sharing of competence and the corresponding need for unity in the external representation, resulting from the application of Article 10 EC, that obliges the Member States to apply the agreement provisionally at the same time as the Community.

Remarkably enough, the Community and the Member States are not required, where the provisional application of the agreement is concerned, to issue a declaration outlining the subject matters that come within their respective competences. The precise reason is not clear. The explanation must be sought in the legal difference between ratification and provisional application. Parties can agree to apply part of, or the entire, agreement provisionally. This does not, however, entail a definitive consent to be bound. Article XXIX(2) of the Agreement on the international dolphin conservation programme illustrates this best. This article provides,

> "Provisional application by a State or regional economic integration organisation shall terminate on the entry into force of this Agreement for that State or regional economic integration organisation or on notification by that State or regional economic integration organisation to the depositary in writing of its intention to terminate provisional application".

An international agreement that has been ratified, that is, the party has expressed its consent to be bound, is binding in its entirety on the contracting party concerned. A party that agrees to apply an international agreement provisionally has signed the agreement. Although signature followed by provisional application can be seen as an indication that the party will, in all likelihood, ratify the agreement, it is not obliged to do so. Provisional application of an agreement or parts of an agreement does not generate the full range of rights and obligations for either of the parties. The only restriction placed on the parties can be found in the rule embodied in Article 18 of both Vienna Conventions. This rule provides that parties that have signed, but not yet ratified an international agreement, must refrain from all actions that run contrary to the object and purpose of the agreement.

4.5 Reservations

The Protocol to the 1979 Convention on Long-range Transboundary Air Pollution by Heavy Metals[126] contains no provision explicitly prohibiting or permitting reservations. The same applies to the Convention on the Protection of the Rhine[127] and the Convention on the Transboundary Effects of Industrial Accidents.[128] On the other hand, Article 42 of the Agreement on the implementation of the provisions of the United Nations Convention on the Law of the Sea of 10 December 1982 relating to the conservation and management of straddling fish stocks and highly migratory fish stocks[129] expressly prohibits the making of reservations or exceptions to the Agreement. A similar provision can be found in Article 28 of the Convention on the Conservation and Management of Fishery Resources in the South-East Atlantic Ocean.[130] Other agreements such as the United Nations Convention to combat desertification[131] (Article 37); the Kyoto Protocol[132] (Article 26) and the International Cocoa Agreement 2001[133] (Article 59), prohibit the making of reservations to the Convention, Protocol and any of the provisions of the Agreement respectively. These prohibitions should be read as also including the prohibition to enter exceptions.

Article 12(1) of the Kyoto Convention[134] provides that the General Annex binds all contracting parties. Therefore, reservations to the General Annex as a whole are not permitted. Although no specific reference is made to the Convention as such, the conclusion must be that reservations concerning the Convention itself are also prohibited. A contracting party may accept one or more of the specific annexes or one or more of the chapters in the General Annex. Reservations to the standards mentioned in these annexes and chapters are not permitted. However, Article 12(2) permits that parties to the Convention may, at the time of ac-

[126] OJ 2001, L 134/41.

[127] OJ 2000, L 289/31. This is an agreement between Germany, France, Luxembourg, the Netherlands, Switzerland, and the European Community.

[128] OJ 1998, L 326/5.

[129] OJ 1998, L 189/16.

[130] OJ 2002, L 234/40.

[131] OJ 1998, L 83/3.

[132] OJ 2002, L 130/4.

[133] OJ 2002, L 342/2.

[134] OJ 2003, L 86/23.

ceptance or at any time thereafter, notify "the depositary of the *recommended practice(s)* in respect of which it enters reservations" (emphasis added).[135] If they notify the depositary and indicate the date on which this withdrawal will take effect, parties may withdraw these reservations in whole or in part. Paragraph 3 furthermore provides,

> "Each Contracting Party bound by a specific annex or chapter(s) therein shall examine the possibility of withdrawing any reservations to the recommended practices entered under the terms of paragraph 2 and notify the Secretary General of the Council of the results of that review at the end of every three-year period commencing from the date of the entry into force of this Convention for that Contracting Party, specifying the provisions of its national legislation which, in its opinion, are contrary to the withdrawal of the reservations".[136]

It was pointed out earlier that the subject of reservations remains a highly contentious issue under international law. This contention does not limit itself to agreements between states, but is also present in the case of international agreements involving the participation of international organisations. The diverse nature of international organisations and their corresponding, internal rules can add to the uncertainties surrounding reservations. Mixed agreements in particular have the potential to render the matter even more complicated and contentious than it already is. This is determined by the unique manner in which the Community and the Member States share competence and, correspondingly, participate in international agreements.

Article 2(1)(d) of the 1969 and the 1986 Vienna Conventions defines a reservation as a unilateral statement, however phrased or named, made by a state or international organisation at the time of the signing, ratification, approval, or accession to an international agreement and which has the object to exclude or modify the legal effects of certain provisions of that international agreement. Reservations are generally seen as an incident to the conclusion of international agreements. General reservations are, therefore, explicitly excluded in the various multilateral agreements.

There are certain occasions where the international agreement permits certain types of reservations. If the agreement is silent on the matter, parties are permitted to enter reservations, provided these reservations are compatible with the 'ob-

[135] The seventh recital of the preamble to Council Decision 2003/231/EC concerning the accession of the European Community to the Kyoto Convention, OJ 2003, L 86/21, indicates that the Community is initially to accede only to the Convention and the Appendices I and II. Accession to the revised annexes contained in Appendix III is to take place at a later date. Article 1 of the Council Decision confirms this.

[136] Article XIV of the Convention on the Conservation of Migratory Species of Wild Animals, OJ 1982, L 210/11, also prohibits general reservations, but allows for the entry of specific reservations in accordance with the provisions of Article XIV and XI. These reservations have to do with Appendixes I and II to the Convention.

ject and purpose' of the agreement.[137] Where an international agreement expressly permits the entry of reservations, parties to the agreement are bound to accept the reservation, unless they can prove that the proposed reservation exceeds the actual authorization. In those instances where the international agreement is silent on the matter of reservations, it is up to each contracting party to decide whether it will accept or not a proposed reservation. The legal effects of the parts of the agreement that are the subject of the reservation will be nullified or modified only as between the party that has entered the reservation and the parties that have accepted it.[138]

Although it is up to the Community and the Member States to decide who will become a party to the agreement[139], the refusal by one or more Member States or some specific Member State(s) to ratify the agreement could be interpreted by the other contracting party as a *de facto* reservation.[140] This would be the case where the participation of all the Member States in the agreement is essential in order to achieve the full effects of the agreement. Examples are certain environmental agreements, such as the Vienna Convention for the Protection of the Ozone Layer[141] and the Agreement on the international conservation programme[142] or certain restricted international agreements.[143]

The non-participation of one or more Member States is likely, and in certain cases even bound, to modify the (territorial) application of the agreement or even its effect. Although the Member State is bound by Community law, Article 10 EC, to undertake al the necessary steps to assist the Community in carrying out its obligation under the agreement, its non-participation means that it itself is not bound, as a party, by the agreement. The Member State does not have to engage in any activity corresponding to those of a contracting party in order to put into effect the provisions of the international agreement. This point can best be illustrated by the following example. Article 20 of the United Nations Convention to combat desertification[144] requires parties to the Convention to contribute adequate financial resources for the financing of the Convention. Member States of the Community that are not parties to the Convention are under no obligation to contribute such financial resources. They would have to assist the Community,

---

[137] Article 19 of the 1969 and 1986 Vienna Conventions.

[138] See also P. Reuter, *supra* note 51, at 82-84.

[139] International agreements frequently contain a provision permitting that a regional economic integration organisation, either alone or jointly with its member states, can become a party. Examples include Article 25 of the Rotterdam Convention, OJ 2003, L 63/29. Furthermore, Article 19 of the 1986 Vienna Convention provides that the participation of an international organisation in an international agreement is governed by the rules of the organisation.

[140] P. Allott, 'Adherence To and Withdrawal From Mixed Agreements' in H.G. Schermers and D. O'Keeffe, *Mixed Agreements* (1983), at 111.

[141] 26 *I.L.M.* (1987), at 1529.

[142] OJ 1999, L 132/3.

[143] For example, the Convention on the Conservation and Management of Fishery Resources in the South-East Atlantic Ocean, OJ 2002, L 234/40.

[144] OJ 1998, L 83/3.

though, to meet its financial obligations. At the same time they would be entitled to have a share of the funds attributed to the Community as a result of its participation in the agreement.

Even declarations issued at the time of the signing or ratification of the agreement concerning the division of competence between the Member States and the Community could arguably have the effect of a reservation. The Community declaration usually makes reference to the changing internal situation of the Community. As long as this is the purpose of the declaration, there should be no risk that it can be misinterpreted. The situation changes when the Community makes an interpretive declaration.[145] Interpretive declarations made by a contracting party, usually at the time of signature or ratification, are often used as a reservation.[146] To avoid such an effect, international agreements frequently contain provisions expressly prohibiting reservations, but also the use of interpretive declarations that can have such an effect.[147]

The Community's competence is never fixed, unless it is non-existent or exclusive. The gradual transferral of competence from the Member States to the European Community, sometimes as a result of a judgement of the European Court of Justice, implies a direct modification of the legal obligations of the Community and the Member States. Where the European Community and the Member States are seen and treated as one, there is no complication. But where they act separately, the transfer of competence can have legal effects similar to a reservation. It is not unusual that mixed agreements contain a provision requiring the Community and the Member States to notify the depositary of the agreement on all changes in competence that may occur as a result of the internal workings of the Community.[148]

Temple Lang argues that the notification of changes concerning the international organisation's competence is only relevant to the other contracting parties to the extent that these changes entail a change in the obligations undertaken.[149]

---

[145] Shaw makes a distinction between mere interpretive declarations and qualified interpretive declarations. The latter can constitute a reservation. M.N. Shaw, *International Law* (2003), at 822-825.

[146] A. Aust, *supra* note 13, at 101-103.

[147] Article 42 of the United Nations Convention relating to the conservation and management of straddling stocks, OJ 1998, L 18916, prohibits reservations and exceptions to the Agreement. Article 43 provides that "Article 42 does not preclude a State or entity, when signing, ratifying or acceding to this Agreement, from making declarations or statements, however phrased or named, with a view, *inter alia*, to the harmonisation of its laws and regulations with the provisions of this Agreement, provided that such declarations or statements do not purport to exclude or modify the legal effect of the provisions of this Agreement in their application to that State or entity".

[148] Article 34(3) of the United Nations Convention to combat desertification, OJ 1998, L 83/3, provides that "They, regional economic integration organisations, shall also promptly inform the Depositary, who shall in turn inform the parties, of any substantial modification in the extent of their competence". A similar provision can be found in Article 29(4) of the Convention on the Transboundary Effects of Industrial Accidents, OJ 1998, L 326/5.

[149] J. Temple Lang, *supra* note 3, at 171-175

He points out that a modification of competence does not necessarily correspond with any given provision of the international agreement at issue. What the other parties, therefore, want to know is not the extent of the Community's competence *per se*, but rather 'the extent of the obligations undertaken'. The parties want the assurance that the European Community, one or more Member States, or the Community and one or more Member States acting together accept all the obligations enshrined in the agreement. No obligation may be left without any of the parties on the Community side being bound to carry it out.[150]

Therefore, where a modification in the division of competence between the Community and the Member States can result in it not being clear whether some or certain obligations are accepted and will be carried out by the Community and/or (some of) the Member States, this could be qualified as a *de facto* reservation. As mentioned before, it is a standard requirement that the depositary, and the other contracting parties, is immediately notified of any changes concerning the internal division of competence between the European Community and its Members.[151]

Another issue worth looking into is whether the Community or the Member States can reject an authorized reservation entered by one or more Member States or the Community. Technically speaking this is possible. The rules of international treaty law apply to the Community and the Member States as they do to any other party. However, the European Community's and Member States' behaviour is also governed by the internal rules of the Community, Article 10 EC. These rules have an overriding character in this matter.

Where the Community and the Member States hold parallel powers, the refusal by either to accept a reservation entered by the other would not have direct legal consequences for their joint participation in the agreement. The consequence would be that the agreement would not apply between these parties. This would create a rather awkward reality between them, but there would be no breach of Community law. As long as the resulting contractual situation does not carry any negative consequences for the functioning of the Community system and the Community is able to perform all its corresponding obligations under the agreement, there would be no breach of Article 10 EC.

In the case of concurrent competence it is not possible for the European Community and the Member States to make non-identical reservations or refuse to accept each other's reservation.[152] Not only there is the risk that the reservation will be made with regard to matters that fall under the competence of the other, but

[150] *Ibid.*

[151] This does not mean that all modifications must be notified. Only to the extent that the modifications can have a direct bearing on who is responsible for the performing of the obligations must these changes be notified.

[152] Rosas argues that reservations and objections to reservations would be 'highly problematic' without Community coordination. He says that Member States may not enter into reservations or object to reservations to parts of the agreement that come within the Community's exclusive competence. A. Rosas, *supra* note 102, at 211.

this reality will in all likelihood undermine the unity of the external representation of the Community.[153] The conclusion has to be that it flows directly from Article 10 EC, and the case-law of the Court of Justice, that it is not possible for the Community and the Member States to enter separate reservations that are not accepted by the other or enter reservations with regard to matters not within the scope of their respective competence.

Furthermore, where the Community accedes to an international agreement to which one or more Member States are a party, it has to accept all reservations made or accepted by the Member States. Where such reservations already exist between Member States, they will, in accordance with Article 307 EC, have to make the necessary changes to allow the Community to become a party to the agreement without compromising the internal functioning of the Community and allow the Community to achieve its goals.

The same principle applies where a candidate Member State accedes to the European Union. Article 307 EC obliges the new Member State and the European Community, among others, to take all necessary steps to eliminate any and all obstacles to their joint participation in international agreements. Of course these changes depend on the willingness of the other contracting parties to accept them. It was stipulated, however, that these parties are primarily interested in obtaining assurances that the accepted responsibilities will be carried out, and less about the exact division of competence between the Community and the Member States. Changes that (will) enhance this guarantee will usually be accepted without any objection.

4.6 Entry into force of mixed agreements

In principle, the entry into force of mixed international agreements is similar to the entry into force of any other international agreement. International treaty law provides that it is up to the parties to the agreement to stipulate the conditions for the entry into force of the agreement. In the absence of any express reference to the entry into force of the international agreement, international treaty law, and more specifically Article 24 of the 1969 and the 1986 Vienna Conventions, provides that the agreement will enter into force as soon as the consent to be bound of all parties involved has been achieved.

It was stated that in international law the conclusion of international agreements is the closest thing to a legislative process. But where national laws are binding on all parties irrespective of whether they agree with the law, international agreements are only binding on the parties that have expressed their consent to be bound. It is, therefore, imperative that the parties to an agreement know when the agreement has entered into force and thus when they become bound by its provisions.

[153] *Ibid.*

Article 58(1) of the International Cocoa Agreement 2001[154] provides that

> "This Agreement shall enter into force definitively on 1 October 2003, or any time thereafter, if by such date governments representing at least five exporting countries accounting for at least 80% of the total exports of countries listed in Annex A and governments representing importing countries having at least 60% of total imports as set out in Annex B have deposited their instruments of ratification, acceptance, approval or accession with the depositary. It shall also enter into force definitively once it has entered into force provisionally and these percentages requirements are satisfied by the deposit of instruments of ratification, approval or accession".

Article 25(1) of the Kyoto Protocol[155] stipulates that

> "This Protocol shall enter into force on the ninetieth day after the date on which not less than 55 Parties to the Convention, incorporating Parties included in Annex I which accounted in total for at least 55 per cent of the total carbon dioxide emissions for 1990 of the Parties included in Annex I, have deposited their instruments of ratification, acceptance, approval or accession".

Paragraph 4 of the same Article states that

> "For the purposes of this Article, any instrument deposited by a regional economic integration organisation shall not be counted as additional to those deposited by States members of the organization".

Article 36(1) of the United Nations Convention to combat desertification[156] provides that:

> "The Convention shall enter into force on the 90th day after the date of deposit of the 50th instrument of ratification, acceptance, approval or accession".

Paragraph 3 further adds that

> "For the purposes of paragraphs 1 and 2, any instrument deposited by a regional economic integration organisation shall not be counted as additional to those deposited by States members of the organisation".

Article 27 of the Convention on the Conservation and Management of Fishery Resources in the South-East Atlantic Ocean[157] stipulates that

---

[154] OJ 2002, L 342/2.
[155] OJ 2002, L 130/4.
[156] OJ 1998, L 83/3.
[157] OJ 2002, L 234/40.

> "This Convention shall enter into force 60 days after the date of deposit with the Depositary of the third instrument of ratification, accession, acceptance or approval at least one of which has been deposited by a coastal State. For each State or regional economic integration organisation, which, subsequent to the date of entry into force of this Convention, deposits an instrument of ratification or accession, this Convention shall enter into force on the 30th day following such deposit".

Paragraph 1 of Article 40 of the Agreement relating to the conservation and management of straddling stocks[158] provides that

> "This Agreement shall enter into force 30 days after the date of deposit of the 30th instrument of ratification or accession".

Article 18(1) of the Kyoto Convention[159] states that

> "This Convention shall enter into force three months after five of the entities referred to in paragraphs 1 and 5 of Article 8 thereof have signed the Convention without reservation of ratification or have deposited their instruments of ratification or accession".

Analysis of these and similar provisions in other multilateral agreements provides the following conclusions. First of all, all these agreements make express reference to the entry into force of the same. The importance of the agreement may require a high number of ratifications[160] or that specific states ratify the agreement before they enter into force.[161] Furthermore, there are a number of multilateral agreements that accept the instrument of ratification or accession of the European Community and other regional economic integration organisations as one of the instruments required for the entry into force of the agreement.[162]

In some cases it is provided that instruments of the organisations will not be counted in addition to the instrument of the member states. These agreements usually permit that the organisation can become a party to the agreement without any of its members. The provisions must thus be read as meaning that if none of the members of the organisation has ratified the agreement by the time the minimum number of ratifications has been achieved, the ratification of the organisation will just be counted as one of the ratifications required for the entry into force of the agreement. If the required number of ratications has not been achieved yet, and one of the member states of the organisation ratifies the agreement, the ratification of the organisation will no longer be counted as one of the ratifications necessary for the entry into force of the agreement.

---

[158] OJ 1998, L 189/16.

[159] OJ 2003, L 86/23.

[160] For example, the United Nations Convention to combat desertification requires the deposit of 50 instruments of ratification to enter into force (Article 36(1).

[161] Examples include the International Cocoa Agreement 2001 and the Convention on the Conservation and Management of Fishery Resources in the South-East Atlantic Ocean.

[162] For example, the Kyoto Convention.

In the case of bilateral agreements the following examples can de cited. Article 129(3) of the Agreement on the European Economic Area, EEA,[163] provides that

> "This Agreement shall enter into force on 1 January 1993, provided that all Contracting Parties have deposited their instruments of ratification or approval before that date. After that date this Agreement shall enter into force on the first day of the second month following the last notification. The final date for such a notification shall be 30 June 1993. After that date the Contracting Parties shall convene a diplomatic conference to appreciate the purpose".

The second paragraph of Article 112 of the Agreement on Partnership and Cooperation between the European Communities and their Member States and the Russian Federation[164] stipulates that

> "This Agreement shall enter into force on the first day of the second month following the date on which the Parties notify each other that the procedures referred to in the first paragraph have been completed".

Article 93(3) of the ACP-EC partnership Agreement[165] determines that

> "This Agreement shall enter into force on the first day of the second month following the date of deposit of the instruments of ratification of the Member States and of at least two-thirds of the ACP States, and of the instrument of approval of this Agreement by the Community".

Article 6 of the Protocol adjusting the Europe Agreement between the EC and its Member States and the Republic of Latvia on account of the accession of Austria, Finland and Sweden to the European Union[166] stipulates that

> "This Protocol shall be approved by the Community and Latvia in accordance with their own procedures. The Contracting Parties shall take the necessary measures to implement this Protocol".

And Article 7 of the same Protocol furthermore provides that

> "This Protocol shall enter into force on the first day of the second month following notification of the completion of the procedures referred to in Article 6 by the contracting parties".

---

[163] OJ 1994, L 1/3.
[164] OJ 1997, L 327/3.
[165] OJ 2000, L 317/1.
[166] OJ 1999, L 317/3.

Article 34(3) of the Interregional Framework Cooperation Agreement between the European Community and its Member States and the Southern Cone Common Market[167] and its member countries determines that

> "This Agreement shall enter into force on the first day of the month following that in which the Parties notify each other of the completion of the procedures necessary for this purpose".

As with the conclusion of mixed multilateral international agreements, the entry into force of these bilateral agreements does not take into consideration the specific internal intricacies of the Community, nor should it. Other parties will be unwilling to enter into any treaty obligation if this were the case.[168] The general rule is that the bilateral agreements enter into force on the first day of either the first or second month following notification of completion of the internal procedures necessary for the ratification or approval of the agreement. With the exception of the Cotonou Agreement, that requires that at least two-thirds of the ACP countries must have ratified the Agreement, mixed bilateral agreements enter into force after all parties concerned have ratified them. On the Community side this means the Community and all the Member States concerned.[169]

This bilateral practice is in sharp contrast to the multilateral setting. What usually happens, and this should be deplored, is that the position of the Community in a multilateral setting is usually a disadvantageous one. Its position is defined in relation to that of its Member States and not as an independent entity endowed with competences separate from the Member States.

Once the minimum number of ratifications has been met, the agreement will enter into force. Interesting for the contracting parties is who on the side of the Community and the Member States has ratified the agreement. If it is the Community alone, then it will assume all obligations and rights embodied in the agreement. If only one or more of the Member States have ratified the agreement, it/they will each be a contracting party assuming individually the full range of ob-

[167] Also known as Mercosur (in Spanish), or Mercosul (in Portuguese), consisting of Brazil, Argentina, Paraguay and Uruguay. Chile and Bolivia are associate members.

[168] This might be the case with some bilateral agreements. A common feature in the Europe Agreements, the EEA Agreement and the Lomé and Cotonou Conventions is the dominant role played by the European Community. Although this dominance does not apply to the actual ratification process, it cannot be said that the Community and its Member States are equal partners of the other contracting parties.

[169] It is standard practice to mention explicitly in the bilateral agreement the Member States of the European Community that will become a party to the agreement. In the case of the ACP-EC Partnership Agreement the Member States are not mentioned explicitly. But Article 100 of the Agreement mentions that the Agreement is "drawn up in two copies in the Danish, Dutch, English, Finnish, French, German, Greek, Italian, Portuguese, Spanish and Swedish languages, all texts being equally authentic". These authentic languages corresponded to all the official languages of the Community at that time. Therefore, the conclusion is that all the Member States of the Community had to become a party to the Agreement.

ligations and rights that are enshrined in the agreement. If the European Community and one or more of the Member States have ratified the agreement, they will collectively assume the obligations embodied in the agreement and collectively be entitled to the rights provided for in the agreement. As indicated before, a number of international agreements require that the Community and the Member States issue a declaration outlining the extent of each party's competence and corresponding acceptance of obligations under the agreement. And in some instances, any change in this division of competence must also be notified to the depositary. Such a practice denies the Community its position as a subject of international law alongside states and entitled to exercise the full range of its competences at international level.

4.6.1 **Article 18 of the Vienna Conventions**

Article 18 of the 1969 and 1986 Vienna Conventions, which constitutes a rule of customary international treaty law[170], is of particular importance in the case of mixed agreements. The article provides that

> "A State or international organisation is obliged to refrain from acts which would defeat the object and purpose of a treaty when:
>
> (a) that State or that organisation has signed the treaty or has exchanged instruments constituting the treaty subject to ratification, act of formal confirmation, acceptance or approval, until that State or that organisation shall have made its intention clear not to become a party to the treaty; or
>
> (b) that State or that organisation has expressed its consent to be bound by the treaty, pending the entry into force of the treaty and provided that such entry into force is not unduly delayed".

It can be argued that Article 18 of the Vienna Conventions complements at international level what Article 10 EC does at the internal, Community, level. The European Court of Justice has consistently held that, where by reason of the internal division of competence it is necessary that the Community and the Member States become a party to an international agreement, they must act together with regard to every aspect of the international agreement.[171] This joint action is necessary to preserve the unity of the external representation of the Community.

This means that the Member States must support the Community in its efforts to negotiate, conclude and implement international agreements, where such agreements are necessary for the achievement of the objectives of the European

[170] D.J. Harris, *Cases and Materials on International Law* (1991), at 750.

[171] Ruling 1/78, *Draft IAEA Convention*, [1978] ECR 2151; Opinion 1/78, *Natural Rubber*, [1979] ECR 2871; Opinion 2/91, *ILO*, [1993] ECR I-1061; Opinion 1/94, *WTO*, [1994] ECR I-5267 and Opinion 2/00, *Cartagena Protocol on Biosafety*, [2001] ECR I-9717.

Community. Even if parts of the agreement come under the exclusive competence of the Member States they must undertake all the necessary steps to assist the Community in meeting its obligations with regard to the issues coming under the Community's exclusive competence. This also means that when the Community and one or more Member States have signed an international agreement the Community and the Member States must refrain from any action that would defeat the object and purpose of the agreement.

The rule of customary international law embodied in Article 18 of both Vienna Conventions requires that states and international organisations refrain from all acts that would defeat the 'object and purpose' of the agreement prior to its entry into force. This obligation applies where the state or international organisation has signed the agreement, but not yet ratified or acceded to the agreement and consent to be bound is subject to ratification or accession (paragraph 1). It equally applies when a state or organisation has expressed its consent to be bound, but the agreement has not yet entered into force and the entry into force is not unduly delayed (paragraph 2). The precise scope of this provision is unclear but it means at least that the state or international organisation must refrain from those acts that would affect its ability to fully comply with the provisions of the international agreement.[172] This obligation remains in effect until the state or organisation concerned ratifies the agreement or indicates that it does not intend to become a party to the agreement.

In the *Opel Austria* Case[173] the Court of First Instance made an explicit reference to the principle embodied in Article 18 of the Vienna Conventions.[174] The case involved a direct challenge to a Council Regulation imposing a countervailing duty on the import of car parts produced by Opel in Austria.[175] The Regulation had been adopted after the Community had ratified the EEA Agreement but before it had entered into force.

The Court of First Instance started out by providing that the principle of good faith embodied in Article 18 of the Vienna Conventions constitutes a rule of customary international law and was therefore binding on the Community (paragraph 90). But rather than looking at the precise application of the principle as outlined in international law, the Court moved from international law to Community law. It held that the prohibition not to act in violation of the object and purpose of a signed agreement was the equivalent of the Community principle concerning the protection of legitimate expectations rather than the other way around (paragraphs 94-95). As a result the Council Regulation was not annulled

---

[172] A. Aust, *supra* note 13, at 93-95.

[173] Case T-115/94, [1997] ECR II-39.

[174] See P.J. Kuijper, The Court and the Tribunal of the EC and the Vienna Convention on the Law of Treaties 1969 in *LIEI* 1998/1, at 13-16 and C. Timmermans, The EU and Public International Law in 4 *E.F.A. Rev.* (1999), at 191-193.

[175] Council Regulation 3697/93, OJ 1993, L 343/1.

because it violated a principle of international law, but because it violated a general principle of Community law.

Although the case was eventually settled on the basis of Community law and it involved a situation whereby the Community had already ratified the EEA Agreement and the date of its entry into force was known, the Court of First Instance has made it clear that the principle of good faith is binding on the Community. As a rule of (customary) international treaty law it is also binding on the Member States. The case involved actions by a Community institution, namely, the Council. All Community institutions must refrain from actions that can result in a defeat of the object and purpose of any of the agreements the Community has signed, but not yet ratified.

Article 300(7) EC provides that an agreement, to which the Community is a party, is binding on the institutions. The principle applies *mutatis mutandis* to an agreement signed but not yet concluded. This puts the European Community's advisory procedure in a specific position. The Court of Justice is barred from interpreting an international agreement in such a manner that its Advisory Opinion could be qualified as a defeat of the object and purpose of the agreement (Article 10 EC). But because the Court's Opinion is dependent on the questions put before it by the institutions or the Member States, these must also refrain from asking such questions that could result in an Opinion from the Court that is contrary to the object and purpose of the agreement.[176] The subject of the interpretation of international agreements by the Court of Justice and the Court of First Instance will be dealt with in the next chapter.

Within the Community context there are two distinct ways in which the principle embodied in Article 18 of the Vienna Conventions can be involved. The first has to do with the Community and the Member States as signatories of an international agreement. It has already been pointed out that both the case-law of the Court of Justice and Article 10 EC leave no doubt as to the Community's and Member States' obligation to act together to preserve the unity of the external representation of the Community. This means that the Community, and the Member States that have signed the agreement, must refrain from actions that would defeat the object and purpose of the agreement. Although in this case there will be a direct reference to Article 10 EC, the international law principle of good faith is equally applicable.

The second element concerns a situation in which the Community has signed an international agreement, but frustrates the object and purpose of the agreement as a direct result of the action of one or more Member States that have no intention to sign or ratify the agreement. This would be the case if the Member State(s) concerned block(s) the decision within the Council resulting in an unnecessary delay of the ratification process. Although Community law, in particular the Articles 226 and 227 EC, provides the Commission and the other Member States with the tools to take legal actions against the Member State(s) involved,

[176] Of course, the European Court of Justice is not obliged to answer the questions put before it where it ascertains that it would be improper or contrary to Community law or international law to answer the questions.

this will not alter the fact that the Community will be in breach of its international obligations.

4.7 Application of mixed agreements

4.7.1 Territorial application of mixed agreements

The general rule of international treaty law is that unless the parties to an international agreement make an express statement indicating a different intention, an international agreement is binding upon each party in respect of its entire territory.[177] Philip Allott points out that it can be argued that 'the problem of partial participation in mixed agreements is analogous to the problem of the territorial application of treaties'.[178] For indeed, a Member State may decide to refrain from ratifying an international agreement, and therefore not be bound by its provisions on the basis of international law, but having the agreement still being applied to it because the European Community is a party to the agreement.[179] This may cause problems in the actual implementation of the agreement.

The problem is that Member States that are not a party to an international agreement, to which the Community is a party, will also be entitled to the rights embodied in the agreement. However, as a rule of international law, third parties derive neither rights nor obligations from an international agreement to which they are not a party.[180] In the case of mixed agreements this principle does not apply, because Member States can never really be seen as a third party. Although the Member State may decide not to become a party to the actual agreement, its involvement in the Community process eliminates any recourse to the third party principle embodied in Article 34 of the Vienna Conventions.[181] Still, not all international agreements require that they be given legal effect in the territory of the contracting parties. But where such territorial application is necessary the aforementioned problems may arise.

There are two ways that parties can pursue to circumvent any problem arising of the non-participation of Member States in an international agreement. The first is by limiting the rights of non-participating Member States. An example is the 1982 United Nations Law of The Sea Convention.[182] Article 4(5) provides that

> "Participation of such an international organisation shall in no case confer any rights under this Convention on Member States of the organisation which are not State Parties to this Convention."

---

[177] Article 29 of the 1969 and 1986 Vienna Conventions. See also M.N. Shaw, *supra* note 145, at 650-651.

[178] P. Allott, *supra* note 140, at 115.

[179] Article 300(7) EC.

[180] Article 34 of the 1969 and 1986 Vienna Conventions.

[181] Article 34 of the 1986 Vienna Convention provides, "A treaty does not create either obligations or rights for a third State or a third organisation without the consent of that State or that organisation".

[182] 21 *I.L.M.* (1982), at 1261.

The precise scope of this provision is unclear. If a Member State of an international organisation, such as the European Community, has to undertake certain obligations to guarantee the full effect of the agreements, should it not be entitled to reap the benefits of its association with that organisation? It cannot be argued that the Member States should also become a party to all mixed agreements. There are some instances where this is simply not feasible.[183]

The second way to solve the problem, and this solution is more commonly used, is to limit the territorial application of the agreement altogether. The added benefit of this solution is that it takes into account the problem of the territorial scope of an international organisation. Article 29 of the 1986 Vienna Convention clearly establishes that the concept of territory and territorial application is directly connected with states. Because the Community is neither a state nor a traditional international organisation, the use of provisions defining the territorial application of agreements to which it is a party, therefore, becomes very meaningful.[184]

Looking at the Community practice the following conclusion can be drawn. All mixed bilateral agreements contain provisions regarding their territorial application. The general rule is that the international agreement applies to the territories in which the EC Treaty applies and under the conditions specified in the Treaty.[185] Some agreements may contain additional clauses, but this is the standard formula.

Examples include Article 121 of the Europe Agreement with the Slovak Republic[186], which provides that

> "This Agreement shall apply, on the one hand, to the territories in which the Treaties establishing the European Economic Community, the European Atomic Energy Community, and the European Coal and Steel Community are applied and under the conditions laid down in those Treaties and, on the other hand, to the territory of the Slovak Republic".

Article 33 of the Interregional framework cooperation Agreement with the Southern Cone Common Market[187] stipulates that

> "This Agreement shall apply, on the one hand, to the territories in which the Treaty establishing the European Community is applied and under the conditions laid down in that Treaty and, on the other hand, to the territories in which the Treaty establishing the Southern Common Market is applied under the conditions laid down in that Treaty and its additional protocols".

---

[183] See also C-D. Ehlermann, 'Mixed Agreements: A list of Problems' in H.G. Schermers and D. O'Keeffe (eds.), *Mixed Agreements* (1983), at 12-13.

[184] See P. Manin, *supra* note 34, at 478-479.

[185] The conditions can be found in Article 299 EC.

[186] OJ 1994, L 359/2.

[187] OJ 1996, L 69/4.

Article 92 of the ACP-EC Partnership Agreement[188] states that

> "Subject to the special provisions regarding the relations between the ACP States and the French overseas departments provided for therein, this Agreement shall apply, on the one hand, to the territories in which the Treaty establishing the European Community is applied and under the conditions laid down in that Treaty and, on the other hand, to the territories of the ACP States".

Article 126(1) of the original EEA Agreement provides that the Agreement applies to the territories to which the EC and the ECSC Treaties apply and under the conditions laid down in these Treaties and to the territories of the Republics of Austria, Finland and Iceland, and the Principality of Liechtenstein, the Kingdoms of Norway and Sweden, and the Swiss Confederation.[189]

In the case of multilateral mixed agreements the practice is more diverse. In some instances the agreement itself will have provisions concerning the territorial application of the agreement and in other instances the Council Decision concluding the agreement will limit the territorial application of the agreement[190] or the Community will issue a declaration limiting the territorial application of the agreement.[191]

Article 10(1) of the Kyoto Convention[192] provides that

> "Any Contracting Party may, at the time of signing this Convention without reservation of ratification or of depositing its instrument of ratification or accession, or at any time thereafter, declare by notification given to the depositary that this Convention shall extend to all or any of the territories for whose international relations it is responsible. Such notification shall take effect three months after the date of receipt thereof by the depositary. However, this Convention shall not apply to the territories named in the notification before this Convention has entered into force for the Contracting Party concerned".

Article 4 of the Convention on the Conservation and Management of Fishery Resources in the South-East Atlantic Ocean states that

> "Except as otherwise provided, this Convention applies within the Convention area, being all waters beyond areas of national jurisdiction in the area bound by a line joining the following points along parallels of latitude and meridians of longitude:

---

188 OJ 2000, L 317/1.

189 OJ 1994, L 1/3. The Protocol Adjusting the Agreement on the European Economic Area amended this Agreement, OJ 1994, L 1/572.

190 An example is Article 1(3) of Council Decision 2002/971/EC authorizing the Member States to ratify or accede to the HNS Convention, OJ 2002, L 337/55, which excludes Denmark.

191 See the Community Notification to the Secretary General of the Customs Cooperation Council adopted in accordance with Article 11 of the Revised Kyoto Convention. OJ 2003, L 71 E/56.

192 OJ 2003, L86/23.

– beginning at the outer limit of waters under national jurisdiction at a point 6º south, thence due west along the 6º south parallel to the meridian 10º west, thence due north along the 10º west meridian to the equator, thence due west along the equator to the meridian 20º west, thence due south along the 20º west meridian to a parallel 50º south, thence due east along the 50º south parallel to the meridian 30º east, thence due north along the 30º east meridian to the coast of the African continent".

Article 3(1) of the Agreement relating to the conservation and management of straddling stocks and highly migratory fish stocks[193] stipulates that

"Unless otherwise provided, this Agreement applies to the conservation and management of straddling fish stocks and highly migratory fish stocks beyond areas under national jurisdiction, except that Articles 6 and 7 apply also to the conservation and management of such stocks within areas under national jurisdiction, subject to the different legal regimes that apply within areas under national jurisdiction and in areas beyond national jurisdiction as provided for in the Convention".

Article V(1) of the Convention on the conservation of migratory species of wild animals[194] provides that

"The object of each Agreement shall be to restore the migratory species concerned to a favourable conservation status or to maintain it in such a status. Each Agreement should deal with those aspects of the conservation and management of the migratory species concerned which serve to achieve that object".

And paragraph 2 of the same Article states that

"Each Agreement should cover the whole of the range of the migratory species concerned and should be open to accession by all Range States of that species, whether or not they are Parties to this Convention".

Article 2 of the Convention for the prevention of marine pollution from land-based sources[195] stipulates that

"The present convention shall apply to the maritime area within the following limits:

(a) those parts of the Atlantic and Arctic Oceans and the dependent seas which lie north of 36º north latitude and between 42º west longitude and 51º east longitude, but excluding:

(i) the Baltic Sea and Belts lying to the south and east of lines drawn from Hasenore Head to Gniben Point, from Korshage to Spodbjerg and from Gilbjerg to Kullen and

[193] OJ 1998, L 189/16.
[194] OJ 1982, L 210/11.
[195] OJ 1975, L 194/6.

(ii) the Mediterranean Sea and its dependent seas as far as the point of intersection of the parallel of 36º north latitude and the meridian of 5º36' west longitude;

(b) that part of the Atlantic Ocean north of 59º north latitude and between 44º west longitude and 42º west longitude".

Article XIII of the Agreement establishing the General Fisheries Commission for the Mediterranean states that

> "The members of the Commission shall, when accepting this Agreement, state explicitly to which territories their participation shall extend. In the absence of such a declaration, participation shall be deemed to apply to all the territories for the international relations of which the member is responsible. Subject to the provisions of Article XIV, the scope of territorial application may be modified by a subsequent declaration".[196]

Although a general conclusion with regard to the territorial application of mixed agreements cannot be drawn, it can be argued that whereas mixed bilateral agreements usually make reference to the territories to which the EC Treaties apply, in general multilateral agreements do not. The latter has more to do with the subject matter of the multilateral agreements than with any other consideration on the part of the other contracting parties.[197]

4.7.2 **Successive mixed agreements**

The subject of successive agreements was dealt with in Section 3.6.3 of the preceding Chapter. The analysis concerned successive international agreements to which the Community alone became a party. Mixed agreements follow a similar pattern. The difference being that on the European side the Community and the Member States are the contracting parties.

The various modalities that could occur are that (a) the Community and (some or all of) the Member states conclude a successive agreement with the same parties (some or all) the Member States had concluded an earlier agreement with; (b) the Community and (some or all of) the Member States conclude an agreement with some of the original contracting parties; (c) the Community, (some or all of) the Member States and (some or all of) the new Member States sign an agree-

---

[196] Although the Community and the Member States have not issued a declaration concerning the territorial application of this Agreement, the provisions of Article XIII are unlikely to be the source of any controversy. The Community and the Member States have issued a Single declaration on the exercise of the competence and voting rights according to Article II(6) of the General Fisheries Commission for the Mediterranean states Agreement, OJ 1998, L 190/36. This Single declaration stipulates the areas in which the Community and the Member States, respectively, have an exclusive competence and the areas where there is a shared competence and who has the voting rights. In line with the AETR judgement, the party that possesses the internal competence also possesses the external competence.

[197] See also *supra* Section 3.6.2.

ment with the same parties to a previous agreement; (d) the Community, (some or all of) the Member States and (some or all of) the new Member States conclude an agreement with some of the parties to the previous agreement.

Similar to the situation in which the European Community assumes the exclusive internal competence, in the case of sub (a), parties will be aware that the Community has assumed part of the internal competence in a given area. In the case of multilateral agreements, the contracting parties will most likely require that the Community and the Member States issue a declaration stipulating the precise limits of the Community's competence. In accordance with the paragraphs 2 and 3 of Article 30 of the Vienna Conventions the parties will determine the compatibility of the two agreements. A similar conclusion applies to sub (c).

In the case of sub (b) the original agreement will remain in force with regard to the Member States and the contracting parties of the original agreement that have not become a party to the new agreement. Article 30 of the 1969 Vienna Convention will govern their contractual relationship to the extent that they are a party to the Convention or customary international law in the event that they are not a party to the 1969 Vienna Convention. The new agreement will apply between the Community, the Member States that have become a party to the new agreement, and the other contracting parties that have also ratified the new agreement. Either the 1969 Vienna Convention or customary international law will govern the contractual relationship. This analysis applies, *mutatis mutandis*, to sub (d). In the event of an incompatibility between the two agreements, Article 307 EC obliges the Community and the Member States to undertake all necessary steps to eliminate these incompatibilities.[198]

4.8 Invalidity, termination and suspension of mixed agreements

International agreements that have entered into force are governed by the principle of *pacta sunt servanda*.[199] This means that the parties that have consented to be bound by the agreement must perform all duties embodied in the agreement and do so in good faith. Supplementing this principle is the rule that agreements that have entered into force will remain valid for the duration of the agreement.[200] Article 42 of both Vienna Conventions provides that the validity, continuance in force and of the consent to be bound can only be questioned on the basis of international (treaty) law.

The main rule is that an international agreement can only be suspended, terminated or denounced in accordance with express provisions provided for in the agreement. Unless the agreement expressly allows for the partial suspension or denunciation, the suspension or denunciation will affect the agreement as a

[198] See in this regard also Article 30(6) of the Vienna Conventions.

[199] Article 26 of the 1969 and 1986 Vienna Conventions.

[200] Article 42 of the 1969 and 1986 Vienna Conventions.

whole. In the absence of specific provisions governing the denunciation, termination or suspension of an international agreement, the rules of the Vienna Conventions or customary international law apply.

International agreements, both bilateral and multilateral, usually contain provisions regarding the termination of the agreement. Some agreements are automatically terminated after a certain period[201]; others terminate after a certain period but have provisions regarding the extension of the duration[202] and some agreements are concluded for an indefinite period of time.[203] Where international agreements contain no provision concerning their duration it is usually assumed that they are concluded for an indefinite period of time. Denunciation or withdrawal from such international agreements will only be possible where the parties intended this possibility or this right can be deduced from the provisions of the agreements.[204]

Similarly most agreements contain provisions concerning the denunciation or withdrawal from the same. Denunciation of a bilateral agreement automatically means that the agreement is terminated, whereas withdrawal from a multilateral agreement will not affect its continuing in force between the remaining parties. In some cases the agreement can be denounced at any time, but in general parties have to wait a certain time between the entry into force of the agreement for the party concerned and its withdrawal from the agreements.[205]

Contrary to termination and denunciation, international agreements rarely contain provisions concerning the (partial) suspension of the agreement. Agreements generally contain elaborate dispute settlement procedures that are specifically designed to avoid such unilateral actions. Furthermore, the legal effects of partial suspension of an agreement are to a certain extent similar to those of a reservation. And as pointed out earlier the possibility to make reservations to multilateral agreements is very rare in international treaty practice. Any party wishing to suspend an international agreement unilaterally will, therefore, have to do so in conformity with the general rules of international treaty law.

In any event the party wishing to suspend, terminate or denounce the agreement must state the reason for the alleged invalidity. The general rule is that international agreements are voidable, not void. This means that the agreement will

---

[201] Article 95(1) of the ACP-EC Partnership Agreement provides that the Agreement is 'concluded for a period of twenty years, commencing on 1 March 2000', OJ 2000, L 317/1.

[202] Article 106 of the EC-Russia Partnership Agreement stipulates that the Agreement will be in force for a period of ten years and it will be renewed automatically year by year unless either of the parties denounces it six months prior to its expiry, OJ 1997, L 327/3. Article 63 of the International Cocoa Agreement 2001 states that the Agreement will remain in force for five years after its entry into force unless it is extended in conformity with the procedure outlined in paragraph 3 or terminated earlier under paragraph 4, OJ 2002, L 342/2.

[203] See Article 34 of the Interregional framework cooperation Agreement between the European Community and the Southern Cone Common Market, OJ 1996, L 69/4.

[204] M.N. Shaw, *supra* note 145, at 845.

[205] Although there is no specific rule of thumb analysis shows that this period usually varies between 2 and 5 years.

remain in force until a party proves that a breach has occurred. The agreement will cease to apply from that moment on. Examples of such grounds include fraud, error, material breach and fundamental change of circumstances. However, in the case of coercion of a state or international organisation or conflict with an existing or emerging peremptory norm of international law the agreement is void.[206]

From a Community perspective the procedural rules governing the suspension of a mixed international agreement are the same rules that apply if the Community alone is a party to the agreement.[207] Their own constitutional provisions determine the procedural rules for the suspension, denunciation or termination of an agreement by the Member States. This is not to say, however, that each Member State can pursue its own course of action regardless of the other Member States or the Community. The Court's statement that the Community and the Member States must cooperate closely in the negotiation, conclusion and implementation of mixed agreement, also applies to the suspension, denunciation and termination of international agreements.

There are thus two sets of rules that apply where mixed agreements are concerned. The first set are the rules of international treaty law and the second the internal rules of the Community. International treaty law governs the suspension, denunciation and termination of international agreements. But where an agreement, or in the absence of express provisions to that extent, international treaty law permits the suspension, denunciation or termination of an international agreement, as a result of breach by one or more contracting parties, this does not automatically mean that either the Community or one or more Member States can suspend, denounce or terminate the application of the agreement.

Mixed agreements involve a shared competence between the Community and the Member States. If it concerns a case of parallel competences, it should be possible, in principle, for either the Community or one or more Member States to suspend, denounce or terminate unilaterally the part of the agreement that comes within their respective competence. Even so, the Community and the Member States prefer to act jointly. This is exactly what happened in the case of the 1983 Agreement between the European Community, the Member States and the Socialist Federal Republic of Yugoslavia. As a result of the ongoing conflict in the early 1990s, the Council adopted Regulation 3300/91/EC suspending the trade concessions granted to the Yugoslav Republic.[208] The Council's decision was preceded by a joint statement of the Community and the Member States of 4 October 1991, demanding that the breach of the cease-fire agreement signed the

---

[206] I. Brownlie, *Principles of Public International Law* (2003), at 590-591.

[207] Article 300(2) EC. The Council of Ministers will have to adopt an internal act authorizing the suspension or withdrawal from the agreement. It is not necessary, however, that the same legal basis as the one used for the conclusion of the agreement is used. See also I. MacLeod *et al*, *supra* note 3, at 163.

[208] OJ 1991, L315/1. The Council used Article 133 EC as the legal basis for its Decision.

same day be respected before midnight of 7 October 1991.[209] Failure to meet this demand would result in the termination of the existing agreement. Article 60 of the Agreement provided that the Agreement would remain in force for six months after a unilateral denunciation. To circumvent this restriction the Council decided to invoke the *clausula rebus sic stantibus* and the supervening impossibility to perform as the basis for the termination of the agreement.[210]

However, where the suspension could affect the object and purpose of the international agreement, because the parallel competences complement each other, suspension, denunciation or termination will have to be based on a mutual decision of the Community and the Member States. Not only would the unilateral suspension, denunciation or termination entail a breach of the international obligations, it would also be a breach of Community law, in particular Article 10 EC. In this case the Council's decision will have to be accompanied by a decision of the Representatives of the Member States meeting within the Council and both the Community and all the Member States party to the agreement will have to suspend, denounce or terminate the agreement at the same time.

In case of concurrent competences, unilateral partial suspension or termination by either the Community or the Member States is not permitted. As pointed out earlier, Article 10 EC, and the Court's case-law, makes it clear that the Community and the Member States have to assist each other and cooperate closely in order to facilitate all aspects of the international agreement. Neither is permitted to act in a manner that would compromise their duty to perform by common accord in the execution of an international agreement to which they are a party.[211] Nor can either act in a manner that can affect or alter the scope of an international agreement. Unilateral suspension, denunciation or termination is not possible, but a Member State wishing to do so could request permission of the Community and the other Member States. If the arguments put forward by the Member State are acceptable to the Community and the other Member States, it may be authorized to implement its decision in accordance with the relevant rules of the international agreement or international treaty law.[212]

Bleckmann summarises the Community reality well when he states that

> "(...) The mixed agreements create rights and obligations for the E(E)C and all its Member States vis-à-vis the third States. (...) These rights and duties cannot be separated one from another, they form a contractual unity. Indeed, the obligations of the E(E)C extend to the execution of the agreements by the Member States. The obligations of the Member States on the other hand extend to the cooperation with the E(E)C

[209] See P.J. Kuijper, 'Trade Sanctions, Security and Human Rights and Commercial Policy' in M. Maresceau, *The European Community's Commercial Policy after 1992: The Legal Dimension* (1993), at 413-417.

[210] *Ibid.* See also Case C-162/96, *Racke*, [1998] ECR I-3655.

[211] D. O'Keeffe, 'Exclusive, Concurrent and Shared Competence' in A. Dashwood and C. Hillion (eds.), *The General Law of EC External Relations* (2000), at 197-198.

[212] I. MacLeod *et al*, *supra* note 3, at 163-164.

> and all other Member States in the execution of these agreements. It must be the consequence of such a legal unity of all rights and duties of the Community and its Member States vis-à-vis the third States that the ulterior legal destiny of the mixed treaties must be uniform. If the Community or one of its Member States may indeed individually dispense itself from the execution of the mixed agreement by reference to the general rules of the international law of treaties, though it continues to be a member of the Community, the mixed agreement, which only functions on the basis of the E(E)C and all its Member States, cannot be further executed. As the obligation to cooperate within the E(E)C is concretized by the mixed agreement, a partial suspension of these agreements vis-à-vis only one Member State may on the other hand block the functioning of the E(E)C as well".[213]

In fact, because international agreements usually view the Community and the Member States as a whole, failure to comply with the aforementioned internal reality of the Community could result in the suspension, denunciation or termination of the agreement by any one of the contracting parties vis-à-vis the Community.[214] The proper execution of the agreement by the Community and the remaining Member States would be hampered by the unilateral actions of the Member States suspending, denouncing or terminating the agreement. This could be construed as forming a fundamental change of circumstances. Parties to the agreement could invoke this ground to suspend, denounce or terminate the agreement. This argument makes the need to act by common accord even stronger.

4.9 Conclusions

In the conclusion of the previous chapter it was argued that neither the Vienna Conventions on the international law of treaties nor customary international law, are equipped to fully take into account the unique nature of the European Community. In international relations the European Community takes an intermediate position between states and traditional intergovernmental organisations. Although, as a subject of international law, international treaty law governs its external treaty actions, the internal rules and workings of the Community system present a number of challenges to international treaty law that need to be addressed. These challenges will require changes in the rules that will allow the Community to act as a full member of the international community in its own right.

The analyses conducted in this chapter show that the addition of mixed agreements, which form an important part of the Community's external treaty practice,

[213] A. Bleckmann, *supra* note 4, at 163.

[214] Remarkably enough whereas international agreements usually contain elaborate provisions concerning the conclusion of international agreements and the exercise of any corresponding voting rights, none are included with regard to the withdrawal from the agreement. In this case the organisation is simply treated as a party, without any regard for the actual consequences. This once again underlines the actual misconceptions that exist in other countries and the rules of international treaty law with regard to the unique character of the European Community.

requires an even more urgent reassessment of the current rules of international treaty law. States wishing to interact with the Community and its Member States are still caught up in old-fashioned notions of states and international organisations, and especially in the important position of states in the international relations. These states are hampered by a certain fear that the Community and its members may take (unfair) advantage of their joint participation in international relations. The internal struggle of the Member States of the European Community to cling to their right of external representation only complicates matters further.

Chapter 5
TREATY INTERPRETATION AND DISPUTE SETTLEMENT

5.1 INTRODUCTION

The purpose of this chapter is to analyse the Community's and the Union's practice in relation to two remaining matters of paramount importance to international treaty law, that is, treaty interpretation and dispute settlement. All the contracting parties must apply international agreements that have entered into force and they must do so in good faith.[1] A corollary of this good faith application of the agreement is its proper interpretation by the parties to the agreement. All organs of the states that are a party to an international agreement are permitted to interpret the agreement. The same rule applies to international organisations, where each organ, within the limits of its powers, is permitted to interpret an international agreement to which those organisations are a party. Generally, however, national courts, the judicial organs of international organisations or other international tribunals or arbitration panels, carry out the interpretation of international agreements.[2]

Arguably the most contentious aspect of the international treaty practice of the Community involves the interpretation of international agreements. This conclusion has less to do with the unique position of the Community in international relations and more with the unique role played by the European Court of Justice and the Court of First Instance in the interpretation and application of international agreements. The Court of Justice, already in the *Van Gend en Loos* Case[3], pointed out that although the Community was created under international law, it did not merely constitute another branch of international law. Rather it constituted a new legal order for the purpose of which the Member States had limited their sovereignty, albeit in a limited number of fields. And in the *Les Verts* Case the Court held that the EC Treaty formed the constitutional document on which the Community was founded.[4] International activities of the Community are, therefore, always interpreted in the light of the Community's constitutional framework.

Under Community law, international agreements concluded by the Community are binding on the Community and the Member States.[5] The European Court

---

[1] The principle of *pacta sunt servanda* codified in Article 26 of both Vienna Conventions.

[2] P. Reuter, *Introduction to the Law of Treaties* (1995), at 95-98.

[3] Case 26/62, [1963] ECR 1.

[4] Case 294/83, [1986] ECR 1339. See on the same matter Opinion 1/91, *EEA I*, [1991] ECR I-6079.

[5] Article 300(7) EC.

of Justice has held that these international agreements 'form an integral part of Community law'.[6] However, contrary to international adjudication, disputes before the European Court of Justice regarding the interpretation of international agreements to which the Community is a party, never involve a dispute between the Community and other contracting parties. On the contrary, the European Court of Justice is called upon to interpret international agreements as part of its advisory opinion[7] or to settle disputes regarding the actual implementation of the agreement within the Community or the Member States.[8] These are all Community procedures and as a result, parties to the actual agreement are barred from providing their opinion as to the precise manner in which the agreement should be interpreted and applied.

The result of this procedure is that the European Court of Justice gives an interpretation that may be different from the actual meaning of the agreement and which can result in a dispute between the Community and its contracting parties. Especially, in those cases in which provisions of the international agreement are identically worded as provisions in the EC Treaty. Although the interpretation given by the Court only binds the Community and the Member States and not the other contracting parties[9], the other parties may construe an interpretation given by the Court that is different from the interpretation of the provisions in the EC Treaty, as a fundamental change of circumstances. After all, if the provisions were supposed to have a different meaning they should have been phrased differently.

The purpose of the first part of this chapter is, therefore, to analyse the Court's case-law, and more particularly, the manner in which the Court has interpreted international agreements. This will be done in order to determine whether the Court, and thus the Community, has interpreted international agreements in conformity with the general rule of treaty interpretation.

Treaty interpretation and dispute settlement are closely connected. In fact, most disputes arising out of the actual execution of international agreements have their origin in differing interpretations of the provisions of agreements. Although proper care is taken to draft an agreement in a clear and unambiguous manner, there is no agreement that cannot cause disputes over its actual interpretation between the parties. This is inherent to the fact that agreements are the result of political negotiations between two or more parties with diverging interests achieving a compromise that is acceptable to all. The problem is further exacerbated by the fact that the negotiating parties seldom have the same official language. But even in cases where the parties utilize the same official language there

[6] Case 181/73, *Haegeman*, [1974] ECR 449, at paragraph 5.

[7] Articles 234 and 300(6) EC. In the case of Article 300(6) EC the European Court of Justice is called upon to interpret international agreements to which the Community is not a party, but which it wants to conclude or accede to.

[8] Articles 230 and 284 EC.

[9] H.G. Schermers and D.F. Waelbroeck, *Judicial Protection in the European Union* (2001), at 297-299.

can be disputes concerning the correct interpretation of provisions in the agreement.

International treaty law itself is silent as to any particular form of dispute settlement as a result of divergent interpretations and applications of international agreements. Parties have to act in good faith, but they are free to develop their own system of dispute settlement within their contractual relationship. The only overriding rule is the principle embodied in Article 33 of the Charter of the United Nations. This provision requires the parties to settle their disputes through friendly means and in conformity with the rules of international law.

It is standard practice in international relations to insert a system of dispute settlement into international agreements. These mechanisms vary from political dialogue to judicial dispute settlement procedures. The Community participation in international agreement brings with it a number of uncertainties for the other parties. It was pointed out in the two preceding chapters that parties are unaware of the precise scope and implications of the unique internal structure of the European Community and the European Union. In their treaty relations with the Community these parties try to avail themselves of a number of techniques to circumvent any problems that may occur in the actual implementation of the agreement as a result of the Community participation. These techniques vary from the demand that the Member States participate in the agreement, despite the Community's exclusive competence in that regard, to the demand that the Community and the Member States issue a declaration outlining the precise limits of their respective competences. Yet, neither of these tools provides all the necessary safeguards that the parties so desire. Still, the rights of the parties are directly correlated with the obligations of the Community and the Member States.

One effective manner to safeguard these rights is through a normative system that spells out the procedures that must be followed whenever there is an alleged breach of the aforementioned obligations. In the second part of this Chapter a number of the existing systems that have been inserted in the various bilateral and multilateral agreements to which the Community is a party will be analysed. The purpose will be to establish what kind of systems have been set up to guarantee parties that whomever has the duty to perform on the Community side will perform and be held accountable if necessary.

5.2 Competence to interpret international agreements

International treaty law provides a general rule of treaty interpretation but is silent as to who has the competence to interpret agreements in force. Treaty law leaves it to the parties to decide on the basis of their own constitutional tradition who has the authority to interpret the agreement. The rules of treaty interpretation enshrined in the Articles 31-33 of both Vienna Conventions, which constitute a *lex specialis* in relation to the fundamental principle of *pacta sunt servanda* contained in Article 26 of the Vienna Conventions, only require that agreements must be interpreted in good faith having account of the text, context and object and purpose of the agreements.

The parties to the agreements, both states and international organisations, must execute international agreements that have entered into force and in order to do so they must interpret them the same.[10] Or as Louis Henkin puts it "the obligation and authority to implement or enforce a treaty involves also the obligation and authority to interpret what the treaty requires".[11] But as stated before the decision as to who is competent to interpret the agreement is left to the individual parties.

It is not uncommon for international agreements to confer the competence to interpret the agreements, on an *ad hoc* tribunal, the International Court of Justice or any other type of (judicial) institutional structure the parties may so choose.[12] Although parties may agree that the interpretation provided by such organs will not have binding force, they are just advisory opinions, such interpretations will have a certain authoritative character that will assist the national institutions in the interpretation and application of the agreements. Thus the European Court of Justice in the *Nederlandse Spoorwegen* Case[13] held that

> "It is true that these classifications [of the Customs Cooperation Council] do not bind the Contracting Parties but they have a bearing on interpretation which is all the more decisive because they emanate from an authority entrusted by the contracting parties with ensuring uniformity in the interpretation and application of the nomenclature.
> When, furthermore, such an interpretation reflects the general practice followed by the Contracting States, it can be set aside only if it appears incompatible with the wording of the heading concerned or goes manifestly beyond the discretion conferred on the Customs Cooperation Council" (paragraphs 24-25).

And in the *Deutsche Shell* Case the Court stated that

> "(...) Although the recommendations of the Joint Committee cannot confer upon individuals rights which they may enforce before national courts, the latter are nevertheless obliged to take them into consideration in order to resolve disputes submitted to them, especially when, as in this case, they are of relevance in interpreting the provisions of the Convention".[14]

The parties can also agree to negotiate and adopt an additional agreement containing a common interpretation of the initial agreement. This additional agree-

[10] P. Reuter, *supra* note 2, at 95.

[11] L. Henkin, *Foreign Affairs and the Constitution* (1972), at 167. See also K.C. Kennedy, Treaty Interpretation by the Executive Branch: The ABM Treaty and "Star Wars" Testing and Development in 80 *AJIL* (1986), at 854-877.

[12] I. Brownlie, *Principle of Public International Law* (2003), at 602. The 1982 Law of the Sea Convention is an example of an international agreement that recognizes the jurisdiction of the International Court of Justice to settle disputes and, therefore, also the jurisdiction to interpret the Convention, 21 *I.L.M.* (1982), at 1261. See also the *Qatar* v *Bahrain* Case, I.C.J. Reports (1994), at 112.

[13] Case 38/75, [1975] ECR 1439.

[14] Case C-188/91, [1993] ECR I-363, paragraph 18.

ment will be regarded as the authentic interpretation and it will prevail over all other interpretations.[15] However, in the absence of such devices it is up to each state or international organisation to designate the organ(s) that has (have) the competence to interpret the agreement. Reuter states that

> "In the case of states, the organs having concluded the treaty are the most qualified to do so, but their courts also have to interpret an increasing number of treaties (...). In international organisations, it is generally accepted that each organ, within its function, is called upon to interpret the treaties which concern it although the interpretations of some, especially judicial, organs may in some cases be binding on the organ as well".[16]

In the case of the European Union this would mean that all five institutions, that is, the Council, the Commission, the European Parliament, the European Court of Justice and the Court of First Instance, and the Court of Auditors, but also the European Central bank, to the extent that the agreement was concluded on the basis of Article 111 EC, have the competence to interpret international agreements to which the Community is a party or where the adoption of Community legislation may lead to a conflicting situation with an agreement to which the Member States are a party.[17]

This conclusion is confirmed by article 300(7) EC, which provides that agreements concluded by the Community are binding on the institutions and the Member States.[18] For the institutions to carry out their individual responsibilities to ensure the Community's compliance with its treaty obligation it is necessary that the institutions have the competence to interpret international agreements. Such to assess the level of cooperation required within the limits of their individual powers.

Because international agreements are binding on the Member States, they, too, have the competence to interpret international agreements where they are called upon to perform certain tasks in order to assist the Community to meet its international obligations. This principal does not only apply in cases where the Community and the Member States are joint parties to an international agreement, but equally where the Community has concluded an agreement exercising its exclusive competence. The interpretation of the national courts is part of the judicial

---

[15] P. Reuter, *supra* note 2, at 95. See also Article 31(2)(b) of both Vienna Conventions.

[16] *Ibid*, at 95-96.

[17] In the light of their advisory role in the legislative procedure, the Economic and Social Committee and the Committee of the Regions also have the authority to interpret international agreements.

[18] In Case 142/88, *Hoesch*, [1989] ECR 3413, the Court held that the arrangement between the United States and the European Community on the restriction on the export of steel pipes and tubes was an international agreement within the meaning of Article 300 EC. It went on to say that "such an arrangement is characterized by the fact that its provisions are binding on the Community institutions and on the Member States pursuant to the Treaty and must be implemented in good faith in respect of the other contracting party in accordance with the applicable rules of public international law" (paragraph 30).

review necessary to ensure a uniform application of the agreement in all Member States. The term 'Member States' should be understood as meaning all organs of the state, including the national courts.[19]

The competence of the Commission to interpret international agreements flows from Article 211 EC, which entrusts the Commission with the task to "ensure that the provisions of this Treaty and the measures taken by the institutions pursuant thereto are applied". The measures taken by the institutions include not only internal legislative acts but also international agreements to which the Community is a party or where the Community has *de facto* replaced the Member States as a party to the agreement.[20] As chief negotiator of the Community and the initiator of all legislative acts within the Community, the Commission has the competence to interpret international agreements. Without the necessary competence to interpret international agreements to which the Community is a party, the Commission would not be able to carry out its duties properly as determined by Article 211 EC. This includes the power to take legal action where the Council, the European Parliament or any one of the Member States has failed to perform their part under the agreement.[21]

Or as the Court held in the *International Dairy Products* Case

> "Under Article 155 (now 211) of the EC Treaty, the Commission is responsible for ensuring application of the Treaty and, accordingly, compliance with international agreements concluded by the Community which, pursuant to Article 228 (now 300(7)) of the Treaty, are binding both on the Community institutions and the Member States. For the Commission to succeed in that task, it must not be hindered in the exercise of its power under Article 169 (now 226) of the Treaty to bring proceedings before the Court where a Member State has failed to fulfil its obligations under such an agreement. The initiation of proceedings before the Court by the Commission cannot therefore depend on the outcome of consultations within the Article 113 (now 133) Committee; a fortiori, it cannot hinge on whether a consensus between the Member States has first been found to exist within the Committee with regard to the interpretation of the Community's commitments under an international agreement".[22]

---

[19] In fact, the majority of the cases before the European Court of Justice involving the interpretation of international agreements are preliminary rulings initiated by national courts seeking guidance from the Court on how to interpret international agreements or provisions of the same. It is for each Member State individually to decide which of its organs has the competence to interpret the international agreement.

[20] Starting with the *Haegeman* Case it has become established case-law that international agreements are an act of one of the institutions. Case 181/73, [1974] ECR 449, paragraph 4. In the *International Fruit Company* Case, Joined Cases 21-24/72, [1972] ECR 1219, the Court held that the Community had assumed the powers previously exercised by the Member States in the area governed by the GATT Agreement and that the provisions of this agreement were binding on the Community.

[21] Articles 226, 228, 230 and 232 EC.

[22] Case C-61/94, [1996] ECR I-3989, paragraph 15.

Henkin, referring to the competence of the President of the United States of America with regard to the subject of treaty interpretation, states, "for international purposes, no doubt, the President determines the United States' position as to the meaning of a treaty. Domestically, too, since the President has usually the principal, often the sole, responsibility to execute a treaty, the treaty means what he says it means".[23] A similar reasoning applies *mutatis mutandis* with regard to the competence of the Council of Ministers of the European Union to interpret international agreements.

Under Articles 111, 133 and 300 EC and 24 and 38 TEU it is the Council that concludes international agreements. That is, it is the Council that expresses, on behalf of the Community and the Union, the Community's and Union's consent to be bound by an international agreement. The Council's competence to engage in international treaty obligations brings with it the corollary that the Council is empowered to interpret international agreements. This reasoning is in line with the powers of the Council as provided for in Article 202 EC and Articles 13 and 14 TEU.

With regard to the role of the legislature in the interpretation of international agreements to which the United States is a party, Henkin observes, "Congress, too, has occasion to interpret a treaty when it considers implementing legislation or other legislation on the same subject".[24] Although the European Parliament does not have the right of initiative, in legislative matters it "shall participate in the process leading up to the adoption of Community acts by exercising its powers under the procedures laid down in Articles 251 and 252 and by giving its assent or delivering advisory opinions".[25] From the foregoing it is evident that the Parliament must have the competence to interpret international agreements if it is to carry out its task as co-legislator of the Community effectively.

Article 111(3) EC stipulates that the Council "on a recommendation from the Commission and after consulting the ECB, shall decide the arrangements for the negotiation and for the conclusion of such agreements". In this context the European Central Bank performs a role that is similar to the role performed by the European Parliament under the provisions embodied in the first part of Article 300(3) EC. The task carried out by the Central Bank under Article 111 EC is part of its basic tasks as outlined in Article 105(2) EC. Where the ECB is therefore called upon to provide an advisory opinion on a proposed international agreement or in the fields provided for under Article 105(4) EC it shall have the competence to interpret that international agreement.

With so many parties capable of interpreting international agreements at the internal level of the Community, there is an inherent risk of divergent interpretations of international agreement. Although interpretations of the European Court of Justice do not bind the other contracting parties, it does override at the internal

---

[23] L. Henkin, *supra* note 11, at 167.

[24] *Ibid.*

[25] Article 192 EC.

level the interpretations of the Community organs and the Member States. Invoking its task as embodied in Article 220 to "ensure that in the interpretation and application of this Treaty the law is observed" the Court in the *Kupferberg* Case held

> "It follows from the Community nature of such provisions that their effect in the Community may not be allowed to vary according to whether their application is in practice the responsibility of the Community institutions or of the Member States and, in the latter case, according to the effects in the internal legal order of each Member State which the law of that State assigns to international agreements concluded by it. Therefore it is for the Court, within the framework of its jurisdiction in interpreting the provisions of agreements, to ensure their uniform application throughout the Community".[26]

Much has been written about the case-law of the European Court of Justice asserting its jurisdiction to interpret international agreement.[27] This competence is not only limited to agreements to which only the Community is a party, but also extends to mixed agreements[28] and international agreements where the Community has *de facto* replaced the Member States as the contracting party.[29] Although the Court has had several previous instances to rule on the applicability of rules of international law in the Community system, with regard to the law of treaties, the leading case is the *Haegeman* Case.[30] In this case the European Court of Justice held that

> "The Athens Agreement was concluded by the Council under Articles 228 (now 300) and 238 (now 310) of the Treaty as appears from the terms of the decision dated 25 September 1961.
> This Agreement is therefore, insofar as concerns the Community, an act of one of the institutions of the Community within the meaning of subparagraph (b) of the first paragraph of Article 177 (now 234).

---

[26] Case 104/81, [1982] ECR 3641, paragraph 14.

[27] Examples include H.G. Schermers *et al*, *supra* note 9; I. MacLeod, I. Hendry and S. Hyett, *The External Relations of the European Communities* (1996); D. McGoldrick, *International Relations Law of the European Union* (1997); K.R. Simmonds, The Community's Declaration upon the Signature of the U.N. Convention on the Law of the Sea in 23 *C.M.L. Rev.* (1986), at 521; A. Davies, Bananas, Private Challenges, the Courts and the Legislature in 22 *YEL* (2002), at 299; K. Lenaerts and E. De Smijter, The European Community's Treaty-making Competence in 16 *YEL* (1996), at 1; G. Bebr, Agreements Concluded by the Community and Their Possible Direct Effect: From International Fruit Company to Kupferberg in 20 *C.M.L. Rev.* (1983), at 35; E. Leray and A. Potteau, Réflexions sur la cohérence du système de contrôle de la légalité des accords internationaux conclus par la Communauté européenne in 34 *RTD eur.* (1998); at 535 and C. Weber, Wirtschaftsabkommen im System der Europaischen Gemeinschaft – Die Rechtsprechung des Europäischen Gerichtshof in 35 *AVR* (1997), at 295.

[28] See Case 12/86, *Demirel*, [1987] ECR 3719.

[29] Joined Cases 21-24/72, *International Fruit Company*, [1972] ECR 1219.

[30] Case 181/73, [1974] ECR 449.

The provisions of the Agreement, from the coming into force thereof, form an integral part of Community law.
Within the framework of this law, the Court accordingly has jurisdiction to give preliminary rulings concerning the interpretation of this agreement" (emphasis added).[31]

But whereas the Court in the *Haegeman* Case merely qualified agreements as being part of Community law, in the *Kupferberg* Case the Court went even further.[32] It held that

> "In ensuring respect for the commitments arising from an agreement concluded by the Community institutions the Member States fulfil an obligation not only in relation to the non-member country concerned but also and above all in relation to the Community which has assumed responsibility for the due performance of the agreement. That is why the provisions of such an agreement, as the Court has already stated (...), form *an integral part of the Community legal system*" (emphasis added).[33]

And in the *Demirel* Case the European Court of Justice extended its jurisdiction to mixed agreements.[34] It started out by repeating its ruling in the *Haegeman* Case.[35] In response to the claim by the German and British governments that the Court's interpretative jurisdiction did not extend 'to provisions whereby Member States have entered into commitments with regard to Turkey'[36] the Court stated,

> "In that connection it is sufficient to state that that is precisely not the case in this instance. Since the agreement in question is an association agreement creating special, privileged links with a non-member country which must, at least to a certain extent, take part in the Community system, Article 238 (now 310) must necessarily empower the Community to guarantee commitments towards non-member countries in all fields covered by the Treaty. Since freedom of movement for workers is, by virtue of Article 48 (now 39) et seq. of the EEC (now EC) Treaty, one of the fields covered by that Treaty, it follows that commitments regarding freedom of movement fall within the powers conferred on the Community by Article 238 (now 310). Thus the question whether the Court has jurisdiction to rule on the interpretation of a provision in a mixed agreement containing a commitment which only the Member States could enter into in the sphere of their own powers does not arise" (paragraph 9).

And in the *Hermès* Case[37], the Court elaborated the position it adopted in the *Demirel* Case. The European Court of Justice's ruling in the *Demirel* Case did not provide a definitive answer as to whether the Court is also permitted to interpret the parts of a mixed agreement that come under the exclusive competence of

[31] *Ibid*, paragraphs 3-6.
[32] Case 104/81, [1982] ECR 3641.
[33] *Ibid*, paragraph 13.
[34] Case 12/86, [1987] ECR 3719.
[35] Case 181/73, [1974] ECR 449.
[36] Case 12/86, *Demirel*, [1987] ECR 3719, paragraph 8.
[37] Case C-53/96, [1998] ECR I-3603.

the Member States or whether its jurisdiction restricted itself to the Community part of the international agreement. The Court held that it had jurisdiction because the Community and the Member States have concluded the WTO Agreement "without any allocation between them of their respective obligations towards the other contracting parties".[38] The Court stated furthermore that under Article 99 of Regulation 40/94 the courts, including the European Court of Justice, had jurisdiction to "apply national rules with a view to ordering provisional measures for the protection of rights arising under a Community trade mark" and they had to do so "in light of the wording and purpose of Article 50 of the TRIPs Agreement".[39]

The Court has also held that it has jurisdiction to interpret arrangements adopted by the Joint Committee set up on the basis of the Convention on a Common Transit Procedure[40] and decisions adopted by the Council of Association established by the EC-Turkey Association Agreement.[41] On the other hand, in the *Vandeweghe* Case, the Court held that it had "no jurisdiction under Article 177 (now 234) of the EEC (now EC) Treaty to give a ruling on the interpretation of provisions of international law which bind Member States outside the framework of Community law".[42]

Although the arguments put forward by the European Court of Justice to assert its jurisdiction to interpret international agreements to which the Community is a party are sound, they are not entirely convincing. It is interesting in this respect to contrast the Court's reasoning with the ruling of the US Supreme Court in *Foster* v *Neilson*.[43] In this case Chief Justice John Marshall, writing the decision of the Supreme Court, held that

> "A treaty is in the nature of a contract between two nations, not a legislative act. It does not generally affect, of itself, the object to be accomplished, especially so far as its operation is infra-territorial, but is carried into execution by the sovereign power of the respective parties to the instrument
>
> In the United States, a different principle is established. *Our Constitution declares a treaty to be the law of the land. It is consequently to be regarded, in courts of justice as equivalent to an act of the legislature whenever it operates of itself, without the aid*

[38] Case C-53/96, paragraph 24.

[39] Ibid, paragraph 28. See also A. Dashwood, 'Preliminary Rulings on the Interpretation of Mixed Agreements' in D. O'Keeffe (ed.), *Judicial Review in European Union Law. Liber Amicorum in Honour of Lord Slynn of Headley* (2000), at 167-175.

[40] Case C-188/91, *Deutsche Shell*, [1993] ECR I-363.

[41] Case C-192/89, *Sevince*, [1990] ECR I-3461.

[42] Case 130/73, [1973] ECR 1329, paragraph 2. See also Case C-162/98, *Hartmann*, [1998] ECR I-7083. In the *Eurocontrol* Case, Case C-364/92, [1994] ECR I-43, Eurocontrol disputed the Court's jurisdiction to interpret the Convention establishing Eurocontrol or the Multilateral Agreement relating to the Collection of Route Charges. The Court dismissed this argument by stating that it was not asked to interpret the Convention, but to interpret the Articles 82 and 87 of the EC Treaty (paragraph 10).

[43] 27 U.S. 253 (1829) (USSC+).

> *of any legislative provision.* But when the terms of the stipulation import a contract, when either of the parties engages to perform a particular act, the treaty addresses itself to the Political, not the Judicial, Department, and the Legislature must execute the contract before it can become a rule for the Court" (emphasis added).

And in the *Head Money* Cases, Justice J. Miller delivering the opinion of the US Supreme Court argued

> "A treaty is primarily a contract between independent nations. It depends for the enforcement of its provisions on the interest and the honour of the governments which are parties to it. If these fail, its infraction becomes the subject of international negotiations and reclamations, so far as the injured party chooses to seek redress, which may, in the end, be enforced by actual war. It is obvious that, with all this, the judicial courts have nothing to do, and can give no redress. But a treaty may also contain provisions which confer certain rights upon the citizens or subjects of one of the nations residing in the territorial limits of the other, which partake of the nature of municipal law and which are capable of enforcement as between private parties in the courts of the country. (...) The Constitution of the United States places such provisions as these in the same category as other laws of Congress by its declaration that this Constitution and the laws made in pursuance thereof, and all the treaties made or which shall be made under the authority of the United States, shall be the supreme law of the land.
> *A treaty, then, is a law of the land, as an act of Congress is whenever its provisions prescribe a rule by which the rights of the private citizen or subject may be determined. And when such rights are of a nature to be enforced in a court of justice, that court resorts to the treaty for a rule of decision for the case before it as it would to a statute*" (emphasis added).[44]

The reasoning of the US Supreme Court is thus that where an agreement is self-executing, that is when it has direct effect, it can be considered an act of the legislature and therefore an act amenable to judicial interpretation.

The European Court of Justice uses a much broader approach to assert its jurisdiction to interpret international agreements. The Court states that all agreements concluded by the Council on behalf of the Community constitute an act of one of the institutions of the Community. Therefore, the starting point is the same, namely, that the agreement constitutes an act of the legislature, *in casu*, the Council. However, it is not the agreement *per se*, but rather the act adopted by the Council ratifying the agreement, which is an act of the Council. That was exactly the issue raised by the Commission in the admissibility stage of France's challenge to the arrangement concluded between the Commission and the US Federal Trade Commission.[45] The Commission contended that the case should be dismissed because France had challenged the validity of the agreement rather than the validity of the act concluding the agreement. Consequently, the Court lacked the competence to rule on the legality of the agreement.

[44] 112 U.S. 580 (1884) (USSC+).
[45] Case C-327/91, [1994] ECR I-3641.

Advocate General Tesauro disagreed with the Commission.[46] In paragraph 9 of his Conclusion he submitted that the case-law of the European Court of Justice did not rule out the possibility of challenging an agreement directly. On the contrary, he asserted that the weight of evidence proved that such a challenge was possible.

In the end, the Court annulled the decision of the Commission concluding the cooperation agreement between the Community and the US Federal Trade Commission without ruling on the validity of the agreement itself. Without answering the question as to whether agreements can be directly challenged the Court merely stated that the Agreement was intended to produce legal effects. As a result the act concluding the Agreement also produced legal effects and was therefore amenable to judicial review under Article 230 EC.

Although not saying so expressly the Court in fact recognized and applied the principle embodied in Article 46 of the Vienna Conventions. This provision prohibits that a state or international organisation invoke the violation of an internal rule as a grounds for the termination of an international agreement. By not ruling on the validity of the agreement itself the Court avoided putting the Community in a position in which the US authorities could claim a wrongful act because of an incorrect use of the right to terminate an international agreement as a result of a breach of internal rules.

The more correct approach for the Court to assert its jurisdiction to interpret agreements should be the use of Article 300(7) EC.[47] As already mentioned, this provision obliges the institutions to engage in or refrain from those activities that will assist or hinder the Community in performing its international obligation. In the performance of its duty, which is to ensure that in the interpretation and application of the EC Treaty the law is observed the Court does not only have the right, but rather the duty to ascertain whether, in the context of a direct challenge on the basis of Article 230 EC or within the framework of a preliminary ruling (Article 234 EC) the Community and the Member States have met their legal duties. This power of the Court, therefore, includes the power to interpret international agreements to which the Community is a party.

The bottom line is, that although all the institutions of the Community have the competence to interpret international agreements to which the Community is a party or has *de facto* substituted the Member States as a party, the final say on the interpretation, from a Community standpoint, rests with the European Court of Justice. The interpretation of international agreements is first and foremost a legal operation.[48] International treaty law, in particular the Articles 31-33 of both Vienna Conventions, governs this process.

---

[46] Conclusion of Advocate General Tesauro in Case C-327/91, [1994] ECR I-3641.

[47] See also Case 104/81, *Kupferberg*, [1982] ECR 3641.

[48] S. Torres Bernárdez, 'Interpretation of Treaties by the International Court of Justice Following the Adoption of the 1969 Vienna Convention on the Law of Treaties' in G. Hafner, G. Loibl, L. Sucharipa-Behrmann and K. Zemanek (eds.), *Liber Amicorum Professor Seidl-Hohenveldern – in honour of his 80th birthday (1998)*, at 722.

5.2.1 Article 31 of the Vienna Conventions

Although it was not until *Opinion 1/91*[49] that the European Court of Justice explicitly applied Article 31 of the 1969 Vienna Convention, there have been numerous occasions in which the Court has been called upon to interpret international agreements and has done so, albeit indirectly, in accordance with the provisions of Article 31 of the Vienna Conventions. As pointed out in the previous Section, the Court has asserted its jurisdiction to interpret international agreement. It can do so in the context of an annulment procedure, Article 230 EC, the preliminary ruling, Article 234 EC, infringement action, Article 226 EC and the action for damages, Article 284 EC. The Court also has jurisdiction to interpret the provisions of a proposed international agreement, Article 300(6) EC.[50]

Article 31 of the 1969 Vienna Convention[51] provides

> "1. A Treaty shall be interpreted in good faith in accordance with the ordinary meaning to be given to the terms of the treaty in their context and in the light of its object and purpose.
>
> 2. The context for the purpose of the interpretation of a treaty shall comprise, in addition to the text, including its preamble and annexes:
>
> (a) any agreement relating to the treaty which was made between all the parties in connexion with the conclusion of the treaty;
> (b) any instrument which was made by one or more parties in connexion with the conclusion of the treaty and accepted by the other parties as an instrument related to the treaty.
>
> 3. There shall be taken into account, together with the context:
>
> (a) any subsequent agreement between the parties regarding the interpretation of the treaty or the application of its provisions;
> (b) any subsequent practice in the application of the treaty which establishes the agreement of the parties regarding its interpretation;
> (c) any relevant rules of international law applicable in relations between the parties.
>
> 4. A special meaning shall be given to a term if it is established that the parties so intended".

[49] Opinion 1/91, *EEA I*, [1991] ECR I-6079.

[50] This includes existing agreements to which the Community intends to accede. See in this regard Opinion 2/94, *ECHR*, [1996] ECR I-1759.

[51] The text of Article 31 of the 1986 Vienna Convention is identical.

The provisions of Article 31 represent a compromise between the various schools of thought regarding the interpretation of international agreements.[52] These schools of thought are the "intention of the parties"[53], the 'textual or ordinary meaning'[54], and the 'teleological' school.[55] Although there is no specific hierarchy among the three different approaches, it is evident that the emphasis is on the textual or ordinary approach. This is understandable as one must start from the premise that that which is written in the international agreement represents the actual intention of the parties.[56] Article 31 makes it clear, however, that the provisions must be read in their context having regard of the 'object and purpose' of the agreement.

Various international courts and tribunals have had a long tradition of using the general rule of Article 31 as the source for the interpretation of agreements. Already in the *Competence of the General Assembly for the Admission of a State to the United Nations* Case, the International Court of Justice held that "the first duty of a tribunal which is called upon to interpret and apply the provisions of a treaty is to endeavour to give the effect to them in their natural and ordinary meaning in the context in which they occur".[57] And in the *Interpretation of Peace Treaties* Case, the International Court of Justice held that "the principle of interpretation expressed in the maxim: *Ut res magis valeat quam pereat*, often referred to as the rule of effectiveness, cannot justify the Court in attributing to the provisions for the settlement of disputes in the Peace Treaties a meaning which, (...), would be contrary to their letter and spirit".[58]

Despite several references by various judges to the Articles 31-33 of the 1969 Vienna Convention in their dissenting and separate opinion, it was not until the *Arbitral Award* Case that the International Court of Justice, for the first time, made an express reference to Article 31.[59] The Court pointed out that an arbitration agreement qualifies as an agreement between states and that this agreement

[52] P. Reuter, *supra* note 2, at 97-98; D.J. Harris, *Cases and Materials on International Law* (1991), at 766-767; I. Brownlie, *supra* note 12, at 603-604 and M.N. Shaw, *International Law* (2003), at 838-839.

[53] The aim of this type of interpretation is to try establish the intentions of the parties, and to interpret these intentions.

[54] The purpose is to establish the object of the agreement in the light of the ordinary or apparent meaning of its terms.

[55] The teleological aim focuses on the object and purpose of the agreement and thus utilises a wider scope than the two other approaches.

[56] This has been the position of the International Law Commission. The Commission took the position that the most important issue is the intention of the parties as expressed in the text of the agreement.

[57] I.C.J. Reports (1950), at 4. In the *Elettronica Sicula* Case the Court made a reference to Article 33(4) of the 1969 Vienna Convention, but only because this provisions was invoked by Italy. I.C.J. Reports (1989), at 15.

[58] I.C.J. Reports (1950), at 221. Harris points out that in this case the Court refused to apply the teleological approach instead of the literal interpretation. In the opinion of the Court the text was clear enough to provide the solution. D.J. Harris, *supra* note 52, at 768.

[59] I.C.J. Reports (1991), at 53. See also S. Torres Bernárdez, *supra* note 48, at 722-733.

has to be interpreted in accordance with the general rules of international law governing the interpretation of international agreements. Making a reference to the Court's own case-law on the interpretation of international agreement, the Court went on to state that the Articles 31 and 32 of the 1969 Vienna Convention constitute a codification of existing customary international law.

As pointed out before, the European Court of Justice has been called upon in numerous occasions to interpret international agreements. Yet in neither of these cases the Court has indicated whether it conducted its interpretation on the basis of the rule embodied in Article 31 of the 1969 Vienna Convention and whether it considered these provisions as a codification of customary international law. The interpretation of international agreements by the Community Court depends on the manner in which they take effect within the Community legal order. If the international agreement takes effect within the Community without any act of transformation, it must be interpreted in accordance with the rules of international treaty law. If, however, the agreement is incorporated into the Community legal order, it must be interpreted in accordance with the corresponding Community legislation.[60]

Looking at the Court's case-law we notice that the Court, and the Court of First Instance, has indeed interpreted international agreements different from similarly or identically worded provisions of the EC Treaty. Thus the Court in the *Polydor* Case, after it had agreed that the terms in the Agreement between the Community and Portugal were similar in several respects, held that the similarity of terms was not sufficient reason to apply to the provisions of the Agreement its existing case-law on the free movement of goods within the Community.[61]

In the *Opel Austria* Case the Court of First Instance ruled, "It is clear from the case-law that in order to determine whether the interpretation of a provision contained in the EC Treaty must be extended to an identical provision contained in an agreement such as the EEA Agreement, that provision should be analyzed in the light of both the purpose and the objective of the Agreement and in its context".[62] And in *Opinion 1/91* the Court stated, "The fact that the provisions of the agreement and the corresponding Community provisions are identically worded does not mean that they must necessarily be interpreted identically".[63]

This approach utilized by the European Court and the Court of First Instance creates the impression that the Courts use different techniques of interpretation. Anne Peters points out that this is not the case.[64] The different interpretation is merely the result of the Court taking the diverging objectives of different treaties into account.[65] Although it is not entirely incorrect to take into account the objec-

[60] C. Weber, *supra* note 27, at 303.

[61] Case 270/80, *Polydor*, [1982] ECR 329, at paragraph 15.

[62] Case T-115/94, [1997] ECR II-43, paragraph 106.

[63] Opinion 1/91, *First EEA Opinion*, [1991] ECR I-6084, paragraph 14.

[64] A. Peters, The Position of International Law Within the European Community Legal Order in 40 *GYIL* (1997), at 23-26.

[65] *Ibid.*

tives of the EC Treaty when interpreting an international agreement to which the Community is a party, Article 31 itself does not permit such a comparative analysis.[66] Each agreement should be interpreted in the light of its own context and its own object and purpose. If the Community does not want to extend the principles of the Community system to its association agreements it should include provisions to this effect or phrase the provisions differently.[67]

The Court's interpretation technique demonstrates the overriding importance the European Court of Justice places on the object and purpose of the agreement. Rather than looking at the literal meaning of the text, the Court tends to interpret the wording of the international agreement in the light of the object and purpose of the agreement compared to the object and purpose of the EC Treaty.[68] Hence, there is a certain communitarian approach to the rules of treaty interpretation.[69]

The Court, in *Opinion 1/91*, held that

> "An international treaty is to be interpreted not only on the basis of its wording but also in the light of its objectives. Article 31 of the Vienna Convention of 23 May 1969 on the law of treaties stipulates in this respect that a treaty is to be interpreted in good faith in accordance with the ordinary meaning to be given to its terms in their context in the light of its object and purpose".[70]

And in the *Chiquita Italia* Case the Court ruled, "the question of the direct effect of provisions contained in an agreement concluded by the Community with non-member countries invariably involves an examination of the spirit, general scheme and terms of that agreement".[71]

---

[66] In fact Article 31, paragraph 2, only permits instruments made by one or more parties in connexion with the conclusion of the agreement, which were accepted by the other parties. It can be argued, however, that because the Court's interpretation does not bind the other parties, it can use the EC Treaty as a comparative source in order to give a proper interpretation of an international agreement and assure its correct application within the Community. Still, where such an interpretation is distinctly different from the general interpretation given by all parties, the Court's action cannot be construed as representing a *bona fide* implementation of the international agreement.

[67] Note that where the Court's early case-law seemed to indicate that whether international agreements could have direct effect depended on considerations of reciprocity, the Court's rulings in the *Bresciani* Case, tentatively, and in the *Kupferberg* and *Polydor* Cases, more emphatically, indicate that reciprocity could be an additional tool but was not a mandatory requirement for an agreement or provisions of the agreement to have direct effect. See also J. Klabbers, International Law in Community Law: The Law and Politics of Direct Effect in 22 *YEL* (2002), at 263-298.

[68] See also P.J. Kuijper, The Court and Tribunal of the EC and the Vienna Convention on the Law of Treaties 1969 in *LIEI* 1998/1, at 2-4.

[69] Kuijper asserts that the Court uses the unique character of the Community to draw a distinction between the Community Treaty and other international agreements. This difference is subsequently used to interpret the provisions. *Ibid.*

[70] Opinion 1/91, [1991] ECR I-6079, paragraph 14.

[71] Case C-469/93, [1995] ECR I-4533. This formula was also used in the *Van Gend & Loos* Case, Case 26/62, [1963] ECR 1. See also J. Klabbers, *supra* note 67, at 274.

In the *Anastasiou* Case the Court stated that

> "Although, in accordance with the rules on the interpretation of treaties (see Article 31 of the Vienna Convention on the Law of Treaties of 23 May 1969, (...)), substantial importance properly attaches to the object and purpose of a treaty and to any subsequent practice in its application, it is important to note that Article 5 of the Association Agreement reflects only one of its objectives and must be reconciled with the other general aims of the Agreement and with the actual provisions interpreted (...)".[72]

The early cases indicate a development whereby the Court has interpreted international agreements or provisions of international agreements but without making it clear as to whether it applied Article 31 of the 1969 Vienna Convention. Based upon the Court's later case-law, it can be readily concluded that, although the Court of Justice now adheres to the general rule embodied in Article 31, it applies the principles embodied in said article in a Community manner, placing emphasis on the object and purpose (teleological interpretation) rather than the literal meaning. Or to put it differently, the Court adheres to the general scheme of Article 31 of the Vienna Conventions, but not to the ordinary text.[73]

International agreements must be interpreted in their context. Paragraph 2 of Article 31 of the Vienna Conventions provides that the context of an international agreement for purposes of interpretation comprises the treaty, including its preamble and annexes and any agreement or instrument related to the agreement and adopted in connection with its conclusion. The growing number of parties to international agreements brings with it the need to draw up additional agreements outlining differing opinions of the parties with regard to certain provisions. These arrangements are an important aid to interpretation and also facilitate the actual treaty-making process. After all, parties to an agreement may accept that one of the parties may, for political reasons, want to raise a certain point, although they do not agree on its inclusion in the main agreement.[74] These additional instruments come in different forms, such as agreed minutes or an exchange of letters.[75]

Decisions of the Council of Ministers of the European Union, approving international agreements, frequently include an interpretive declaration on these agreements or some provisions of the agreements. Although it is questionable to what extent the Court is bound by such provisions, they can serve as an addi-

---

72 Case C-432/92, [1994] ECR I-3087, paragraph 43.

73 However, in Opinion 2/00, *Cartagena Protocol on Biosafety*, [2001] ECR I-9713, the Court referred to the entire text of Article 31 of the Vienna Convention on the Law of Treaties and applied the provisions accordingly.

74 A. Aust, *Modern Treaty Law and Practice* (2000), at 190-191.

75 Aust refers to the explanatory reports approved by the government experts who were involved in drafting the conventions of the Council of Europe. These documents are usually adopted and published at the same time as the actual conventions and are a valuable source of interpretation of the conventions. A. Aust, *supra* note 74, at 191.

tional source for the Court when it interprets the agreement. Especially, where these statements have not been met with any opposition from the other contracting parties. The Court, in the *Bresciani* Case, indicated that reciprocity is not a pre-requisite for the interpretation of an agreement.[76] It is therefore not necessary that declarations made by the Council are expressly accepted or refuted by the other contracting parties. Still, the Court may be inclined to give less emphasis to these declarations and statements made by the Council when it is not clear what their precise status is.

In its interpretation of international agreements the European Court of Justice has used a variety of additional sources to assist it in providing the proper interpretation of provisions of international agreements. Thus the Court in the *Chiquita Italia* Case compared the GATT to the Fourth ACP-EEC Convention and ruled that it had a different nature.[77] In the *Gözütok* Case the Court held that the aptness of its interpretation of the *ne bis in idem* principle as enshrined in Article 54 of the Convention implementing the Schengen Agreement was the only interpretation that gave "precedence to the object and purpose of the provision rather than to procedural or purely formal matters" in order to ensure that the aforementioned principle had proper effect.[78]

Other examples include the *Kolpak* Case, in which the European Court of Justice compared the EC-Poland Association Agreement with the EC-Slovakia Association Agreement and held that they did not differ "in regard to their objectives or the context in which they were adopted".[79] In the *Interfood* Case the agreements between the Community and its GATT partners regarding the customs tariff were treated as a possible source of assistance in interpreting the rules of classification applicable to the GATT.[80] In the *Bresciani* Case, the express reference in Article 2(1) of the Yaoundé Convention to Article 13 of the EC Treaty was reason enough for the Court to interpret the provision in the same manner as Article 13 EC.[81] And in the *Haegeman* Case the Community Court held that the interpretation of paragraph 2 of Protocol 14 annexed to the EC-Greece Association Agreement had to take place "in the light of the general structure both of the Athens Agreement, of which it forms part, and of the totality of the provisions contained in the Protocol itself".[82]

[76] Case 87/75, [1976] ECR 129, paragraphs 22-23.

[77] Case C-469/93, [1995] ECR I-4533.

[78] Joined Cases C-187 and C-385/01, [2003] ECR I-1345, paragraphs 33-35.

[79] Case C-438/00, [2003] ECR I-4135, paragraphs 25-26.

[80] Case 92/71, [1972] ECR 231, paragraph 6.

[81] Case 87/75, [1976] ECR 129, paragraph 25.

[82] Case 181/73, [1974] ECR 449, paragraph 10. In the *Deutsche Shell* Case reference was made to recommendations from the Joint Committee as a source for interpretation by the national courts. Case C-188/91, [1993] ECR I-363, paragraph 18. See also Case 38/75, *Nederlandse Spoorwegen*, [1975] ECR 1439; Case 104/81, *Kupferberg*, [1982] ECR 3641 and Joined Cases 21-24/72, *International Fruit Company*, [1972] ECR 1219.

The Court has also used the interpretation of international agreements by the Commission as the correct one.[83] Without indicating what motivated it to accept the Commission's interpretation, the Court in the *Nederlandse Spoorwegen* Case adopted the Commission's interpretation of the 1950 Convention on Nomenclature for the Classification of Goods in Customs Tariffs.[84] Similarly, the Court adhered to the Commission's interpretation of three different agreements in order to establish the effect of allowing Member States the power to require a licence for the export of the relevant products to non-member countries.[85] And in the *Dürbeck* Case, the fact that the special GATT group relied on the uncontested information provided by the Commission to hold that the protective measures adopted by the Commission did not infringe the Articles I and II of the GATT, was sufficient reason to accept the Commission's interpretation.[86] In the *Kziber* Case the Court followed the Commission's interpretation of article 41(1) of EC-Morocco Cooperation Agreement on the concept of social security in relation to an identical concept in Regulation 1408/71 on the application of social security schemes to employed persons and family moving within the Community.[87]

Prima facie, the Court's use of additional sources to establish the context of an international agreement or assist it in the actual interpretation of an agreement is in line with Article 31 of the Vienna Conventions. The auxiliary items listed in Article 31(2) should not be seen as the only additional sources that can be used to determine the context of an international agreement. The Court's use of additional sources is clearly intended to arrive at the proper interpretation of the agreement and to avoid ascertaining a meaning that is ambiguous, obscure or manifestly absurd or unreasonable.[88] The difference with the aim of Article 31 of the Vienna Conventions is, however, that the Court aims at avoiding an interpretation that would primarily be contrary to, ambiguous or manifestly absurd in the light of the objectives of the Community system, and not the meaning of the international agreement as such. The Court does not seek to avoid a manifestly absurd interpretation in the light of the intention of the parties to the agreement but rather it looks for an interpretation that is compatible with the Community Treaty.

Under Article 300(6) EC the Court's opinion can be requested on the compatibility of an envisaged international agreement with the EC Treaty. Therefore, the Court's jurisprudence on the interpretation of international agreements should be seen in the light of the Court's task under Article 300(6) EC. Whenever the Court is called upon to interpret an international agreement, it will have to do so in a

[83] G. Gaja, 'Trends in Judicial Activism and Judicial Self-restraint Relating to Community Agreements' in E. Cannizzaro (ed.), *The European Union as an Actor in International Relations* (2002), at 130-132.

[84] Case 38/75, [1975] ECR 1439.

[85] Case 225/78, *Bouhélier*, [1979] ECR 3151.

[86] Case 112/80, [1981] ECR 1095.

[87] Case C-18/90, [1991] ECR I-199.

[88] Article 32 of the Vienna Conventions.

manner that will render the end result compatible with the EC Treaty. However, in pursuing this aim, the Court cannot go so far as to interpret an agreement in a manner that is completely at odds with the (general) intention of the parties to the agreement. If such a conflicting situation does occur, it is evident that the agreement should not have been concluded in the first place. It will then be for the Commission and the Council to remedy this situation. For example, through the re-negotiation of the entire agreement, an amendment of the provisions that is not compatible with the EC Treaty, or an amendment of the EC Treaty itself.

It should be mentioned, though, that the European Court of Justice, in its application of Article 31 of the Vienna Convention has rarely made express reference to the remaining elements contained in this article. On occasion the Court has taken some of these various other elements of treaty interpretation into consideration. In the *Anastasiou* Case the Commission, supported by the United Kingdom, invoked the grounds of subsequent practice to justify the acceptance of movement certificates issued by authorities other than those of the Republic of Cyprus.[89]

Brownlie points out that, although subsequent practice by individual parties has its merits[90], reference to subsequent practice is generally accepted where it establishes the understanding of all the parties concerning the interpretation of the agreement.[91] He stipulates, however, that the application of the concept where international organisations are concerned is different and more complex. In the traditional intergovernmental framework, member states that oppose a certain practice, but are outvoted by the other members, are not bound by the subsequent practice. Brownlie also states that the practice of the organs of the organisations may be influenced or governed by political or opportunistic motives. Only after the reasons behind the practice have become evident can the legal relevance of the practice be ascertained.[92]

The fact that all parties must accept the subsequent practice is obvious, because agreeing to an authoritative interpretation through a subsequent practice clearly establishes the intention of the parties. Therefore, to be considered subsequent, the practice must be consistent, common to or accepted by all parties.[93] It is, however, not necessary that all parties engage in the practice. It only has to be proved that all parties have, albeit tacitly, accepted the practice. It has to be stressed, though, that the subsequent practice must be resorted to within the context of the general rule of interpretation embodied in Article 31(1) of the Vienna Conventions.[94]

---

[89] Case C-432/92, [1994] ECR I-3087, paragraphs 31-35.

[90] This would be the case where this practice is known to and accepted by the other parties. D.J. Harris, *supra* note 52, at 771. See also the *Anglo-Iranian Oil Co.* Case, I.C.J. Reports (1952), at 20.

[91] I. Brownlie, *supra* note 12, at 605.

[92] *Ibid.*

[93] A. Aust, *supra* note 74, at 194-195.

[94] S. Torres Bernárdez, *supra* note 48, at 745.

The supranational character of the Community creates a different reality. Formal decisions can be taken by qualified majority vote. If a Member State opposes the use of a certain practice in the application of an international agreement it should utilize one of the various tools available under the EC Treaty to challenge such a practice. If a Member State fails to do so it cannot, at a later stage, invoke its initial opposition to deny the effects of a subsequent practice. It should be stressed, however, that such a conclusion would only apply in the case of a binding Council decision. If the practice came about informally, it would require the approval of all the Member States.

In the *South West Africa* Case, the International Court of Justice held that "Interpretations placed upon legal instruments by the parties to them, though not conclusive as to their meaning, have considerable probative value when they contain recognition by a party of its own obligations under an instrument".[95] In the *Anastasiou* Case, the Commission, in recognition of the practice by most Member States of accepting movement certificates by authorities other than the authorities of the Republic of Cyprus, distributed specimen stamps and authorized signatures as used by the Turkish Community in the northern part of Cyprus. Greece was the only Member States that had explicitly objected to this practice. The remaining Member States tolerated the practice as long as it occurred covertly.

The Court dismissed the argument put forward by the Commission and the United Kingdom. The Court recognized that Article 31 of the 1969 Vienna Convention does attach proper attention to the subsequent practice of the parties. But the Court held that Article 5 of the association agreement reflected only one of the objectives of the agreement. This objective had to be reconciled with the other general aims of the agreement.[96] The Court also pointed out that events that took place did not "establish unequivocally, within the meaning of Article 31 of the Vienna Convention, the existence of an agreement between the parties regarding the interpretation of the relevant provisions of the 1977 Protocol".[97] This conclusion was supported by the fact that the official position of the Republic of Cyprus, as one of the contracting parties, that only products accompanied by movements issued by the official government, was in direct contrast with the Commission's practice (paragraph 51).

Kuijper correctly points out that a distinction should be made between agreements concluded by the Community alone and mixed agreement.[98] Although in the case of an exclusive Community competence the Member States may be called upon to assist the Community in carrying out its contractual obligations, it cannot be denied that they do so as Members of the European Union and not as contracting parties. As a result, practices of the Member States cannot be consid-

[95] I.C.J. Reports (1966), 6, at 135-136.

[96] Paragraph 43.

[97] Paragraph 50.

[98] P.J. Kuijper, *supra* note 68, at 7-9.

ered as subsequent practice where this behaviour reflects a clear break with the ordinary meaning of the agreement.

Of course, where such a practice is openly condoned or endorsed by the relevant institutions of the Community, it can be argued that the practice of the Member States has become the practice of the Community. The difficulty is to establish the precise moment where the collective behaviour of the Member States becomes the behaviour of the institutions, in particular the Council. One thing is clear though, all the Member States must engage in the practice or at least, albeit tacitly, accept it. Where one or more Member States oppose the practice, it can never be considered a Council practice. This is even so where the Commission and the European Parliament endorse the practice. Therefore, in this instance one cannot speak of a subsequent practice of the Community.

Kuijper also points out that 'hidden' activities cannot be taken into consideration when one wants to determine subsequent practice.[99] The fact that, in the *Anastasiou* Case, only the United Kingdom was willing to admit to the practice probably influenced the Court's decision. The Member States were willing to continue the practice as long as everyone agreed to look the other way. Once it came out into the open no one was willing to admit to the existence of the practice.

In the case of mixed agreements, a distinction must be made between parallel competences and concurrent competences. In the case of concurrent competences it is not possible to establish a clear delimitation between the Community and the Member States' respective competences. Therefore, the subsequent practice requires the participation of the Community and all the Member States that are a party to the agreement. The situation of parallel competences presents a different scenario. Technically speaking, it is possible to separate the Community part of the agreement from the part of the agreement that falls under the competence of the Member States. In this regard it could be argued that the collective behaviour of the Member States can be construed as an established subsequent behaviour. It is difficult to see, however, how the Court of Justice could uphold this argument.

In the *Anastasiou* Case the Court made it clear that one must have regard of the entire object and purpose of the agreement, not only one specific part.[100] The Court held that the subsequent practice of the parties must be relevant to establish the authoritative interpretation of a provision in the light of the object and purpose of the entire agreement. Therefore, similar to a situation of concurrent competences, both the Community and the Member States that are a party to the agreement must engage in a certain practice before it can be considered subsequent practice in the sense of Article 31 of the Vienna Conventions.

Article 31(4) of the Vienna Conventions provides that a special meaning must be given to a term if the parties intended it to have this special meaning. The ap-

---

[99] *Ibid.*

[100] Case C-432/92, [1994] ECR I-3087, paragraph 43.

parent meaning of a term in its context is irrelevant in this regard. The party invoking the special meaning must, therefore, prove that this was the intention of all the parties.[101] Shaw points out that the standard of proof is fairly high, because this situation involves derogation from the ordinary meaning of the word.[102]

It is unlikely that the European Court of Justice will give effect to a special meaning of a term. Given the fact that the Court places added emphasis on the object and purpose of the agreement in the light of the object and purpose of the EC Treaty, it will be very difficult for a party to convince the Court of the special meaning of a term in an international agreement.

5.2.2 **Article 32 of the Vienna Conventions**

Article 32 of both Vienna Conventions permits the use of supplementary means of interpretation either to confirm the meaning resulting from the application of Article 31 of the Vienna Conventions, or when the interpretation in accordance with Article 31 leaves the meaning ambiguous, obscure or leads to a result that is manifestly absurd or unreasonable. In this instance parties can have recourse to the preparatory work, *traveaux préparatoires*, of the agreement or the circumstances of the conclusion of the agreement.

In the preparation of the 1969 Vienna Convention, the International Law Commission deliberately refrained from providing a definition for the concept '*traveaux préparatoires*'. The Commission was afraid that this could lead to the possible exclusion of relevant information.[103] At the Vienna Convention, the United States argued in favour of using the preparatory documents on the same footing as the text of the international agreement to establish the intention of the parties. The parties argued, among others, that preparatory instruments are confusing, unequal and partial, and, therefore, rejected the proposal. In fact, according to the French delegation, the adopted text is the most recent expression of the common intention of the parties and should therefore prevail.[104]

In its analysis of international agreements, the European Court of Justice has never had recourse to the preparatory documents of these agreements, nor has it taken the circumstances of their conclusion into account. This is not surprising given the fact that the Court never has recourse to preparatory documents when interpreting the EC Treaty or secondary Community legislation. Kuijper points

---

[101] A. Aust, *supra* note 74, at 196. In the *Eastern Greenland* Case, Norway alleged that the word Greenland should not be understood in the geographical sense but rather as meaning the colonies or colonized area of the West coast. The Permanent Court of International Justice dismissed Norway's contention stating that "The geographical meaning of the word Greenland (...) must be regarded as the ordinary meaning of the word. If it is alleged by one of the Parties that some unusual or exceptional meaning is to be attributed to it, it lies on that Party to establish its contention". P.C.I.J. Reports (1933), Series A, No. 53, at 49

[102] M.N. Shaw, *supra* note 52, at 844.

[103] See also D.J. Harris, *supra* note 52, at 774.

[104] *Ibid*, at 774-775.

out that the Court regards the Council as some kind of 'black box', which produces certain instruments.[105] The Court does not, however, venture into analysing the inner workings of the Council.

Similarly, the Community Court never looks into the process that takes place between the Community institutions involved in the negotiation and conclusion of the agreement. These are political processes that come within the discretion of the parties and which the Court does not consider to be of its concern. Similarly, it is impossible for the Court to know, in the case of mixed agreements, what has transpired in the national parliaments. Even if it did have access to this information, it would be extremely difficult to establish some kind of common practice.

5.2.3 **Article 33 of the Vienna Conventions**

When an international agreement is authenticated in two or more languages the text is equally authoritative in each language. Especially, in the case of bilateral agreements concluded by the Community or by the Community and the Member States jointly, the authentic text is standard in all the official languages of the Community and the official language(s) of the other contracting party.[106] In the case of multilateral agreements it is more common practice to limit the number of official languages to only a few.[107]

In the *Mavromatis Palestine Concessions* Case, the Permanent Court of International Justice held that

> "(...) Where two versions possessing equal authority exist one of which appears to have a wider bearing than the other, it is bound to adopt the more limited interpretation which can be made to harmonise with both versions and which, as far as it goes, is doubtless in accordance with the common intention of the Parties".[108]

Contrary to its international counterpart, the European Court of Justice has never indicated whether it takes the various authentic texts into consideration. In the interpretation of the EC Treaty or secondary legislation, the Court frequently has recourse to the various authentic texts to establish the precise meaning of a term. Even in the case of general principles of law, the Court sometimes looks into the

---

[105] P.J. Kuijper, *supra* note 68, at 10-11.

[106] Article 130 of the EC-Latvia Europe Agreement provides that "This Agreement is drawn up in duplicate in the Danish, Dutch, English, Finnish, French, German, Greek, Italian, Portuguese, Spanish, Swedish, and Latvian languages, each of these texts being equally authentic". OJ 1998, L 26/3. On the other hand the Fourth ACP-EEC Convention is only authentic in the Community languages, but not in the languages of the ACP countries (Article 369). OJ 1991, L 229/3. A similar situation applies in the EC-ASEAN Cooperation Agreement (Article 9). OJ 1980, L 144/2.

[107] The United Nations Convention to combat desertification is authentic in Arabic, Chinese, French, Russian and Spanish (Article 40). OJ 1998, L83/3. And Article 32 of the Convention on the Transboundary Effects of Industrial Accidents provides that the Convention is authentic in English, French and Russian. OJ 1998, L 326/5.

[108] P.C.I.J. Reports (1926) Series A, No. 2.

specific meaning of the principles in various languages. However, in the case of an international agreement the Court never considers the various language versions as an additional source of interpretation. It primarily uses the object and purpose of both the international agreement and the EC Treaty to find the correct interpretation. This is even so where the agreement has provisions, which are identically worded as provisions of the EC Treaty.

5.3 Dispute settlement

5.3.1 **Characteristics of treaty disputes**

International agreements that have entered into force must be applied in good faith. If the text is clear and unambiguous the agreement must be applied in accordance with its provisions. If the text is not clear, the agreement must be interpreted before it can be applied. The overwhelming number of treaty disputes arises from differing interpretations between parties. With the exception of certain international agreements, such as a peace treaty or an agreement establishing the international borders between two states, international agreements find their actual application in the interactions between private parties or between a private party and a government institution. In these instances these private parties will try to rely on or, especially in the case of the government agency, deny the direct effect of the agreement.

In the case of the European Community, the European Court of Justice has asserted its jurisdiction to interpret international agreements to which the Community is a party in an authoritative fashion. It was pointed out that this unilateral interpretation of the agreement carries with it the risk of an interpretation that is distinctly different from the interpretation the other parties intended the agreement to have. But the actual implementation of the agreement by either party could equally generate a dispute. Another source of dispute arises when one or more parties are no longer satisfied with one or more parts of the agreement. In this particular case, a dispute involving the interpretation or application of the agreement can be used as a pretext to renegotiate (parts of) the agreement.[109]

Despite several attempts to that effect, the international community has never succeeded in drawing up some form of binding third-party dispute settlement

[109] Kaplan *et al* wrote that "(...) disputes about treaty interpretation or the application of rules of customary law are often a means of asserting what is really a desire for legislative reform; that is, for changing the content of the rules. To the extent that this is true disputes about the law are not bona fide legal disputes, but rather an aspect of political manoeuvre. (...). Related to the foregoing is the fact that many disputes which appear to be disputes about the correct interpretation of a treaty or customary law have hidden motivation". M.A. Kaplan and N. deB. Katzenbach, *The Political Foundations of International Law* (1961), at 277-278. See also S. Rosenne, *Developments in the Law of Treaties 1945-1986* (1989), at 277-281.

procedure dealing with parts or all of the law of treaties.[110] This is not to say that international treaty law lacks any form of dispute settlement mechanisms. Rather, there are no hard and fast rules.[111] There is no specific method by which disputes concerning the interpretation or application of international agreements must be solved. It is left to the parties to set up the necessary mechanisms to settle such disputes. The Articles 65, 66 and the Annex of the Vienna Conventions merely provide the procedures that must be followed with respect to the invalidity, termination, withdrawal from or suspension of the operation of an international agreement and the procedures for judicial settlement, arbitration and conciliation.[112]

These articles require the parties to settle their dispute in accordance with the means provided for in Article 33 of the United Nations Charter. Article 33 of the UN Charter elaborates the general principle embodied in Article 2(3) of the same Charter. Article 2(3) requires parties to settle international disputes by peaceful means.[113] Consequently, the procedures for the settlement of treaty disputes are the same as the procedures for the settlement of any other international dispute. Furthermore, the procedure is the same irrespective of whether the dispute arises in the ambit of a bilateral or multilateral agreement. The dispute is usually between only two of the parties.[114]

Dispute settlement mechanisms can be divided into 'voluntary' and 'compulsory'. They can also be divided into 'binding' and 'non-binding'. A third form of division is into 'judicial' and 'non-judicial' forms of dispute settlement. A voluntary dispute settlement mechanism is one upon which parties agree once a dispute arises. A compulsory dispute settlement mechanism is agreed upon *ex ante*, a so-called 'compromissory clause', and is usually included among the provisions of the agreement or is attached as a separate agreement to the main agreement. A judicial dispute settlement mechanism involves the use of a court, tribunal or arbitration panel. The settlement of a dispute is binding if the parties agree that the decision will be binding whatever the outcome. This means that even judicial forms of dispute settlement can be non-binding if such is the express wish of the parties. Like all other aspects of treaty law the dispute settlement is governed by the will of the contracting parties.[115]

In the following paragraphs a number of dispute settlement mechanisms in some bilateral and multilateral agreements will be analyzed. The purpose is to determine what common features are present. Bilateral agreements will be the focus of attention in Section 5.4. Starting with the 1982 Law of the Sea Convention, multilateral agreements tend to display dispute settlement mechanisms that are

---

[110] See S. Rosenne, *supra* note 109, at 259-268.

[111] A. Aust, *supra* note 74, at 285.

[112] S. Rosenne, *supra* note 109, at 296-352 and M.N. Shaw, *supra* note 52, at 858.

[113] The most usual forms of dispute settlement are negotiation, mediation and good offices, conciliation, arbitration and judicial settlement.

[114] A. Aust, *supra* note 74, at 285-286.

[115] A. Aust, *supra* note 74, at 286. See also S. Rosenne, *supra* note 109, at 296-352.

closely tailored along the model of the Articles 65, 66 and the Annex of the Vienna Conventions. In these cases the (possible) participation of the Community and the Member States has a strong influence on the choice of the dispute settlement mechanism. Multilateral agreements will be analysed in Section 5.5.

It was argued that the contracting parties, in the absence of previous knowledge of the precise extent of the Communities competence in relation to its Member States, utilize a number of techniques designed to guarantee that the obligations under the agreement will all be met on the Community side and that the Community and the Member States will not benefit twice from their joint participation. The *ex ante* inclusion of precise dispute settlement mechanisms, and more precisely elaborate procedural requirements, is designed as a fail safety in the event disputes arise concerning the interpretation and application of an agreement. Detailed and elaborate provisions, such as those in the 1982 Convention on the Law of the Sea, are thus included to safeguard the interest of the non-Community contracting parties.[116]

5.4 Bilateral agreements

Although all bilateral agreements concluded by the Community or the Community and one or more Member States contain provisions dealing with dispute prevention and dispute settlement, none is as elaborate as the Agreement establishing the European Economic Area, EEA.[117] In fact, the EEA Agreement represents the most ambitious and comprehensive agreement ever concluded by the European Community and its Member States.[118] This comprehensive character is not only related to the forms of political cooperation and dispute settlement but also applies to the substantive and institutional provisions of the Agreement. The comprehensive character is also evident in the depth of the mechanisms available to solve any potential or existing dispute. As elaborate as the provisions in other agreements may be, none approaches the level of interconnectedness that pervades the EEA Agreement. The EEA Agreement thus becomes the yardstick against which the dispute settlement mechanisms of other bilateral agreements can be measured.

---

[116] See also J. Heliskoski, *Mixed Agreements as a Technique for Organizing the International Relations of the European Community and Its Member States* (2001), at 157-158.

[117] The EEA Agreement is neither a bilateral nor a multilateral agreement, but rather a mix of both. It is a bilateral agreement as far as it operates between the European Community and the EFTA States, but a multilateral agreement with regard to the EFTA States.

[118] See, for example, A. Toledano Laredo, The EEA Agreement: An overall view in 29 *C.M.L. Rev.* (1992), at 1199-1213; R.C. Gladstone, The EEA Umbrella: Incorporating Aspects of the EC Legal Order in 20 *L.I.E.I.* (1994)/1, at 461; C. Reymond, Institutions, Decision-making Procedure and Settlement of Disputes in the European Economic Area in 30 *C.M.L. Rev.* (1993), at 449 and S. Norberg, The Agreement on a European Economic Area in 29 *C.M.L. Rev.* (1992), at 1171.

5.4.1 Political dialogue

Political dialogue is a recurring element in association agreements concluded by the Community. The political dialogue is not a dispute settlement mechanism as such. Rather, its purpose is to provide the Community, the Member States and the other contracting party (parties) with an alternative to dispute settlement and, even worse, a possible unilateral denunciation of the association agreement. It enables the parties to discuss all matters associated with the interpretation and application of the agreement. Any positive outcome of such a political dialogue guarantees the uniform interpretation and application of the agreement. Although its use varies according to the type of association agreement and the level of association between the Community and the associated state(s), its role in helping the parties find common solutions and avoiding potential disputes is invaluable.

The Cotonou Agreement[119] contains a number of mechanisms aimed at avoiding disputes between the parties, and works towards common interpretations and application of the Agreement. These mechanisms can be found in Title II, The Political Dimensions.[120] Title II deals with a wide variety of subjects ranging from the essential elements such as human rights protection and good governance to migration issues. Article 8(1) provides that "the Parties shall regularly engage in a comprehensive, balanced and deep political dialogue leading to commitments on both sides". The objective of the political dialogue is to exchange information, and to establish agreed priorities and shared agendas, and covers all the aims and objectives laid down in the Cotonou Agreement.[121] The dialogue is also intended to facilitate consultations in international fora. One of its key objectives is to avoid a Party denouncing the Agreement.[122] In the case of the essential elements mentioned in Title II of the Cotonou Agreement, the dialogue is formal and intended to lead to far-reaching decisions.[123]

The focus of the political dialogue is either on specific political issues of mutual concern, or on issues of general significance for the attainment of the objec-

[119] Partnership Agreement between the members of the African, Caribbean and Pacific Group of States of the one part, and the European Community and its Member States, of the other part, signed in Cotonou on 23 June 2000 and entered into force on 1 April 2003, OJ 2000, L 317/3. The 76 ACP States plus the European Community and its 15 Member States have ratified the Cotonou Agreement, http://www.europa.eu.int/comm/development/body/cotonou/index_en.htm. The Agreement was ratified by the Community on the basis of Council Decision 2003/159/EC of 19 December 2002, OJ 2003, L 65/27. The Cotonou Agreement was applied provisionally between 2 August 2000 and its entry into force following Decision No 1/2000 of the ACP-EC Council of Ministers, OJ 2000, L195/46, and Decision 2000/771/EC of the Representatives of the Governments of the Member States, meeting within the Council, OJ 2000, L 317/375.

[120] Articles 8-13.

[121] Article 8(2).

[122] Ibid.

[123] See Article 9 of the Cotonou Agreement. See also K. Arts, ACP-EU Relations in a New Era: The Cotonou Agreement in 40 *C.M.L. Rev.* (2003), at 102-104 and B. Martenczuk, From Lomé to Cotonou: The ACP-EC Partnership Agreement in a Legal Perspective in 5 *E.F.A. Rev.* (2001), at 467-474.

tives of the Agreement.[124] Article 8(6) requires that the political dialogue be conducted in a flexible manner. The dialogue can be formal or informal and conducted within and outside the institutional framework, in the appropriate format and at the appropriate level including regional, sub-regional or national level.[125] The term 'flexible' should not be interpreted as only referring to these forms of dialogue, but also to the level of government representatives involved. The Cotonou Agreement does not indicate who can request such a dialogue to take place, but it is self-evident that such dialogue can occur at the request of any party or grouping of parties. The dialogue can also take place without a formal request. The dialogue can take place between some or all of the parties. It must, however, always involve the Community, the Community and one or more Member States, or one or more Member States on the one hand and one or more ACP States on the other hand.[126]

The political dialogue is intended to find negotiated solutions to all matters and to avoid the occurrence of disputes between the parties. Although no such express reference is made, the dialogue does not restrict the rights of the parties to move to the forms of dispute settlement provided in the Articles 96-98 of the Agreement. Parties are not obliged to seek a negotiated solution in accordance with the provisions in Title II, but this is preferred. This is made clear by the first sub-paragraph of Article 12, which requires the Community to inform the ACP States in good time of its intention to adopt a measure that may affect the interests of the ACP States. The ACP States may request that consultations take place. These consultations are to take place promptly.[127]

The provisions on political dialogue in the EC-Latvia Europe Agreement[128] were included in Title II of the Agreement (Articles 4-7). They were different in

---

[124] Article 8(4). These issues include such matters as arms trade, drugs and organized crime and religious discrimination.

[125] The institutional structure consists of the Council of Ministers, the Committee of Ambassadors and the Joint Parliamentary Assembly.

[126] Article 3 of Council Decision 2003/159/EC provides that in consultations the Community will be represented by the Presidency of the Council and the Commission. This provision is part of the provisions dealing with the procedures embodied in the Articles 96 and 97 of the Cotonou Agreement. Although no specific reference is made to the political dialogue the Article must be read as also including this procedure. Similarly, no such specific reference is made in the Internal Agreement between the Representatives of the governments of the Member States meeting within the Council on measures to be taken and procedures to be followed for the implementation of the ACP-EC Partnership Agreement, OJ 2000, L 317/376. Article 1 of the Internal Agreement requires that where a common position is to be adopted by the representatives of the Community concerning matters for which the Member States are competent the Council shall act unanimously on a proposal from the Commission or from a Member State. In the course of its external activities, the Commission may also maintain all appropriate contacts provided the Council is kept abreast of all developments.

[127] Article 12, sub-paragraph 2. The Community is obliged to accept the submissions of the ACP States, but must inform them in advance, where possible, of the decisions it will adopt (sub-paragraphs 3-5).

[128] Europe Agreement establishing an Association between the European Communities and their Member States, of the one part, and the Republic of Latvia, of the other part, OJ 1998, L 26/3. The

character from the provisions of the Cotonou Agreement. This is understandable given the differing object and purpose of the Europe Agreement in relation to the Cotonou Agreement. Whereas the political dialogue between the Community and the ACP States shall be comprehensive, balanced and deep leading to commitments on both sides, the political dialogue between the Community and Latvia shall be developed and intensified. Although both processes can lead to similar results, the starting point is different and the aim is different. This should be read in light of origins of the agreements. The Cotonou Agreement represents a continuation of the relationship between the Community and the ACP States that dates back to the Yaoundé Conventions. It marks the follow-up of the Lomé Conventions. The EC-Latvia Agreement was concluded in response to the developments in Central and Eastern Europe in 1989 and thereafter, and was intended to prepare Latvia for membership of the European Union. The Agreement represented the first step in this new relation and correspondingly the political dialogue had to start from the beginning and it had to be intensified progressively.

The political dialogue shall

> "Accompany and consolidate the rapprochement between the European Union and Latvia, support the political and economic changes underway in that country or already realized, and contribute to the establishment of close links of solidarity and new forms of cooperation between the Parties".[129]

It promoted, among others, cooperation in areas covered by the Union's Common Foreign and Security Policy and security and stability in Europe.[130]

The political dialogue between the parties was to take place within the multilateral framework.[131] This was in stark contrast with the flexible formula in the Cotonou Agreement. Although, in the latter case, dialogues primarily take place within the institutional framework, the Agreements also permit *ex ante* informal talks. In the case of the Europe Agreement the parties had to agree on other forums, but according to the forms and practices established with the associated countries of central Europe.[132]

Article 6(2), fourth indent, permitted that, with the agreement of the Parties, dialogue could be established by "any other means which would make a useful contribution to consolidating, developing and stepping up this dialogue". Where, however, the political dialogues were at ministerial level they were to take place within the Association Council.[133] In principle, the parties could agree that meetings at ministerial level also take place in other informal settings. But the specific

---

Agreement was ratified by the Community on the basis of Council Decision 98/98/EC of 19 December 1997, OJ 1998, L 26/1.

[129] Article 4.

[130] Article 4, third and fourth indent.

[131] Article 5.

[132] Ibid.

[133] Article 6(1).

importance attached to these meetings in the Agreement made this highly unlikely. The Cotonou Agreement does not place such *ex ante* restrictions on the political dialogue at ministerial level. The level of flexibility embodied in the Cotonou Agreement clearly exceeds that of the Europe Agreements.

Contrary to the Cotonou Agreement, the political dialogue of the Europe Agreements was not regarded as an alternative to dispute settlement. Although the progressive character of the dialogue had the advantage that it could lead to political solutions pre-empting the need for official dispute resolution this was not an aim in itself. The political dialogue in the Europe Agreement had the primary aim of setting up a negotiating process to accompany the developments in the associated countries and to lead the way for convergence and membership. Because the accession criteria, as set out in Article 49 TEU, and the so-called Copenhagen criteria, already made reference to such concepts as respect for human rights, democracy and the rule of law, there was no need for additional reference in the Europe Agreements. Therefore, the political dialogue also involved these matters.

The provisions on political dialogue in Title II of the EC-Russia Cooperation Agreement bare a strong resemblance with the provisions of the Europe Agreement.[134] The political dialogue is intended to lead to more intense political relations, but because the EC-Russia Cooperation Agreement does not envisage membership of the Union, as is the case with the Europe Agreements, the political relations are of a different order. The political dialogue in the Cooperation Agreement includes concerted efforts by the parties pertaining to "the observance of the principles of democracy and human rights".[135]

The level of commitment on these matters is of a differing intensity than the level embodied in the Europe Agreements and the Cotonou Agreement. The dialogue is to take place within pre-established forums with little room for flexibility.[136] Similarly, the political dialogue of the Cooperation Agreement is not a political alternative to dispute settlement. But like the Europe Agreements it can have such an impact or effect.

The Agreement between the Council of the European Union, Iceland and Norway on the Schengen Agreement[137] does not contain any express reference to a

[134] Articles 6-9.

[135] Article 6, third indent.

[136] Article 8, third indent, permits the creation of other means, including the possibility of expert meetings that would contribute to consolidating and developing the dialogue.

[137] Agreement concluded by the Council of the European Union and the Republic of Iceland and the Kingdom of Norway concerning the latter's association with the implementation, application and development of the Schengen acquis, OJ 1999, L 176/36. The Agreement was concluded on the basis of Council Decision 1999/437/EC of 17 May 1999, OJ 1999, L 176/31. Although the Council concluded this Agreement, it must be assumed that the European Union is a party to the agreement. This is the case because the Council does not possess international legal personality and cannot, therefore, conclude international agreements. See also Chapter 2, The external competence of the European Union.

political dialogue. This is not to say that there is no room for negotiations within the co-operative structure. The Republic of Iceland and the Kingdom of Norway are to be associated with the activities covered in the Annexes A and B of the Agreement.[138] Within the mixed Committee set up on the basis of Article 3(1) any concern entertained by Iceland and Norway shall be given due consideration.[139] However, these concerns only relate to problems they encounter in respect of a particular act or measure, or questions concerning the development of provisions of concern to them, or the implementation of the same.

The Agreement does not make reference to a more general dialogue concerning matters falling under the Schengen Agreement. This does not exclude the right of either of the parties to put such matters on the agenda if the need arises. But whereas the aforementioned association agreements explicitly create room for such dialogue, the Council-Iceland-Norway Agreement does not. In principle one would have to look at the Schengen Agreement to see what kind of arrangements have been made. Although the Schengen Agreement provides for close co-operation between the parties it is not an agreement to which either the Community or the Union is a party. Many of the provisions of the Schengen Agreement have been progressively incorporated into the European Community in accordance with the provisions of Title IV of the EC Treaty.

Dialogue between the Community, the Member States and the EFTA States associated in the European Economic Area can take place in various forums[140], but the primary setting is the Joint Committee.[141] It is essentially a permanent setting for the exchange of information and consultations between the European Commission and the EFTA States.[142] Because of the dominance of the Community in the EEA relation and the close association of the EEA system with the Community[143], the parties must be kept abreast in due time of all developments within the Community.[144] The Joint Committee shall, therefore, where such becomes necessary, adopt those decisions concerning amendments of the Annexes of the EEA Agreement that are as closely as possible to the measures adopted by the Community. These decisions will allow the simultaneous application of the Community legislation and the amended annexes. If no decision can be reached,

[138] Article 1.

[139] Article 4(2), second indent.

[140] Dialogue can also take place at the level of the EEA Council, which brings together representatives of the EC Council of Ministers, the Commission and the government of each EFTA State. Article 5 of the EEA Agreement authorizes the contracting parties to raise any matter of concern at the level of the EEA Council or the Joint Committee.

[141] The Joint Committee consists of representatives of the Commission and each of the EFTA States.

[142] Article 92(1) provides that the main purpose of the Joint Committee is to guarantee an effective implementation and execution of the EEA Agreement through exchanges of views and information.

[143] The EEA contains a body of law that is identical to EC law.

[144] This includes the monitoring of any developments within the case-law of the European Court of Justice and the EFTA Court regarding EC provisions that are identical to EEA provisions.

the Joint Committee will examine all other possibilities to ensure the proper functioning of the EEA Agreement.[145]

Prima facie, the EEA procedure bears a strong resemblance to the procedures in the aforementioned agreements, especially the Cotonou Agreement. However, on closer inspection it becomes evident that the permanent character of the dialogue and the extent and purpose of the dialogue is much more intensive than the dialogue in the three other bilateral agreements. As pointed out before, this is because of the level of association between the Community and the EFTA States. The European Court of Justice has frequently ruled that identical provisions in the EC Treaty and the association agreements should not necessarily have the same interpretation. This case-law does not apply to the EEA Agreement.[146] The EEA Agreement is a clear extension of the EC common market. And although the EEA is not a common market in itself, it is clearly more than an ordinary free trade association. In fact, only four common policy areas are excluded, namely, agriculture and fisheries, a common external trade policy, border controls that are simplified but not abolished, and a common policy on taxation.[147] It is in this framework that the political dialogue takes place and must be understood.

5.4.2 Consultation

The consultation procedure can be used to find a negotiated settlement to an existing dispute or as a means to avoid a dispute from materializing. The difference with the political dialogue is that the consultation procedure is always focused on a specific matter relating to the interpretation, application or implementation of an international agreement. The political dialogue, on the other hand, can be of a more general nature and does not necessarily involve issues concerning the interpretation, application or implementation of the agreement.[148]

The Cotonou Agreement provides for two situations involving the consultation procedure, namely, regarding human rights, democratic principles and the

---

[145] Article 99(4) requires the parties to cooperate in good faith throughout the information and consultation phases in order to facilitate the work of the Joint Committee.

[146] Article 6 of the EEA Agreement provides that on the date of the signature of the Agreement all provisions of the Agreement that are identical to Community provisions must be interpreted and applied in accordance with the relevant rulings of the European Court of Justice.

[147] See S. Norberg, *supra* note 118, at 1172-1173.

[148] Analysis of a number of bilateral agreements shows that the consultation procedure is the preferred form of dispute settlement, or an instrument to find a common solution regarding any specific matter. Examples of other agreements in which the consultation procedure plays a prominent role are the Agreement on international humane trapping standards between the European Community, Canada and the Russian Federation, OJ 1998, L 42/43; the Agreement between the European Economic Community and the People's Republic of China on trade in textile products, OJ 1990, L 352/2; the Agreement between the European Community and the Government of Canada regarding the application of their competition laws, OJ 1999, L 175/50 (in this Agreement the consultation procedure is in fact the only mechanism available to the parties) and the Stabilization and Association Agreement between the European Union and the Republic of Croatia and Interim Agreement, Press release of 30 October 2001 – Press: 398 Nr 13344/01, http://www.europa.eu.int.

rule of law (Article 96) and with regard to corruption (Article 97). In the EC-Latvia Agreement consultation could be requested within the Association Council concerning measures adopted by one party against another for failure to fulfil an obligation under the Agreement (Article 123(2), second sub-paragraph). Article 102 of the EC-Russia Cooperation Agreement permits that the parties may agree to consult each other promptly through appropriate channels on any matter concerning the interpretation or implementation of the Agreement and other relevant aspects of the relations between the parties. Under Article 3(4) of the Council-Iceland-Norway Agreement, Iceland and Norway are only to be consulted on matters mentioned in Article 1 of the Agreement.

Of all these procedures the ones embodied in the Cotonou Agreement are the most elaborate. Although, as pointed out before, their use is not dependent on a prior use of political dialogue, Article 96 of the Cotonou Agreement shows a clear preference for the use of dialogue prior to the use of the consultation procedure.[149] In fact, parties will only have recourse to the consultation procedure under Article 96 if the political dialogue has not generated the necessary positive results or it involves an urgent matter. In the case of the Fiji Islands, the unconstitutional replacement of the democratically elected government and the failure to restore democracy fully, were considered serious enough to use the procedure of Article 96 of the Cotonou Agreement.[150] Consultations were also held with the government of Liberia under the Articles 96 and 97.[151]

The consultation procedure must be initiated no later than 15 days (Article 96) or 21 days (Article 97) upon the invitation of any one of the parties. In both cases the consultations are not to last longer than 60 days. On the European side, the Community and the Member States act as one party. This is obvious because acting separately would provide the Community and the Member States an unfair advantage. However, in the case of a political dialogue the Community and the Member States may act separately. Article 98 also recognizes, at the initial stage, disputes between individual parties on the Community side and one or more ACP States. However, for the application of the arbitration procedure the Community and the Member States act together.

The procedural aspects on the Community side are governed by the Internal Agreement between the Representatives of the governments of the Member

[149] Article 97 does not make special reference to the political dialogue. However, serious cases of corruption are considered a violation of the Agreement on the basis of Article 9(3), second sub-paragraph.

[150] Council Decision 2001/334/EC, concluding consultations with the Republic of the Fiji Islands under Article 96 of the ACP-EC Partnership Agreement, OJ 2001, L 120/33. In a letter to the President of the Republic of the Fiji Islands the Council notified the President that the notification of the 9th EDF allocation and the financing and implementation of new programmes under the 6th, 7th and 8th EDF National Indicative Programmes would be suspended until Fiji had returned to democracy. OJ 2001, L 120/34.

[151] Council Decision 2002/274/EC of 25 March 2002, OJ 2002, L 96/23. See also Council Decision 2003/632/EC of 25 August 2003, adopting measures concerning Liberia under Article 96 of the ACP-EC Partnership Agreement in a case of special emergency, OJ 2003, L 220/3.

States, meeting within the Council.[152] The Annex to the Internal Agreement provides that on the initiative of the Commission or a Member State, the Council is to adopt a decision to hold consultations with the party or parties concerned. The Council will adopt this decision by qualified majority and the Presidency and the Commission shall represent the Community.[153]

If the consultations do not lead to an acceptable solution for the parties involved or if consultation is refused, appropriate measures may be taken.[154] These measures must be in accordance with international law and proportional. The article makes no reference to the possible denunciation of the Agreement, but recognizes, as a measure of last resort, the suspension of the Agreement. In all likelihood this also includes the suspension of part of the Agreement if this part can be separated from the Agreement without affecting its general functioning. Parties do, however, have the general right to denounce the Agreement upon six months' notice.[155]

The provisions of Articles 96 and 97 of the Cotonou Agreement are in sharp contrast with the provisions of the Council-Iceland-Norway Agreement. No effect is given to the failure to reach some form of political compromise between the parties. But that is because, as indicated earlier, the consultation procedure is not intended as a dispute settlement mechanism. Similarly, the EC-Russia Cooperation Agreement does not make any reference to the effects of a failed consultation.[156] Neither did the EC-Latvia Agreement make reference to any particular effects. However, in this case consultation was directly related to the adoption of measures against a party considered to be in breach of its obligations under the Agreement and had to be requested by the other party. One can assume that if the consultations did not generate a positive outcome, the complaining party could proceed and adopt the proposed measures or invoke the dispute settlement procedure.

The Annexes to the EEA Agreement contain all the secondary Community law that has been integrated into the EEA structure. The integration does not occur automatically but is the result of consultations between the Community and the EFTA States. These consultations must start at the earliest possible stage. Articles 99 and 100 of the EEA Agreement allow for the participation of experts of the EFTA States in Community committees that assist the Commission in the preparation of draft Community measures. These experts must be treated in the

---

[152] OJ 2000, L 317/376.

[153] Article 1.

[154] Article 96(2)(a), fourth sub-paragraph.

[155] Article 99.

[156] Article 107 requires that the party that considers adopting measures against an offending party must inform the Cooperation Council of these appropriate measures. No reference is made to a consultation procedure, but such a procedure is not explicitly excluded. Parties are free to make use of such a procedure, but the complaining party can also apply these measures immediately. The only restriction is that it has to use those measures that disturb the functioning of the Agreement the least (paragraph 2, second sub-paragraph).

same way as Community experts and the consultations must take place as soon as new legislation is being considered or prepared by the Commission. Proposals that have been sent to the Council of Ministers of the European Union are also sent to the EFTA States. The parties may decide to hold preliminary exchanges of views within the Joint Committee, followed by additional consultations at the most important moments before the measure is adopted at the Community level. If these consultations do not generate a satisfactory solution, supplementary efforts can be made to work out a negotiated solution. If no such agreement is possible the parties can invoke one of the various (dispute settlement) mechanisms available.

None of the aforementioned agreements requires the parties to consult on an implementation of the agreements that is in parallel with corresponding Community provisions. All consultations are strictly restricted to the actual interpretation and application of the agreement itself or the occurrence of disputes that might compromise the interpretation and application of the agreement. Internal measures must be in conformity with the provisions of the agreements, but in principle there is no obligation to consult on these matters. Parties can request such consultations. Usually though the consultations will only take place after possibly conflicting measures have been adopted. The EEA Agreement sets a different precedent in that the adoption of internal Community measures with EEA relevance will be the subject of consultation from the moment of their preparation until their final adoption and beyond.

5.4.3 **Conciliation**

The conciliation procedure is not a standard feature in bilateral agreements concluded by the Community. Within the structures of international agreement the prominence is usually on diplomatic or negotiated solutions and consultations, and to a lesser extent on arbitration or on some other form of dispute settlement. The consultation procedure, either within the context of the political dialogue or as part of the dispute settlement procedures is the preferred mechanism of the Community. Of the agreements analyzed in this part of the chapter, the only agreement containing a conciliation procedure is the EC-Russia Cooperation Agreement.

The conciliation procedure is part of the dispute settlement procedure embodied in Article 101 of the EC-Russia Cooperation Agreement. Recourse to the conciliation procedure is, however, not automatic. Even in this instance, preference is given to a diplomatic solution. Disputes concerning the interpretation or application of the Agreement must first be brought before the Cooperation Council.[157] The Cooperation Council may settle the dispute by means of a recommenda-

[157] Article 101(1).

tion.[158] Recommendations are usually non-binding forms of dispute settlement. If parties agree with the settlement they will proceed to implement the decision. If there is no agreement within the Cooperation Council or if either of the parties disagrees with the final recommendation, the parties may agree to use the conciliation procedure.[159]

This procedure appears to give a certain added weight to the recommendations of the Cooperation Council. After all, if the parties agree with the recommendations they must implement them. Failure to accept the recommendation can result in the imposition of the conciliation procedure.[160] However, the third sub-paragraph of Article 101(3) provides that the recommendations taken by the conciliators shall not be binding. Here once again, if the parties agree with the recommendation they must implement them. If either of the parties is of the opinion that the subject of dispute centres on an essential part of the agreement and no agreement is reached, that party could unilaterally denounce the agreement in accordance with the provisions of Article 106 of the Agreement. However, this is not in the interest of either party. One can, therefore, readily assume that parties will strive to reach a solution that is acceptable to all and implement this decision, whether it is a recommendation from the Cooperation Council or a recommendation from the conciliators.

Within the EEA structure there is a limited role for conciliation but this procedure does not involve the parties to the Agreement. Conciliation is to be sought by the Joint Committee where the European Commission and its EFTA counterpart, the EFTA Surveillance Authority, hold different interpretations concerning the rules on state aid. The procedure can only be used when the Commission and the Surveillance Authority have varying views concerning interim measures adopted by one or more contracting parties to offset the negative effects of state aid granted by another contracting party.[161]

5.4.4 **Arbitration**

The Council-Iceland-Norway Agreement does not denominate the dispute settlement procedure. It simply states in Article 11(1) that in the case of a dispute concerning the application of the Agreement or where a decision of European Court of Justice on the application of the Agreement is substantially different from the application given by courts of Iceland and Norway the dispute shall be placed on

[158] Article 101(2). The wording suggests that other forms of dispute settlement are open to the Cooperation Council. However, this provision must be read as meaning that the Cooperation Council does not have to settle the dispute.

[159] Article 101(3)

[160] Each of the parties appoints a conciliator. The Cooperation Council appoints the third conciliator. The Community and its Member States act as one party. The decision of the conciliators is taken by majority vote (Article 101(3)). The Cooperation Council may set the rules of procedure for dispute settlement (Article 101(4)).

[161] Article 64(1).

the agenda of the Mixed Committee. The Agreement is silent as to the legal effects of the Committee's decision. Article 11(3), second sub-paragraph provides that the Agreement is considered as terminated if no final settlement is reached. In the light of this far-reaching effect in the case of no solution, it is correct to assume that the decisions of the Mixed Committee are binding on the parties. After all, a decision of which the end result is not acceptable to one of the parties is the same as no solution to the dispute.

As in the case of the EC-Russia Cooperation Agreement, the EC-Latvia Europe Agreement provides for recourse to, in this case Association Council, before invoking the arbitration procedure.[162] The Association Council may settle the dispute by means of a decision.[163] The Association Council can also adopt a recommendation. The decision is binding on the parties[164], but the legal effects of other types of solutions offered by the Association Council are unclear. The choice for other forms of solutions will be the outcome of consultations and negotiations. The Agreement provides a negotiated way out of a dispute. It can be readily assumed that such solutions will be accepted as being binding and agreed upon by consensus. This is all the more so, because the Association Council could eventually adopt a binding decision if a negotiated solution or an informal recommendation proves to be impossible. If no settlement can be reached within the Association Council, either of the parties may have recourse to arbitration.[165] Each party appoints an arbitrator, the third arbitrator will be appointed by the Association Council (paragraph 4). The arbitrators' decision is taken by majority vote and is binding on the parties (paragraph 4, fourth sub-paragraph).

The dispute settlement mechanism of the Cotonou Agreement is similar to the dispute settlement mechanism of the EC-Latvia Agreement. Disputes are to be submitted before the Council of Ministers (Article 98(1)). However, if the dispute occurs between meetings of the Council of Ministers, the parties may agree to bring the matter before the Committee of Ambassadors. If the Council of Ministers, or the Committee of Ambassadors, cannot reach a settlement, either party may request a settlement of the dispute by arbitration (Article 98(1)). Each party shall appoint an arbitrator, but it can ask the Secretary General of the Permanent Court of Arbitration to appoint the second arbitrator (Article 98(2)(a)). The two arbitrators must appoint the third arbitrator but can also request that the Secretary General of the Permanent Court of Arbitration appoint the third arbitrator (Article 98(2)(b)). The decisions of the arbitrators are binding (Article 98(2)(d)).[166] No reference is made to the legal effect of the Council of Minister's decision. Still,

[162] Article 113.

[163] Article 113(2).

[164] Article 113(3).

[165] Article 113(3).

[166] Unless parties agree on different rules of procedures, the procedure laid down in the optional arbitration regulation of the Permanent Court of Arbitration for International Organisations will be applied.

the possibility of arbitration and the binding nature of the arbitration panel's decision mean that parties will not simply dismiss the Council's decision. This would be tantamount to a continuation of the dispute. The possibility of subsequent binding arbitration, therefore, gives added weight to the decision of the Council of Ministers.

Another point worth considering is that a party may dispute the invocation of the procedures of Articles 96 and 97 of the Cotonou Agreement. After all, Article 98 explicitly refers to disputes concerning the interpretation or application of the Agreement. A party could invoke Article 98 to challenge the validity of any measure adopted on the basis of either Article 96 or Article 97. In the case of Article 96, except in cases of special urgency, the matter must have been brought before the Council of Ministers. If the consultations do not result in a satisfactory solution, either party could adopt the measures it deems necessary. The party affected by the measure could resort to arbitration immediately. A new consideration by the Council of Ministers is not necessary. In case of Article 97, there is no involvement of the Council of Ministers. In this instance parties would have to put the dispute before the Council before recourse to the arbitration procedure. The measures themselves cannot, on the basis of Article 98, be challenged directly, but rather the application of the procedure of Article 96 is.

Although the EEA Agreement permits the use of arbitration, its role is subordinate to other political mechanisms and forms of dispute settlement available under the Agreement. Recourse to arbitration is restricted to the field of the safeguard measures. The main rule embodied in the EEA Agreement is that disputes between the parties must be settled at political level within the Joint Committee. Failure to reach a negotiated solution can result in the suspension of the affected part of the EEA Agreement, but even this is a political decision. However, if there are "serious economic, societal or environmental difficulties of a sectorial or regional nature" and these difficulties cannot be resolved, parties retain the right to adopt unilateral safeguard measures.[167] These measures must be restricted in scope and duration. Prior to the adoption of such safeguard measures, the party involved must notify the Joint Committee of its intention. Consultations will be held to find a negotiated solution. The Joint Committee must solve disputes arising as a result of the scope or duration of the safeguard measure within three months. If no such solution can be found, any party may refer the dispute to arbitration.

Each party appoints one arbitrator. The arbitrators will nominate a third arbitrator who cannot be of the same nationality of either of the two other arbitrators. The panel adopts its decisions by majority and the decisions are binding on the parties concerned.[168]

---

[167] Article 112(1). These safeguard measures apply to all parties to the Agreement (Article 112(3)).

[168] Article 111 and Protocol 33 of the EEA Agreement.

5.4.5 Judicial procedures

The absence of judicial procedures to settle disputes in the Community's bilateral agreements is noteworthy. As pointed out, in the bilateral sphere political dialogue, consultation and some form of dispute settlement are common features. None of the agreements, with the exception of the EEA Agreement, provides for judicial settlement, not even the use of the European Court of Justice. With the exception of the Council-Iceland-Norway Agreement none of the agreements analyzed even offer the possibility for the parties to the agreement to submit statements of case or written observations to the Court of Justice.[169] This is remarkable, because disputes could arise as a result of an interpretation given by the Court. These interpretations could run counter to the perceived intention of the other parties. Even if recourse were to be had to any one of the procedures provided for, it is obvious that the decision of the Court cannot be overruled. But it is unclear whether the Court can be bound, with regard to any future cases, by any decision adopted by the Parties.

In a number of cases, the European Court of Justice has held that interpretations by bodies set up by an agreement can be a useful tool, but they are not binding on the Court.[170] On the other hand, the Court has held that implementing measures adopted by the EC-Turkey Association Council can have direct effect and are, therefore, binding.[171] It is unclear whether this also extends to decisions adopted to settle a dispute between the parties. The answer depends on the legal effect of the decision. If the decision is binding, there can be instances where the decision can have direct effect and consequently it is binding on the Court. The Court, like all other Community institutions, must take all the necessary steps to give full effect to international agreements to which the Community is a party. This includes binding resolutions to a dispute concerning the interpretation or application of the agreement. If the recommendation or decision is not binding, then it is up to the Court to decide whether it wants to use the decision as a reference in the settlement of a case before it.

The European Court of Justice plays an important role in the interpretation and application of the EEA Agreement, and more importantly, its Annexes. There is the general provision of Article 6 of the EEA Agreement that requires the parties to adhere to the decisions of the Court issued prior to the signing of the EEA Agreement. Disputes within the Joint Committee concerning new secondary legislation that has to be implemented within the EEA structure can also be brought, by common accord, before the Court of Justice. The Court will give a preliminary

---

[169] Article 9(2) of the Council-Iceland-Norway Agreement. This option is only open with regard to preliminary references concerning the interpretation of any provision referred to in Article 2 of the Agreement.

[170] See Case 38/75, *Nederlandse Spoorwegen*, [1975] ECR 1439 and Case C-188/91, *Deutsche Shell*, [1993], ECR I-363.

[171] Case C-192/89, *Sevince*, [1990] ECR I-3461.

ruling on the interpretation of the contested measure. The EEA Agreement itself is silent as to the legal effects of such rulings[172] but in *Opinion 1/92* the Court held that these rulings are binding on the parties.[173]

It must also be pointed out that in the performance of its task, especially in the field of dispute settlement, the Joint Committee has powers that, to a certain extent, resemble judicial powers. In *Opinion 1/92* the European Court of Justice expressed some concern with regard to the Joint Committee's judicial powers, but in the end ruled that these powers were compatible with the EC Treaty.[174]

Another matter worth mentioning is the EFTA Court. This Court has limited jurisdiction, in that it can only settle disputes between the EFTA States. During the negotiations of the EEA Agreement the initial proposal had been to create an EEA Court to settle disputes between the EEA partners with regard to the interpretation and application of the EEA Agreement. This was held to be incompatible with the EC Treaty as the EEA Court would have the power to rule on the interpretation of secondary Community law.[175]

5.5 MULTILATERAL AGREEMENTS

The increased participation of international organisations in international affairs, and more particularly in multilateral agreements, demands a shift not only in the way international agreements are negotiated and concluded, but also in the manner in which issues such as liability for non-performance and the settlement of disputes arising from the interpretation and application of the agreements are regulated. The problem is exacerbated by the enormous diversity of internal rules of the organisations, and more particularly, the internal relation between the international organisations and their members. In this regard the European Community is a case in point. The division of powers between the Community and the Member States requires an international approach that permits the Community to assert its own identity at international level and which at the same time permits the Member States to continue to participate in international affairs to the full extent of their statehood. However, the (gradual) internal transfer of sovereignty from the Member States to the Community, and the corresponding shift in the international participation by both the Community and the Member States[176], presents prospective international partners with an unprecedented reality for which international law has yet to find a proper and uniform response.

Analysis of the Community's treaty practice has demonstrated the various solutions provided by the Community's contracting partners, especially in the mul-

[172] Article 107. This article also creates the possibility for EFTA States to allow a court or tribunal to ask the European Court of Justice for the interpretation of an EEA rule.

[173] *EEA II*, [1992], ECR I-2821.

[174] *Ibid.*

[175] Opinion 1/91, *EEA I*, [1991] ECR I-6079.

[176] See Case 22/70, *AETR*, [1971] ECR 263.

tilateral setting. It became clear that these arrangements, aimed at establishing precise delimitations between the Community's and the Member States' competence, as elaborate as they may be, cannot in themselves, settle all outstanding matters and provide the parties with all the necessary assurances they would have had if they had to deal with the Member States alone. This is in part due to the gliding scale in which the transfer of competence from the Member States to the Community takes place. But it is also because of the repeated attempts made by the other parties to avoid that the Community and the Member States gain any advantage from their joint participation in the agreement. This approach can be born out of ideological concerns or simple distrust. The bottom line, as far as these third parties are concerned, is that the joint participation of the Community and the Member States should not result in an increase of their individual rights to the detriment of the other parties.[177]

It becomes obvious that such diverging positions cannot yield compromissory results that could meet the wishes and demands of all the parties to the international agreement. Especially the Community may be reluctant to participate in any international agreement that would restrict its participation considerably or make its participation subordinate to the (role performed by the) Member States, notably concerning matters falling within its exclusive competence. One alternative way to reconcile such opposing positions is through the creation of an elaborate system of dispute settlement mechanisms. But here again another problem comes to the forefront. Traditional international dispute settlement is directed towards disputes between states and frequently involves such established institutions as the International Court of Justice. Yet, Article 34 of the Statute of the Court clearly stipulates that only states can be a party to the Court's contentious proceedings. So far no attempts have been made to alter this situation. The aforementioned reconciliation process, therefore, does not only need to find a compromise between the two opposing positions regarding the Community's participation and the need for additional assurances towards the third countries, but also requires the development of a system of dispute settlement that will allow the Community to act in defence of its own prerogatives and be able to respond to any claim concerning possible substandard performance.

Heliskoski argues that "the problems posed by mixed agreements can be alleviated and the various opposing aspirations reconciled, through rules of a procedural nature".[178] He points out that it is possible to create mechanisms, which leave it to the Community and the Member States themselves to decide to whom particular matters under the agreement should be attributed. However, this has always been the crux of the matter. The position of the Community, the Member

[177] This approach was very evident throughout the negotiations of the 1982 Law of the Sea Convention. See also T. Treves, 'The European Community and the Law of the Sea Convention: New Developments' in E. Cannizzaro (ed.), *The European Union as an Actor in International Relations* (2002), at 279-281.

[178] J. Heliskoski, (2001), *supra* note 116, at 157.

States, and more particularly, the European Court of Justice has always been that the precise division of competence between the Community and the Member States is an internal matter. It is precisely this 'internal matter' that the other contracting parties want to see settled *ex ante*, that is, before the Community and the Member States assume the obligations embodied in an international agreement. Furthermore, the anxieties of the other contracting parties do not restrict themselves to mixed agreements, but equally apply to situation in which the Community has an exclusive competence.

Therefore, what one comes to expect is that the more important, complex and global an international agreement, the more elaborate and detailed the procedural aspects of any dispute settlement mechanism will be. This reality is clearly evidenced by the dispute settlement mechanisms in the 1986 Vienna Convention on the Law of Treaties between States and International Organisations or between International Organisations or such agreements as the 1982 Vienna Convention on the Law of the Sea. But not only these agreements set up elaborate systems of dispute settlement that can serve the international community as possible examples. As the Chairman of the Ad Hoc Group on Article 13 of the United Nations Framework Convention on Climate Change puts it

> "The procedures set forth in the conventions established under the ILO, the dispute settlement regime established by the WTO/GATT, the human rights instruments and the Implementation Committee of the Montreal Protocol, provide examples of a range of consultative and dispute resolution mechanisms that have evolved as a result of time, experience and political expediency".[179]

This statement shows that international partners have a plethora of political and dispute settlement mechanisms from which to choose, mechanisms that have proven their worth, to balance their needs and their desire for certainty with the Community's right to assert its own identity at international level. Nevertheless, the systems used so far have been designed to preserve the existing *status quo*, that is either the Community alone or the Member States but never concurrent. Analysis of three additional multilateral agreements will illustrate this point.

5.5.1 Negotiations and consultations

All international agreements provide either explicitly or implicitly for constant negotiations between the parties in order to facilitate the implementation or application of the agreements, or to avoid or settle any dispute arising from diverging interpretations of the agreements. International agreements are usually accompanied by the setting up of an institutional framework specifically designed to coordinate these political dialogues.

---

[179] *Report of the Ad Hoc Group on Article 13 on the Work of Its Second Session*, Held at Geneva on 10 July 1996, FCCC/AG 13/1996/2 of 18 July 1996.

Under the provisions of the International Cocoa Agreement 2001[180] the International Cocoa Council primarily carries out this function.[181] In this process the International Cocoa Council can delegate some of its powers to the Executive Committee, except, among others, the settlement of disputes under Article 50 of the Agreement. In the case of the United Nations Framework Convention on Climate Change, hereinafter referred to as UNFCCC,[182] the role of supreme political body is performed by the Conference of Parties, COP. Although subsidiary bodies can assist the Conference of Parties, such as the subsidiary body for implementation (Article 10), their role is rather limited. Finally, in the Convention on Biological Diversity reference is also made to a Conference of Parties. But whereas Article 7(2) of the UNFCCC expressly refers to the Conference of Parties as being 'the supreme body' of the Convention, the Convention on Biological Diversity does not make such an express reference. However, analysis of the provisions on the powers of the Conference of Parties under the Biodiversity Convention shows a strong similarity with those of the UNFCCC. Therefore, the conclusion is that there is no difference between the two. It should be pointed out that all decisions of the International Cocoa Council are binding on the parties.[183] No reference is made to the legal nature of the decisions of both the Conferences of Parties. Looking at the wording of the provisions the conclusion is that the decisions can be both binding and non-binding.

Before analysing the relevant provisions of the agreements in question, note should be taken of the scope and aim of the agreements. It was pointed out that one could expect the dispute settlement mechanisms to be more elaborate if the agreements are more important, complex and global in nature. Of the three agreements it is clear that the International Cocoa Agreement 2001 is the most limited in scope. It lacks a preamble and its primary objective is "to promote international cooperation in the world cocoa economy".[184] Looking at the two remaining agreements it could be argued that, although both are of great importance to the international community, the UNFCCC appears to be the more important of the two. This can be deduced in part from their respective preambles. In the first recital the UNFCCC states an acknowledgment of the Parties that "change in the Earth's climate and its adverse effects are a common concern of mankind". And the sixth recital makes reference to the fact that "the global nature of climate change calls for the widest possible cooperation by all countries and their participation in an effective and appropriate international response (...)". The biodiversity Convention 'merely' states that the Contracting Parties are "conscious of the intrinsic value of biological diversity and of the ecological, genetic, social,

[180] OJ 2002, L342/2.

[181] Articles 6 and 7.

[182] OJ 1993, L33/13.

[183] Article 12 (4). All decisions of the Council are taken by a simple distributed majority vote unless the Agreement provides for a special vote (Article 12(1)).

[184] Article 1(a).

economic, scientific, educational, cultural, recreational and aesthetic values of biological diversity and its components". The conclusion on the apparent greater importance of the UNFCCC in relation to the Biodiversity Convention is supported by the objectives of both agreements as formulated in Article 2 UNFCCC and Article 1 Biodiversity Convention respectively.[185]

The political dialogue within the International Cocoa 2001 Agreement restricts itself primarily to consultations between the members concerning the interpretation or application of the Agreement. The parties must afford each other adequate opportunity for consultations. Under the Biodiversity Convention parties are free to cooperate outside the structure of the Conference of Parties on a range of matters, but it is up to the Conference of Parties to review the implementation of the Convention. Article 23(1) only requires the Conference of Parties to hold regular meetings, but leaves it to the parties to determine when such meetings will take place.[186] The UNFCCC Conference of Parties does not restrict itself to conduct regular meetings to assess the implementation of the Convention but also permits convening such sessions with regard to any related legal instrument the Conference of Parties adopts.[187] Whereas the Biodiversity Convention only requires the Parties to meet at regular intervals, the UNFCCC obliges the Parties to meet every year unless the Conference of Parties decides otherwise.[188]

Although both the UNFCCC and the Biodiversity Convention Conferences of Parties provide the parties with ample opportunity for regular contacts to negotiate any matter concerning the implementation of the Conventions, only Article 13 of the UNFCCC requires the Conference of Parties to establish "a multilateral consultative process, available to the parties at their request, for the resolution of questions regarding the implementation of the Convention". This so-called Ad Hoc Group on Article 13 meets at regular intervals. However, due to uncertainty concerning the precise scope of Article 13, so far the Ad Hoc Group has not been able to set up a comprehensive consultative system for the parties.

5.5.2 **Dispute settlement**

Of the three agreements discussed the dispute settlement mechanism of the International Cocoa 2001 Agreement is, as is to be expected, the simplest. Disputes

---

[185] The ultimate objective of the UNFCCC is to achieve stabilization of greenhouse gas concentrations in the atmosphere at a level that would prevent dangerous anthropogenic interference with the climate system. The objective of the Biodiversity Convention is the conservation of biological diversity, the sustainable use of its components and a fair and equitable share of benefits arising from the utilization of genetic resources.

[186] Extraordinary meetings can also be held if the Conference of Parties deems it necessary or at the request of any Party, provided that within six months after the Party has submitted the request to the Secretariat it is supported by at least one-third of the Parties (Article 23(2)).

[187] Article 7(2).

[188] Article 7(4). The provision on extraordinary sessions is identical to those of the Biodiversity Convention.

concerning the implementation or application, which are not settled in accordance with the consultation procedure or otherwise, can be referred to the International Cocoa Council.[189] Before the Council adopts its final decision, members holding not less than one-third of the total votes or any five members, can request to seek the opinion of an *ad hoc* advisory panel. The Council has to take the advice of the panel into consideration, but no reference is made with regard to the time the panel should be granted to give its opinion and the weight of this advisory opinion in the decision of the Council.

In accordance with standard practice and in order to allow the panel to perform its task properly, it must be given a reasonable amount of time in accordance with the urgency and the complexity of the matter. Its advisory opinion, though not binding, must be given due consideration by the Council. If the Council disregards the panel's advice it would, at least, have to provide sufficient reasons why it does so. It should not be forgotten that the panels are not installed on the basis of a request of one member, but rather of a substantial number of members. This stresses the importance of the advisory opinion from the perspective of the requesting members. Neither is it clear by which majority the Council adopts its final decision, but in light of the frequent use of the simple distributed majority vote, including the decision to suspend a member's voting rights in accordance with the provisions of Article 51, it must be assumed that the same procedure applies in the context of Article 50.[190]

The dispute settlement mechanism of the Biodiversity Convention is more elaborate than the International Cocoa Agreement 2001, but bears a strong resemblance with the dispute settlement procedure of the UNFCCC. Both Conventions require the parties to seek a negotiated solution to their dispute.[191] The Biodiversity Convention allows the parties, in the event that no negotiated solution can be reached, to seek jointly good offices of or request mediation by a third party (paragraph 2). The UNFCCC formulates the provision more broadly. Parties are to seek settlement of their dispute through negotiation or any other peaceful means. Under the UNFCCC parties could thus decide to use third party mediation, good offices or any form of dispute settlement immediately, rather than go through bilateral negotiations. The Biodiversity Convention, on the other hand, makes bilateral negotiations a pre-requisite for any other form of dispute settlement.

Both Conventions require the parties, when ratifying, accepting, approving or acceding to the Conventions, to declare in writing to the depositary which other

[189] Article 50(1).

[190] In the case of voting rights, the European Community has a number of votes equal to the number of Member States party to the Agreement. However, they are not permitted to exercise their voting rights concurrently. No special reference is made to the participation of the Community and the Member States in the dispute settlement mechanism, but is evident that disputes will involve either the Community or one or more Member States. The Community and the Member States cannot, therefore, jointly be held liable for the same breach of the Agreement.

[191] Article 27(1) Biodiversity Convention and Article 14 UNFCCC.

forms of dispute settlement they prefer. The UNFCCC permits states to choose submission of the dispute to the International Court of Justice and/or arbitration (paragraph 2). International organisations can only opt for arbitration. The Biodiversity Convention does not make such a distinction. It merely states that a state or regional economic integration organisation may declare in writing whether it accepts arbitration or submission to the International Court of Justice or both. In this sense the Biodiversity Convention is more evolutionary than the UNFCCC. After all, a change of the Statute of the International Court of Justice would automatically permit access of international organisations to the Court if their declarations included submission to the International Court of Justice. In the case of the UNFCCC, the organisation would in principle have to submit a new declaration. However, the declaration issued under Article 14 (2) of the UNFCCC remains in force in accordance with its terms. Parties could limit such durations in order to better respond to new developments. No such provision is made in the Biodiversity Convention. Still, it must be said that the Biodiversity Convention, with regard to a possible acceptance of the jurisdiction of the International Court of Justice is better suited than the UNFCCC.

Part I of Annex II to the Biodiversity Convention provides an elaborate arbitration procedure. Article 1 requires the claimant party to notify the secretariat that the parties are referring a dispute to arbitration. The notifying state must outline the subject matter of the dispute, but if the parties cannot agree on the subject matter it will be for the president of the arbitration tribunal to determine the same. The remainder of the provisions outline the additional procedural requirements.[192] Article 16 provides that the decision of the arbitration tribunal shall be binding on the parties. The decision is without the possibility of appeal unless such an option has been agreed upon in advance. The arbitration procedure of the UNFCCC is to be determined by the Conference of Parties. So far the COP has not succeeded in developing such a procedure, neither for the UNFCCC nor for the Kyoto Protocol[193], which utilizes the same dispute settlement mechanisms as the UNFCCC.[194]

The UNFCCC and the Biodiversity Convention both permit the use of a conciliation procedure, but on different terms. Under the UNFCCC conciliation is possible if, after 12 months following notification by one party to another that a dispute exists between them, and the parties have not been able to settle their dispute through arbitration or judicial settlement, whichever is applicable, the dispute shall be submitted at the request of any of the parties to the dispute to conciliation.[195] The period of 12 months is clearly intended as a cooling off period during which parties can reconsider their position and try yet again to work

---

[192] Articles 2-17 of Part 1 of Annex II.

[193] OJ 2002, L130/4.

[194] See also R. Lefeber, From The Hague to Bonn to Marrakesh and beyond: A negotiating history of the compliance regime under the Kyoto Protocol in 14 *Hague Yb.* (2001), at 25-54.

[195] Article 14(5).

out a negotiated solution to their dispute. It also guarantees that parties will constructively work towards a settlement on the basis of arbitration or a ruling of the International Court of Justice. If no agreement can be reached, parties will have to wait one full year before they can proceed to the next phase and that is conciliation. In the meantime unilateral measures are not permitted.

Under the Biodiversity Convention conciliation is only possible if the parties to the dispute have not accepted the same or any procedure.[196] This means that the arbitral or judicial procedures will be finalized and the dispute settled. Prolonging the dispute beyond this stage is impossible. This is confirmed by Article 13 of Part 1 of Annex II, which grants a party to the arbitration procedure the right to request a continuation of the procedure, should the other party fail to appear before the tribunal. The rules of procedure under the UNFCCC have yet to be elaborated. Therefore, it is understandable that the conciliation alternative had to be included in the Convention. In the absence of such procedural rules parties would be free to adopt any unilateral measure to settle their dispute. This could seriously undermine the proper functioning of the Convention.

In the case of conciliation both Conventions contain the rules of procedure. Article 14(6) of the UNFCCC provides that each party shall appoint an equal number of members of the conciliation commission. The members of the commission will jointly appoint a chairman. The decision of the commission is recommendatory and must be considered in good faith by the parties. The Conference of Parties can adopt additional procedures relating to conciliation (paragraph 7). The provisions on conciliation under the Biodiversity Convention can be found in Part 2 of Annex 2. Article 1 provides that the conciliation commission shall consist of five members, two appointed by each party and the president chosen by the members of the commission. The decisions are to be taken by majority vote and constitute a proposal for the resolution of the dispute. The parties must consider this proposal in good faith.

5.6 Conclusions

The European Court of Justice, as the main judicial organ of the European Union, has asserted its jurisdiction to give authoritative interpretations concerning agreements to which the Community is a party. This authority does not restrict itself to agreements concluded on the basis of the Community's exclusive competence, but it also extends to mixed agreement and agreements in regard to which the Community, at the internal level, has assumed competence to act, and acts of institutions set up on the basis of international agreements. The underlying reason being that these agreements, having been concluded by the Council, become part of the Community legal order from the moment of their entry into force. In per-

[196] Article 27(4).

forming this task, the Court must not only ensure a uniform interpretation and application of the agreements inside the Community, but it must also make sure that the agreements are implemented in accordance with the intention of the parties and the rules of international law.

The interpretation of international agreements is of fundamental importance for its proper implementation and application. It is, therefore, imperative that the parties to the agreements adhere to the same rule of interpretation. Such an approach provides the contracting parties, at least, with a minimum set of guarantees concerning uniform interpretation. It is, therefore, surprising to note that the European Court of Justice does not display a strict compliance to the rules of treaty interpretation as embodied in the Articles 31-33 of the Vienna Convention.

The Court's attitude is remarkable because, more than any other Community institution, it must provide the assurance that the Community will honour its international treaty commitments. On the other hand, the Court's approach is not surprising because in its case-law the Court has consistently made it clear that binding as international agreements may be on the Community, in the Community legal order these agreements are subordinate to the EC Treaty. This subordination is due to the unique character of the Community as a separate legal order. The Court has consistently denied the application of principles and rules of international law as far as the internal workings of the Community system is concerned. It is against this background that the Court interprets provisions of international agreements. As a result, the Court tends to adhere to the general scheme embodied in the Articles 31-33, but not to the ordinary text. The Court places emphasis on the object and purpose of the agreements in light of the object and purpose of the EC Treaty.

With regard to dispute settlement matters a mixed picture is discernible. In the bilateral setting the Community usually has a relatively dominant position in relation to its negotiating partners. This is the case within the European Economic Area, Cotonou or the Europe Agreements, to name just a few. As a result, the dispute settlement mechanisms are more in line with the wishes of the Community, while giving proper consideration to the interests of the other parties. From the European Community, being itself an entity in which negotiations play a crucial role in the integration process, one can come to expect that it will give preference to negotiated solutions in its external treaty relations over other (binding) forms of dispute settlement. Analysis of a number of bilateral agreements confirms this prediction. The agreements display a strong emphasis on political dialogue and consultations. Even in those instances where dispute settlement mechanisms exist, the procedures include the possibility of additional negotiations or consultations. It is only where such negotiated solutions are not forthcoming or do not guarantee the desired outcome, that the agreements permit, as a last resource, access to other forms of dispute settlement such as arbitration and conciliation. Remarkably, however, little or no use is made of judicial forms of dispute settlement.

In the multilateral setting the Community can exert less influence and pressure. Still, the multilateral agreement, pretty much like the bilateral agreement, gives preference to the negotiation and consultation processes to avoid the occurrence of disputes or to settle actual disputes concerning the interpretation and application of agreements. Where recourse to binding dispute settlement is provided for, the options range from dispute settlement within the main political body to arbitration and the possible use of the International Court of Justice. In the case of multilateral agreements the procedural aspects of dispute settlement tend to be lengthy and elaborate. The decision by the parties to include such lengthy and elaborate provisions is directly related to the participation of international organisations, such as the Community, in the agreement. The detailed provisions are seen as a safeguard measure to ensure that neither the Community nor the Member States can elude their treaty obligations or acquire additional privileges, because of the Community's unique internal structure and the joint participation of the European Community and the Member States at international level.

FINAL REMARKS AND RECOMMENDATIONS

The purpose of this study was to conduct an in-depth comparative legal analysis of the relationship between the Community and the Union's external treaty-making practice and the international law of treaties. A number of factors formed the basis for this study. First, there is an extensive *acquis* of international agreements, both bilateral and multilateral, concluded between the European Community or the European Union and third states and other international organisations. Second, the Community and the Member States, acting together as one contracting party, have concluded a large number of these agreements. A third factor is that the two Vienna Conventions, to the extent that they embody customary treaty law, govern the Community and the Union's treaty practice. Although most of the substantive provisions of the Vienna Conventions qualify as customary law, questions remain as to which are not customary law and the precise scope of those that constitute customary law. Therefore, it is unclear to what extent the Community and the Union are affected by these rules. The involvement of the Member States, as joint contracting parties, further complicates this matter, as most of the Member States are a party to the 1969 Vienna Convention on the law of treaties. The end result is a very mixed, and potentially, confusing situation.

In international relations the European Community and the European Union occupy a singular and unique position. This unique position is the direct result of the internal constitutional structure of the Community and the Union, which presents these organisations with state-like characteristics. And although the two entities are distinctly different in nature, it cannot be denied that they occupy a place of prominence in the international community. Still, the existence of three separate entities[1] representing the same group of Member States creates a rather confusing and ambiguous reality at both the internal and external level. The European Constitution adopted on 18 June 2004 by the Brussels Intergovernmental Conference, is designed specifically to put an end to the complexity resulting from this legal reality.

At the external level the uncertainty is compounded by the fact that the Member States of the European Union have not lost their status as sovereign nations and are, therefore, capable of exercising all external activities related to their statehood. This includes the power to conclude international agreements. The unique combination of an organisation, with state-like characteristics, and its Member States operating together in the conclusion of international agreements brings about questions as to whether the current legal regime governing interna-

[1] This includes the European Atomic Energy Community, Euratom.

tional treaty relations provides sufficient guarantees to cover the contractual relations between on the one hand the Community, the Union or the Community and the Member States and on the other hand third countries and other international organisations.

Analysis has revealed a close adherence on the part of the Community and the Union to the rules embodied in both the 1969 and the 1986 Vienna Convention to the extent that these rules represent customary international law. Yet adherence to these principles does not mean strict compliance. The practice of the Community and the Union reveals that in a number of situations the existing rule is interpreted to fit the internal structure of the Community and the Union rather than the other way around. As a result, other contracting parties may be left in doubt as to the manner in which treaty law applies to the Community, the Union and the Member States. To counter this uncertainty, parties may be tempted to include safeguard provisions in the actual agreements. This will, of course, have a limiting effect on the exercise of the Community and the Union's external treaty-making competence.

There are two ways to solve this ambiguity. One would be to alter the internal framework of the two organisations. However, this implies a reversal of the integration process, and from a Union standpoint this is unacceptable. Besides, even if such a reversal were contemplated, there is no guarantee that the existing rules of international treaty law would provide the necessary answers. The problem is not so much the rules, but rather the extent to which these rules apply.

The second option is a modification of the rules of international treaty law. This second option is more practical, but it is questionable whether there is a consensus in the international community to do so. However, the existing international legal regime was set up at a time of strong ideological opposition and limited participation of international organisations in international relations. The international legal regime does not take full account of the enormous diversity that exists at present among international organisations. But whereas states represent, at international level, a homogenous group, the same cannot be said of international organisations. Their objectives, tasks and structures are as diverse as their numbers. And more than any organisation, the Community and the Union feel the constraints imposed upon them by the existing international rules.

Legal certainty, especially in the light of the large number of agreements concluded by the European Community and the European Union, requires a renewed codification of the rules of international treaty law governing the external treaty relations of the two. This is especially so in the case of mixed agreements. The enlargement process and a further extension of the scope of the powers of the Community and of the Union will inevitably result in a further increase in treaty relations between the Community, the Union, the Member States on the one hand, and third countries and international organisations on the other hand. Where the Community or the Union acts as a single contracting party the current rules of international treaty law provide ample guarantees. However, the same cannot be said of mixed agreements. International treaty law simply does not deal with this subject matter. Only a renewed codification of the law of treaties can remedy this situation.

The renewed codification process can be brought about in one of three ways. The first involves a re-assessment of the provisions of the 1986 Vienna Convention. The advantage of this option is that the groundwork has already been done. All that will be required is a refining of those provisions that do not adequately recognize the diversity among international organisations and do not take into account the manner in which the Community and the Union interact with third parties in their treaty relations. Still, this solution does not definitively solve the question concerning the underlying relationship between the two Conventions. The European Union is unwilling to conclude a convention on the law of treaties that puts it at a disadvantage vis-à-vis third countries.

The second option proposes the inclusion of provisions, which make specific reference to the European Union, in the 1969 Vienna Convention. The modification must relate to the European Union, as it will exist after the new European Constitution has come into force. This will be in 2007, at the earliest. It would serve no purpose to codify the existing hybrid structure of the Union into the law of treaties. The new convention on the law of treaties would not solve the current uncertainties and it would have to be modified once the new European Constitution comes into effect. The disadvantage of this option is that it places the Union on a different level vis-à-vis other international organisations. Although there is ample justification for such differential treatment, it is obvious that this solution will be met with strong opposition from states and other international organisations. In particular such organisations as the World Trade Organisation, which already presents a strong resemblance with certain Community-like features, will object.[2] The only way their wishes can be accommodated is through the inclusion of some broad concepts in the new convention on the law of treaties. However, this would be a repeat performance of the 1986 Vienna Convention and would, therefore, defeat the purpose of the renewed codification process.

The third, and recommended, option is the merging of the existing Vienna Conventions into one single convention on the law of treaties. The merging of the existing Vienna Conventions must include the amendment of certain provisions in order to deal with all aspects of the external treaty relations of international organisations. This third option should also be preferred by the European Union because it is more in line with current Union practice. Although the Commission favours reference to the 1969 Vienna Convention, the Court of Justice and the Court of First Instance have frequently referred to both the 1969 and 1986 Vienna Conventions. The use of a single convention eliminates any ambiguity that may exist with regard to the underlying relations between the two existing

[2] Compare the compulsory dispute settlement procedures of the Community with the procedures of the World Trade Organisation.

Conventions. It will also provide greater clarity with regard to the rules that constitute customary treaty law. More importantly, the new and modified convention will regulate effectively mixed agreements.

Mixed agreements are a unique instrument in international relations. It is the primary type of agreement concluded by the Community and its use is only likely to increase. Yet, despite its extensive use by the Community to date, no provisions of treaty law have been adopted to regulate their application. Any amendment of the existing international law of treaties must include provisions that regulate the use of mixed agreements, and more precisely the consequences of their use.

Although it is accepted that states and international organisations are distinct entities, the merger of the Vienna Conventions guarantees equality in their contractual relations. This is not the same as saying that their general status under international law is the same. Only in their contractual relations do states and international organisations act on the same level.

In the light of the foregoing, and the research as a whole, the following alterations to some of the provisions of the Vienna Conventions are proposed. The intention of these proposals is to provide clear answers to the most important shortcomings of international treaty law that need to be remedied. The structure of the thesis has followed the standard sequence for the negotiation, conclusion, coming into force and application of international agreements. The following proposals on the contrary will accompany the numerical order used in the Vienna Conventions. This is done for the sake of clarity. The existing texts of the corresponding articles that do not need amendment have not been reproduced. Only the proposed modifications that should be added have been mentioned. An explanatory note follows each provision.

Article 2 (Definitions)

> (...)
> This includes treaties concluded between an International Organisation and one or more Member States, on the one hand, and one or more states or one or more International Organisations, on the other hand.
>
> (...)
> An International Organisation means an Intergovernmental Organisation to which its Member States have attributed competences over a range of matters, including the authority to make decisions binding on the Members.

The current definition of the term ‘treaty’ does not include the so-called ‘mixed agreements’. Although this type of agreements is permitted, express reference to their use will improve the legal certainty surrounding their application. The extent of the rights and obligations of the Community, Union and the Member

States vary depending on whether they act separately or in unison. International treaty law should cover this diversity.

The 1969 and the 1986 Vienna Conventions define an international organisation as an intergovernmental organisation. International organisations can be defined in accordance to their composition, the relationship between the organisation and the members, its tasks, objectives and powers or a combination of some or all of these factors. Although it is evident that the definition should not include non-governmental organisations, it is not necessary that the organisation is composed of only states. It is imperative, however, that the definition includes a reference to the relationship between the organisation and the member states, and more particularly, the legal effects of the rules of the organisation on its member states. International practice indicates a desire on the part of states to make a distinct reference to the binding nature of legislation adopted by the organisation vis-à-vis its member states. A definition of the concept 'international organisation' should include a codification of this practice.

In his draft articles on responsibility of international organisations, Special Rapporteur Giorgio Gaja defined an international organisation as "an organisation which includes States among its members insofar it exercises in its own capacity certain governmental functions".[3] In its proposal, seeking authorisation to negotiate accession to the International Civil Aviation Organisation, the Commission indicated a preference for the definition of the term 'regional economic integration organisation' as used by the Statute of the Food and Agriculture Organisation. The concept is defined as "one constituted by sovereign States, a majority of which are a Member of the Organisation, and to which its Member States have transferred competence over a range of matters within the purview of the Organisation, including the authority to make decisions binding on its Member States in respect of those matters".[4]

The proposed definition contains elements of both definitions. By qualifying the organisation as 'intergovernmental', it is obvious that the majority, but not necessarily all the members are states. Although the term 'governmental functions' presupposes the capacity to adopt (binding) legislation it is more appropriate to include an express reference to that effect in the definition. This avoids any misunderstanding with regard to the precise scope of the powers attributed to the organisation. Finally, not all international agreements come about within the framework of international organisations. Express reference to membership of an additional organisation has therefore a restrictive effect.

---

[3] Special Rapporteur, Mr. Giorgio Gaja, *First report on responsibility of international organisations*, 2003, A/CN.4/532.

[4] SEC(2002)381 final.

Article 8 (Subsequent confirmation of an act performed without authorization)

(...)

> Where a person represents an International Organisation and its Member States on the one hand, a Member State of the Organisation cannot claim that the act relating to the adoption of a treaty is without legal effect, when the decision authorizing the person to act was adopted in accordance with the established procedures or practices within the Organisation.

It is commonplace within the Community that the decision to appoint a single negotiator on behalf of the Community and the Member States is taken unanimously. It involves the exercise of sovereign state powers and this requires the consent of all Member States concerned. However, this consent is not always given through an express decision. Throughout the Uruguay Round of Trade Negotiations the Commission was tacitly given the authority to negotiate on behalf of the Community and the Member States. When the internal rules or practices of the organisation permit that, in the event of a mixed agreement, the parties may appoint a single person to adopt the final text, a Member State should not be allowed to object to the text, by stating that no formal internal decision had been adopted.

Article 9 (Adoption of the text)

(...)

> Where an International Organisation and its Member States act as one party in the preparation of the text of a treaty, their individual consents will be required for the adoption of the treaty. Where the organisation acts on the basis of an exclusive competence, the Member States are not permitted to vote on the adoption of the final text, even if they have participated in the preparation of the final text.

This provision is intended to provide international organisations with the right to fully exercise their external powers without unnecessary restrictions. At the same time it guarantees that the Member States will be allowed to execute their treaty powers to the extent that these powers have not been transferred to the organisation. It can happen that what started out as a shared competence between the organisation and its members has transformed, in the course of the negotiations, into an exclusive competence of the organisation as a result of the internal transfer of competence from the member states to the organisation. The pre-emption that occurs at the internal level should also be present at the external level.

Article 18 (Obligation not to defeat the object and purpose of a treaty)

> (...)
> A State is obliged to refrain from acts which would defeat the object and purpose of a treaty when the International Organisation, of which it is a Member, has signed the treaty, irrespective of whether the State has not signed the treaty itself.

Within the European Community Article 10 EC guarantees that Member States will refrain from actions that may defeat the object and purpose of an agreement signed by the Community. If a similar provision is absent in the constituting treaty of an international organisation or its scope is not clear, a member state may act in a manner that makes it difficult or impossible for that organisation to comply with its treaty obligations. Although international treaty law provides that the contractual relations of a state or international organisation cannot in itself create rights and obligations for third parties, this rule cannot be applied when the organisation has signed the agreement with the approval of its member states.

Article 19 (Formulation of reservations)

> (...)
> An International Organisation may enter a reservation except in cases where the International Organisation and its Member States act as a joint contracting party and the reservation was not accompanied by an identical reservation of the participating Member States.
>
> A Member State of an International Organisation may enter a reservation except in cases where the International Organisation and its Member States act as a joint contracting party, and the reservation was not accompanied by an identical reservation of the Organisation and all other participating Member States.

It was pointed out in Chapter 4, that the existence of parallel powers between the Community and the Member States means that, in principle, both can enter reservations with regard to the part of the agreement that comes within their competence without the need for the other to enter a similar reservation. It is obvious that this will result in a complex and confusing situation. It is impossible for third parties to determine whether the division of competences between the Community and the Member States is on the basis of parallel or concurrent competences. Nor can they establish the precise delimitation of these competences. It was also mentioned that the division of competences, even in the case of parallel competences, could alter over time. The other contracting parties would have to keep themselves abreast of all the developments within the Community. This is an unacceptable situation. Consequently, the Community, or the Union, and the Member States must be treated as one single unit when they enter reservations.

It may appear that this provision is not in the interest of the European Union. However, this is not the case. The provision guarantees that the Member States of the Union will not transgress on the powers reserved for the European Union under the EU Treaty. It should be seen as an external complement to the concept of Union loyalty.

Article 29 (Territorial scope of treaties)

> (...)
> The territory of an international Organisation includes the entire territory of the Member States to which the provisions of its constituting treaty and additional protocols apply. The International Organisation may agree to extend the scope of an international treaty it is a party to, to other areas in which the Member States have granted it jurisdiction, provided that such extension does not defeat the object and purpose of this international treaty.

The purpose of this article is to safeguard the rights of third parties with respect to the territory of the entire organisation. The non-participation of a Member State should not result in that Member State enjoying the benefits of the organisation's participation in the agreement, but at the same time refusing to accept the corresponding obligations. In some instances this can have serious repercussions on the actual application of the agreement. For example, the non-participation of one or more Member States in an open skies agreement between the Community, the Member States and a third country could have a far-reaching impact on air transport to and from the Community.

Article 58 (Suspension of the operation of a multilateral treaty)

> (...)
> Unless otherwise provided Member States of an International Organisation or the International Organisation may not unilaterally suspend the operation of a treaty or provisions of the treaty when the International Organisation and the Member States are joint contracting parties.

This provision is self-evident. When an international organisation and its member states act as joint contracting parties neither should be permitted to suspend, unilaterally, the operation of the agreement or provisions of the agreement. Although the member states will continue to be bound by the agreement, because of their membership of the organisation, they should not be allowed to engage in any activity that will create uncertainty with regard to the application of the agreement or which is capable of defeating its object and purpose.

Article 61 (Supervening impossibility of performance)

> (...)
> There is no impossibility of performing a treaty when an International Organisation and its Member States act as joint contracting parties, and the Organisation and the remaining participating Member States have assumed the obligations of a defaulting Member State.

The mere fact that a member state is not capable to perform its part of the agreement should not constitute a sufficient breach for the immediate termination of the agreement. In the case of mixed agreements the parties assume the totality of the obligations without it being clear which part will be performed by the member states and which part by the organisation. As long as the organisation and the member states guarantee the full effect of the agreement it shall remain in force.

Article 62 (Fundamental change of circumstances)

> (...)
> A fundamental change may not be invoked if the change is the result of a shift in the division of competences between the International Organisation and its Member States and the Organisation and its Member States are joint contracting parties. However, when the International Organisation acquires an exclusive competence with regard to the subject matter of the treaty, parties may invoke a fundamental change of circumstances unless it is evident that the change will not affect their rights or defeat the object and purpose of the treaty.

The European Community and the European Union are characterised by a system of shared competences between the organisations and the Member States. The level of competence attributed to these organisations determines the extent to which the Community and the Union are empowered to act. The attribution can be through an express provision or through the actual exercise of legislative powers, pre-emption. This internal shift in competence should not be a pretext for third parties to denounce an agreement to which the Community, or the Union, and the Member States are parties. After all, the Community, or the Union, and all the Member States continue to guarantee the full application of the agreement. On the other hand, parties frequently conclude international agreements with the Community because the participation of one or more Member States in the agreement is assured. The subsequent acquisition by the Community or the Union of an exclusive competence could be regarded as a fundamental change of circumstances. The third parties want the continued participation of the Members, but Community law precludes this. In the light of these internal changes, third parties should be allowed to reconsider their options.

As pointed out before, it is expected that the new European Constitution will result in a more homogenous representation of the Union at international level.

However, this homogenous activity can only reach its full effect if the rules governing the Union and its Member States' treaty relations are more in tune with their unique form of internal cooperation. A similar reasoning can be applied to other international organisations. Therefore, the time has come for the International Law Commission to redefine existing international treaty law.

Only a renewed codification of the international law of treaties will guarantee the full effectiveness of the European Community and the European Union's treaty-making powers and practice.

SELECTED BIBLIOGRAPHY

Allo, A-P.,
'Les Accords Administratifs entre l'Union Européenne et les Organisations Internationales' in D. Dormoy (ed.), *L'Union européenne et les organisations internationals* (1997), at 56-67

Allott, P.,
'Adherence To and Withdrawal From Mixed Agreements' in D. O'Keeffe and H.G. Schermers (eds.), *Mixed Agreements* (1983), at 97-121

Amerasinghe, C.F.,
Liability to third parties of member states of international organisations: Practice, principle and judicial precedent in 85 *AJIL* (1991), at 259-280

Arnold, R.,
Der Abschluss gemischter Verträge durch die Europäischen Gemeinschaften in 19 *AVR* (1980-1981), at 419-456

Arts, K.,
ACP-EU Relations in a New Era: The Cotonou Agreement in 40 *C.M.L. Rev.* (2003), at 95-116

Aust, A.,
Modern Treaty Law and Practice (2000)

Auvret-Finck, J.,
L'Avis 2/91 Relatif à la Convention No 170 de l'OIT in 3-4 *CDE* (1995), at 443-460

Balekjian, W.H.,
'Mixed Agreements: Complementary and Concurrent Competences?' in D. O'Keeffe and H.G. Schermers (eds.), *Mixed Agreements* (1983), at 141-151

Barav, A.,
'The division of external relations power between the European Economic Community and the Member States in the case-law of the Court of Justice' in A. Bleckmann and C.W.A. Timmermans (eds.), *Division of powers between the European Communities and their Member States in the field of external relations* (1980), at 29-64

Barents, R.,
Het Verdrag van Amsterdam in Werking (1999)

Barents R. and Brinkhorst, L.J.,
Grondlijnen van Europees Recht (2003)

Barents, R.,
Naar een Europese Constitutie? Part I in *NTER* (2002), at 305-312

Barents, R.,
Naar een Europese Constitutie? Parts II-VI in *NTER* (2003), at 39-47, at 100-108, at 167-173, at 138-144 and 218-224

Bebr, G.,
Agreements Concluded by the Community and their Possible Direct Effect: From International Fruit Company to Kupferberg in 20 *C.M.L. Rev.* (1983), at 35-73

Bekkers, V.J.J.M.,
'Europese integratie en subsidiariteit' in V.J.J.M. Bekkers, H.T.P.M. van den Hurk and G. Leenknegt (eds.), *Subsidiariteit en Europese integratie. Een oude wijsheid in een nieuwe context* (1995), at 1-17

Bekkers, V.J.J.M., Hurk, H.T.P.M. van den and Leenknegt, G.,
'Subsidiariteit als Europese rechtsnorm' in V.J.J.M. Bekkers, H.T.P.M. van den Hurk and G. Leenknegt (eds.), *Subsidiariteit en Europese integratie. Een oude wijsheid in een nieuwe context* (1995), at 163-180

Bell, J., Byron, S. and Whittaker, S.,
Principles of French Law (1998)

Bernhardt, R.,
'Europäisches Gemeinschaftrecht und das Recht internationaler Organisationen: Gemeinsamkeiten und Unterschiede, in G. Hafner, G. Loibl, A. Rest, L. Sucharipa-Behrmann and K. Zemanek (eds.), *Liber Amicorum Professor Seidl-Hohenverldern-in honour of his 80th birthday* (1998), at 25-36

Blaustein, A. and Flanz, F. (eds.),
Constitutions of the Countries of the World. Special Supplement France (1994)

Bleckmann, A.,
'The competence of the EEC' in A. Bleckmann and C.W.A. Timmermans (eds.), *Division of powers between the European Communities and their Member States in the field of external relations* (1980), at 3-14

Bleckmann, A.,
'The Mixed Agreements of the EEC in Public International Law' in D. O'Keeffe and H.G. Schermers (eds.), *Mixed Agreements* (1983), at 155-165

Bogdandy, A. von,
The Legal Case for Unity: The European Union as a Single Organisation with a Single Legal System in 36 *C.M.L. Rev.* (1999), at 887-910

Bono, R.G.,
The International Powers of the European Parliament, the Democratic Deficit and the Treaty on European Union in 12 *YEL* (1992), at 85-138

Bot, B.R.,
Negotiating Community Agreements: Procedure and Practice in 7 *C.M.L. Rev.* (1970), at 286-310

Bourgeois, J.H.,
The EC in the WTO and Advisory Opinion 1/94: An Echternach Procession in 32 *C.M.L. Rev.* (1995), at 763-787

Breitenmoser, S.,
Die Europäische Union zwischen Völkerrecht und Staatsrecht in 55 *ZaöRV* (1995), at 951-992

Brownlie, I.,
Principles of Public International Law (2003)

Brölmann, C.,
'The 1986 Vienna Convention on the Law of Treaties: The History of Draft Article 36*bis*' in J. Klabbers and R. Lefeber (eds.), *Essays on the Law of Treaties. A collection of essays in honour of Bert Vierdag* (1998), at 121-140

Bulterman, M.,
Human Rights in the Treaty Relations of the European Community. Real Virtues or Virtual Reality? (2001)

Bunn-Livingstone, S.,
Juricultural Pluralism vis-à-vis Treaty Law. State Practice and Attitudes (2002)

Calliess, C. and Ruffert, M. (eds.),
Kommentar des Vertrages über die Europäische Union und des Vertrages zur Gründung der Europäischen Gemeinschaft – EUV/EGV – (2002)

Campbell, D. and Cotter, S.,
The Law of the European Community. A Commentary on the EC Treaty (1998)

Canor, I.,
"Can Two Walk Together, Except They Be Agreed?" The Relationship between International Law and European Law: The incorporation of United Nations sanctions against Yugoslavia into European Community law through the perspective of the European Court of Justice in 35 *C.M.L. Rev.* (1998), at 137-187

Castillo de la Torre, F.,
Case Law: Opinion 1/00 in 39 *C.M.L. Rev.* (2002), at 1373-1393

Chalmers, D.,
'Legal Base and the External Relations of the European Community' in N. Emiliou and D. O'Keeffe (eds.), *The European Union and World Trade Law* (1996), at 46-61

Cheyne, I.,
International Agreements and the European Community Legal System in 19 *E.L.Rev.* (1994), at 581-598

Cheyne, I.,
'Haegeman, Demirel and their progeny' in A. Dashwood and C. Hillion (eds.), *The General Law of E.C. External Relations* (2000), at 20-41

Cheyne, I.,
'International instruments as a source of Community Law' in A. Dashwood and C. Hillion (eds.), *The General Law of E.C. External Relations* (2000), at 254-275

Close, G.L.,
Self-restraint by the EEC in the exercise of its External Powers in 1 *YEL* (1981), at 45-68

Cockborne, J-E. De, Defalque, L., Durand, C-F., Prahl, H. and Vandersanden, G.,
Commentaire Megret. Le Droit de La CEE. Préambules, Principes, Libre Circulation des Marchandises Volume I (1992)

Costonis, J.J.,
The Treaty-making Power of the European Economic Community: The Perspective of a Decade in 5 *C.M.L. Rev.* (1967-1968), at 421-457

Cottier, T. and Caplazi, A.,
Das Genehmigungsverfahren beim Abschluss völkerrechtlicher Abkommen in der Europäischen Union (1998)

Council of Europe (ed.),
Treaty Making – Expression of Consent by States To Be Bound by a Treaty (2001)

Craig P. and de Búrca, G.,
EU Law. Text, Cases and Materials (2002)

Cremona, M.,
'Human Rights and Democracy Clauses in the EC's Trade Agreements' in N. Emiliou and D. O'Keeffe (eds.), *The European Union and World Trade Law* (1996), at 62-77

Cremona, M.,
'External Relations and External Competence: The Emergence of an Integrated Policy' in P. Craig and G. de Búrca (eds.), *The Evolution of EU Law* (1999), at 137-175

Cremona, M.,
Rhetoric and Reticence: EU External Commercial Policy in a Multilateral Context in 38 *C.M.L. Rev.* (2001), at 359-396

Cremona, M.,
The Draft Constitutional Treaty: External Relations and External Action in 40 *C.M.L. Rev.* (2003), at 1347-1366

Croley, S.P. and Jackson, J.H.,
WTO Dispute Procedures, Standard of Review, and Deference to National Governments in 90 *AJIL* (1996), at 193-213

Curtin, D.,
The Constitutional Structure of the Union: A Europe of Bits and Pieces in 30 *C.M.L. Rev.* (1993), at 17-69

Curtin, D. and Dekker, I.,
The EU as a 'Layered' International Organisation: Institutional Unity in Disguise in P. Craig and G. de Búrca (eds.), *The Evolution of EU Law* (1999), at 83-136

Dashwood, A.,
The Limits of European Community Powers in 21 *E.L.Rev.* (1996), at 113-128

Dashwood, A.,
'Implied External Competence of the EC' in M. Koskenniemi (ed.), *International Law Aspects of the European Union* (1998), at 113-123

Dashwood, A.,
External Relations Provisions of the Amsterdam Treaty in 35 *C.M.L. Rev.* (1998), at 1019-1045

Dashwood, A. and Heliskoski, J.,
'The classic authorities revisited' in A. Dashwood and C. Hillion (eds.), *The General Law of E.C. External Relations* (2000), at 3-19

Dashwood, A.,
'Preliminary Rulings on the Interpretation of Mixed Agreements' in D. O'Keeffe (ed.), *Judicial Review in European Union Law. Liber Amicorum in Honour of Lord Slynn of Hadley* (2000), at 167-175

Dashwood, A.,
Case Law: Opinion 2/00 in 39 *C.M.L. Rev.* (2002), at 353-368

Davies, A.P.,
Bananas, Private Challenges, the Courts and the Legislature in 22 *YEL* (2002), at 299-326

De Búrca, G.,
The Principle of Subsidiarity and the Court of Justice as an Institutional Actor in 36 *JCMS* (1998), at 217-235

Dixon, M. and McCorquodale, R.,
Cases and Materials on International Law (1991)

Dormoy, D.,
'Le statut de l'Union européenne dans les organisations internationales' in D. Dormoy (ed.), *L'Union européenne et les organisations internationals* (1997), at 36-55

Editorial Comments. Dispute Settlement and Countermeasures in the International Law Commission in 88 *AJIL* (1994), at 471-477

Editorial Comments. Remedies Along with Rights: Institutional Reform in the New GATT in 88 *AJIL* (1994), at 477-488

Editorial Comments. The European Union – A new international actor in 38 *C.M.L.Rev.* (2001), at 825-828

Eeckhout, P.,
'Expliciete en impliciete externe bevoegdheden na Maastricht – Status quaestionis' in Asser Instituut Colloquium Europees Recht, *Externe bevoegdheden van de Europese Unie* (1993), at 1-15

Eeckhout, P.,
'The External Dimension of the Internal Market and the Scope and Content of a Modern Commercial Policy' in M. Maresceau (ed.), *The European Community's Commercial Policy after 1992: The Legal Dimension* (1993), at 79-101

Eeckhout, P.,
The Domestic Legal Status of the WTO Agreement: Interconnecting Legal Systems in 34 *C.M.L. Rev.* (1997), at 11-58

Ehlermann, C.-D.,
'Mixed Agreements: A List of Problems' in D. O'Keeffe and H.G. Schermers (eds.), *Mixed Agreements* (1983), at 3-21

Elias, O.,
General International Law in the European Court of Justice: From Hypothesis to Reality? In 31 *Neth.Yb.Int'l.L.* (2000), at 3-34

Emiliou, N.,
Towards a clearer demarcation line? The division of external relations power between the Community and Member States in 31 *JCMS* (1993), at 76-86

Emiliou, N.,
'The Allocation of Competence Between the EC and its Member States in the Sphere of External Relations' in N. Emiliou and D. O'Keeffe (eds.), *The European Union and World Trade Law* (1996), at 31-45

Emiliou, N.,
The Death of Exclusive Competence? in 21 *E.L.Rev.* (1996), at 294-311.

Feenstra, J.J.,
'A Survey of the Mixed Agreements and their Participation Clauses' in D. O'Keeffe and H.G. Schermers (eds.), *Mixed Agreements* (1983), at 207-248

Fiedler, W.,
'Entwicklungslinien im Recht der Staatensukzession' in G. Hafner, G. Loibl, A. Rest, L. Sucharipa-Behrmann and K. Zemanek (eds.), *Liber Amicorum Professor Seidl-Hohenveldern – in honour of his 80th birthday* (1998), at 133-156

Fischer, P.,
'Is there a European identity in the field of law? Some considerations on the nature and scope of European Law' in G. Hafner, G. Loibl, A. Rest, L. Sucharipa-Behrmann and K. Zemanek (eds.), *Liber Amicorum Professor Seidl-Hohenveldern – in honour of his 80th birthday* (1998), at 157-174

Flaesch-Mougin, C.,
Le Traite de Maastricht et les Competences Externes de la Communaute

Europeenne: à la recherche d'une politique externe de l'union in 3-4 *CDE* (1993), at 351-398

Flory, T. and Martin, F-P.,
Remarques à Propos dês Avis 1/94 et 2/92 de la Cour de Justice des Communautés Européennes au regard de l'Évolution de la Notion de Politique Commerciale Commune in 3-4 *CDE* (1996), at 379-400

Foster, N.G. and Sule, S.,
German legal system and laws (2002)

Freckmann, A. and Wegerich, T.,
The German Legal System (1999)

Fried, R.,
The Relations between the EC and International Organisations. Legal Theory and Practice (1995)

Gaja, G.,
'The European Community's Rights and Obligations under Mixed Agreements' in D. O'Keeffe and H.G. Schermers (eds.), *Mixed Agreements* (1983), at 133-140

Gaja, G.,
'Trends in Judicial Activism and Judicial Self-restraint Relating to Community Agreements' in E. Cannizzaro (ed.), *The European Union as an Actor in International Relations* (2002), at 117-134

Gautron, J-C.,
'L'Union européenne et le concept d'organisation internationale' in D. Dormoy (ed.), *L'Union européenne et les organisations internationals* (1997), at 15-35

Gauttier, P.,
Horizontal Coherence and the External Competences of the European Union in 10 *European Law Journal* (2004), at 23-41

Gladstone, R.C.,
The EEA Umbrella: Incorporating Aspects of the EC Legal Order in *LIEI* 1994/1, at 61-94

Goucha Soares, A.,
Pre-emption, Conflicts of Powers and Subsidiarity in 23 *E.L.Rev.* (1998), at 132-145

Granvik, L.,
'Incomplete Mixed Environmental Agreements of the Community and the Principle of Bindingness' in M. Koskenniemi (ed.), *International Law Aspects of the European Union* (1998), at 255-272

Grawert, R.,
Wie soll Europa organisiert werden? – Zur konstitutionellen "Zukunft Europas" nach dem Vertrag von Nizza- in 38 *Europarecht* (2003), at 971-991

Griller, S. and Gamharter, K.,
'External Trade: Is There a Path Through the Maze of Competences?' in S. Griller and B. Weidel (eds.), *External Economic Relations and Foreign Policy in the European Union* (2002), at 65-112

Grimes, J.M.,
Conflicts Between EC Law and International Treaty Obligations: A Case Study of the German Telecommunications Dispute in 35 *Harvard International Law Journal* (1994), at 535-564

Groeben, H. von der, Thiesing, J. and Ehlermann, C.-D. (eds.),
Kommentar zum EU-/EG-Vertrag (1997)

Groux, J.,
'Mixed Negotiations' in D. O'Keeffe and H.G. Schermers (eds.), *Mixed Agreements* (1983), at 87-96

Hafner, G.,
'The Amsterdam Treaty and the Treaty-making power of the European Union. Some critical comments' in G. Hafner, G. Loibl, A. Rest, L. Sucharipa-Behrmann and K. Zemanek (eds.), *Liber Amicorum Professor Seidl-Hohenveldern – in honour of his 80th birthday* (1998), at 257-284

Ham, A.D.,
International Cooperation in the Anti-trust Field and in Particular the Agreement Between the United States of America and the Commission of the European Communities in 30 *C.M.L. Rev.* (1993), at 571-597

Hancher, L.,
Constitutionalism, the Community Court and International Law in 25 *Neth.Yb.Int'l.L.* (1994), at 259-298

Hardy, M.,
Opinion 1/76 of the Court of Justice: The Rhine Case and the Treaty-Making Powers of the Community in 14 *C.M.L. Rev.* (1977), at 561-600

Harris, D.J.,
Cases and Materials on International Law (1991)

Hartley, T.C.,
The Foundations of European Community Law. An Introduction to the Constitutional and Administrative Law of the European Community (2003)

Hartley, T.C.,
Constitutional Problems of the European Union (1999)

Hartley, T.C.,
International Law and the Law of the European Union – A Reassessment in 33 *Neth.Yb.Int.L.* (2002), at 1-35

Hausmaninger, H.,
The Austrian Legal System (1998)

Heliskoski, J.
Should There Be a New Article on External Relations? In M. Koskenniemi (ed.), *International Law Aspects of the European Union* (1998), at 273-287

Heliskoski, J.,
Mixed Agreements as a Technique for Organizing the International Relations of the European Community and its Member States (2001)

Hellion, C.,
Institutional Aspects of the Partnership between the European Union and the Newly Independent States of the Former Soviet Union: Case studies of Russia and Ukraine in 37 *C.M.L. Rev.* (2000), at 1211-1235

Herrmann, C.W.,
Monetary Sovereignty over the Euro and External Relations of the Euro Area: Competences, Procedures and Practice in 7 *E.F.A. Rev.* (2002), at 1-24

Hillgruber, C.,
Das Verhältnis der Europäischen Gemeinschaften und der Europäischen Union zu ihren Mitgliedstaaten – staats- und völkerrechtlich betrachtet in 34 *AVR* (1996), at 347-375

Hilpold, P.,
'Human Rights Clauses in EU-Association Agreements' in S. Griller and B. Weidel (eds.), *External Economic Relations and Foreign Policy in the European Union* (2002), at 359-383

Holdgaard, R.,
The European Community's Implied External Competence after the Open Skies Cases in 8 *E.F.A. Rev.* (2003), at 365-394

Hongju Koh, H.,
The President Versus the Senate in Treaty Interpretation: What's All the Fuss About? In 15 *Yale.J.Int'l.L.* (1990), at 331-344

Hyett, S.,
The duty of cooperation: a flexible concept in A. Dashwood and C. Hillion (eds.), *The General Law of E.C. External Relations* (2000), at 248-253

Jackson, J.H.,
Status of treaties in domestic legal systems: A policy analysis in 86 *AJIL* (1992), at 310-340

Jans, J.,
European Environmental Law (2000)

Kaddous, C.,
L'arrêt France c. Commission de 1994 (Accord Concurrence) et le contrôle de la <<légalité>> des accords externes en vertu de l'Article 173 CE: La difficile reconciliation de l'orthodoxie Communautaire avec l'orthodoxie internationale in 3-4 *CDE* (1996), at 613-633

Kamiel, M.,
The exclusive treaty-making power of the European Community up to the period of the Single European Act (1996)

Kaplan, M.A. and deB. Katzenback, N.,
The Political Foundations of International Law (1961)

Kapteyn, P.J.G.,
Het Advies 1/76 van het Europese Hof van Justitie, de externe bevoegdheid van de Gemeenschap en haar deelneming aan een Europees oplegfonds voor de binnenscheepvaart in *SEW* 4 (1978), at 276-288

Kapteyn P.J.G. and VerLoren van Themaat, P.,
Introduction to the Law of the European Communities (Third Edition edited and further revised by L. Gormley, 1998)

Kapteyn, P.J.G. and VerLoren van Themaat, P.,
Het recht van de Europese Unie en van de Europese Gemeenschappen (2003)

Karagiannis, S.,
L'Expression <<accord envisage>> dans l'Article 228 § 6 du Traite CE in 1-2 *CDE* (1998) at 105-136

Kälin, W.,
'Implementing Treaties in Domestic Law: from "Pacta Sunt Servanda" to "Anything Goes"?' in V. Gowlland-Debbas (ed.), *Multilateral Treaty-making* (2000), at 111-128

Kennedy, K.C.,
Treaty interpretation by the Executive Branch: The ABM Treaty and "Star Wars" testing and development in 80 *AJIL* (1986), at 854-877

Keukeleire, S.,
Het buitenlands beleid van de Europese Unie (1998)

King Gamble, J.,
Multilateral Treaties: The significance of the name of the instrument in 10 *Calif.W.Int'l.L.J.* (1980), at 1-24

Klabbers, J.,
Qatar v. Bahrain: the concept of "treaty" in international law in 33 *AVR* (1995), at 361-376

Klabbers, J.,
The Concept of Treaty in International Law (1996)

Klabbers, J.,
'Presumptive Personality: The European Union in International Law' in M. Koskenniemi (ed.), *International Law Aspects of the European Union* (1998), at 231-253

Klabbers, J.,
Re-inventing the Law of Treaties: The contribution of the EC Courts in 30 Neth.Yb.Int'l.L. (1999), at 45-74

Klabbers. J.,
International Law in Community Law: The Law and Politics of Direct Effect in 22 *YEL* (2002), at 263-298

Koenig, C. and Pechstein, M.,
Die EU-Vertragsänderung in 33 Europarecht (1998), at 130-150

Kokott, J. and Rüth, A.,
The European Convention and Its Draft Treaty Establishing a Constitution for Europe: Appropriate Answers to the Laeken Questions? In 40 *C.M.L. Rev.* (2003), at 1315-1345

Kooijmans, P.H.,
Internationaal publiekrecht in vogelvlucht (2002)

Koskenniemi, M.,
'International Law Aspects of the Common Foreign and Security Policy' in M. Koskenniemi (ed.), *International Law Aspects of the European Union* (1998), at 27-44

Kotuby, C.T.,
External Competence of the European Community in The Hague Conference on Private International Law: Community Harmonisation and Worldwide Unification in 48 *NILR* (2001), at 1-30

Koutrakos, P.,
The Interpretation of Mixed Agreements under the Preliminary Reference Procedure in 7 *E.F.A. Rev.* (2002), at 25-52

Kronenberger, V.,
'Common Foreign and Security Policy: International law aspects of the association of Third States with the common positions of the Council of the European Union' in V. Kronenberger (ed.), *The EU and the International Legal Order: Discord or Harmony?* (2001), at 351-369

Kuijper, P.J.,
'Trade Sanctions, Security and Human Rights and Commercial Policy' in M. Maresceau (ed.), *The European Community's Commercial Policy after 1992: The Legal Dimension* (1993), at 387-422

Kuijper, P.J.,
'The Community and State Succession in Respect of Treaties' in D. Curtin and T. Heukels (eds.), *Institutional Dynamics of European Integration. Essays in Honour of Henry G. Schermers* (1994), at 619-640

Kuijper, P.J.,
The Court and the Tribunal of the EC and the Vienna Convention on the Law of Treaties 1969 in *LIEI* 1998/1, at 1-23

Lane, R.,
New Community Competences under the Maastricht Treaty in 30 *C.M.L. Rev.* (1993), at 939-979

Lanotte, J. vande,
Inleiding tot het Publiek Recht. Deel 2: Overzicht van het Publiek Recht (1997)

Leal-Arcas, R.,
The European Community and Mixed Agreements in 6 *E.F.A. Rev.* (2001), at 483-513

Leal-Arcas, R.,
Exclusive or Shared Competence in the Common Commercial Policy: From Amsterdam to Nice in *LIEI* 2003/1, at 3-14

Lecheler, H.,
Die Pflege der auswärtigen Beziehungen in der Europäischen Union in 32 *AVR* (1994), at 1-23

Leclerc S.,
Les Communications de la Commission et le Marché Interiéur. A propos de l'arrêt rendu par la Cour de justice des Communautés européennes lê 20 mars 1997 dans l'affaire C-57/95, Rec. 1997, p. I-1640 à I-1652 in 1-2 *CDE* (1998), at 161-175

Leenen, A.Th.S.,
Gemeenschapsrecht en volkenrecht (1984)

Lefeber, R.,
'The Provisional Application of Treaties' in J. Klabbers and R. Lefeber (eds.), *Essays on the Law of Treaties. A collection of essays in honour of Bert Vierdag* (1998), at 81-95

Lefeber, R.,
From The Hague to Bonn to Marrakesh and beyond: A negotiating history of the compliance regime under the Kyoto Protocol in 14 *Hague Yb.* (2001), at 25-54

Léger, P. (ed.),
Commentaire article par article des traits UE et CE (2000)

Lenaerts, K. and Ypersele, P. van,
Le principe de subsidiarité et son contexte: étude de l'article 3B du Traité CE in 1-2 *CDE* (1994), at 3-83

Lenaerts, K. and De Smijter, E.,
The European Community's Treaty-making Competence in 16 *YEL* (1996), at 1-57

Leray, E. and Potteau, A.,
Réflexions sur la coherence du système de contrôle de la légalité des accords internationaux conclus par la Communauté européenne in 34 *RTD eur.* (1998), at 535-571

Le Sueur, A., Herberg, J. And English, R.,
Principles of Public Law (1999)

Louis, J-V.,
Le Projet de Constitution: Continuité ou Rupture? in 3-4 *CDE* (2003), at 215-223

Lukaschek, A. and Weidel, B.,
'Exclusive External Competence of the European Community' in S. Giller and B. Weidel (eds.), *External Economic Relations and Foreign Policy in the European Union* (2002), at 113-150

MacLeod, I., Hendry, I.D. and Hyett, S.,
The External Relations of the European Communities (1996)

Manin, P.,
The European Communities and the Vienna Convention on the Law of Treaties between States and International Organisations or between International Organisations in 24 *C.M.L. Rev.* (1987), at 457-481

Maresceau, M. and Montaguti, E.,
The Relations between the European Union and Central and Eastern Europe: A legal appraisal in 32 *C.M.L. Rev.* (1995), at 1327-1367

Marquardt, S.,
'The Conclusion of International Agreements under Article 24 of the Treaty on European Union' in V. Kronenberger (ed.), *The EU and the International Legal Order: Discord or Harmony?*, at 333-349

Martenczuk, B.,
From Lomé to Cotonou: The ACP-EC Partnership Agreement in a Legal Perspective in 5 *E.F.A. Rev.* (2000), at 461-487

Maunu, A.,
The Implied External Competence of the European Community after the ECJ Opinion 1/94 – Towards Coherence or Diversity? in *LIEI* 1995/2, at 115-128

McGoldrick, D.,
International Relations Law of the European Union (1997)

McNair, I.,
The Law of Treaties (1961)

Megret, J.,
Le Droit de la Communauté Économique Européenne. Commentaire du Traité et des Textes Pris pour son application, Volume 12 (1980)

Michel, V.,
2004: Le défi de la répartition des compétences in 1-2 *CDE* (2003), at 17-86

Middeldorp, G. and Ooik, R.H. van,
Van verdeelde Open Skies naar een uniform Europees extern luchtvaartbeleid in *NTER* 2003, at 1-10

Mitsilegas, V.,
The New EU-USA Cooperation on Extradition, Mutual Legal Assistance and the Exchange of Police Data in 8 *E.F.A. Rev.* (2003), at 515-536

Neuhold, H.,
'The provisions of the Amsterdam Treaty on the CFSP: cosmetic operation or genuine progress?' in G. Hafner, G. Loibl, A. Rest, L. Sucharipa-Behrmann and K. Zemanek (eds.), *Liber Amicorum Professor Seidl-Hohenverldern – in honour of his 80th birthday* (1998), at 495-510

Nuehold, H.,
'Organs Competent to Conclude Treaties for International Organisations and the Internal Procedure Leading to the Decision to Be Bound by a Treaty and Negotiation

and Conclusion of Treaties by International Organisations' in K. Zemanek (ed.), *Agreements of International Organisations and the Vienna Convention on the Law of Treaties*, ÖZoR, Supplementum 1 (1971), at 195-268

Neuwahl, N.A.E.M.,
Joint Participation in International Treaties and the Exercise of Power by the EEC and Its Member States: Mixed Agreements in 28 *C.M.L. Rev.* (1991), at 717-740

Neuwahl, N.A.E.M.,
Case Law: Opinion 2/91 in 30 *C.M.L. Rev.* (1993), at 1185-1195

Neuwahl, N.A.E.M.,
Shared Powers or Combined Incompetence? More on Mixity in 33 *C.M.L. Rev.* (1996), at 667-687

Neuwahl, N.A.E.M.,
'The WTO Opinion and implied external powers of the Community: a hidden agenda?' in A. Dashwood and C. Hillion (eds.), *The General Law of E.C. External Relations* (2000), at 139-151

Neuwahl, N.A.E.M.,
'Legal Personality of the European Union – International and Institutional Aspects' in V. Kronenberger (ed.), *The EU and the International Legal Order: Discord or Harmony?* (2001), at 3-22

Norberg, S.,
The Agreement on a European Economic Area in 29 *C.M.L. Rev.* (1992), at 1171-1198

Obradovic, D.,
Repatriation of Powers in the European Community in 34 *C.M.L. Rev.* (1997), at 59-88

O' Keeffe, D.,
'Exclusive, concurrent and shared competence' in A. Dashwood and C. Hillion (eds.), *The General Law of E.C. External Relations* (2000), at 179-199

Okowa, P.,
The European Community and International Environmental Agreements in 15 *YEL* (1995), at 169-192

Osakwe, C.,
'The Concept and Forms of Treaties Concluded by International Organisations' in K. Zemanek (ed.), *Agreements of International Organizations and the Vienna Convention on the Law of Treaties*, ÖZoR, Supplementum 1 (1971), at 165-193

Peers, S.,
Common Foreign and Security Policy 1999-2000 in 21 *YEL* (2001), at 531-567

Pernice, I.,
Völkerrechtliche Verträge internationaler Organisationen – Tendenzen und mögliche Grundlagen einer Assimilierung von internationalen Organisationen und Staaten im Lichte der Wiener Konvention über das Vertragsrecht internationaler Organisationen – in 48 *ZaöRV* (1988), at 229-250

Pescatore, P.,
International Law and Community Law – A comparative analysis in 7 *C.M.L. Rev.* (1970), at 167-183

Pescatore, P.,
External Relations in the Case-law of the Court of Justice of the European Communities in 16 *C.M.L. Rev.* (1979), at 615-645

Pescatore, P.,
'Treaty-making by the European Communities' in F. Jacobs and S. Roberts (eds.), *The Effect of Treaties in Domestic Law* (1987), at 171-195

Pescatore, P.,
Guest Editorial: Nice – Aftermath in 38 *C.M.L. Rev.* (2001), at 265-271

Peters, A.,
The Position of International Law Within the European Community Legal Order in 40 *GYIL* (1997), at 9-77

Petersmann, E-U.,
'Constitutional Principles Governing the EEC's Commercial Policy' in M. Maresceau (ed.), *The European Community's Commercial Policy after 1992: The Legal Dimension* (1993), at 21-61

Phinnemore, D.,
Stabilisation and Association Agreements: Europe Agreements for the Western Balkans? in 8 *E.F.A. Rev.* (2003), at 77-103

Plender, R.,
'The European Court's Pre-emptive Jurisdiction: Opinions under Article 300(6) EC' in D. O'Keeffe (ed.), *Judicial Review in European Union Law. Liber Amicorum in Honour of Lord Slynn of Hadley* (2000), at 203-220

Pocar, F.,
'The Decision-making Processes of the European Community in External Relations' in E. Cannizzaro (ed.), *The European Union as an Actor in International Relations* (2002), at 3-16

Reisman, W.M.,
Necessary and Proper: Executive Competence to Interpret Treaties in 15 *YaleJ.Int'l.L.* (1990), at 316-330

Reuter, P.,
Introduction to the Law of Treaties (Translated by José Mico and Peter Haggenmacher, 1995)

Reymond, C.,
Institutions, Decision-making Procedure and Settlement of Disputes in the European Economic Area in 30 *C.M.L. Rev.* (1993), at 449-480

Rideau, J.,
'L'Ordre juridique communautaire et la participation de la Communauté européenne aux organisations internationales' in D. Dormoy (ed.), *L'Union européenne et les organisations internationals* (1997), at 68-101

Riedel, E. and Will, M.,
'Human Rights Clauses in External Agreements of the EC' in P. Alston, M. Bustelo and J. Heenan (eds.), *The EU and Human Rights* (1999), at 723-754

Rosas, A.,
'Mixed Union – Mixed Agreements' in M. Koskenniemi (ed.), *International Law Aspects of the European Union* (1998), at 125-148

Rosas, A.,
'The European Union and mixed agreements' in A. Dashwood and C. Hillion (eds.), *The General Law of E.C. External Relations* (2000), at 200-220

Rosenne, S.,
Developments in the Law of Treaties 1945-1986 (1989)

Sack, J.,
The European Community's Membership of International Organisations in 32 *C.M.L. Rev.* (1995), at 1227-1256

Schermers, H.G.,
The Direct Application of Treaties with Third States: Note concerning the Polydor and Pabst Cases in 19 *C.M.L. Rev.* (1982), at 563-569

Schermers, H.G.,
'A typology of Mixed Agreements' in D. O'Keeffe and H.G. Schermers (eds.), *Mixed Agreements* (1983), at 23-33

Schermers, H.G. and Blokker, N.M.,
International Institutional Law (2003)

Schermers, H.G. and Waelbroeck, M.,
Judicial Protection in the European Union (2001)

Schilling, T.,
A New Dimension of Subsidiarity: Subsidiarity as a Rule and a Principle in 14 *YEL* (1995), at 203-255

Schweisfurth, T.,
The Treaty-making Capacity of the CMEA in Light of a Framework Agreement Between the EEC and the CMEA in 22 *C.M.L. Rev.* (1985), at 615-647

Schorkopf, F.,
Die Untätigkeit des Rates der Europäuschen Union im Gesetzgebungsverfahren in 35 *Europarecht* (2000), at 365-402

Schreuer, C.,
Die Bedeutung internationaler Organisationen im heutigen Völkerrecht in 22 *AVR* (1984), at 363-404

Schrwarze, J.,
Ein pragmatischer Verfassungsentwurf – Analyse unde Bewertung des vom Europäischen Verfassungskonvent vorgelegten Entwurfs eines Vertrags über eine Verfassung für Europa- in 38 *Europarecht* (2003), at 535-573

Schutter, O. de and Lejeune, Y.,
L'Adhesion de la Communauté à la Convention Européenne des Droits de l'Homme à propos de l'Avis 2/94 de la Cour de Justice des Communautés in 3-4 *CDE* (1996), at 555-606

Shaw, M.N.,
International Law (2003)

Simmonds, K.R.,
'The UN Convention on the Law of the Sea 1982 and the Community's Mixed Agreements Practice' in D. O'Keeffe and H.G. Schermers (eds.), *Mixed Agreements* (1983), at 199-206

Simmonds, K.R.,
The Community's Declaration upon Signature of the U.N. Convention on the Law of the Sea in 23 *C.M.L. Rev.* (1986), at 521-544

Smith, M.,
'The Commission and external relations' in G. Edwards and D. Spence (eds.), *The European Commission* (1997), at 264-289

Smulders, B.M.P.,
Kritische kanttekeningen bij de gevolgen van het 'ontwerp-verdrag tot vaststelling van een grondwet voor Europa' voor het institutionele evenwicht in *NTER* 2003, at 246-252

Tagaras, H.N.,
L'Effet Direct dês Accords Internationaux de la Communauté in 1-2 *CDE* (1984), at 15-53
Temple Lang, J.,
The Ozone Layer Convention: A new solution to the question of Community participation in "mixed" international agreements in 23 *C.M.L. Rev.* (1986), at 157-176
Temple Lang, J.,
The ERTA judgment and the Court's case-law on competence and conflict in 6 *YEL* (1986), at 183-218
Temple Lang, J.,
Community Constitutional Law: Article 5 EEC Treaty in 27 *C.M.L. Rev.* (1990), at 645-681
Temple Lang, J.,
The Duties of National Authorities Under Community Constitutional Law in 23 *E.L.Rev.* (1998), at 109-131
Tiilikainen, T.,
To Be or Not to Be?: An Analysis of the Legal and Political Elements of Statehood in the EU's External Identity in 6 *E.F.A. Rev.* (2001), at 223-241
Timmermans, C.W.A.,
Het recht als multiplier in het Europese integratieproces. Iets over bevoegdheids-verhoudingen tussen Gemeenschap en Lid-Staten (1978)
Timmermans, C.W.A.,
'Division of external powers between Community and Member States in the Field of harmonisation of national law – A case study' in A. Bleckmann and C.W.A. Timmermans (eds.), *Division of powers between the European Communities and their Member States in the field of external relations* (1980), at 15-28
Timmermans, C.W.A.,
German Unification and Community Law in 27 *C.M.L. Rev.* (1990), at 437-449
Timmermans, C.W.A.,
The EU and Public International Law in 4 *E.F.A. Rev.* (1999), at 181-194
Timmermans, C.W.A.,
'Organising joint participation of E.C. and Member States' in A. Dashwood and C. Hillion (eds.), *The General Law of E.C. External Relations* (2000), at 239-247
Toledano Laredo, A.,
The EEA Agreement: An Overall View in 29 *C.M.L. Rev.* (1992), at 1199-1213
Tomuschat, C.,
'Liability for Mixed Agreements' in D. O'Keeffe and H.G. Schermers (eds.), *Mixed Agreements* (1983), at 125-132
Tomuschat, C.,
A United Germany within the European Community in 27 *C.M.L. Rev.* (1990), at 415-436
Tomuschat, C.,
'Abkommen der Gemeinschaft' in H. von der Groeben (ed.), *Kommentar zum EG-/EU-Vertrag* (1997), at 488-494
Torres Bernárdez, S.,
'Interpretation of Treaties by the International Court of Justice Following the Adoption of the 1969 Vienna Convention on the Law of Treaties' in G. Hafner, G.

Loibl, A. Rest, L. Sucharipa-Behrmann and K. Zemanek (eds.), *Liber Amicorum Professor Seidl-Hohenverldern – in honour of his 80th birthday* (1998), at 721-748

Trachtman, J.P.,
The Domain of WTO Dispute Resolution in 40 *Harvard International Law Journal* (1999), at 333—377

Treves, T.,
'The European Community and the Law of the Sea Convention: New Developments' in E. Cannizzaro (ed.), *The European Union as an Actor in International Relations* (2002), at 279-296

Tridimas, T. and Eeckhout, P.,
The External Competence of the Community and the Case-Law of the Court of Justice: Principle versus Pragmatism in 14 *YEL* (1994), at 143-177

Tridimas, T.,
'The WTO and OECD Opinions' in A. Dashwood and C. Hillion (eds.), *The General Law of EC External Relations* (2000), at 48-60

Tridimas, T.,
'The WTO and OECD Opinions' in A. Dashwood and C. Hillion (eds.), *The General Law of E.C. External Relations* (2000), at 48-60

Vanhamme, J.,
Volkenrechtelijke beginselen in het Europees recht (2001)

Vignes, D.,
'L'Absence de personalité juridique de l'Union européenne: Amsterdam persiste et signe' in G. Hafner, G. Loibl, A. Rest, L. Sucharipa-Behrmann and K. Zemanek (eds.), *Liber Amicorum Professor Seidl-Hohenverldern – in honour of his 80th birthday* (1998), at 757-770

Waelbroeck, M.,
'The Emergent Doctrine of Community Pre-emption – Consent and Re-delegation' in T. Sandalow and E. Stein (eds.), *Courts and the Free Markets. Perspectives from the United States and Europe, Volume II* (1982), at 548-580

Ward, A.,
'Community Development Aid and the Evolution of the Inter-institutional Law of the European Union' in A. Dashwood and C. Hillion (eds.), *The General Law of E.C. External Relations* (2000), at 42-47

Weber, C.,
Wirtschaftsabkommen im System der Europäischen Gemeinschaft – Die Rechtsprechung des Europäischen Gerichtshofs in 35 *AVR* (1997), at 295-315

Weidel, B.,
'The Community Export Control System for Dual Use Goods – A Story of Reconquering Lost Grounds?' In S. Griller and B. Weidel (eds.), *External Economic Relations and Foreign Policy in the European Union* (2002), at 419-444

Weiler, J.H.H.,
'The External Legal Relations of Non-Unitary Actors: Mixity and the Federal Principle' in D. O'Keeffe and H.G. Schermers (eds.), *Mixed Agreements* (1983), at 35-83

Wellenstein, E.,
Twenty-five Years of European Community External Relations in 16 *C.M.L. Rev.* (1979), at 407-423

Wessel, R.A.,
The International Legal Status of the European Union in 2 *E.F.A. Rev.* (1997), at 109-129

Wessel, R.A.,
Revisiting the International Legal Status of the EU in 5 *E.F.A. Rev.* (2000), at 507-537

Wessel, R.A.,
The Inside Looking out: Consistency and Delimitation in EU External Relations in 37 *C.M.L. Rev.* (2000), at 1135-1171

Wessel, R.A.,
'De Europese Unie in de internationale rechtsorde' in Mededelingen van de Nederlandse Vereniging voor Internationaal Recht, *De Plaats van de Europese Unie in het veranderende bestel van de volkenrechtelijke organisatie* (2001), at 1-77

Westlake, M.,
The Council of the European Union (1995)

White, N.D.,
The law of international organisations (1996)

Witte, B. de,
'Internationale verdragen tussen lidstaten van de Europese Unie' in Mededelingen van de Nederlandse Vereniging voor Internationaal Recht, *De plaats van de Europese Unie in het veranderende bestel van de volkenrechtelijke organisatie*, Preadviezen (2001), at 79-131

Witte, B. de,
The European Constitutional Treaty: Towards an Exit Strategy for Recalcitrant Member States? In 10 *MJ*1 (2003), at 3-8

Wouters, J.,
De Europese Unie als internationale actor na het Verdrag van Nice in *NTER* 2002, at 62-69

Wouters, J.,
Exit the Convention, Come the IGC. Some reflections on the Convention as a Method for Constitutional Change in the EU in 10 *MJ*3 (2003), at 225-232

Zwaan, J.W. de and Vrouenraets, M.,
'The future of the third pillar: An evaluation of the Treaty of Amsterdam' in T. Heukels, N. Blokker and M. Brus (eds.), *The European Union after Amsterdam* (1998), at 203-214

Zwaan, J.W. de,
The Legal Personality of the European Communities and the European Union in 30 *Neth.Yb.Int'l.L* (1999), at 75-113

Zwaan, J.W. de,
The Netherlands (judiciary and authorities) and Article 10 of the EC-Treaty. Report for FIDE 2000, XIX Congress, Helsinki 1-3 June 2000 in *SEW* 4 (2000), at 132-154

Zwaan, E. de,
Alles of Nice. IGC 2000: adequate voorbereiding van de uitbreiding? In *AA* 50 (2001), at 312-324

Zwaan, J.W. de,
De toekomst van de Europese Unie. Een aantal constitutionele kanttekeningen in 50 *AA* (2001), at 301-311

Zwaan, J.W. de and Bultena, A.J.,
Ruimte van vrijheid, veiligheid en rechtvaardigheid. De samenwerking op het gebied van Justitie en Binnenlandse Zaken in de Europese Unie (2002)

TABLE OF CASES

European Court of Justice

Case 26/62, *Van Gend en Loos*, [1963] ECR 1
Case 6/64, *Costa/ENEL*, [1964] ECR 585
Case 14/70, *Bakels*, [1970] ECR 1009
Case 22/70, *AETR*, [1971] ECR 263
Case 7/71, *Commission* v *France*, [1971] ECR 1003
Case 92/71, *Interfood*, [1972] ECR 231
Joined Cases 21-24/72, *International Fruit Company*, [1972] ECR 1219
Case 39/72, *Commission* v *Italy*, [1973] ECR 101
Case 8/73, *Massey-Ferguson*, [1973] ECR 897
Case 130/73, *Vandeweghe*, [1973] ECR 1329
Case 181/73, *Haegeman*, [1974] ECR 449
Case 38/75, *Nederlandse Spoorwegen*, [1975] ECR 1439
Case 87/75, *Bresciani*, [1976] ECR 129
Joined Cases 98 and 99/75, *Carstens Keremik*, [1976] ECR 252
Joined Cases 3, 4 and 6/76, *Kramer and others*, [1976] ECR 1279
Case 41/76, *Donckerwolcke*, [1976] ECR 1921
Case 50/76, *Amsterdam Bulb* v *Produktschap voor Siergewassen*, [1977] ECR 137
Joined Cases 69 and 70/76, *Dittmeyer*, [1977] ECR 238
Case 61/77, *Commission* v *Ireland*, [1978] ECR 417
Case 94/77, *Zerbone*, [1978] ECR 99
Case 120/78, *Cassis de Dijon*, [1979] ECR 649
Case 225/78, *Bouhelier*, [1979] ECR 3151
Case 61/69, *Denkavit*, [1980] ECR 1205
Case 798/79, *Chem-Tec*, [1980] ECR 2646
Case 804/79, *Commission* v *United Kingdom*, [1981] ECR 1045
Case 812/79, *Burgoa*, [1980] ECR 2787
Case 112/80, *Dürbeck*, [1981] ECR 1095
Case 270/80, *Polydor*, [1982] ECR 329
Case 17/81, *Pabst and Richarz*, [1982] ECR 1331
Case 104/81, *Kupferberg*, [1982] ECR 3641
Case 230/81, *Luxembourg* v *European Parliament*, [1983] ECR 255
Case 266/81, *SIOT*, [1983] ECR 731
Case 14/83, *Von Colson*, [1984] ECR 1891
Joined Cases 294-297/83, *Les Verts*, [1986] ECR 1339
Case 44/84, *Hurd*, [1986] ECR 29
Case 152/84, *Marshall*, [1986] ECR 723
Case 174/84, *Bulk Oil*, [1986] ECR 559
Case 178/84, *Commission* v *Germany*, [1987] ECR 1274
Case 187/85, *Fediol*, [1988] ECR 4155

Case 188/85, *Fediol II*, [1988] ECR 4193
Case 12/86, *Demirel*, [1987] ECR 3719
Case 45/86, *Commission* v *Council*, [1987] ECR 1493
Case 136/86, *BNIC* v *Aubert*, [1987] ECR 4789
Case 204/86, *Greece* v *Council*, [1988] ECR 5233
Case 70/87, *Fediol III*, [1989] ECR 1781
Case C-2/88 Imm, *Zwartveld*, [1990] ECR I-3365 and [1990] ECR I-4405
Case 142/88, *Hoesch*, [1989] ECR 3413
Case C-69/89, *Nakajima*, [1991] ECR I-2069
Case C-79/89, *Brown Boveri*, [1991] ECR I-1884
Case C-106/89, *Marleasing*, [1990] ECR I-4135
Case C-192/89, *Sevince*, [1990] ECR I-3461
Case C-213/89, *Factortame*, [1990] ECR I-2433
Case C-300/89, *Titanium Dioxide*, [1991] ECR I-2867
Case C-340/89, *Vlassopoulou*, [1991] ECR I-2357
Joined Case C-6 and C-9/90, *Francovich*, [1991] ECR I-5357
Case C-18/90, *Kziber*, [1991] ECR I-199
Case C-286/90, *Poulson*, [1992] ECR I-6048
Joined Cases C-181 and C-248/91, *Bangladesh*, [1993] ECR I-3685
Case C-188/91, *Deutsche Shell*, [1993] ECR I-363
Case C-237/91, *Kazim Kus*, [1992] ECR I-6781
Case C-271/91, *Marshall II*, [1993] ECR I-4367
Case C-316/91, *European Parliament* v *Council (EDF)*, [1994] ECR I-625
Case C-327/91, *France* v *Commission*, [1994] ECR I-3641
Case C-364/92, *Eurocontrol*, [1994] ECR I-43
Case C-405/92, *Driftnets*, [1993] ECR I-6133
Case C-432/92, *Anastasiou*, [1994] ECR I-3087
Case C-350/92, *Spain* v *Council*, [1995] ECR I-1985
Joined Cases C-46 and C-48/93, *Brasserie du Pêcheur*, [1996] ECR I-1131
Case C-65/93, *European Parliament* v *Council*, [1995] Ecr I-643
Case C-280/93, *Germany* v *Council*, [1994] ECR I-4973
Case C-360/93, *European Parliament* v *Council*, [1996] ECR I-1195
Case C-469/93, *Chiquita Italia*, [1995] ECR I-4533
Case C-25/94, *Commission* v *Council*, [1996] ECR I-1469
Case C-61/94, *International Dairy Arrangement*, {1996] ECR I-3989
Case C-70/94, *Werner*, [1995] ECR I-3189
Case C-83/94, *Leifer*, [1995] ECR I-3231
Case C-84/94, *United Kingdom* v *Council*, [1996] ECR I-5755
Case C-233/94, *Germany* v *European Parliament and Council*, [1997] ECR I-2405
Case C-268/94, *Portugal* v *Council*, [1996] ECR I-6207
Case C-84/95, *Bosphorus*, [1996] ECR I-3953
Case C-124/95, *Centro-Com*, [1996] ECR I-81
Case C-177/95, *Ebony Maritime*, [1997] ECR I-1131
Case C-183/95, *Affish*, [1997] ECR I-4315
Case C-53/96, *Hermès*, [1998] ECR I-3637
Case C-54/96, *Dorsch Consult*, [1997] Ecr I-4983
Case C-149/96, *Portugal* v *Council*, [1999] ECR I-8395
Case C-162/96, *Racke*, [1998] ECR I-3655

Case C-336/96, *Gilly*, [1998] ECR I-2793
Case C-321/97, *Andersson*, [1999] ECR I-3551
Case C-162/98, *Hartmann*, [1998] ECR I-7083
Case C-193/98, *Pfennigmann*, [1999] ECR I-7747
Joined Cases C-300 and C-392/98, *Parfums Christian Dior*, [2000] ECR I-11307
Case C-29/99, *Commission* v *Council*, [2002] ECR I-11221
Case C-438/00, *Kolpak*, [2003] ECR I-4135
Joined Cases C-187 and C-385/01, *Gözütok*, [2003] ECR I-1345

Opinions and Rulings of the European Court of Justice

Opinion 1/75, *OECD Local Cost Standard*, [1975] ECR 1355
Opinion 1/76, *Rhine Navigation*, [1977] ECR 741
Ruling 1/78, *Draft IAEA Convention*, [1978] ECR 2151
Opinion 1/78, *Natural Rubber*, [1979] ECR 2871
Opinion 1/91, *EEA I*, [1991] ECR I-6079
Opinion 2/91, *ILO*, [1993] ECR I-1064
Opinion 1/92, *EEA II*, [1992] ECR I-2821
Opinion 2/92, *OECD II*, [1995] ECR I-521
Opinion 1/94, *WTO*, [1994] ECR I-5267
Opinion 2/94, *ECHR*, [1996] ECR I-1759
Opinion 3/94, *Bananas*, [1995] ECR I-4577
Opinion 1/00, *ESA*, [2002] ECR I-3498
Opinion 2/00, *Cartagena Protocol on Biosafety*, [2001] ECR I-9717

Court of First Instance

Case T-29/92, *SPO*, [1995] ECR II-289
Case T-115/94, *Opel Austria*, [1997] ECR II-39
Case T-254/97, *Chemnitz*, [1999] ECR II-
Case T-211/02, *Tideland Signal*, [2002] ECR II-

Permanent Court of International Justice

Mavromatis Palestine Concessions Case, P.C.I.J. Reports (1926) Series A, No. 2
Legal Status of Eastern Greenland Case, P.C.I.J. Reports, Series A/B, No. 53

The International Court of Justice

Reparations for Injuries Suffered in the Service of the United Nations Case, I.C.J. Reports (1949), at 174
Competence of the General Assembly for the Admission of a State to the United Nations Case, I.C.J. Reports (1950), at 4
South West Africa Case, I.C.J. Reports (1966), at 6
Interpretation of Peace Treaties Case, I.C.J. Reports (1950), at 221
Convention on the Prevention and Punishment of the Crime of Genocide Case, I.C.J. Reports (1951), at 15
Anglo-Iranian Oil Case, I.C.J. Reports (1952), at 20

Nuclear Test Cases, I.C.J. Reports (1974), at 253
Interpretation of the Agreement between the WHO and Egypt Case, I.C.J. Reports (1980), at 73
Elettronica Sicula Case, I.C.J. Reports (1989), at 15
Arbitral Award Case, I.C.J. Reports (1991), at 53
Qatar v *Bahrain Case*, I.C.J. Reports (1994), at 112
Hungary v *Slovakia (Gabcíkovo-Nagymaros Project)*, I.C.J. Reports (1997), at 7
Germany v *United States of America (La Grand Case)*, I.C.J. Reports (2001)

United States Supreme Court

Foster v *Neilson*, 27 U.S. 253 (1829) (USSC+)
Head Money Cases, 112 U.S. 580 (1884) (USSC+)

SELECTED DOCUMENTS

Official Journal of the European Union

OJ 1975, L 194/5
Council Decision of 3 March 1975 concluding the convention for the prevention of marine pollution from land-based sources (including the text of the Convention)

OJ 1977, L 240/1
Council Decision of 25 July 1977 concluding the Convention for the protection of the Mediterranean Sea against pollution and the Protocol for the prevention of the pollution of the Mediterranean Sea by dumping from ships and aircraft (including the texts of the Convention and the Protocol)

OJ 1977, L 240/35
Council Decision of 25 July 1977 concluding the Convention for the protection of the Rhine against chemical pollution and an Additional Agreement to the Agreement, signed in Berne on 29 April 1963, concerning the International Commission for the Protection of the Rhine against Pollution (including the text of the Agreement)

OJ 1978, L 378/1
Council Regulation (EEC) No 3179/78 of 28 December 1978 concerning the conclusion by the European Economic Community of the Convention on Future Multilateral Cooperation in the Northwest Atlantic Fisheries (including the text of the Convention)

OJ 1980, L 71/1
Council Decision of 10 December 1979 concerning the conclusion of the Multilateral Agreements resulting from the 1973 to 1979 trade negotiations (including the text of the Agreements)

OJ 1980, L 144/1
Council Regulation (EEC) No 1440/80 of 30 May 1980 concerning the conclusion of the Cooperation Agreement between the European Economic Community and Indonesia, Malaysia, the Philippines, Singapore and Thailand – member countries of the Association of the South-East Asian Nations (including the text of the Agreement)

OJ 1981, L 252/26
Council Decision of 4 September 1981 on the conclusion of the Convention on the conservation of Antarctic marine living resources (including the text of the Convention)

OJ 1981, L 313/1
Council Decision of 30 June 1981 on the notification of the provisional application by the European Economic Community of the International Cocoa Agreement 1980

OJ 1982, L 210/10
Council Decision of 24 June 1982 on the conclusion of the Convention on the conservation of migratory species of wild animals (including the text of the Convention)

OJ 1982, L 342/1

Council Decision of 31 March 1982 on the signature and notification of provisional application of the Sixth International Tin Agreement (including the text of the Agreement)

OJ 1984, L 272/1

Council Regulation (EEC) No 2876/84 of 21 September 1984 on the conclusion of an Agreement between the European Economic Community and the Government of the United States of America concerning fisheries off the coasts of the United States (including the text of the Agreement)

OJ 1984, L 292/7

Council Regulation (EEC) No 3114/84 of 6 November 1984 on the conclusion of an Arrangement in the form of an exchange of letters between the European Economic Community and the Government of Canada on the establishment of a scientific observation programme in the Regulatory Area of the NAFO Convention

OJ 1985, L 250/1

Council Regulation (EEC) No 2616/85 of 16 September 1985 concerning the conclusion of a Trade and Economic Cooperation Agreement between the European Economic Community and the People's republic of China

OJ 1987, L 62/22

Council Decision of 3 November 1986 concerning the conclusion of the Agreement in the form of an Exchange of Letters between the European Economic Community and the United States of America on the Mediterranean preferences, citrus and pasta (including the text of the Agreement)

OJ 1990, L 213/3

Decision of the Representatives of the Governments of the Member States of the European Coal and Steel Community, meeting within the Council

OJ 1990, L 304/1

Council Regulation (EEC) No 3155/90 of 29 October 1990 extending and amending Regulation (EEC) No 2340/90 preventing trade by the Community as regards Iraq and Kuwait

OJ 1990, L 352/1

Council Decision of 24 September 1990 concerning the conclusion of the Agreement between the European Economic Community and the People's republic of China on trade in textile products

OJ 1991, L 229/1

Decision of the Council and the Commission of 25 February 1991 on the conclusion of the Fourth ACP-EEC Convention (including the text of the Agreement)

OJ 1991, L 315/1

Council Regulation (EEC) No 3300/91 of 11 November 1991 suspending the trade concessions provided for by the Cooperation Agreement between the European Economic Community and the Socialist Federal republic of Yugoslavia

OJ 1992, L 301/31

Council Decision of 13 July 1992 on the conclusion of an Agreement between the European Economic Community and the Government of the United States of America concerning the application of the GATT Agreement on Trade in Civil Aircraft on trade in large civil aircraft (including the text of the Agreement)

OJ 1993, L 125/1

Council Decision of 10 May 1993 concerning the conclusion of an Agreement in the form of a Memorandum of Understanding between the European Economic Community and the United States of America on government procurement (including the text of the Memorandum of Understanding)

OJ 1993, L 309/1

Council Decision of 25 October 1993 concerning the conclusion of the Convention on Biological Diversity (including the text of the Convention)

OJ 1993, L 337/172

Council Decision of 23 November 1993 concerning the conclusion of an Agreement in the form of an exchange of letters between the European Community and Romania on the reciprocal establishment of tariff quotas for certain wines (including the text of the Agreement)

OJ 1993, L 337/177

Council Decision of 23 November 1993 concerning the conclusion of an Agreement between the European Community and Romania on the reciprocal protection and control of wine names (including the text of the Agreement)

OJ 1993, L 348/1

Decision of the Council and the Commission of 13 December 1993 on the conclusion of the Europe Agreement between the European Communities and their Member States, of the one part, and the Republic of Poland, of the other part (including the text of the Agreement)

OJ 1994, L 1/1

Decision of the Council and the Commission of 13 December 1993 on the conclusion of the Agreement on the European Economic Area between the European Communities, their Member States and the Republic of Austria, the Republic of Finland, the Republic of Iceland, the Principality of Liechtenstein, the Kingdom of Norway, the Kingdom of Sweden and the Swiss Confederation (including the text of the Agreement)

OJ 1994, L 33/11

Council Decision of 15 December 1993 concerning the conclusion of the United Nations Framework Convention on Climate Change (including the text of the Convention)

OJ 1994, L 76/34

Council Decision of 10 March 1994 concerning the amendments to the reservations entered by the Community in respect of some provisions of certain Annexes to the international Convention on the simplification and harmonization of customs procedures

OJ 1994, L 202/19

Council Decision of 21 February 1994 concerning the conclusion of an Agreement in the form of an exchange of letters between the European Community and the Republic of Poland amending Annex IVb to the Interim Agreement between the European Coal and Steel Community and the European Economic Community, of the one part, and the Republic of Poland, of the other part, and to the Europe Agreement between the European Communities and their Member States, of the one part, and the Republic of Poland, of the other part (including the text of the Agreement)

OJ 1994, L 223/23

Council Decision of 18 July 1994 concerning the conclusion of the Cooperation Agreement between the European Community and the Republic of India on Partnership and Development (including the text of the Agreement)

OJ 1994, L 294/26

Council Decision of 11 July 1994 on the conclusion of an Agreement in the form of an exchange of letters concerning fish, amending the Interim Agreement on trade and trade-related matters between the European Economic Community and European Coal and Steel Community, of the one part, and the Czech and Slovak Federal republic, of the other part, and the Europe Agreement establishing an association between the European Communities and their Member States, of the one part, and the Slovak Republic, of the other part (including the text of the Agreement)

OJ 1994, L 336/1

Council Decision of 22 December 1994 concerning the conclusion on behalf of the European Community, as regards matters within its competence, of the agreements reached in the Uruguay Round multilateral negotiations (1986-1994) (including the text of the Agreements)

OJ 1994, L 357/1

Council and Commission Decision of 19 December 1994 on the conclusion of the Europe Agreement between the European Communities and their Member States, of the one part, and Romania, of the other part (including the text of the Agreement)

OJ 1994, L 359/1

Decision of the Council and the Commission of 19 December 1994 concerning the conclusion of a Europe Agreement establishing an association between the European Communities and their Member States, of the one part, and the Slovak Republic, of the other part (including the text of the Agreement)

OJ 1995, L 95/45

Decision of the Council and the Commission of 10 April 1995 concerning the conclusion of the Agreement between the European Communities and the Government of the United States of America regarding the application of their competition laws (including the text of the Agreement)

OJ 1995, L 298/4

Council Decision of 4 December 1995 concerning the joint action, adopted by the Council on the basis of Article J.3 of the Treaty on European Union, on continued support for European Union administration of the town of Mostar

OJ 1995, L 308/79

Council Decision of 17 April 1995 on the signature and the provisional application of the Agreement between the European Community and Canada on fisheries in the context of the NAFO Convention (including the text of the Agreement)

OJ 1995, L 317/34

Council and Commission Decision of 4 December 1995 on concluding the Additional Protocol to the Europe Agreement establishing an association between the European Communities and their Member States, of the one part, and the Republic of Poland, on the other part (including the text of the Protocol)

OJ 1995, L 317/39

Council and Commission Decision of 4 December 1995 concluding the Additional Protocol to the Europe Agreement establishing an association between the European

Communities and their Member States, of the one part, and Romania, of the other part (including the text of the Protocol)

OJ 1996, L 115/42

Council and Commission Decision of 22 April 1996 concluding the Additional Protocol to the Europe Agreement establishing an association between the European Communities and their Member States, of the one part, and the Slovak Republic, of the other part (including the text of the Protocol)

OJ 1997, L 26/1

Decision of the Council and the Commission of 19 December 1997 on the conclusion of the Europe Agreement establishing an association between the European Communities and their Member States, of the one part, and the Republic of Latvia, of the other part (including the text of the Agreement)

OJ 1997, L 327/1

Council and Commission Decision of 30 October 1997 on the conclusion of the Partnership and Cooperation Agreement between the European Communities and their Member States, of the one part, and the Russian Federation, of the other part (including the text of the Agreement)

OJ 1997, C 340/93

Protocol integrating the Schengen *acquis* into the framework of the European Union

OJ 1998, L 26/1

Decision of the Council and the Commission of 19 December 1997 on the conclusion of the Europe Agreement establishing an association between the European Communities and their Member States, of the one part, and the Republic of Latvia, of the other part (including the text of the Agreement)

OJ 1998, L 42/40

Council Decision of 26 January 1998 concerning the conclusion of an Agreement on international humane trapping standards between the European Community, Canada and the Russian Federation and of an Agreed Minute between Canada and the European Community concerning the signing of the said Agreement (including the text of the Agreement)

OJ 1998, L 83/3

United Nations Convention to combat desertification in those countries experiencing serious drought and/or desertification, particularly in Africa

OJ 1998, L 156/1

Council Decision of 27 April 1998 concerning the conclusion of the Agreement amending the fourth ACP-EC Convention of Lomé, signed in Mauritius on 4 November 1995

OJ 1998, L 189/14

Council Decision of 8 June 1998 on the ratification by the European Community of the Agreement on the implementation of the provisions of the United Nations Convention on the Law of the Sea of 10 December 1982 relating to the conservation and management of straddling stocks and highly migratory fish stocks (including the text of the Agreement)

OJ 1998, L 190/34

Council Decision of 16 June 1998 on the accession of the European Community to the General Fisheries Commission for the Mediterranean (including the text of the Agreement)

OJ 1998, L 194/15

Council Decision of 18 June 1998 concerning the Agreement between the European Community, the European Space Agency and the European Organisation for the Safety of Air Navigation on a European contribution to the development of a global navigation satellite system (GNSS) (including the text of the Agreement)

OJ 1998, L 237/8

Council Decision of 27 November 1997 concerning the conclusion of an Agreement in the form of an exchange of letters between the European Community and the Republic of Poland regarding a Protocol on a European Conformity Assessment Agreement within the framework of the Europe Agreement between the European Communities and their Member States, of the one part, and the Republic of Poland, of the other part (including the text of the Protocol)

OJ 1998, L 326/5

Convention on the transboundary effects of industrial accidents

OJ 1999, L 132/1

Council Decision of 26 April 1999 on the signature by the European Community of the Agreement on the International Dolphin Conservation Programme (including the text of the Agreement)

OJ 1999, L 142/1

Common Position of 27 May 1999 adopted by the Council on the basis of Article 34 of the Treaty on European Union, on negotiations relating to the Draft Convention on Cyber Crime held in the Council of Europe

OJ 1999, L 151/20

Council Decision of 11 May 1999 concerning the conclusion of the Agreement between the European Community and Hong Kong, China on cooperation and mutual administrative customs matters (including the text of the Agreement)

OJ 1999, L 175/50

Agreement between the European Communities and the Government of Canada regarding the application of their competition laws

OJ 1999, L 176/31

Council Decision of 17 May 1999 on certain arrangements for the application of the Agreement concluded by the Council of the European Union and the Republic of Iceland and the Kingdom of Norway concerning the association of those two States with the implementation, application and development of the Schengen *acquis*

OJ 1999, L 176/36

Agreement concluded by the Council of the European Union and the Republic of Iceland and the Kingdom of Norway concerning the latter's association with the implementation, application and development of the Schengen acquis

OJ 1999, L 176/53

Agreement in the form of exchanges of letters between the Council of the European Union and the Republic of Iceland and the Kingdom of Norway concerning committees which assist the European Commission in the exercise of its executive powers (including the text of the Agreement)

OJ 1999, L 317/1

Council Decision of 18 May 1998 on the conclusion of a Protocol adjusting trade aspects of the Europe Agreement establishing an association between the European Communities and their Member States, of the one part, and the Republic of Latvia, of the other part, to take account of the accession of the Republic of Austria, the

Republic of Finland and the Kingdom of Sweden to the European Union and the outcome of the Uruguay Round negotiations on agriculture, including improvements to the existing preferential arrangements (including the text of the Protocol)

OJ 2000, L 15/2

Agreement concluded by the Council of the European Union and the Republic of Iceland and the Kingdom of Norway on the establishment of rights and obligations between Ireland and the United Kingdom of Great Britain and Northern Ireland, on the one hand, and the Republic of Iceland and the Kingdom of Norway, on the other, in areas of the Schengen *acquis* which apply to these States

OJ 2000, L 89/15

WIPO Performances and Phonograms Treaty

OJ 2000, L 195/46

Decision No 1/2000 of the ACP-EC Council of Ministers regarding transitional measures valid from 2 August 2000 until the entry into force of the ACP-EC Partnership Agreement

OJ 2000, L 197/35

Council Decision of 17 July 2000 on the acceptance, by the European Community, of the amendment to the Agreement establishing the General Fisheries Commission for the Mediterranean with a view to establishing an autonomous budget for that organization (including the text of the Agreement)

OJ 2000, L 283/18

Council and Commission Decision of 12 October 2000 on the conclusion of the Protocol to the Partnership and Cooperation Agreement establishing a partnership between the European Communities and their Member States, of the one part, and the Russian Federation, of the other part (including the text of the Protocol)

OJ 2000, L 289/31

Convention on the Protection of the Rhine (Translation)

OJ 2000, L 317/3

Partnership Agreement between the members of the African, Caribbean and Pacific Group of States of the one part, and the European Community and its Member States, of the other part, signed in Cotonou on 23 June 2000

OJ 2000, L 317/376

Internal Agreement between the representatives of the governments of the Member States, meeting within the Council on measures to be taken and procedures to be followed for the implementation of the ACP-EC Partnership Agreement

OJ 2001, L 30/44

Council Decision of 8 December 2000 on the signing, on behalf of the European Community, of the United Nations Convention against transnational organised crime and its Protocols on combating trafficking in persons, especially women and children, and the smuggling of migrants by land, air and sea

OJ 2001, L 43/20

Decision No 1/2001 of the ACP-EC Committee of Ambassadors of 30 January 2001 concerning the adoption of the Rules of Procedure of the ACP-EC Council of Ministers

OJ 2001, L 43/24

Decision No 2/2001 of the ACP-EC Committee of Ambassadors of 30 January 2001 concerning the adoption of the Rules of Procedure of the ACP-EC Committee of Ambassadors

OJ 2001, L 48/31

Council Decision of 29 January 2001 concluding the consultation procedure with Haiti under Article 96 of the ACP-EC Partnership Agreement

OJ 2001, L 50/7

Decision No 4/2000 of the EU-Slovak Association Council of 27 December 2000 amending, through the setting-up of a Joint Consultative Committee, Decision No 1/95 establishing the rules of procedure of the Association Council

OJ 2001, L 93/40

Agreement between the European Community and the Republic of Iceland and the kingdom of Norway concerning the criteria and mechanisms for establishing the State responsible for examining a request for asylum lodged in a Member State or in Iceland or Norway

OJ 2001, L 120/33

Council Decision of 9 April 2001 concluding consultations with the Republic of the Fiji Islands under Article 96 of the ACP-EC Partnership Agreement

OJ 2001, L 125/1

Council Decision of 9 April 2001 concerning the conclusion of the Agreement between the European Union and the Federal Republic of Yugoslavia (FRY) on the activities of the European Union Monitoring Mission (EUMM) in the FRY (including the text of the Agreement)

OJ 2001, L 134/40

Council Decision of 4 April 2001 on the approval, on behalf of the European Community, of the Protocol to the 1979 Convention on Long-range Transboundary Air Pollution on Heavy Metals (including the text of the Protocol)

OJ 2001, L 241/1

Council Decision of 30 August 2001 concerning the conclusion of the Agreement between the European Union and the Former Yugoslav Republic of Macedonia (FYROM) on the activities of the European Union Monitoring Mission (EUMM) in FYROM (including the text of the Agreement)

OJ 2001, C 1/7

Exchange of Letters between the World Health Organisation and the Commission of the European Communities concerning the consolidation and intensification of cooperation

OJ 2002, L 50/64

Council Decision of 18 February 2002 concluding consultations with Zimbabwe under Article 96 of the ACP-EC Partnership Agreement

OJ 2002, L 96/23

Council Decision of 25 March 2002 concluding consultations with Liberia under Articles 96 and 97 of the ACP-EC Partnership Agreement

OJ 2002, L 130/1

Council Decision of 25 April 2002 concerning the approval, on behalf of the European Community, of the Kyoto Protocol to the United Nations Framework Convention on Climate Change and the joint fulfilment of commitments thereunder (including the text of the Protocol)

OJ 2002, L 201/48

Council Decision of 25 June 2002 concerning the conclusion, on behalf of the European Community, of the Cartagena Protocol on Biosafety (including the text of the Agreement)

OJ 2002, L 234/40

Convention on the Conservation and Management of Fishery Resources in the South-East Atlantic Ocean

OJ 2002, L 256/7

Council Decision of 19 September 2002 authorising the Member States, in the interest of the Community, to sign, ratify or accede to the International Convention on Civil Liability for Bunker Oil Pollution Damage, 2001 (the Bunkers Convention) (including the text of the Convention

OJ 2002, L 293/1

Council Decision of 30 September 2002 concerning the conclusion of the Agreement between the European Union and Bosnia and Herzegovina (BiH) on the activities of the European Union Police Mission (EUPM) in BiH (including the text of the Agreement)

OJ 2002, L 334/1

Council Common Position of 10 December 2002 concerning restrictive measures against Somalia

OJ 2002, L 334/3

Council Joint Action of 10 December 2002 amending and extending the mandate of the Special Representative of the European Union in Afghanistan

OJ 2002, L 337/55

Council Decision of 18 November 2002 authorising the Member States, in the interest of the Community, to ratify or accede to the International Convention on Liability and Compensation for Damage in Connection with the Carriage of Hazardous and Noxious Substances by Sea, 1996 (the HNS Convention) (including the text of the Convention)

OJ 2002, L 342/1

Council Decision of 18 November 2002 concerning the conclusion on behalf of the European Community of the International Cocoa Agreement 2001 (including the text of the Agreement)

OJ 2003, L 26/1

Council Decision of 17 December 2003 on the signing of the Agreement between the European Union and the Republic of Iceland and the Kingdom of Norway on the application of certain provisions of the Convention of 29 May 2000 on Mutual Assistance in Criminal Matters between the Member States of the European Union and the 2001 Protocol thereto (including the text of the Agreement)

OJ 2003, L 53/62

Council Common Position 2003/140/CFSP of 27 February 2003 concerning exception to the restrictive measures imposed by the Common Position 2002/402/CFSP

OJ 2003, L 53/63

Council Joint Action 2003/141/CFSP of 27 February 2003 amending Joint Action 2002/210/CFSP on the European Union Police Mission

OJ 2003, L 63/27

Council Decision of 19 December 2002 concerning the approval, on behalf of the European Community, of the Rotterdam Convention on the Prior Informed Consent Procedure for certain hazardous chemicals and pesticides in international trade (including the text of the Convention)

OJ 2003, L 65/27

Council Decision of 19 December 2002 concerning the conclusion of the Partnership Agreement between the African, Caribbean and Pacific Group of States, of the one part, and the European Community and its Member States, of the other part, signed in Cotonou on 23 June 2000

OJ 2003, L 80/36

Agreement between the European Union and the North Atlantic Treaty Organisation on the security of information

OJ 2003, L 82/45

Council Decision 2003/222/CFSP of 21 March 2003 concerning the conclusion of the Agreement between the European Union and the Former Yugoslav Republic of Macedonia on the status of the European-led Forces (EUF) in the Former Yugoslav Republic of Macedonia (including the text of the Agreement)

OJ 2003, L 86/21

Council Decision of 17 March 2003 concerning the accession of the European Community to the Protocol of Amendment to the International Convention on the simplification and harmonisation of customs procedures (Kyoto Convention) (including the text of the Protocol)

OJ 2003, L 93/50

Agreement between the European Union and the Republic of Albania on the activities of the European Union Monitoring Mission (EUMM) in the Republic of Albania

OJ 2003, L 101/22

Council Common Position 2003/280/CFSP of 16 April 2003 in support of the effective implementation of the mandate of the ICTY

OJ 2003, L 106/36

Council Common Position 2003/ 297/ CFSP of 28 April 2003 on Burma/Myanmar

OJ 2003, L 181/27

Agreement on extradition between the European Union and the United States of America

OJ 2003, L 181/34

Agreement on mutual legal assistance between the European Union and the United States of America

OJ 2003, L 220/3

Council Decision of 25 August 2003 adopting measures concerning Liberia under Article 96 of the ACP-EC Partnership Agreement in a case of special urgency

OJ 2003, L 313/79

Agreement between the European Union and the Government of Latvia on the participation of the Republic of Latvia in the European-led forces (EUF) in the former Yugoslav Republic of Macedonia

OJ 2003, C 67/10

Resolution of the EEA Consultative Committee of 26 June 2002 on enlargement and the future of the EEA

OJ 2004, L 12/54

Agreement between the European union and the Slovak Republic on the participation of the armed forces of the Slovak Republic in the European Union-led Forces (EUF) in the Former Yugoslav Republic of Macedonia

OJ 2004, L 16/65

Council Decision 2004/75/CFSP of 11 December 2003 concerning the conclusion of the Agreement between the European Union and the Former Yugoslav Republic of Macedonia on the status and activities of the European Union Police Mission (EUPOL Proxima) in the Former Yugoslav Republic of Macedonia (including the text of the Agreement)

OTHER SELECTED DOCUMENTS

COM(1995) 504 final

Proposal for a Council Decision concerning the conclusion of the interregional framework cooperation Agreement between the European Community and its Member States, of the one part, and the Southern Cone Common Market and its member countries, of the other part (including the text of the Agreement)

COM(1999) 435 final

Proposal for a council Decision on Signature by the European Community of the Convention of 28 May 1999 for the Unification of Certain Rules for International Carriage by Air (the Montreal Convention)

COM(2001) 187 final

Proposal for a Council Decision authorising the Federal Republic of Germany to conclude with the Republic of Poland an agreement containing measures derogating from Articles 2 and 3 of the Sixth Council Directive (77/388/EEC) of 17 May 1977 on the harmonisation of the laws of the Member States relating to turnover taxes

COM(2001) 583 final

Proposal for a Council Decision on objection to be made on behalf of the European Atomic Energy Community to a reservation formulated by the Islamic Republic of Pakistan at the time of its accession to the Convention on the Physical Protection of Nuclear Material

COM(2002) 127 final

Proposal for a Council Decision concerning the conclusion, on behalf of the Community, of the Cartagena Protocol on Biosafety

COM(2002) 520 final

Proposal for a Council Decision on the signing by the European Community of the Council of Europe Convention on contact concerning children

COM(2002) 628 final

Proposal for a Council Decision concerning the accession of the European Community to the Protocol of Amendment to the International Convention on the simplification and harmonisation of customs procedures (Kyoto Convention) (including the text of the Convention)

COM(2003) 104 final

Communication from the Commission to the Council and the European Parliament, Wider Europe – Neighbourhood: A New Framework for Relations with our Eastern and Southern Neighbours

COM(2003) 712 final

Proposal for a Council Decision on the signing and the provisional application of bilateral agreements between the European Community and certain third countries (Azerbaijan, Kazakhstan, Tajikistan and Turkmenistan) on trade in textile products

SP(2000)3785/5

Commission Notice of 31 January 2001, Guide pratique de l'accord-cadre sur les relations entre le Parlement européen et la Commission européenne

SEC(2002)381 final

Recommendation from the Commission to the Council in order to authorize the Commission to open and conduct negotiations with the International Civil Aviation Organization (ICAO) on the conditions and arrangements for accession by the European Community and Recommendation from the Commission to the Council in order to authorize the Commission to open and conduct negotiations with the International Maritime Organization (IMO) on the conditions and arrangements for accession by the European Community

United Nations, FCCC/AG13/1996/2

Framework Convention on Climate Change: Report of the Ad Hoc Group on Article 13 on the work of its second session, held at Geneva on 10 July 1996

http://www.europa.eu.int

European Union, Selected instruments taken from the Treaties, Book I, Volume I (1999)

http://www.europa.eu.int

Signature of the Euro-Mediterranean Association Agreement between the European Community, its Member States and Lebanon

http://www.europa.eu.int

Signature of the Association Agreement between the European Community and Its Member States and the Republic of Chile 18 November 2002

http://www.europa.eu.int

Signature of the Agreement on maritime transport between the European Community and China 6 December 2002

http://www.europa.eu.int

Press Release by the Danish Presidency: EU and Iran to start negotiations on Trade and Cooperation agreement 12 December 2002

http://www.europa.eu.int

EU-Presidency and Commission Joint Press Release on the opening of the negotiations with Iran 12 December 2002

CONV 305/02

The European Convention: Final report of Working Group III on Legal Personality

CONV 850/03

The European Convention: Draft Treaty establishing a Constitution for Europe

United Nations: Charter of the United Nations in 39 *AJIL* (1945), at 190

United Nations: Statute of the International Court of Justice in 39 *AJIL* (1945), at 215

Convention for the Protection of Human Rights and Fundamental Freedoms in 45 *AJIL* (1951), at 24

Vienna Convention on the Law of Treaties in 8 *I.L.M.* (1969), at 679

Convention for the Prevention of Marine Pollution from Land-based Sources in 13 *I.L.M.* (1974), at 352

Vienna Convention on the Succession of States in Respect of Treaties in 17 *I.L.M.* (1978), at 1488

Conference of the Plenipotentiaries of the Coastal States of the Mediterranean Region for the Protection of the Mediterranean Sea against Pollution from Land-based Sources: Final Act in 19 *I.L.M.* (1980), at 863

A/CONF.62/121 (21 *I.L.M.* (1982), at 1245)

Third United Nations Conference on the Law of the Sea: Final Act

Vienna Convention on the Law of Treaties between States and International Organizations or between International Organizations in 25 *I.L.M.* (1986), at 543

Final Act of the Conference of Plenipotentiaries on the Protection of the Ozone Layer in 26 *I.L.M.* (1987), at 1520

Contracting Parties to the Convention for the Prevention of Marine Pollution from Land-based Sources: Protocol amending the Convention in 27 *I.L.M.* (1988), at 625

UNEP/IG.80/L.12 (28 *I.L.M.* (1989), at 652)

United Nations Environment Programme: Final Act of the Conference of Plenipotentiaries on the Global Convention on the Control of Transboundary Movements of Hazardous Wastes

Tractatenblad 1994 No. 183

Memorandum of Understanding on the European Union Administration of Mostar

A/CN.4/528

International Law Commission, Fifty-fifth Session (5 May to 6 June and 7 July to 8 August 2003)

A/CN.4/532

United Nations General Assembly: First report on responsibility of international organizations by Mr. Giorgio Gaja, Special Rapporteur

A/CN.4/535 and A/CN.4/535/Add. 1

United Nations General Assembly: Eighth report on reservations to treaties by Mr. Alain Pellet, Special Rapporteur

INDEX

www.ingramcontent.com/pod-product-compliance
Lightning Source LLC
Chambersburg PA
CBHW072242240926
51846CB00012B/142
* 9 7 8 9 0 6 7 0 4 1 8 2 9 *